Unorthodox Kin

Unorthodox Kin

PORTUGUESE MARRANOS AND
THE GLOBAL SEARCH FOR BELONGING

Naomi Leite

UNIVERSITY OF CALIFORNIA PRESS

University of California Press, one of the most distinguished university presses in the United States, enriches lives around the world by advancing scholarship in the humanities, social sciences, and natural sciences. Its activities are supported by the UC Press Foundation and by philanthropic contributions from individuals and institutions. For more information, visit www.ucpress.edu.

University of California Press
Oakland, California

Library of Congress Cataloging-in-Publication Data

Names: Leite, Naomi, 1972– author.
Title: Unorthodox kin : Portuguese Marranos and the global search for
   belonging / Naomi Leite.
Description: Oakland, California : University of California Press, [2017] |
   Includes bibliographical references and index.
Identifiers: LCCN 2016027927 (print) | LCCN 2016028590 (ebook) |
   ISBN 9780520285040 (cloth : alk. paper) | ISBN 9780520285057 (pbk. : alk.
   paper) | ISBN 9780520960640 (ebook)
Subjects: LCSH: Kinship—Cross-cultural studies. | Ethnology—Philosophy. |
   Portugal—Kinship. | Portugal—Religious life and customs.
Classification: LCC GN487 .L45 2017 (print) | LCC GN487 (ebook) |
   DDC 305.892/40469—dc23
LC record available at https://lccn.loc.gov/2016027927

Manufactured in the United States of America

26 25 24 23 22 21 20 19 18 17
10 9 8 7 6 5 4 3 2 1

For my teachers, all

Making sense of other people is never easy, and making sense of how other people make sense can be very difficult indeed.

KEITH BASSO
Portraits of the Whiteman

For events in times or places outside our own experience, we have nothing to go on but the stories other people tell us. Past events exist, after all, only in memory, which is a form of imagination. The event is real *now,* but once it's *then,* its continuing reality is entirely up to us, dependent on our energy and honesty.

URSULA LEGUIN
Tales from Earthsea

CONTENTS

Anthropologists, like everyone else, live in the flow of time. When we write of the field research that forms the basis of our work, it is already past. The events of this book are now history; today, the people whose stories and observations I recount might express themselves differently; organizations I describe may no longer exist, or may now have a different character and emphasis; individuals who feature prominently may no longer be involved in Marrano affairs in the same way, if at all; several, in fact, have died. But if the details of the story I tell are specific to just one time and place, the questions explored are not. Experiences of self-discovery and (in)voluntary affiliation, belonging and exclusion, kinship and relatedness, enchantment and wonder are basic to human existence, though their shape may vary widely across geographical and cultural settings. How and to what extent these experiences are molded by interaction with others, particularly as global interconnectivity enables our closest relationships to span vast distances, is a puzzle with which we are all faced, in one way or another, in our own lives. The story of Portugal's urban Marranos and their search for belonging offers a glimpse of just one among many answers.

. . .

The seed of this book was sown more than two decades ago, when in the span of a few days both my maternal grandfather, Harry Fischer, and my paternal grandmother, Nancy Leite, called independently to say they had taped a public television broadcast I would want to see. It was *The Last Marranos,* a documentary film about a secret community of "hidden Jews" discovered in an isolated Portuguese village, where they had lived disconnected from the

Jewish world for hundreds of years. I had just finished my first semester of graduate school in anthropology, and my grandparents knew I planned on research in Portugal but did not yet have a field project. For my uncomplicatedly Jewish grandfather, it was a fascinatingly exotic topic, the proper stuff of anthropology, yet also an uplifting story about his people; for my non-Jewish grandmother, it was a tantalizing indication that her late Portuguese American husband's family tales of lost Jewish origins might actually hold some truth. For me, the fledgling anthropologist, it was a ripe example of the complexities of individual and collective identity, though truth be told, I was as intrigued by my grandparents' different but equally pronounced investment in the subject matter as by the community itself. In the end, I did not base my research in that village, but I did go on to conduct fieldwork on people who identify as Marranos in contemporary Portugal—and on the extraordinary interest the story of Portugal's hidden Jews attracts from abroad. Although the project has evolved substantially since those two long-ago phone calls, credit for this book's genesis belongs to them.

Beyond my grandparents, I have incurred many debts in the course of the research and writing of this book, which first took shape as the focus of my doctoral research at the University of California, Berkeley. It would be difficult to overstate my gratitude to Nelson Graburn—teacher, PhD advisor, coauthor, mentor, friend—whose enthusiasm, support, and sharp intellectual engagement with my work over the past two decades have been a blessing many times over. Stanley Brandes, too, has been a mentor over many years, sharing his engaged and compassionate approach to ethnographic research, writing, and teaching and nurturing my instinct for narrative ethnography. The influence of both men on this book runs deep. During my graduate career Margaret Conkey, Alan Dundes, Harvey Stahl, George Lakoff, Rosemary Joyce, Emily Martin, and Edward Bruner provided intellectual guidance and mentorship at key moments, for which I am deeply grateful. Each is godparent to this project in a different way.

The research on which this book is based took place over a twelve-year period, from my first exploratory forays to Portugal (summers, 1996–98) and participant observation on Marrano-related Jewish heritage tours and conferences (2002, 2004) to eighteen months of concentrated fieldwork in Lisbon and Porto, Portugal's two largest cities (June 2004–January 2006) and shorter follow-up visits thereafter (2007, 2008). Fieldwork was generously supported by a National Science Foundation Graduate Research Fellowship, a Maurice Amado Research Fellowship in Sephardic Studies, a doctoral fellowship from the Memorial Foundation for Jewish Culture, and a multiyear Fialon Fellowship from the Institute of European Studies, UC Berkeley, which also supported dissertation writing. I thank those institutions, as well as the Portuguese Studies Program, Graduate Division, and Department of Anthropology at UC Berkeley for additional research funds.

By definition, ethnographic fieldwork depends upon the cooperation of strangers; in the best of worlds, some become dear friends. That was my experience. Countless people contributed their time, knowledge, honesty, and energy to this project, some in a fleeting conversation during a tourist visit or a Marrano association meeting, others in discussions that spanned months or years. Individuals shared their observations, reflections, life stories, humor, and raw emotions, allowing me to join them in private meetings, in their homes, on tour buses and in hotel rooms, in private cars, and even in such intensely personal moments as appearing before a rabbinic court. People suggested articles, offered contacts, showed me their own writings and photographs, and shared lodging while traveling. I owe an immeasurable debt to each and every one. I hope I have adequately honored their experiences and insights and that they found some benefit in sharing their time with me. Above all, I thank the people of the organizations here called HaShalom, Menorá, and Kehilá, who opened their doors to a shy but nosy anthropologist and offered a temporary place of belonging. I continue to be overwhelmed by the trust they placed in me. For all, I have great affection and *saudades*. My gratitude is immense.

While all names in this book are pseudonyms, those who participated in my research will likely recognize themselves in these pages. I find it difficult to articulate how grateful I am to those I call Catarina Queirós, Dulce Oliveira, Joaquim Martins, Cécile Rodrigues, Nuno and Luisa Sanches, and Ricardo Carvalho, whose generosity, hospitality, and true friendship were vital. Without the dear woman I have named Graciana Mayer, who took me under her wing from the start, this research would never have begun. I am equally indebted to the people I call Anshel Rappaport, Frank Albertson, and Rabbi Ezra and Chaya Kaplan, who readily offered their candid observations and affectionate support during the many hours we spent together. I thank the European Masorti *beit din* that convened on March 30, 2006, for their open ear and willingness to allow my presence, and particularly "Rabbi Asher" for taking the time to talk with me in depth about the status of B'nai Anusim and the nature of conversion.

Both before and during my fieldwork, many individuals shared their knowledge of Jewish culture, texts, religious practices, history, and folklore, lending context and nuance to my sense of how Marranos fit into the bigger picture. I am especially grateful to Ken Goldberg, Seymour Fromer, Fred Rosenbaum, Sandy and Joseph Goldberg, staff and students at Lehrhaus Judaica, Dolores Sloan, Stephen Gomes, Leo Abrami, William (Ze'ev) Brinner, and Moshe Lazar for their knowledgeable and enthusiastic engagement.

In Portugal and after, wonderful friends, colleagues, and extended kin enriched my understanding of Portuguese culture and helped me navigate its more confusing currents, among them Eva Graburn and Pedro Martins, Camila Castro, Irene Whitmore, Graça Cravinho, David Cabral, Miguel Vale de Almeida, António Medeiros, João de Pina-Cabral, Sandra Seskin, the Salazar Leite family, and Brian and Joana Winter. My Porto housemates, José Gata, Ana Fernandes, and Bridget Saavedra Scanlon, gamely tolerated my endless questions and odd work hours. Most of all I am grateful to "Catarina Queirós," whose kindness, wit, moral support, and furry menagerie were gifts I can never sufficiently return, and Sérgio Castro Pinheiro, lost too soon, who gave me perspective, unflagging support, and a home on both sides of the Atlantic. Although our paths diverged before his untimely death in 2010, his knowledge and humor are woven into the fiber of this book, his mark on my life indelible.

After the immersion of fieldwork, writing can be a lonely business. Two transoceanic writing groups sustained me throughout. To the Writing Women, who kept me on track over the many months of writing the first draft, and the Little Engines That Can, who saw the manuscript through to completion, I owe my heartfelt thanks: Paula Mota Santos, Sarah Werning, Rebekkah Carney, Rachel Giraudo, Kate Abramson, Irina Wenk, Maki Tanaka, Alisa Velonis, Laura Bathurst, Rebecca Ghent, and Mary Mostafanezhad. I am blessed by their humor, generosity, and honest interventions, and find it hard to imagine a more supportive community for getting things done. Onward, Engines!

Numerous people have responded to drafts of this work presented at conferences and invited lectures. In particular, members of audiences at the London School of Economics, the Graduate Institute of Geneva, the University of Lausanne, Brunel University London, and Stockholm University offered comments and questions that sharpened the book's overall framing. I was fortunate to participate in the March 2014 Wenner-Gren workshop on spiritual kinship, "The Sacred Social," held at the University of Virginia, which provided a stimulating context to rethink some of my material. I thank the organizers for inviting me and all of the participants, especially Fenella Cannell, Susan McKinnon, Gillian Feely-Harnik, and Don Seeman, for their thoughtful feedback. A postdoctoral fellowship from the Memorial Foundation for Jewish Culture supported revision of the manuscript, with space and time provided by the Harris Center for Judaic Studies and College of Arts and Sciences of the University of Nebraska–Lincoln. I now finish this book at SOAS, University of London, where I am particularly grateful to Head of Department David Mosse for ensuring that I had time to complete it and to Caroline Osella and Gabriele vom Bruck for their timely and supportive contributions.

Throughout my career, Nelson Graburn has modeled a remarkably collaborative, warm, unpretentious way of being a scholar, focused on sharing ideas and fostering personal connections. Following his example has helped me build an extraordinary intellectual community of my own. I treasure the many conversations I have had over the years with these dear colleagues and friends, whose thinking has inevitably influenced mine: Misha Klein, Paula Mota Santos, Alexis Bunten, Laura Bathurst, Elizabeth Roberts, Rachel Giraudo, Irina Wenk, David Picard, Valerio Simoni, Michael Di Giovine, Mary Mostafanezhad, Alysoun Quinby, and Charlie Carroll.

Several people generously read and commented on drafts of this manuscript. Caroline Chen, Jinfu Zhang, and Brad Erickson gave helpful feedback on chapters early on. For their insightful comments on complete drafts, my gratitude to Nelson Graburn, Stanley Brandes, Edward Bruner, David Shneer, Stacy Eisenstark, Misha Klein, Elizabeth Leite, and Jason Head. Two colleagues deserve special recognition: Rupert Stasch, whose thoughtful, detailed commentary helped to clarify the manuscript's framing, and Paula Mota Santos, who read multiple drafts, offering her expertise as an anthropologist and a Portuguese native on both the ethnographic material and the arguments it supports. At the University of California Press, editor Reed Malcolm was an author's dream: patient but firm, engaged, and empathetic. His colleagues Stacy Eisenstark, Zuha Khan, Jessica Moll, and Tom Sullivan skillfully steered the manuscript from acquisition through to production, fielding my many queries with grace. Victoria Baker's artful and incisive indexing brought the project to a close.

For their steadfast love, intellectual curiosity, and infectious delight in discovering different ways of living, seeing, and being, I thank my parents. My brother, Adam, has been a wellspring of wisdom and support throughout a tumultuous decade. I cherish our evolving relationship as siblings and fellow academics. Misha Klein, the sister I didn't have, has accompanied this project from the beginning as a beloved friend, interlocutor, and colleague. Ashley Smith performed miracles; without her, this book would not be.

And to Jason, who already knows: amidst the many ways of making kin, recognition is ours. Thank you, my always and eternal husband, for finding me and bringing me home.

A NOTE ON TRANSLATION AND TERMINOLOGY

All translations in this book are my own, unless otherwise noted, including quotations from Portuguese-language publications. Isolated foreign terms generally appear first in the original language, italicized, with parenthetical translation preceded by an abbreviation: Pt. = Portuguese; Sp. = Spanish; Ital. = Italian; Heb. = Hebrew; Yid. = Yiddish.

One term used throughout this book, *Marrano,* has a long and controversial history. Until recently it was common in Jewish circles, both scholarly and vernacular, as the primary term for Jews forcibly converted to another religion who secretly maintained their faith (Roth 1941). Its etymology is poorly documented, but most scholars point to the Spanish *marrano,* "swine," an Inquisition-era epithet for secret Jews. Over the past two decades its use has become controversial, particularly in the American Southwest, where numerous individuals trace their ancestry to Jews who fled the Spanish Inquisition and argue vociferously for abolition of this "abusive" term (Kunin 2009: 2; Hordes 2005: 5–7). Out of respect, scholars generally now use *crypto-Jew* or *converso* (Sp.; convert). Others opt for *anusim* (Heb.; forced/coerced ones), the term used in centuries of rabbinic legal rulings involving individuals forced to abandon Judaism. In light of this terminological sensitivity I use *crypto-Jewish descendant* when referring to individuals from the Portuguese and Spanish diasporas who travel to Portugal in search of Jewish roots and/ or participate in social media relating to hidden Jewish ancestry.

In Portuguese, however, *marrano* is not a pejorative term, neither in reference to oneself nor in reference to others. If anything, it carries connotations of heroism, resistance, and survival (Mea 1998, 2005). It first appeared in colloquial Portuguese in the twentieth century, and today its sole meaning is "secret Jew" or descendant thereof (Pimentel and Monteiro 1999: 14;

Carvalho 1999: 31–32). Since the 1920s it has been the preferred term among urban Portuguese who identify as descendants of forced converts, in reference both to themselves and to their ancestors (Mea and Steinhardt 1997). Most participants in my research were emphatic that the term should be maintained for historical and political reasons discussed in this book. It is in recognition of its particular meaning in Portuguese, and specifically its usage by "Marranos" themselves, that I retain it here.

Introduction

AN ETHNOGRAPHY OF AFFINITIES

af·fin·i·ty, *noun*
    I. (a) sympathy marked by community of interest: kinship;
(b) i. an attraction to or liking for something; **ii.** an attractive
force between substances or particles that causes them to enter
into and remain in chemical combination
    II. (a) likeness based on relationship or causal connection,
analogy; **(b)** a relation between biological groups involving
resemblance in structural plan and indicating a common origin[1]

PARTIAL RELATIONS

On a sunny Sunday morning in August, Ricardo Carvalho, a thirty-five-year-
old shipping clerk from a nondescript northern Portuguese suburb, checks
his watch and quickly drinks the last of his espresso. Gesturing for me to
follow, he walks briskly across the café esplanade to the sidewalk and pauses
for me to catch up, then resumes his story as we hurry to meet the tour bus.
He is telling me about having dinner with an American rabbi a few months
ago, another in a string of stories he's shared about encounters with Jews visiting from abroad. They come to him through word of mouth, or via his website, or by happenstance, in person, when he and they both happen to attend
Shabbat (Sabbath) services at the grand twentieth-century synagogue in
Porto, Portugal's second-largest city. He takes visitors on walking tours of
Porto's medieval Jewish quarter and recounts eight centuries of Portuguese
Jewish history, asking nothing in exchange but their time; for Ricardo, the
opportunity to meet and perhaps befriend these foreigners is an end in itself.
Whether an independent tourist couple, a Jewish heritage tour group, a
rabbi, a historian passing through, or outreach activists seeking "lost" or

"hidden" Jews of Portuguese origin, the specifics are less important to him than the simple fact that they are Jews—and that they invariably seem as interested in him as he is in them.

On this particular morning it is a group of twenty Italians, all retirees, midway through a package tour of "Jewish Portugal." He has agreed to meet them at the synagogue and lead a short walking tour. As with previous visitors, he will not volunteer that he works as a shipping clerk, nor will they ask his profession; with his wire-rimmed glasses, intellectual bearing, and facility in several languages, tourists invariably take him for an academic or a white-collar professional. In fact he easily could be an academic, given the many years he's spent studying Jewish and European history, linguistics, and religion on his own. But in the Portugal of his youth, a working-class child like Ricardo had few opportunities to become a scholar, just as today, on this sunny morning in 2004, there are few avenues for him to join Portugal's tiny, tight-knit Jewish community. Despite his public activism to raise awareness of Portugal's medieval Jewish heritage, his explanation that he has Jewish ancestry, and his attendance at the Porto synagogue off and on for nearly a decade, most Portuguese Jews do not consider him a Jew at all.

When we arrive at the synagogue's austere iron gates the tour bus has not yet arrived. Waiting, I turn to take in the imposing four-story building. Even after seeing it so many times, I am struck anew by its vast facade and still more by its remarkable history. The largest synagogue in the Iberian Peninsula, it contains not only a spacious, intricately tiled Moorish-style sanctuary, but also classrooms, a library, meeting hall, full kitchen, dining room, ritual bath (Heb., *mikvah*), and lodgings for a rabbi and a caretaker. For most of its existence, however, the opulent building has stood empty; the *mikvah* lay in disrepair for decades, and until quite recently no religious leader had ever lived in the rabbi's quarters. Five hundred years have passed since Porto's Jewish population was large enough to warrant such a building. Instead, as Ricardo explains during his walking tours, it is the physical expression of a dream: that one day the descendants of Portugal's "lost" Jews would return en masse to their ancestral faith, a Jewish community rising phoenix-like from the Inquisition's long cold ashes.

When the synagogue was first being built, in the 1920s, that hope had a certain logic. In 1910 a Jewish traveler stumbled upon a village of *marranos* (Pt.; secret Jews) in the country's mountainous interior. These were the remnant of Portugal's once-substantial Jewish population, forcibly converted en masse to Catholicism in the fifteenth century and hounded continuously by the Inquisition for more than two hundred years thereafter. Over the centuries they developed a clandestine Judaism, living outwardly as Catholics while transmitting fragmentary rituals from one generation to the next. The great synagogue, its construction underwritten with donations from Jews abroad, was intended as a beacon to the thousands of *marranos* rumored still to be hiding throughout Portugal's northern provinces (Mea and Steinhardt 1997). But the hoped-for return never came. For years the doors opened only rarely, primarily for cultural events, the key held in private hands. In the 1980s a small group of expatriates from Israel, the United States, England, and France restored and rededicated the building in collaboration with a few Portuguese citizens whose Jewish grandparents had immigrated from Eastern Europe early in the century.

Today tourists are surprised to learn that the synagogue's leadership consists largely of foreigners like themselves. In fact, Ricardo emphasizes, few who attend Shabbat services have roots deeper than one or two generations in Portuguese soil, if that. Beyond the two or three Catholic-born Portuguese women who converted to Judaism when they married congregants, the only ethnic Portuguese to be found within the synagogue's walls are Ricardo and others who, like him, describe themselves as *marranos* or *b'nei anussins* (Heb.-Pt.; children of the coerced)—descendants of the forced converts of long ago.[2]

Both in Porto and in Lisbon, the nation's capital, over the past few decades dozens of people have come forward and identified themselves as ancestral Jews. Reaction from the Portuguese Jewish community has been at best indifferent: they dismiss the newcomers as non-Jews, not least because neither distant ancestry nor a desire to be Jewish automatically makes one a Jew according to Jewish law. In accompanying several Jewish heritage tour groups through Portugal, on the other hand, I have noted that Jews from abroad tend to view self-titled Marranos in a far more sympathetic light. This August morning marks the first Jewish tour group I will experience from the Marranos' perspective. Standing next to Ricardo, I wonder what the tourists will make of my being there.

Before I can ask what I should do when they arrive, we are joined by Miguel Santos, Ricardo's good friend and fellow Marrano. Just then the bus rounds the corner and pulls to the curb, stopping directly in front of us. The doors open. Italian retirees spill down the steps, one after another. They await no formal introduction, reaching out to clasp hands with each of us in turn, moving briskly as if along a receiving line. "Shalom!" they cry, using the universally recognized Hebrew greeting and looking directly into our eyes. "Shalom! Shalom!" Pointing to the chest, they offer their names: "Giuseppe! Shalom!" Ricardo and Miguel readily answer in kind, having done this before: "Shalom! Ricardo!" "Shalom! Miguel!" I try to follow suit, but with so many outstretched hands and exuberant faces coming at me at once I have difficulty focusing. "Shalom! Naomi!" I announce heartily to no one in particular, shaking hands with one tourist while smiling at another. "Shalom!"

The Italian guide leads his charges into the synagogue for a presentation and tour by a Jewish community representative, this time a Canadian expatriate. Next will come Ricardo's walking tour through the old Jewish quarter. Catching my breath, I realize that I have not retained a single name: I recall a blur of eager faces, broad smiles, clasped hands, effusive goodwill, and no real communication at all. In an earlier stage of my research I arrived at these same gates alongside similar package tourists, accompanying them through Portugal from site to site, community to community. Then, as today, participants were clearly as excited to meet local people as they were to tour the synagogue, and it had been relatively easy to remember the names and faces of the one or two people greeting us at each stop. But from the other side, the encounter is nothing short of overwhelming and, truth be told, a bit disconcerting. I am uncomfortably aware that our visitors have no way of knowing that I am neither Portuguese nor a member of Porto's Jewish community. All they've learned is my name.

Inside, we listen as the community representative outlines the synagogue's history. As soon as he mentions the early twentieth-century discovery of surviving Marranos and their significance to the building, the tourists are visibly more attentive. A clamor of questions: they want to know how many Marranos there were, how they found safe harbor, what their rituals were like, where they've gone, whether their descendants still identify as Jews. At this, Ricardo steps forward and clears his throat. "There are still Marranos in Portugal," he says. "But we're not all rural villagers." Their guide translates and the tourists look at Ricardo in wonder. A Marrano, a secret Jew, the Inquisition's surviving remnant, here, in front of them! But the community representative ignores the interruption and continues his presentation. As soon as we are back outside, the tourists bombard Ricardo with questions, crowding around to hear him. An elegantly dressed woman takes his hand and holds it tightly, listening intently; an elderly man claps him on the back, grinning. They ask his family surnames. Several announce that their own ancestors escaped from Portugal centuries earlier, fleeing the Inquisition. They are thrilled to meet someone here who might be kin.

For Ricardo and Miguel, the tourists offer an encounter with kinship of a different order. For most of their visitors, the word *Marrano* conjures images of families: families practicing secret rituals together, marrying only among other Marrano families, passing their identity and practices from mother to daughter across the centuries. But at the turn of the twenty-first century, those who identify as Marranos in urban Portugal are typically the only ones in their natal family to pursue a connection with Judaism, and most began to do so only in young adulthood. Though many heard as children that they had Jewish ancestors on one side or the other, they were taught no secret prayers growing up, nor was there an emphasis on socializing with other families of the same background. They do not know their Jewish ancestors' names, nor even the approximate location of the last practicing Jew on the family tree. Nonetheless, most associate their Jewishness with kinship: at this moment in history, August 2004, they understand descent—genealogical lineage—to be the primary element binding them to the Jewish people, for whom they feel a great affinity in the abstract but with whom they have few opportunities for direct interaction. Thus to be greeted warmly by visiting Jews is, for Portugal's urban Marranos, to reconnect by proxy with their broken lineage and to experience belonging—however fleetingly—among their own lost tribe.

·   ·   ·

This is a book about the desire for belonging, about identifying with a particular social category and having that claim to affiliation denied. It is about the ways that cultural logics of kinship inform imaginings of self in relation to others, individually and collectively, both back in time and across vast distances, and the ways those same logics work in practice to render some people strangers and others, kin. I open with the encounter between Ricardo, a would-be Jew-by-descent denied Jewish belonging in his local context, and the Italian Jewish tourists, who readily embraced him as a Marrano and potential kinsman, because it highlights how fleeting interactions in distinct social spaces allow different expressions of self, and hence different experiences of belonging or exclusion, to come to the fore. These expressions of self are not random. As I show in the chapters that follow, understandings of oneself and of one's place in different social worlds are culturally patterned and contextually contingent. The defining criteria of Jewishness have always varied widely across cultural contexts, over time, and from one social sphere to another (Cohen 1999; Herskovits 1927); small wonder, then, that "marginal" groups like Ricardo and his counterparts, who understand themselves to be Jewish according to criteria that are to them entirely reasonable, often find that recognition as Jews by others is far from guaranteed.

The warmth and fascination the Italian tourists showed Ricardo and Miguel did not arise from nowhere. They, like so many other Jewish visitors, arrived fully aware of Portugal's dramatic history of secret Judaism, and that history engendered feelings of affinity for all Marranos they encountered during their tour, rural and urban. Indeed, *affinity* was a term I heard over and over throughout my research, in conversations both in English and in Portuguese. As we will see, in Portugal and around the world people from a wide range of backgrounds articulated feelings of connection, resonance, likeness, sympathy, shared essence, and even direct ancestral linkage with the hidden Jews of Portugal's past and their descendants in the present. In Portugal, those who called themselves Marranos also expressed such affinities for Jews in the abstract, for the ancestral population from whom they felt their connection had been severed, and, ultimately, for a small number of individual visitors who returned repeatedly to teach and guide them. The assumption, nature, and consequence of these diverse forms of affinity comprise my central theme.

Ricardo and Miguel, like a great many other participants in my research, were members of organizations created by and for people who believed they had "lost" Portuguese Jewish roots, as well as individuals merely interested in learning about the country's Jewish history. Dismissed by the mainstream Jewish communities and lacking access to educational materials, communal support, and even basic knowledge of Judaism, members of these organizations turned to each other, the internet, and foreign Jewish travelers for information and encouragement. By the early 2000s they were regularly hosting tour groups and international Jewish outreach workers, who traveled to Portugal in hopes of bringing the country's storied Marranos back to the Jewish world at large. My own work in Portugal began in 2002, just as interaction with foreign Jews was rapidly increasing, and continued during eighteen months of intensive fieldwork in Lisbon and Porto (from 2004 to 2006), followed by return visits in 2007 and 2008.

The events recounted in this book took place largely within Portugal, but their imaginative and interpersonal context often reached far beyond its borders. This is a study of global interconnection, not only to the degree that the infrastructure and cultural flows of globalization enable the kinds of imaginings and interactions I explore in the pages that follow, but equally in subjective perceptions of *being connected* to others, both far back in time and widely around the globe. The question of identity, too, is woven throughout this work. From an anthropological perspective, identities are neither fixed nor inherent, but are created and reproduced continuously through social practice and in interaction with others (Holland et al. 1998; Pieterse 2007). While urban Marranos understood themselves to descend from hidden Jews and consciously adopted a set of practices and attitudes they felt were appropriate to that self-designation, their overt exclusion from Portuguese Jewish life, knowledge, and religious practice continuously challenged it. As Ricardo's story shows us, however, Jewish visitors from abroad provided an alternative social space in which to express their evolving sense of self. Viewed simultaneously against the backdrop of Portuguese understandings of identity and ancestry and in light of models of Jewish peoplehood invoked by tourists and other foreign interlocutors, the urban Marranos' constructions of self reveal the dense entanglement of kinship categories with the dynamics of identification and belonging across local, national, and global spheres of encounter.

My analysis proceeds through a series of turning points in the Portuguese Marrano movement, each providing a context for considering a distinct set of theoretical issues regarding identity, the self, social practice, tourism and cross-cultural communication, and (global) kinship. Taken together, they offer a narrative account of the movement itself, beginning with the earliest history of Portuguese hidden Jews through to the consolidation of urban Marrano identity in the 1990s and 2000s, proceeding to analysis of the continual influence of visitors from abroad, and concluding with discussion of the formal "return" of a group of Marranos to their ancestral faith before a London rabbinic court in 2006. Throughout, Jews from other countries—in the abstract, in imaginings sourced from popular media, in face-to-face interaction, and in direct communication online or by telephone—will prove central to Marranos' shifting understanding of themselves ancestrally and in relation to the Jewish world and, above all, to their experiences of kinship or estrangement.

This, then, is a book for anyone interested in the nature of identity and belonging in an era of globalization; in the malleability of social categories, whether chosen or ascribed; in the ways that cultural logics of kinship, prior imaginings, and expressions of emotion inevitably color face-to-face interactions; and in the processes and practices through which individuals come to know themselves and to recognize others as comrades, compatriots, and kin. While the story at the book's heart is that of Portugal's urban Marranos, this is also a larger story of how diverse forms of kinship, relatedness, and belonging evolve across scales of human sociality, from the global to the interpersonal and back again. I offer an ethnography of affinities felt and affirmed or denied, a fine-grained analysis of the mechanisms through which perceptions of likeness, mutuality, and interconnection—in the expansive, implicitly global sense of Jewish peoplehood—are concretized and tested "on the ground," in the resolutely local context of face-to-face interaction.

As with any form of identity, ethnic, religious, or otherwise, the Marranos' experience of *identification*—the process through which one comes to think of oneself as belonging to or essentially connected with a particular social category—occurred within webs of interconnection, both imaginative and intersubjective. These interconnections were everywhere shot through with ideas and expressions of affinity, encompassing not only essential relatedness but also, as the definition that opens this chapter suggests, experiential echoes, analogical resonance, and feelings of attraction, sympathy, and common interest. When grounded in repeated face-to-face encounters, such diffuse feelings of affinity can give rise to family-like bonds, based on mutual expressions of love, care, nurturance, and investment of time and energy. Hence my analysis makes particular note of *affect,* the communicative register in which emotions, feelings, and subjectivities take shape and gather force in relations between individuals (Richard and Rudnyckyj 2009), for it proved a critical factor in the outcome of interactions between Marranos, their foreign visitors, and members of the Portuguese Jewish communities. Ultimately, their story reveals that close physical proximity and face-to-face expressions of affect remain the productive sphere for identification and belonging—even as heightened global interconnectivity generates ever more opportunities for encounter.

PORTUGUESE MARRANOS, RURAL AND URBAN

To identify as a Marrano in contemporary Portugal is to tie oneself to intersecting histories of descent and rupture, both Portuguese and Jewish. In the Middle Ages, Portugal was home to a thriving, centuries-old Jewish community, one of the world's largest, that was abruptly obliterated by mass forced conversion in 1497. Many of the unwilling converts attempted to continue practicing Judaism in secret, but 250 years of Inquisitorial scrutiny rooted out all but the most stalwart. The rest assimilated into the Catholic mainstream. Those few who were able to escape from Portugal joined existing Iberian-origin Jewish communities abroad (Benbassa and Rodrigue 2000).[3] By the eighteenth century, Portugal seemed a country entirely without Jews (Martins 2006). Their absence constituted a profound shift for both the Portuguese nation and world Jewry, a rupture in the historical trajectory of two peoples, remembered by both even today. Among Jews, it is part of the story of the Sephardic diaspora, the branch of the Jewish people made up of descendants of those who fled persecution in Spain and Portugal, and of the heroic Inquisition-era Marranos, who persisted in their faith even at risk of death and survived in small, hidden communities until well into the twentieth century. For the Portuguese, it is a piece of their long and complex ethnic and religious history, according to which the forced converts contributed one more ancestral stream—joining the Celtic, Germanic, Mediterranean, and "Moorish"—said to run in the nation's veins (Bastos 2000).

For those who consider themselves Marranos in urban Portugal today, both that descent and its rupture are deeply personal, often painfully so. Unlike the "rural villagers" from whom Ricardo differentiated himself, who maintained a collective sense of themselves as Jews over centuries by raising each new generation in an isolated, closed community (Garcia 1993), the self-titled Marranos of Portugal's major metropolitan areas came to an ancestral Jewish identity on their own, usually in adulthood, through an extended period of study and introspection. In their solitary quest to become Jews in the present, many described themselves as first discovering and then recovering something brutally wrenched from their ancestors by the Inquisition. Because the distinction between the two groups of "Marranos" is critical to understanding the city-dwellers at the heart of this book, throughout I distinguish the latter as *urban* Marranos. Nonetheless, the rural Marranos— that is, intact communities of secret Jews—will remain visible in the margins throughout, for to this day their fame fuels ancestral imaginings among urban Marranos and shapes the expectations of Jewish visitors from afar.

Marrano Associations

Rather than the family or the village, it was the institution of the *associação* (Pt.; association, society, federation) that brought Portugal's urban Marranos together and cemented their collective identity. *Associações*—voluntary, affinity-based membership organizations—are a common feature of the Portuguese social landscape. Often focused on recreational and cultural interests like sports, film, or the arts, associations also form around regional, national, ethnic, or religious origins (Costa 2002; Sardinha 2009). Immigrant *associações,* for example, typically serve their members both as mutual aid societies and as spaces of familiarity and solidarity. Long-term foreign residents or postcolonial citizens and their descendants create associations to preserve linguistic and cultural heritage, whether in private community celebrations or public folkloric displays, and religious communities typically have ancillary associations as well. As a social institution, then, the Portuguese *associação* encompasses anything from a literary circle of five members to an immigrant-based cultural association of five hundred, from a denominational youth group for Angolan-Portuguese teenagers to a professionally run, nongovernmental organization (NGO) serving the deaf nationwide. Whatever the focus, *associações* have certain features in common: by-laws, membership rolls, regular dues, nonprofit status, and recognition from the state as legal entities advancing shared objectives.

In the early 2000s, each of Portugal's two largest cities had a "Marrano" association: in Lisbon, HaShalom Jewish Association, and in Porto, Menorá Jewish Cultural Association.[4] In the spectrum of *associações,* they occupied a murky niche. Not exactly religious, nor solely cultural, they were created neither as ethnic minority associations nor as identity-based support groups. Their interstitial character became especially apparent in 2005, when the City of Porto inaugurated its Municipal Council of Communities (*Conselho Municipal das Comunidades*). Intended to provide a voice for the city's diverse resident minority populations, the council comprised representatives from twelve different *associações.* The local Jewish community association, Associação Comunidade Israelita do Porto,[5] had a seat alongside groups like the Porto Hindu Association and the Luso-African Methodist Association. Porto's Marrano association, on the other hand, did not. Menorá members explained to me that this was because they were not an immigrant group—on the contrary, by definition their ancestors had lived on Portuguese soil hundreds of years earlier—nor, they said, could they be recognized as an ethnic minority because their physical appearance, cultural practices, and family names were all those of ordinary Portuguese. Moreover, as (ancestral) Jews they were already represented by the Jewish community association, even if the latter did not recognize them among its constituents, and so they could not claim a "community" seat as an association representing a minority religion. Nonetheless, Menorá's president attended the inaugural meeting, inviting me along and chatting comfortably afterward with the council's official members. However different the social niche held by their respective *associações,* council members had collaborated with Menorá on joint events in the past and understood it to be engaged in a similar enterprise: a struggle for recognition, identity, and solidarity.

Menorá and HaShalom were founded within a few years of each other, in 2002 and 1999, respectively. The two groups' leaders communicated frequently about common concerns by text and email, sometimes daily, and collaborated on strategic planning, occasionally making the three-hour train journey between cities to meet face-to-face. At weekly meetings, participants gathered to plan activities and to discuss Jewish history and religious practice, as well as to commiserate over their difficulty joining the local Jewish community. Each association had approximately forty dues-paying members, most of whom knew one another despite the more than two hundred miles separating them. If not already acquainted through personal networks or social media, they met when the associations held joint holiday events or at their annual national meeting, which also attracted participants from other parts of the country. Thus at the beginning of the 2000s it could be said that there was a single urban, ancestrally Jewish community forming in Portugal, a coherent social space distributed across two distinct geographical regions and centered primarily in local associations.

Association Members

Initially, the members of HaShalom and Menorá seemed to me a fairly homogeneous group. Of the thirty most active participants, most were relatively young—in 2005 the average age was forty—and only four had children. The majority were single, either divorced or never married, with roughly equal numbers of men and women. By Portuguese standards they were well educated, having completed at least a year of postsecondary education at a time when just 60 percent of working adults nationwide had attended school past age fifteen.[6] Several were graduate students or professional academics. Regardless of educational attainment, all were avid, proficient researchers. They shared a fascination with anything Jewish—history, culture, politics, religious practice—and were articulate, well read, and passionate about their involvement.

From their dress, demeanor, and communication style, I interpreted them to be upper-middle-class white-collar workers and professionals. Because the Portuguese consider it impolite to ask a relative stranger's occupation and work was rarely discussed at meetings, weeks or months passed before I learned through casual conversation what each person did. In fact they ran the gamut from gardener to filmmaker, trucking dispatcher to translator, psychiatrist to secretary. There were several lawyers, a hairdresser, two poets, a preschool teacher, a bookstore cashier—in short, a mix of professionals and hourly employees in a wide range of sectors, from diverse working- and middle-class backgrounds. Within the context of the Marrano associations, however, these differences were unremarked and evidently unimportant. The only explicit invocations of social identity within the group highlighted what they—the Marranos (*os marranos*) or B'nai Anusim (*os b'nei anussins*)—had in common: a conviction that they had Jewish ancestors; a fundamental sense of themselves as Jewish but no directly transmitted familial legacy of Jewish practice; a desire for acknowledgment of their Jewishness by others; and a shared experience of being individually and collectively marginalized and even openly spurned at the synagogues in Lisbon and Porto.

During my time with the Marrano associations, I became increasingly aware of an additional, more muted commonality: most participants expressed feeling somehow different from the societal mainstream. The subject generally arose indirectly, as an analogy for their marginalization from Portugal's normative Jewish communities, but their sense of being "other" reflects a central aspect of Portuguese social life that is important for understanding their experience. Until the last quarter of the twentieth century Portugal was a profoundly class-stratified society, with a small ruling elite and a vast population of farmers, unskilled laborers, and urban poor. Today the underlying class consciousness, now expanded to a growing middle class, is crosscut by numerous other forms of affiliation and differentiation, a matrix continuously if intuitively used to ascertain who is or is not "one of us" and hence who will have access to one's restricted social networks. These range from regional distinctions—rural/urban, north/south, mainland/island, and, above all, Lisbon versus the rest of Portugal—to hierarchies based on education, pedigree, accent, and employment, among many others. Determinations of who is outside or inside one's group, different from or similar to oneself, are continuously if implicitly negotiated and reproduced in everyday interaction.

There are also numerous forms of social distinction stemming from Portugal's long history as both a colonial power and a country of emigration.

More than a quarter of the core participants in HaShalom and Menorá were *retornados* (returnees), the Portuguese term for the roughly five hundred thousand colonial-settler descendants who arrived en masse in Lisbon from the African colonies in late 1975, fleeing the violent decolonization process. Just as they had been legally classified *brancos de segunda classe* (second-class whites) during the colonial era, because their families had lived and died on African soil for generations (Errante 2003), upon arriving in Portugal the near-destitute refugees found they would be equally "second-class Portuguese"—stigmatized by custom, if not by law, and widely viewed as a burden on the nation. Other members of the *associações* were raised elsewhere, their parents having participated in a massive wave of low-wage labor migration that carried over 1.5 million Portuguese to France, Germany, and Brazil between 1960 and 1990 (Gonçalves 1996). Having returned to Portugal as teens or young adults, they were keenly aware of bearing the stigmatized accent and mannerisms of the countries where they were raised—a telltale sign of impoverished origins, despite their own upward social mobility (Koven 2007). And there were still more forms of social difference: individuals who were gay but closeted; self-made intellectuals from working-class families; middle-class Brazilians who were naturalized Portuguese citizens but felt they would never be socially accepted as fully Portuguese; and more. This is not to say that everyone in the Marrano *associações* felt outside the mainstream, but it was one of the few things this disparate group articulated in common besides a powerful commitment to being Jewish in the present.

But if a sense of marginality or existential difference was a frequent trait among urban Marranos, it was paradoxically not because they were ancestrally Jewish. For reasons discussed in the next chapter, in Portugal it is considered a truism that most Portuguese have some degree of distant Jewish ancestry. Consequently, to trace one's origins to the fifteenth-century forced converts is to articulate a direct and ancient tie to the nation, locating oneself squarely in one of its oldest social categories.[7] It is to do so, moreover, in the idiom of genealogical descent—a potent logic in a society where ancestry and familial identities are key factors in the social constitution of persons (Bouquet 1993; Pina-Cabral 1997). For urban Marranos, ancestral Jewishness was a core aspect of their sense of self: rather than merely carrying "Jewish blood" (*sangue judeu*) as one among many components in the ethnic makeup of the Portuguese people, they understood themselves *to be Jews* by descent—in body and in spirit—and hence felt an essential kinship with the ancestral Jewish population they had rediscovered and, above all, with the Jewish people as a whole. Nonetheless, because their understanding of what makes one "Jewish" differed fundamentally from that of the members of the Jewish communities of Lisbon and Porto, that sense of kinship was not reciprocated within the social space of the local synagogues, or indeed anywhere among Portugal's "mainstream" Jews.

KINSHIP AS CATEGORY, CLASSIFICATION, AND FEELING

For anthropologists, *kinship* is a technical term. It refers to culturally variable systems of social classification according to which some people are more closely related than others, as well as the roles, rights, and obligations that inhere in different types of relationships (Holy 1996: 9). As an analytical category, kinship subsumes both "the family" as a domestic unit and "descent groups" defined by lineage of a common ancestor; both have long been central to anthropological understandings of how societies are organized. While the criteria used to determine kin vary cross-culturally—including, for example, procreation, nurturance, coresidence, and shared substances like blood or food—for most of the twentieth century scholars assumed that these were merely different means of describing the familiar Western genealogical grid of biological descent and marriage (Schneider 1984; Holy 1996).

In recent decades, anthropologists have increasingly used the concept of *relatedness* as an alternative to kinship, marking a shift away from the long-held presumption that biological reproduction is everywhere a constitutive element in reckoning kin (Carsten 2000; Franklin and McKinnon 2001). Instead, by examining culturally particular processes by which people *become* kin—from practices transforming international adoptees into the children of their adoptive parents in contemporary Norway (Howell 2006) to the creation of "chosen" gay and lesbian families in 1980s America (Weston 1991)—we have become aware of the powerful role of sentiments, solidarities, acts of nurturance and care, religious beliefs about the nature of personhood, predestination, and family, resemblance and recognition, and even conscious choice in determining the content and bounds of the category "kin," as locally defined, for those involved.[8] This move to capture how people act upon and feel kinship with specified others in practice, rather than simply noting the "natural facts" of kin ties or stated norms, has, perhaps predictably, been met with protests that "relatedness" is far too vague a concept, so indistinguishable from other forms of social relations that it "cannot be separated in any precise way from the general notion of the social and thus endowed with a meaning which would prevent it from becoming intellectually vacuous" (Holy 1996: 168). But this objection misses a fundamental ethnographic truth: people tell us that they feel connected to others in an essential sense that they articulate in the language of family and concretize in expressions of nurturance and care. Relatedness—whether imagined or lived out face-to-face—is a social fact, and it is not limited to "kinship" as mapped in the traditional genealogical chart. It is precisely the term's flexibility that makes it so analytically useful.

Attending to relatedness rather than the presuppositions of twentieth-century kinship theory also permits us to follow people's feelings and commitments when they lead us across cultural domains and scales of social organization (Franklin and McKinnon 2001; McKinnon and Cannell 2013). In European and European-settler societies, relatedness is typically understood to inhere in shared ancestry, articulated in terms of blood or, increasingly, DNA. But if that were the sole criterion, how would one draw the line between kin and non-kin? After all, if we go back far enough in time all human beings share common ancestors, as do all mammals, even all vertebrates; and there is consequently no necessary limit to which we could count cousins (collateral kin), not even by species. As there is a Western cultural model of "the family of man," defined by common descent, so, too, could we entertain the thought of a "family of hominids." The point at which relatives give way to non-relatives is ultimately a matter of cultural systems of classification (Zerubavel 2012). Rather than presuming definitive distinctions between cultural domains like the nuclear family, descent group, nation, or ethnicity, if we follow this trajectory of thought and view relatedness as equally "real" for those who recognize it at larger scales, the use of kinship terminology for broad collectivities emerges as something other than mere metaphor (Carsten 2004; Nash 2005). Indeed, I suggest that relatedness operates at different scales not distinctly, but as an experiential continuum; and its kinship character is recognizable not only in our research participants' words but also in their reasoning, affect, and actions.

To illustrate the interpenetration of reasoning about different scales of relation, consider the symbolic significance of shared blood (Carsten 2011). In Portugal, blood is a defining symbol of "family" (Pina-Cabral 1991: 128–33), but it is also a key symbol of ethnonational belonging: the discourse of "Portuguese blood" is alive and well in everyday conversation. Is the "blood" of one's family the same "blood" that connects one to the nation? In the case of Jewishness, the two are explicitly one and the same (Schneider 1977: 70): according to Jewish law, Jewishness is carried through the maternal "bloodline," and in many countries—including both the United States and Portugal—Jews and non-Jews make casual reference to "Jewish blood" (Glenn 2002; Boyarin 2013: 107–10). Thus "blood" grounds a continuum of relatedness running from the Jewish nuclear family to the Jewish people at large, "a kinship that is, to be sure, not merely biological or 'racial,' but is nevertheless inherited" (Boyarin 2013: 124). While the relatedness one feels to one's immediate family and the relatedness one feels to the ethnic group or the nation are not necessarily the same, in this case they exist along a spectrum. Again, the quality or subjective feeling of relatedness is a matter of degree, not of kind.

In articulating their Jewishness in terms of descent, urban Marranos relied upon a discourse of lineage that was equally—if differently—intelligible to both Portuguese and Jewish listeners. While their logic did not always mesh with that of their interlocutors, it was nonetheless familiar, and for many foreign visitors it sufficed to render them part of "the Jewish family." And yet here the time-honored anthropological question of how descent groups are reckoned, and especially how individuals are socially emplaced by them—that is, how the person is classified as belonging to a particular social category based on ancestral lineage (Holy 1996)—is turned on its head. Rather than being ascribed to a predetermined descent group by the social facts of their birth and the birth of relevant ancestors before them, urban Marranos in effect decided for themselves the group to which they would belong and pointed to ancestry as the reason. Writing of similarly multi-scalar, deep-time "kinship narratives" used by white-settler descendants to support their claims to Kenyan national belonging, anthropologist Janet McIntosh (2015: 264) notes that they too emphasize "one lineage as the focal point of their rights [to belong] . . . while disregarding other ancestors who came more recently from elsewhere." Nonetheless, she cautions, "the perception of relatedness always involves selective and culturally-based storytelling about which relationships are important to our claims, which are not, and why" (2015: 255). Even when voiced in direct response to challenges to the speaker's identity, such "simplifications of complex lineages" may reflect deeply felt, even mystical beliefs about linkages between ancestral ties, the self, and feelings or emotions (McIntosh 2015: 259–61; Basu 2007; Sturm 2010).

Voluntary claims of ancestral belonging do not always convince, however sincerely they may be offered. During the tourist visit with which this chapter began, we watched as a local Jewish community representative impassively ignored Ricardo's statement of Marrano origins. Moments later, the Italian tourists reacted to the same statement with a shower of attention and interpersonal warmth, demonstrated by close physical proximity, smiles, words, and touch. Why the difference? In part, it is a matter of whether these individuals came to the interaction interested primarily in personhood or in peoplehood, in determining whether one particular individual was legitimately "a Jew" or in welcoming back an entire lost branch of the Jewish family tree.

This is an important illustration of how, as a classificatory system, the logic of kinship can give rise to disconnection and exclusion as much as to recognition and inclusion (Franklin and McKinnon 2001: 15–20). The description of the Jewish people as a "family" is commonplace among Jews worldwide, likely stemming from centuries of liturgical emphasis on collective descent from the biblical patriarchs and matriarchs and the many holidays memorializing trials and triumphs of earlier generations. Not only are prayers directed to "our God, God of our ancestors, God of Abraham, Isaac, and Jacob,"[9] but home-based holidays like Hanukkah and Passover, typically observed by even the most secular of Jews, commemorate events of the past as if they happened directly and collectively to those assembled: "*We* were slaves to Pharaoh in Egypt, and the Lord ... took us out from there with a mighty hand and an outstretched arm," recounts the Passover Haggadah, read aloud each year. Such regular rehearsal of "sociobiographical memory" (Zerubavel 1996) inculcates a sense of shared ancestral experience with all Jews, everywhere, over generations and across oceans.

Nonetheless, the defining criteria of "the Jewish family" vary sharply from one community to the next. Nowhere is this more apparent than in debates over the authenticity of groups seeking recognition as Jews on the basis of collective lineage. Over the past fifty years, not only Iberian Marranos but populations in southern Africa, Central and East Asia, India, South America, and other far-flung locales have claimed to have, or have been identified as having, distant Jewish ancestry (Charmé 2012; Parfitt and Semi 2002).[10] In some cases their kinship narratives specify direct descent from the Ten Lost Tribes, separated from the rest of the Jewish people nearly three thousand years ago (Ben-Dor Benite 2009). But whether traced over thousands of years or merely hundreds, such ancestral claims provoke uncomfortable reflection among Jews on how far out the "branches" of the Jewish family tree can be traced, and on what basis. Ensuing debates make the terms of Jewish identification and belonging explicit, as framed both by those seeking recognition and by those who would accept or deny them (Egorova and Perwez 2013; Seeman 2009); hence they help us tease apart the many strands forming such social identities and the complex processes through which groups recognize others as alien or kin.

What makes a population Jewish? What makes an individual a Jew? Ethnographic studies of *Jewishness*—the qualities and content of being Jewish, whether in one's own eyes or in the eyes of others (Cohen 1999)—in diverse parts of the world have revealed that answers to these questions vary widely, emphasizing everything from religious adherence to fractional ancestry to cultural or linguistic practices (Brink-Danan 2008; Klein 2014; Lehrer 2013: 176–96). Yet whether understood locally in terms of religion, race, ethnicity, tribe, culture, genetic inheritance, or soul (Herskovits 1927; Markowitz 2006), there remains a consistently articulated belief that "the Jews" are a distinct people with a shared history. Indeed, one of the few characteristics people who identify as Jews everywhere seem to share is an awareness that there are people in other lands who are also called "Jews," whose customs may be different but whose destinies are in some sense linked to their own. It is precisely their claim to peoplehood despite the lack of any other consistently unifying feature that makes Jews so "good to think with" about such long-standing anthropological concerns as identity, ethnicity, relatedness, and belonging (Klein 2012; Dominguez 1989). That different individuals may draw upon entirely different domains to explain their sense of identification with Jews from other parts of the world—from ritual observance to ethnicity, shared culture to common descent—reminds us of the extent to which all expressions of social solidarity are, like the identities from which they stem, both socially produced and culturally inflected.

Identifying with the entirety of the Jewish people is one thing; recognizing a given individual as a Jew is another. As anthropologist Daniel Segal (1999: 236) reminds us, understandings of how individuals might know a Jew when they see one—including in their own family tree or even their own soul—are based on *typifications,* received and widely shared perceptions of what defines a particular population. While they do not necessarily reflect empirical reality, typifications reveal underlying cultural assumptions about the nature of identity, difference, descent, and belonging that extend far beyond the particularities of the Jewish case. How a given population distinguishes between Jews and non-Jews indicates a great deal about how they conceive of and ascribe other forms of social identity, too (Hoffman 2001; Klein 2012). In the Portuguese case, constructions of Jewishness draw simultaneously on two distinct systems of social identification, giving rise to two quite different typifications—ancestral (innate) and religious (practiced)—and making the determination of who is or is not "a Jew" a complicated matter indeed.

According to Jewish law, or *halakhah,* there is a straightforward answer to the question of who is a Jew: only the biological offspring of a Jewish mother, herself the biological daughter of a Jewish mother, and so on back in time. For Jews-by-birth, halakhah does not distinguish between those who practice the rituals of Judaism and those who do not. Belief, too, is irrelevant, as is the Jewish status of the father. Only matrilineal descent or, absent a Jewish mother, voluntary conversion under rabbinic supervision will suffice. But in practice, things are decidedly less clear. Conversion is not always an option, however fervent the desire, as a proselyte cannot begin the process without a community willing to accept him or her and, at the very least, a supervising rabbi—not an insignificant hurdle in regions with very small Jewish populations and few if any rabbis. Consequently, a would-be convert may be a longtime adherent to Jewish religious practice and even an accepted participant in a Jewish community without being considered "a Jew." Moreover, a convert to some branches of Judaism, such as the liberal Reform movement or middle-road Masorti movement (known in the United States as Conservative), will not be accepted as a Jew by the rigorously observant Orthodox. And while the Reform movement accepts as Jews individuals with a Jewish father and a non-Jewish mother, Masorti/Conservative and Orthodox Judaism follow halakhah in deeming such individuals categorically non-Jewish (Klein 1996).

Yet there is a marked tendency among observant and secular Jews alike to view individuals with only paternal Jewish ancestry—or even just one great- or great-great-grandparent—as somehow more Jew*ish* than those with none at all (Klein 1996: 201–23; cf. Boyarin 2013: 118–28). Just as in the case of African, Asian, and South American groups claiming collective Jewish lineage, those who follow halakhah may consider individuals with partial ancestry to be "lost" members of the Jewish family, but not Jews, per se. Those with a more expansive, secular definition of Jewishness may see them at once as "lost" kin and as Jews—though not necessarily for the reasons Marranos and other "returning" populations understand themselves in those terms. I return to this point in subsequent chapters, for divergences in social classification proved a crucial aspect of the urban Marranos' dilemma. It was also an important factor in the diverse attitudes and expressions of affect among the two primary groups visiting the Marrano associations: tourists and Jewish outreach workers.

TOURING KIN

Foreign visitors, actual or anticipated, were a continual presence for members of the Marrano *associações* throughout the 2000s. In this sense, as a category of actors they constituted a fixed component of the local organizational dynamic. Termed *pessoas de fora* (Pt.; people from outside [the country]) by urban Marranos, those who made the journey came from diverse points around the globe, in groups, as couples, or alone. Most hailed from the United States, Canada, Brazil, England, France, Italy, Spain, and Israel, but during my fieldwork Jewish visitors also came from South Africa, Australia, Mexico, and even Venezuela and Jamaica. They represented a broad socioeconomic spectrum: schoolteachers, an airline baggage handler, professors, a boutique wine importer, lawyers, real estate agents, and a great many others. Ultimately, toward the end of my research, members of Menorá and HaShalom came to depend on a limited network of middle-class American, Canadian, English, and Israeli individuals for multiple forms of support *as kin,* a dynamic I explore in the book's final chapter.

Pessoas de Fora: *Tourists and Outreach Workers*

While the urban Marranos generally did not distinguish between types of *pessoas de fora,* their visitors tended to see themselves either as leisure travelers (here termed *tourists*) or as Jewish outreach workers. I take *tourists* to be a neutral term, meaning simply "discretionary leisure travelers whose trips begin and end in the same place" (McCabe 2009: 40; cf. Smith 1989: 1). *Jewish outreach workers* (encompassing *outreach activists* and *educators*), on the other hand, are goal-oriented travelers, often emissaries from organizations that focus on finding isolated or "lost" Jewish communities, forging person-to-person contacts, and providing educational and logistical support to facilitate their (re)integration into the Jewish world. In the 1920s two such organizations, one Dutch and one British, formed expressly to reach Marranos throughout the north of Portugal. In addition to underwriting emissaries' travels, these early outreach organizations publicized their efforts throughout Europe and the English-speaking world, generating a stream of curious tourists that has not abated a century later (Mea and Steinhardt 1997). In recent decades, the Israeli Orthodox NGOs Amishav (Heb.; My People Return) and Shavei Israel (Heb.; Returners of Israel), as well as the American-based, multiculturalist and nondenominational Kulanu (Heb.; All of Us), have played a similar role, sending rabbis or volunteers to reach the descendants of forced converts in Belmonte, Lisbon, and Porto—among many such "lost" Jewish groups worldwide—and disseminating news of their efforts via international media outlets (Charmé 2012; Cooper 2006). Independent Jewish educators, too, make the journey, volunteering to teach for a period of days or weeks in isolated Jewish communities. During my time in Portugal, over a dozen foreign visitors came to offer courses representing everything from entirely secular, "ethnic" forms of Judaism to ultra-Orthodox observance, covering topics from basic Jewish history and introductory Hebrew to detailed analysis of ethical principles in the Torah. Independent educators' visits often lasted longer than those of tourists and institutional outreach workers, who typically stayed only a few hours.

Tourism and the Desire for Connection

Why were Jewish tourists so interested in meeting Marranos? In an analysis of travelers' narratives of searching for the Ten Lost Tribes, Alanna Cooper (2006) argues that seeking Jews in other lands is a means of making sense of the condition of diaspora. While her argument is specific to Ten Tribes tales and in particular the tension between images of diaspora as either a utopic state or a profoundly undesirable condition, it captures a broader truth. The Jewish people are by definition globally dispersed, and, as noted above, the presumption of essential connection with fellow Jews everywhere is a common feature of most Jewish identities, whatever their specific cultural or religious flavor. To seek contact with far-flung Jewish populations is thus to affirm one's bond with the tribe at large, and perhaps also to experience their experiences as one's own (Kugelmass 1994: 181). As one American tourist commented to me, "Jews really care about connecting with other Jews. We want to know what's going on with Jews in other countries. It just feels important." This may explain the long-standing practice that journalist Ruth Gay (1971) dubbed "counting Jews": for centuries, Jewish travelers to distant lands have made a point of meeting local Jews (cf. Loeb 1989). They note their number, occupations, foreign customs, and religious practices and then publish an article or travelogue upon their return.[11] The tantalizing tension between familiar and exotic is surely at least partly responsible for their interest: if all Jews are kin by virtue of belonging to a common descent group, literally or metaphorically, then meeting long-lost "cousins" adds both an exciting, distinctive new dimension to "the family" and a reassuring sense of connection across difference.

Anthropologists of tourism have shown, however, that Jews are not unique in this regard. Although it takes a different form in each context, seeking contact with local coethnics while vacationing is a widespread practice, whether the traveler is undertaking genealogical tourism, traveling to an ancestral homeland to explore ethnocultural roots, or, as in the case of African American tourists to Brazil, the Caribbean, and sub-Saharan Africa, "crisscross[ing] the Atlantic hoping to find the 'same' represented by their 'black brothers and sisters' . . . [and thus] reconnecting a fragmented transnational African affiliation" (Pinho 2008: 72). In fact, recent scholarship reveals that the desire for connection is a powerful motivator of many forms of leisure travel, whether connection to local people, to fellow travelers, or to a truer version of one's self (e.g., Basu 2007). In her study of middle-class Canadian travel enthusiasts, for example, anthropologist Julia Harrison (2003: 46) notes a pervasive impulse "to either affirm or renew some kind of human connection across time, space, or cultural difference" (see, e.g., Conran 2006; Simoni 2014). Small wonder, then, that when fulfilled this desire finds expression not only in verbal effusiveness but also in gesture, physical touch, and broad expressions of positive affect—particularly when a language barrier intervenes.

While Harrison suggests it is a desire for sociability and intimacy lacking in everyday life that drives tourists to seek direct encounters and deeper engagements away from home, so too do individuals living in tourist destinations seek encounters and engagements with tourists, and for similar reasons. The urban Marranos' desire to meet foreign Jewish travelers, socialize with them, and thus find avenues to the belonging denied them locally exemplifies a much larger phenomenon: in diverse contexts around the world, anthropologists note that local populations see in tourist interactions a means to a different life—to local respect, to economic stability, to love and marriage, to overseas migration, to expressing a true inner self, or simply to being better understood (e.g., Cohen 1971; Brennan 2004; Simoni 2016). As in Ricardo's case, spending time with people entirely outside one's workaday milieu offers the possibility for different, more "authentic" aspects of the self to gain expression. Hence just as many tourists seek a deeper connection with themselves through leisure travel (Wang 1999), in their encounters with tourists many urban Marranos found a deeper connection—again, however fleetingly—with the (re)discovered Jewish self within.

Imaginaries and Affinities

There would be little reason for travelers and local people to seek contact with one another if they did not carry some preconception of what they would find. While imagination is a faculty of the individual, *imaginaries*—"shared, socially transmitted representational assemblages" of people, places, and events (Salazar and Graburn 2014: 1)—are a collective resource, the sum total of available imagery and ideas circulating in media, advertising, literature, word of mouth, and the like. As a cultural phenomenon, imaginaries give substance and meaning to individual imaginings, providing an interpretive context potentially shared by a great many people but visible only as they surface in specific images and interactions (Leite 2014). The hopes and expectations of urban Marranos were shaped largely by Portuguese imaginaries of the Jewish people at large and of the Jews of the Portuguese past; their foreign visitors, on the other hand, were motivated by imaginaries of *klal yisrael* (Heb.; all Israel, the Jewish people as a whole), or *peoplehood,* with its accompanying imagery of mutual responsibility and interconnection, and of the historical Marranos, understood as stalwart defenders of Jewish identity and faith in the face of torture and even death.

Many tourists described feeling a powerful affinity or "kinship" with Marranos, based on imaginaries drawn from Jewish legend, literature, song, and film. Some found resonance between the Marranos' perilous survival in hiding and events or feelings in their own lives; for others, an interest in Marranos emerged out of a broader identification with "the Jewish people," collectively. One elderly tourist, a Montreal native who grew up in a Yiddish-speaking community in the 1930s, explained his lifelong interest in Marranos and his impetus for traveling to Portugal by commenting that he had always had a strong feeling for *klal yisrael* and then quoting the opening lyrics of a song learned in childhood: "Tell me, Marrano, brother mine . . ." That song,

"Zog, Maran" (Yid.; Tell Me, Marrano), remains popular today, still sung in Yiddish at Passover dinners in Jewish community centers, schools, and synagogues and featured on dozens of commercial recordings. Unsurprisingly, numerous other visitors also mentioned it to me. It is an imagined dialogue, the haunting melody underscoring its tragic lines:

> Tell me, Marrano, brother mine,
> Where have you prepared your seder?
>> In a cave, our hidden meeting place,
>> There I have prepared my seder.
>
> Tell me, Marrano, where, from whom,
> Will you get the white matzo?
>> In a cave, a dark cavern,
>> My wife already kneaded the dough.
> . . .
> Tell me, Marrano, how will you live
> When your voice is heard out-ringing?
>> When the enemy finds me there,
>> I will die singing.[12]

The lyric is an early twentieth-century poem, written during a time of brutal anti-Semitic attacks on Jewish settlements across Eastern Europe. Today the song's use of Yiddish—the language of Eastern European (Ashkenazi) Jews—implicitly invokes an analogy between the suffering of Portugal's Marranos and that of the twentieth-century Ashkenazim. The analogy is familiar to Jewish audiences, based on what historian Yosef Yerushalmi (1982: 5) calls "phenomenological affinities" between the Iberian Inquisitions and European anti-Semitism of the later nineteenth and twentieth century, culminating in the Holocaust. In each case, following a prolonged period of oppression and increasing violence the ruling regime implemented a brutal, methodical process to eliminate the Jewish people, and some survived by hiding their identity. This analogy leads in turn to celebration of the Marrano as a heroic figure, the surviving spark that still burns amidst the Inquisition's ashes, a metaphor of hope for the post-Holocaust generation.

Folded into the Jewish metanarrative of destruction and survival, the Marrano experience has become part of Jewish heritage, indeed of all Jews' potential "symbolic estate," that which "is drawn from the 'heritage' available, and is worked into the actual experience of the persons involved" (Graburn 1982: 3). One can even reenact being a Marrano, attempting to feel what they felt, using items ordered from Jewish gift catalogs—a beautifully produced cookbook of "crypto-Jewish" recipes culled from Inquisition trial records,[13] for example, or a novelty "crypto-Jewish" Hanukkah menorah that when rotated 180 degrees masquerades as a flowerpot—for their story is "our" story. Hence "Zog, Maran," the song commemorating the heroic Marrano and embracing him as a close member of the Jewish family—"brother mine"—across great distances of time and space.

Individuals throughout the Portuguese and Jewish diasporas also discover Marrano history within the self, via genealogical research, familial lore, or pure intuition, as descendants of Inquisition-era Portuguese Jews are now scattered across the globe. They may internalize that history of suffering and survival as their own, a personal heritage carried, as it were, in their veins. This is an ancestral affinity—a sense of connection and sympathy across many generations—shared by the urban Marranos in Portugal. And, of course, both urban Marranos and their counterparts throughout the Portuguese diaspora professed a feeling of affinity for the present-day Jewish people in the abstract, an ineffable sense of connection that was by definition distanced but no less heartfelt for that. The perception of essential connectedness went both ways.

As "lost" Jews, Portugal's Marranos are frequently the object of outreach efforts by organizations seeking to hasten the prophesied "Ingathering of the Exiles"—the return of all Jews to the land of Israel, a prerequisite for the Messiah's arrival—or simply to encourage them to identify openly as Jews and connect with Jews in other countries. While they are sometimes invoked rhetorically as a metaphor for the perils of Jewish assimilation, they are more frequently imagined to have steadfastly maintained their faith. When descendants of Marranos come forward to embrace a Jewish identity, they are often celebrated and even revered as a symbol of Jewish survival despite generations of identity loss.

There are diverse forms of affinity—experiential resonance, mutual connection, biogenetic relatedness, shared history, and shared destiny—at work here, and at the turn of the twenty-first century each of these ways of marking connection with the figure of the Marrano was surrounded by a remarkable degree of cultural production. In an effort to grasp the imaginative context shaping foreign Jews' hopes for and expectations from their encounters in Portugal, I tracked expressions of affinity as they arose in social media, movies, radio programs, novels, folklore, the work of Jewish outreach organizations, Jewish heritage tour marketing, and ultimately conversational emphases among tourists and outreach workers. I found that imaginaries colored every encounter, not to mention the self-image of urban Marranos themselves. For the international production of imagery, text, practice, and metaphor invoking the Marranos as a symbolically charged social category made its way across the Portuguese border, just as it circulated the rest of the globe: on the internet, in film, in literature, in the words and actions of those who made the journey, urban Marranos found themselves mirrored in the eyes of the world.

For their part, urban Marranos, too, imagined the lives and cultures of Jews abroad based on globally circulating media and encounters with tourists and other Jewish visitors in Portuguese cities, as well as during their own travels. They also found resonance in aspects of Jewish theology and practice, Portuguese Jewish history, even the tribulations of the ancient Israelites. Whether expressed by foreign Jews or urban Marranos, these ancestrally, spiritually, and globally mapped forms of affinity—embraced as identity, lived in practice, materialized through travel, and tested in face-to-face inter-action—form the warp and woof of the events and arguments conveyed in this book.

CONNECTIVITY AND PROXIMITY IN A GLOBAL ERA

Although they understood themselves to be fundamentally Jewish by birth, urban Marranos faced a daunting obstacle in their efforts to live as Jews: there were virtually no locally available resources for them to learn how to do so. Lacking all but the most superficial access to the local Jewish communi-ties, they turned instead to the internet, ordering materials from abroad, participating in social media, and corresponding directly with Jews in other countries. Combined with information gathered during their own travels and via their conversations with Jewish tourists and outreach workers, the internet provided a first glimpse of how they might bring their external reality into alignment with their internal sense of self.

Their engagement with foreign Jews, not to mention their utilization of electronic media as a resource for self-making, was made possible by the rapid increase in connectivity and dramatic expansion of social relations brought about by globalization. In considering the implications of global intercon-nectivity, however, we must proceed with caution. It is all too easy to make assumptions about how the urban Marranos experienced their participation in it. To be connected to international networks of people and far-flung sources of knowledge does not necessarily mean that one *feels* connection. The circulation of information online, the rapid rise of social media, and the movement of tourists and other visitors in and out of their social sphere did not provide urban Marranos with a sense of Jewish belonging, nor of being part of "the Jewish people." As one man in Porto said when I asked why he didn't feel personally connected to Jews abroad, given how often he and the others seemed to be communicating with them online, "We don't live on the internet. We live in the real world."

Sociologist John Tomlinson makes a distinction between *connectivity* and *proximity* that helps to elucidate this subjective differentiation between communicating online and living in "the real world." If connectivity refers to the "stretching" of real-time social relations across vast distances, Tomlinson (1999: 4) writes, this must not be mistaken for being equivalent to physical proximity. Even as rhetoric of a "shrinking world" creates the perception of closer contact, "the experience of proximity afforded by these connections coexists with an undeniable, stubbornly *physical distance* between places and people in the world, which the technological and social transformations of globalization have not conjured away."[14] The more carefully we examine the subjective experience of going about daily life in actual geographic places, the clearer it becomes that we need to probe "how far connectivity establishes 'proximity' beyond the technological modality of increasing access" (Tomlinson 1999: 9). Put another way, simply knowing that one has access to and can communicate with particular far-off people does not guarantee the *feeling* of proximity; and globalization's "increasing access," even if brought to fruition in direct interaction, does not necessarily produce experiences of interpersonal engagement, communicative transparency, or intimacy.

In fact, it was everyday proximity, face-to-face relations with other people in their own cities, that initially had the greatest impact on the urban Marranos' feelings regarding the Jewish world. For reasons explored later in this book, Portugal's tiny organized Jewish community was at best unwelcoming and at worst openly and even harshly dismissive. Despite the support, acceptance, and expressions of affection they received online and in fleeting encounters with Jewish tourists and outreach workers from abroad, it was not enough to counterbalance the negative impact of interactions in the immediate social space of the synagogues and other venues where they encountered local Jews. At the same time, their positive sense of themselves as Jews and as Marranos was also profoundly local, based largely on Portuguese cultural logics of ancestry and identity and on the particularities of the Portuguese Jewish past and present. It was only when certain foreign visitors returned again and again, creating lasting, transnational emotional ties based on concrete personal relations, that their lived relationship to the Jewish world began to change, the idiom in which they articulated their Jewishness shifted from ancestry to affiliation, and they came to feel globally connected in a lasting way.

Thus, my intention in this ethnography of Portugal's urban Marrano movement is to offer a broader commentary on the nature of connectivity and social relations under conditions of globalization. In essence, my point is that technological connectivity does not always produce the experience of proximity, and proximity does not necessarily give rise to social intimacy. These are distinct modalities of interaction, and they operate at different registers, with different effects. For all the imagining of one another that people do, I suggest, it is still face-to-face social relations, personal interactions when present in the same physical location, that take primacy. Local encounters remain the productive sphere, at least where identification, relatedness, and belonging are concerned. Yet this should not be mistaken for a simple opposition between the global and the local, for the two constitute each other: global interconnectivity continuously produces new localities, new orders of face-to-face interaction, that in turn inform and shape global processes. The difference between "global" and "local" is not one of kind but, like "relatedness," a matter of scale (Tsing 2000). Nonetheless, we will see that it is often in one's immediate physical setting that experiences of belonging or exclusion carry the greatest and most lasting force.

A SENSE OF THE WHOLE

In 1977 Theron Nuñez, one of the earliest anthropologists to write on tourism, sagely remarked, "Any attempt to study an indigenous population and a tourist population in interaction will probably require talents similar to that of the Roman rider, with a foot on each horse. To make complete, accurate, and empathetic observations of both populations will necessitate a delicate balancing act" (1977: 212). He was right. To explore the relationship between mutual imaginings and face-to-face interactions, I needed to experience the encounter from both sides—from the perspective of the urban Marranos and from the perspective of Jewish heritage tourists and outreach workers who traveled to meet them. As I became aware of the myriad actors, activities, institutions, and images that impinged upon urban Marranos' sense of self, my task became more complicated still. There was a complex but coherent constellation of factors, emanating from physical locations around the world. Such multipartite systems, especially those manifested on a global scale, are inherently challenging for anthropologists (Marcus 1998; Hannerz 2003). We seek a form of "insider" knowledge that can be gained only through close proximity and regular interaction: our hallmark method, participant observation, requires that we quite literally participate in the phenomena we study, ideally as any "native" would, while observing ourselves and others doing the same. Hence I expected that by occupying multiple subject positions in diverse locations over time, I would be better situated to grasp the whole. What follows is an overview of those "locations," both physical and virtual, and the angles of vision they afforded.

Locations

My primary position in the field, over the longest period (from 2004 to 2006), was that of a member of Menorá and HaShalom. For eighteen months I divided my time between them, participating fully as a dues-paying member. In addition to attending each group's weekly meetings, I accompanied members to Introduction to Judaism classes, Jewish-related events, and synagogue services; attended a jointly planned national meeting; and participated alongside them whenever visitors arrived from abroad. When outreach workers offered classes, I too was a student, as most of the material was equally new to me. I was frequently asked to translate orally and in writing, an intermediary role that was both illuminating and ethically complex, particularly during members' emotion-charged, family reunion–style interactions with organized tour groups.

The urban Marranos were educated, often cosmopolitan individuals, all of them avid readers, who understood the idea of anthropological research. They gamely participated in my continuous informal interviewing, joking about when the little notebook in my bag would make its next appearance. Many went out of their way to connect me with others who might be helpful for my work, offering references on Marrano history and actively including me in their organizational planning and activities. I soon learned that my initial impression of homogeneity in the two associations was an artifact of the way I originally encountered them: as a collectivity. I met most members in 2002 and 2004 as a participant observer on package tours of "Jewish

Portugal," in prearranged meetings listed on the itinerary simply as a visit with "local Anusim" or "crypto-Jews." When I subsequently returned as a lone ethnographer, I initially continued to interact with them as a unified group, at meetings, the synagogue, and post-event dinners.

After a few months I began to socialize with them as individuals in cafés, over restaurant dinners with one or two others, and eventually in their homes. Over time I became a confidante, the insider-outsider who could be trusted to listen, even as members knew I was studying them; some became my dear friends. After returning home in early 2006, I stayed in regular contact with members of HaShalom, as several were preparing to go before a London rabbinic court for a ritual process that would result in their formal recognition as Jews. Three months later, I flew to London to accompany them through that process as participant observer, translator, and friend. The nature and duration of this intensive fieldwork, combined with lengthy individual interviews at the conclusion of my research, gave me a deep appreciation for the internal journey participants made over the course of my time with them.

Were it not for the internet, neither I nor the urban Marranos would have been aware of the extraordinarily diverse, international network of people engaged in thinking about Portugal's "lost" Jews and their descendants. Nor, I imagine, would the other participants in my research, many of whom met online and corresponded regularly over vast geographical distances. One crucial nexus was the Nostálgia network.[15] Created and moderated by a South Africa–born descendant of Portuguese hidden Jews, it served from its inception in 1997 as an online information hub and contact point for individuals throughout the Portuguese diaspora who were exploring possible Jewish ancestry. Many urban Marranos joined its discussion forum, a listserv. Also among the more than one thousand subscribers were past and future tourists, genealogists, academics, and staff and supporters of outreach organizations like Kulanu and Shavei Israel. English, Portuguese, French, and Spanish were all accepted languages, with traffic peaking in 2004 at 820 posts emailed to members in a single month.

Although I joined the forum in 2000 and remained a subscriber until 2006, at the turn of the century fieldwork online was quite unusual and I did not treat Nostálgia as a field site per se. Instead, it became a means for me to engage online and, in many cases, face-to-face with a global network of people for whom any and all Portuguese Jews, past or present (and whether referred to as Marranos, crypto-Jews, Jews, or B'nai Anusim), were of great interest. Remarkably, seemingly everywhere I went—Marrano associations, Jewish heritage tours, Marrano-related conferences and lectures, meetings of Jewish outreach organizations, even among tourists attending services at one of Portugal's three synagogues—I encountered Nostálgia subscribers. It was the international nexus for people invested in the memory of Portugal's Inquisition-era Jews and/or their present-day descendants. Through this early social media hub, participants formed friendships from afar that subsequently blossomed face-to-face—in a Portuguese café, on a heritage tour, at a conference, in purposeful travel to visit one another. Indeed, it was through Nostálgia that several urban Marranos—and I—first became aware that HaShalom and Menorá existed. It was also how I initially met outreach activists and Jewish educators who would later visit Portugal and play an important part in my research. More than a hobbyist website, Nostálgia was the sole portal to a kaleidoscopic network of relationships and perspectives.

One of the most fruitful of those perspectives came through a tour bus window. Early in my preparations for fieldwork, Nostálgia founder Graciana Mayer and a handful of subscribers organized two ten-day package tours, held in 2002 and 2004, in conjunction with a secular Jewish outreach organization. These were advertised as "Conference-Tours," emphasizing their scholarly and goal-oriented character as a hybrid of education and outreach, targeting descendants of hidden Jews both on and off the bus. Each tour was designed for a combined audience of people of "lost" Portuguese Jewish ancestry, Jewish outreach workers, and scholars specializing in crypto-Jewish studies, with more of the former participating in the first tour and more of the latter two in the second. In all, the tours attracted fifty-two participants from ten countries on five continents, the overwhelming majority already Nostálgia members. Once living in Portugal, in 2005 I participated in five more tours: a ten-day bus tour titled "On the Trail of Jewish Portugal," designed for European members of a Jewish women's organization and their spouses, and four trips in private cars, where couples found their way to me beforehand via word of mouth, wrote to me for advice planning their itinerary, and consented to have me join them. I also informally interviewed tourists whom I encountered at Jewish heritage sites or following services at the mainstream synagogues, sometimes joining them for part of their journey as well.

Occupying the methodological position of "a tourist among tourists" (Graburn 2002: 25) and thus continuously on the move throughout "Jewish Portugal," my interactions with the Marrano associations and local Jewish communities were brief, framed within a touristic encounter that lasted no more than an hour or two. The long hours on the road, on the other hand, provided ample opportunity for informal but in-depth interviews with participants who were already discussing their observations and reactions with one another (Bruner 2005; Graburn 2002). Afterward, I conducted follow-up interviews whenever and however the opportunity arose—by phone, face-to-face in restaurants and homes in several countries, even over coffee at my own kitchen table. In all, I traveled with and/or interviewed well over one hundred tourists and more than twenty outreach workers.

Finally, in order to situate the urban Marrano movement in its national context I lived as would any middle-class young academic in Porto or Lisbon, participating in each city's social and cultural life. I lived in several different apartments, each in a different neighborhood, sharing lodging with Portuguese friends or fellow foreign students and researchers. To understand the place of religious and ethnic minorities in Portugal, past and present, I attended academic conferences, public lectures, municipal and regional "heritage days," and book launches. I also participated in events hosted by the normative Jewish communities and interviewed staff at the Israeli embassy, interactions that offered unexpected insights into the politics of Jewish belonging both locally and internationally.[16] Even socializing and vacationing with Portuguese friends and my own long-lost kin, third cousins in Lisbon, deepened my understanding. And, of course, I chatted with neighbors, drove, grocery shopped, ate, slept, read, and simply lived there, sharing the pleasures and frustrations of Portuguese urban life.

Multisited Ethnography, Multifaceted Self

> Intervening in an interconnected world, one is always, to varying degrees, "inauthentic": caught between cultures, implicated in others.
>
> JAMES CLIFFORD
> *The Predicament of Culture*

Mine was a peripatetic style of ethnographic research, in the tradition of what has come to be called "multisited ethnography" but has a much longer history as an unnamed but widely practiced field method. Anthropologists have always moved from place to place in the course of their research, participating in the daily activities of the people(s) under study. What has changed is not the method, but the scale on which such mobile research is conducted, just as the scale on which our research subjects' lives are lived—physically or imaginatively—has expanded as well (Appadurai 1996). Where Margaret Mead's (1928) fieldwork in Samoa took her from the beach to thatched houses to inland food-gathering sites to the weaving house, in my case the "site" spanned half the northern hemisphere. I conducted fieldwork not only in Porto, Lisbon, and elsewhere throughout Portugal, but in classrooms, cafés, synagogues, conference rooms, and private homes in California, Texas, Antwerp, and London. Some sites were more conceptual or virtual than physical; the touristic destination called "Jewish Portugal," for example, to which I returned again and again, is overlaid on the geographical landscape of Portugal, an asynchronous space mapped through tourists' imaginative engagement (Leite 2007). Fieldwork online was another form of mobility, as events unfolded simultaneously across physical and virtual domains. Even continents away, their location "in the field" was as close as the laptop on my desk or the phone in my pocket.

Ultimately I came to think of my research not as multisited, but as taking place within what Ghassan Hage (2005: 466) calls a "globally spread, geographically non-contiguous site," a "phenomenal landscape" (Comaroff and Comaroff 2003: 169) that existed not only in my own mind but also, and far more importantly, in the imagination and lived experience of many participants in my research. A single example demonstrates the point. One afternoon a year or so after I returned from Portugal, the phone rang in my Berkeley apartment. It was Anshel, an elderly Canadian outreach activist and longtime Nostálgia subscriber whom I had met repeatedly over the years, calling from New York. We had been communicating via email since our first conversation at a Texas conference in 2003 and especially after traveling together during his several visits to Portugal in 2004 and 2005, when I was his translator and driver. He called occasionally just to chat; recently our discussions had centered on a (short-lived) new outreach NGO he was creating with a group of urban Marranos. But that afternoon he had a specific favor to ask.

"I've been talking with a rabbi in Texas," he said. "He's going to northern Portugal soon. He'd like to talk to someone in the Marrano community. Which of our friends do you think I should send him to? I would put him in touch with Octávio, in Porto, but I've been having trouble tracking him down lately, and I'm not sure who would be better." I immediately thought of Paula, who also lived in Porto, and told him I would find out whether she was willing.

"So, how do you know this rabbi?" I asked, thinking it would be helpful to give Paula some background. She was fluent in four languages and always managed to find Jews on her own trips abroad—New York, Jerusalem, even Germany—and regularly met with foreign tourists and visiting rabbis in Portugal.

"Oh!" Anshel exclaimed. "It's so complicated! The rabbi, who's in Texas, wanted a contact in the north, since he's going to Porto. He wrote to Kulanu, in Washington. They told him to write to Graciana, in South Africa, since she knows everyone, right? Well, you know she's not so involved in the north anymore. She passed him on to Carlos, in Lisbon; you know how he's been really involved in the Porto group since he moved back from Canada. Carlos told the rabbi, 'If you want to meet people, you should talk to Anshel in New York. He's really in touch on a personal level.' So he called me, and now I'm calling you! Can you help?"

I did help. From my desk in Berkeley, I emailed Paula in Porto, who replied within a few hours that she would be happy to meet the rabbi and sent her greetings to Anshel; I gave her email address to Anshel, who shared it with the rabbi in Texas, who in turn emailed me with questions. When Anshel called back later that evening, I told him the rabbi and I were in touch. "Oh, how wonderful," he replied. "I'm so glad the family's expanding!" This multinational chain of personal contacts among far-flung people, all of whom had met face-to-face multiple times—except for the Texas rabbi, whose addition "expanded the family"—brought into sharp relief the globally interconnected and yet unexpectedly intimate nature of "the field" in my work.

Conducting fieldwork of this kind was surprisingly easy from a logistical perspective, though continually moving between sites was often physically exhausting. What proved more difficult was maintaining a stable sense of self, inwardly and outwardly, across the disparate physical locations in which I landed. Undertaking field research in a cultural or national context in which one is a partial participant, a descendant, a "halfie" (Abu-Lughod 1991), or even a "native" anthropologist can open doors otherwise invisible, but also brings destabilizing moments of blurring between self and other, researcher and subject (Halstead 2001; Kondo 1986; Visweswaran 1994). Such moments raise difficult ethical and epistemological questions. This is especially the case in fieldwork involving participant observation from multiple angles within a coherent system, particularly if the researcher can reasonably be read as a "native" or "halfie" in *every* subject position she occupies (Tsuda 2003).

Movement between field settings required that I make continual shifts in positionality in order to maintain focus on "the native's point of view," in the famous phrase of Bronislaw Malinowski, founder of the ethnographic method. My fieldwork began on a tour bus, descending at various sites alongside my fellow travelers to interact with local people. I first met the urban Marranos in the context of the Nostálgia Conference-Tours, both of which included Jewish outreach workers and scholars. Although *on* the bus I was interpreted primarily as Portuguese American (due to my Portuguese surname and command of the language), *off* the bus urban Marranos took me for "a mainstream Ashkenazi Jew," as one Menorá member put it. I was uncertain how to respond to either attribution. My one Portuguese great-grandparent immigrated over a century ago, and I do not identify as culturally Portuguese American. On the other hand, although I am of entirely Ashkenazi descent on my mother's side, I was not raised in a Jewish community, had no Jewish religious education, and grew up aware of only two Jewish holidays, Hanukkah and Passover, both of which were easily made secular. And while I certainly knew that my maternal family was ethnically Jewish, I have no memory of ever entering a synagogue as a child.

While my hybrid, fragmented background, once explained, was perfectly intelligible to many on the bus, particularly the Americans and Brazilians, it made little sense in the Portuguese context. When I returned to do long-term fieldwork, most local people initially continued to interact with me as a Jewish researcher, interpreting me to be like other Jewish researchers and educators who had visited them in the past. Seeing me as a potential resource, they would ask complex questions about Judaism that I was wholly unprepared to answer. Over time, they realized that I too had gained most of my knowledge of Jewish history, religion, and culture in adulthood, and that I was in many ways as estranged from my Jewish background as they were, though mine was of course many generations closer. My mother's decision not to have a Jewish wedding, which meant that my parents had no Jewish wedding contract, or *ketubah*—without which, several urban Marranos (incorrectly) informed me, my own Jewishness could not be established according to Jewish law—rendered me "in the shit, just like us," as one member of HaShalom put it early on.

But this new "insider" position was no more comfortable than being read as a "mainstream" Jew had been, for unlike the urban Marranos I was not seeking to engage in Jewish religious practice. Having seen me first as comfortably Jewish and then as a would-be Jew like themselves, they were understandably misled by my regular attendance at synagogue services and Judaism courses alongside them; although they understood the nature of my research, they had difficulty comprehending my subject position relative to it. As a result, unlike my predecessors who have done fieldwork in Catholic countries and felt the need to downplay their Jewish background (Behar 1996; Brandes 2003; Orlove 1997), in Portugal I often felt compelled to be *more* religiously Jewish than I actually was.[17]

As my fieldwork continued and first tourists and then Jewish educators came to meet with the associations in which I had become an integral member, my shape shifted once again: in the eyes of some tourists, *I* became a "Marrano," because when they asked how I had chosen this research topic I truthfully mentioned that my Portuguese-descendant father had been raised with familial oral history of Portuguese Jewish ancestry. From then on, no matter how I tried to clarify my position, foreign visitors would ask about secret rituals, unexplained practices, or special prayers I might remember from childhood, and were visibly disappointed to hear that there were none. In the eyes of outreach workers and Jewish educators, on the other hand, I was both a fellow Jew working with the Marranos and a student of Judaism like the people among whom I was doing research, both of which were in some senses correct. And expatriate Jews at the synagogues in Lisbon and Porto, some of them academics, often took me to be one of their own.

Everywhere, people seemed not only to want to find a "native" location for me within the system I was studying, but to connect with me because they saw me as being in some way fundamentally like themselves: as they sought connection with one another, so they sought it with me. Over time I came to see that we were all "natives" in a global network of people engaged in thinking about and finding belonging through Portuguese Jewishness—even myself. There seemed to be no outside position I could occupy, no safe ground to which I could retreat. At any given moment someone seemed always to be reading me in a way that felt partial, not quite correct, even inauthentic—an unanticipated outcome of taking on a multisited project that intersected with my own world and so neatly matched the sometimes uncomfortably coexisting facets of my social and internal self.

THE SEARCH FOR BELONGING

On a warm October evening in 2004, twelve Menorá members and I arrived at the Porto synagogue for the annual catered community dinner for Sukkot, the Jewish harvest festival. The rabbi, a Shavei Israel emissary whom the synagogue board grudgingly allowed to work with Marranos on-site, had encouraged us all to attend and asked that we book a spot in advance. The dinner, he said, would be 30€ (US$42) apiece. But on arriving we discovered that the board had increased the price to 40€ (US$50)—cash only. Several Menorá members grumbled (correctly, I later learned) that it was done to reduce their numbers, since only they were charged the fee; dinner was free for dues-paying synagogue members and their families. Although a few left in a huff, there were still almost as many urban Marranos present that evening as there were members of the local Jewish community, nearly all of the latter synagogue board members and their families.

While there was palpable tension from the outset, given the unhappy surprise of the increased ticket price, the situation worsened over the course of the evening. Seated together at the far end of the dining room and unfamiliar with the Orthodox sequence of ritual hand-washing, blessings over bread and wine, and silence before eating, several Menorá members made the faux pas of eating bread too early, talking at the wrong time, and not participating in blessings, prompting the community leaders' wives to shake their heads in dismay. Their children, teenagers all, sat together at an adjacent table and shot furtive, curious glances in our direction. Soon marinated chicken, rice, and vegetables were served "family style," the catering staff bringing each of the eight tables large serving dishes to be passed.

As we were seated at separate tables, community members and Marranos did not share food. For over an hour no one spoke to us—until my dining companions nominated me to ask one of the catering staff for more rice for the table. To my dismay, she walked not to the kitchen, as I had expected, but to the head table, where a still-heaping platter sat directly in front of the community president. Wordlessly, she picked it up and handed it to me as I cringed in embarrassment. Moments later I was up again, this time to the kitchen to ask if there was more chicken. I spoke quietly, hoping some remained on the stove that I could take to my table undetected. But the wife of one of the community leaders, who was helping the catering staff wash dishes, overheard. She whirled around and exclaimed, "Don't ask the caterers to bring you food! Get it from another table. You people have to learn how to live in a community! What's wrong with you? This isn't some country club you can just join!" At that, she marched over to the teenagers' table, picked up their partly emptied platter of chicken, and set it with a thud on our table. Everyone turned to stare. It seemed we had needed only to ask the neighboring table to pass the platter. Our failure to speak had given offense.

It was in that moment that I felt most keenly how urban Marranos were marked as outsiders among the Jews of Portugal, and unwelcome ones, at that. That evening I was shamed for my lack of knowledge, just as they were: I knew as little about Orthodox Jewish observance as they did, if not less; I had no more understanding of the community's behavioral norms than they did, and despite my best efforts seemed to blunder at every turn. The sense of being watched, appraised, and found wanting was overwhelming and, I later learned upon conferring with Menorá members, commonly felt. "You get used to it," shrugged one young woman, her dangling Star of David earrings trembling as she wryly shook her head. "You get used to it." But did they, really?

As I pondered the angry imperative to "learn to live in a community," it struck me that joining a collectivity spread over such a vast scale—here, the Jewish people—is a far more complicated proposition than simply finding a representative group and situating oneself among them. At issue is a question common to all "imagined communities," nations and other social groupings so large that members "will never know most of their fellow-members, meet them, or even hear of them, yet in the mind of each lives the image of their communion ... as a deep, horizontal comradeship" (Anderson 1991: 6–7). Under what conditions do newcomers come to feel personally connected to the whole? If there are rituals to foster integration, to what extent do they bridge the difference between categorical inclusion or relatedness, on a rhetorical level, and emotional experiences of interpersonal belonging? These are questions of identity and identification, of imagination and encounter, of the resolutely local (the person) and the abstractly global (a people), and their answer requires close scrutiny of each of those terms. Belonging, after all, is a particular kind of relation, one that arises amidst subjective experiences of mutual connection (May 2013: 79; cf. Candea 2010). Back in my Porto flat that October night, reflecting on the dinner's painful conclusion, I wondered: if the Jewish people are a globally dispersed family, united by common ancestry or by "adoption" via conversion, how could this small group of self-designated "born" Jews—so roundly rejected in their out-of-the-way corner of the world—possibly find belonging among them?

ONE

Hidden Within, Imported from Without

A SOCIAL CATEGORY THROUGH TIME

ON A BONE-CHILLINGLY COLD DAY IN NOVEMBER, the caretaker of Portugal's sole remaining medieval synagogue told me a story, one I had heard several times before. As we sat huddled by the electric space heater, the only source of warmth in the small, damp stone sanctuary, the elderly man explained that most Portuguese people have "Jewish blood" (*sangue judeu*). To illustrate, he recounted a legend set during the time of King José I, who reigned from 1750 to 1777. "The story goes," he began,

> that King José declared a law that all descendants of Jews must wear yellow hats. So the prime minister, the Marquis of Pombal, went to a store to buy three yellow hats, and then went to the palace to talk to the king with the hats under his arm.
>
> The king looked at him, saw the three yellow hats, and asked: "Oh, Marquis, what are those hats for?" And he said, "Your Majesty, I was following orders when I got these, because I don't know of a single Portuguese in Portugal who doesn't have Jewish blood running in his veins."
>
> The king began to laugh and asked: "So, why do you have three?" The prime minister said: "One is for me, another for the Inquisitor General, and another in case Your Majesty should wish to cover His head."

The caretaker, himself a self-avowed descendant of Jews, would tell this story to most of the visitors who came to the Tomar synagogue—now a museum—that day, whether they were Portuguese or foreign.[1] He would ask Portuguese visitors their surnames, often telling them their names were "New Christian," a statement they readily recognized as meaning that they too had Jewish ancestry. Many were interested and asked questions, or said they already knew; others, like the twenty-five-year-old pharmacist who wandered in out of the rain thinking he was visiting another museum altogether, shook their heads and said, "Oh, I wouldn't know anything about that." The caretaker feels it is important that all of his visitors understand the implications of his country's Jewish past for the Portuguese people of the present, as well as for Jews worldwide. Although he is not a practicing Jew, his wife, who also greets visitors and who is also a descendant of Jews, wears a large Star of David pendant that never fails to attract the attention of the tens of thousands of Jewish tourists who come through the building's doors each year. When foreigners ask if they are Jewish, the caretaker and his wife generally say yes.

The Star of David pendant and avowal of Jewish descent, the story of the three yellow hats and questions about surnames, mean different things to Portuguese visitors than to foreigners, to whom the polyglot caretaker speaks in English, French, Spanish, Italian, even basic Hebrew. For to be "Jewish" in Portugal is no straightforward matter: while the social category "Jews" (*judeus*) has existed in Portuguese society for well over a millennium (Martins 2006), its meaning has varied continuously over the past five hundred years. At different moments in time, Portugal has been described as a place of Jewish refuge; a hostile landscape, stripped of Jewish life; a locus of flourishing but perilous hidden Judaism; a modern European nation with a Jewish population of less than .0001 percent; and a country whose entire population has "Jewish blood." At any given point, was the Portuguese landscape teeming with Jews, or were there none at all? This is a question of social classification, not of descent or faith, for what has changed in each case is nothing more than context: over time the definition of "Jews" and the constitutive components of "Jewishness" have shifted continuously, and with them the population to which they refer.

In this chapter, I pursue two interrelated aims: (1) to track this complex social category across centuries, teasing apart its various meanings and subcategories over time; and (2) to provide the broad historical context—as recorded by historians and as remembered by diverse stakeholders in the present—for the emergence and rapid growth of urban Marrano associations in the late 1990s and 2000s. The role of continual foreign attention and intervention will prove crucial here, as Portuguese Jewishness has always been caught up, one way or another, with an outsiders' gaze. Long ago, there was a population called "Jews" who were both Portuguese and very much part of the Jewish people, writ large; through a series of tragic events, those Jews effectively vanished from the Jewish world, "lost" to their brethren in other countries. They were not forgotten, however, and memory of their loss became the stuff of Jewish legend. Their loss was remembered in Portugal as well, as a lingering presence and as a remembered identity passed down through families and even entire communities. Without that memory, there could be no claims to ancestral Jewishness by the urban Marranos, nor feelings of relatedness from the foreign Jews who came to meet them. At the same time, the story of Portugal's "lost" Jews continuously surfaces in academic texts, popular media in numerous languages, and widely distributed tourist materials, providing fodder for their lasting presence in everyday Portuguese discourse and in the litany of catastrophes that have befallen the Jewish people. In the intervening centuries, however, other populations in Portugal have been identified as "Jews" (or "Jewish"), according variously to self-ascription or to ascription by other Portuguese or by diverse constituencies abroad. If the category's slipperiness becomes confusing as we move along, it is because categorical confusion itself is a defining feature of Jewishness in the Portuguese social landscape, past and present.

From an anthropological perspective, ethnic and religious categories are socially produced and hence malleable. Social boundaries that distinguish one group from another, the cultural and phenotypical characteristics defining this or that ethnicity, inevitably change with time and context. Moreover, as Frederik Barth writes in the classic volume *Ethnic Groups and Boundaries,* social divisions persist irrespective of the specific individuals and characteristics that populate them; such divisions "entail social processes of exclusion and incorporation whereby discrete categories are maintained *despite* changing participation and membership in the course of individual life histories" (1969: 9–10). The category "Jews" persists in Portuguese society even as its criteria and meaning change, and consequently individuals and even entire populations move in and out of its domain. The same is true of "Marranos," a category whose boundaries seem to shift with each speaker, sliding closer to or further from "Jews" or "Catholics" with context and signifying a range of different groups: medieval forced converts to Catholicism who secretly continued to practice Judaism; their descendants, past and present, who over generations developed a syncretic religion, a unique hybrid combining elements of both Judaism and Catholicism; and those today who identify as descendants of the historical Marranos but grew up without any secret rituals at all. While respecting its variable application, in this chapter I use *Marrano* interchangeably with *hidden Jews* and *crypto-Jews* to refer specifically to those individuals, past and present, who practice a secret, syncretic form of Judaism. However, these categories, like all social categories, have a tendency to blur around the edges, and where needed I add explanation.

From a relatively simple religious distinction between Jews and Christians in the medieval era to the extraordinary complexity of the Jewishness attributed to rural villagers by foreign Jews and Portuguese nationalists in the early twentieth century, this chapter traces the tangled history of a remarkably long-lasting social category. In the process, it recounts several historical episodes in which foreign Jews have attempted to make contact with Portuguese Marranos and foster their return to the Jewish people. The best known of these involves Belmonte, a mountain village where an intact community of crypto-Jews maintained a Jewish identity and rituals up to the early twentieth century, when they were first discovered. Although their fame has waxed and waned, these hidden Jews have never disappeared entirely from the Jewish imagination abroad; in the 1980s and 1990s they sought contact with the Jewish world and were discovered anew, causing an international sensation. The urban Marranos among whom I conducted my research had no ancestral ties to that community, but the continual light shone on Belmonte deflected onto them, distorting as much as it illuminated. Their story is deeply embedded in this broader historical, sociological, and imaginative context.

PORTUGUESE JEWS

Let us begin with the medieval era, a time when Portuguese Jews and Catholics were neatly differentiated by an array of social distinctions. Politically the Jews were a distinct corporate entity, led by a head rabbi who reported directly to the king, with a parallel system of governance and justice rooted in rabbinic law (Martins 2006). Although quite economically and socially integrated, their difference was underscored not only by their religious practices but by heavier taxation than was levied on other subjects and by periodic royal decrees requiring that they wear distinctive clothing, hats, or insignias. A new form of differentiation began in the mid-fourteenth century, when Jews were required to live in segregated neighborhoods known as *judiarias* (Jewish quarters), ending a long history of Catholics and Jews living side by side (Ferro Tavares 1995).

Enforced social distinctions notwithstanding, while Jews in neighboring Spain suffered periodic violent oppression, forced conversion, and outright massacres, Portugal's Jews lived relatively undisturbed. Indeed, in the medieval era the Portuguese crown afforded them "rights unparalleled in the rest of Europe" (Gitlitz 1996: 48), such as the right—denied Jews elsewhere—to own land. Some fit the persistent stereotype of prosperous tax collectors, court astrologers, jewelers, mapmakers, and royal physicians (Saraiva 2001), but there were also farmers, millers, weavers, blacksmiths, shoemakers, and small shop-keepers, regularly conducting business with their Christian neighbors and even serving alongside them in the king's army (Ferro Tavares 1982; Martins 2006: vol. 1). By the early fifteenth century Jews could be found from the poorest to the richest levels of Portuguese society, in more than one hundred cities and towns throughout the kingdom. Despite their residential segregation, so socially integrated were they that in the 1420s the cardinal of Lisbon openly reproached Christians and Jews for dining in each other's homes, attending each other's weddings, and celebrating family occasions together (Ferro Tavares 1995: 64). Today, popular histories and tourism materials celebrate this prolonged period of coexistence as a golden age, one said to reflect an inherent Portuguese tendency to embrace and incorporate difference.

Despite the diverse ways Jews were marked as a distinct population, there is little scholarly consensus on their number. Historians' estimates for the fifteenth century range from 30,000 to 75,000, roughly 3 to 8 percent of a national population of one million (Martins 2006: 1:121). The difficulty of fixing an estimate is partly due to the continuous addition of Jews emigrating from Spain. Beginning in 1391, when anti-Semitic riots broke out across Aragon and Castile, and continuing throughout the fifteenth century, they came in droves, fleeing pogroms in which synagogues and entire neighbor-hoods were burned, thousands of Jews killed, and thousands more forcibly converted (Roth 1941, 1964). Initially the refugees were quietly absorbed into Portugal's preexisting Jewish communities, but the situation changed radi-cally with the Spanish Edict of Expulsion in 1492. Given four months to convert or leave, most Spanish Jews chose departure. Crossing the border into Portugal, still an apparent haven of coexistence, was a logical choice.

The Spanish Expulsion had enormous consequence for Portuguese Jewry (Soyer 2007a). During the summer of 1492 alone some 50,000 to 200,000 exiles entered Portugal, joining the thousands of Spanish Jewish families that had already arrived and the many tens of thousands of native-born Jews.[2] The demographic implications are striking: with this sudden influx, by 1493 as much as 20 percent of Portugal's resident population would have been Jewish. Five hundred years later these figures have become central facts of Portuguese history, promulgated in popular texts, on the internet, and on Jewish heritage tours. During my fieldwork, I often heard foreign visitors comment on medi-eval Portugal's importance as a rare place of refuge, a haven where Jewish literature and scholarship flourished. One tourist, a Portuguese American academic of newly discovered Jewish ancestry, exclaimed to me that given the numbers involved, "Portugal was the most Jewish country in the world!"

Remarkable in themselves, these population estimates are more dramatic still for their abrupt reversal: within five years of the Spanish Expulsion, the number of Jews in Portugal would plummet to zero. Initially, Portugal's King João II offered the Spanish Jews sanctuary, provided that they left within eight months. But he failed to make sufficient transport available for their departure; most had no choice but to remain and were declared slaves, their assets seized. The following year, attempting to coerce conversion, the king ordered hundreds of Jewish children taken from their parents, baptized, and—unless the parents converted as well—sent with Christian families to populate the African equatorial island of São Tomé. His successor, Manuel, came to power in 1495 and promptly began negotiations with Ferdinand and Isabella, the famed *reyes católicos* of the Spanish Inquisition, to marry their daughter. Having expelled the Jews from their kingdom, the Spanish monarchs refused the marriage until Manuel agreed to purge his own lands. The resulting Portuguese Edict of Expulsion, issued on December 5, 1496, gave all Jews ten months to convert or leave. Immediately there followed a series of decrees designed "to completely and forever eradicate Judaism—and even its memory—from Portugal" (Saraiva 2001: 11). Synagogues were closed and their communal property, from books to dwellings, seized and redistributed. Privately owned ritual objects and Hebrew books were confiscated and Jewish cemeteries were destroyed. Within two years the *judiarias* would be unrecognizable, the streets renamed and populated entirely by Catholics.

Despite this attempt at total erasure, traces remain. A street called Rua da Judiaria (Judiaria Road) can still be found in Lisbon's Alfama district, as in dozens of other Portuguese towns, and in nearby Sintra there is a Beco da Judiaria (Judiaria Alley). Many villages also have a Rua Nova (New Street), said to be the name given to the main thoroughfare of a *judiaria* upon its transformation into an ordinary neighborhood (Ferro Tavares 1995: 77). Indicative place-names—Monte dos Judeus (Mountain of the Jews), Vale do Judeu (Valley of the Jew)—dot the landscape, rewarding the traveler patient enough to find them. Today these toponyms serve as clues to the location of former *judiarias* and, given the scarcity of other physical remains, are often key sites on heritage tours of "Jewish Portugal" (Leite 2007).

The Edict of Expulsion notwithstanding, Portugal's Jews were never expelled. Yet we know that by the end of 1497, none remained. How can this be so? Historians believe the king could not accept the economic impact of losing such a large segment of his people, particularly a population so "industrious and profitable" (Roth 1964: 160). Instead, as historian Maria José Ferro Tavares (1995: 74) puts it, "under the guise of expulsion, King Manuel laid out a Machiavellian plan that would simultaneously achieve religious homogeneity in the kingdom and allow the continued presence of the minority which he had no intention of seeing leave Portugal." That plan unfolded in numerous decrees designed to curtail emigration and coerce conversion. Immediately after Manuel's Edict of Expulsion, for example, departures from the kingdom were drastically curtailed, many points of embarkation were closed to Jews altogether, and all Jewish children under age fourteen were ordered baptized and placed in Christian homes unless their parents agreed to be baptized with them (Lipiner 1999: 74; Roth 1941: 57–59).

In the end, no ships were provided to ferry the Jews from Portugal, and very likely only a handful managed to escape. Instead, they were eradicated through baptism. In the sensationalistic popular version of how this occurred, repeated to me in the field by numerous travelers and guides, Portugal's entire Jewish population—one hundred thousand or more—gathers at Lisbon's harbor on the specified October day, prepared to depart. They have been summoned there by the king, but no ships await them; instead, they are surrounded by priests who douse them with holy water and declare them Christians. In this version of events Portugal's entire Jewish population vanishes within a span of hours, officially transformed into Catholics. Hardly less dramatic is the account of professional historians, who write that the forced conversion at the harbor involved a smaller crowd of some twenty thousand and took place several months earlier, in May (Ferro Tavares 1995). But Lisbon's mass baptism was only the first of many, in a coordinated effort from one end of the country to the other, throughout the summer of 1497. When the edict's October deadline arrived, there were no Jews left to expel.

NEW CHRISTIANS, CRYPTO-JEWS, MARRANOS

What was eradicated that summer in 1497 was not a people, but a social category. Waking up the morning after his or her baptism, a Portuguese Jew would have changed only in name: still the same person, with the same allegiances, habits, and beliefs, only now officially classified not as a *judeu* (Jew) but a *cristão-novo* (New Christian). With the loss of that social identity came an entirely new way of life. No longer segregated in *judiarias* and no longer living according to their own system of laws and beliefs—indeed, now expressly forbidden to do so—the New Christians were faced with an extraordinary feat of cultural assimilation. From the food they ate, to the holidays they celebrated, to their newly Christianized names, they were required to live as Catholics as quickly as possible. Ironically, the requirements for private religious practice were less stringent. Shortly before the mass baptisms, Manuel decreed that during the next twenty years no inquiries would be made into any new convert's faith. With the entire Jewish population converted so suddenly and involuntarily, that clemency created the possibility for secret practice of Judaism on a massive scale.

Having ostensibly expelled Judaism, but not the Jewish people, the crown then set about dismantling the social distinctions that had reinforced their separate status for generations. Where Jews had been barred from many civil, academic, religious, and court posts, as New Christians they were now deemed eligible. The elite of the former Jewish society were granted nobility, and with it Old Christian status (later called *limpeza de sangue,* purity of blood). Most remarkably, for the first decade following the forced conversions New Christians were forbidden from marrying other New Christians, a policy of enforced intermarriage strengthened by harsh restrictions on emigration (Ferro Tavares 1995; Gitlitz 1996). While New Christians rapidly integrated into Old Christian professional and economic networks, drawing on opportunities afforded by their changed status, the crown's rulings did little to counteract the entrenched social categories that had precipitated them. Ample historical evidence indicates that both Old and New Christians continued to think of the latter not as Catholics, but as Jews. This became devastatingly clear in the Lisbon Massacre of 1506. Revived in popular memory by American novelist Richard Zimler's international best-seller, *The Last Kabbalist of Lisbon* (1998), the surge of extreme violence began on Easter Sunday. Worshipers at Lisbon's São Domingos cathedral witnessed a strange light near a statue of the Virgin Mary and proclaimed it a miracle. When a New Christian man audibly expressed doubt, nearby congregants attacked and killed him for his heresy. Rioting broke out, incited by Dominican friars, and over the next three days nearly two thousand New Christians—adults, children, infants—were slaughtered (Soyer 2007b).[3] According to eyewitnesses, writes historian Renée Melammed (2004: 59), "the crowds and friars called out for the death of the 'Jews.' [Thus] a term that should already have been defunct in this society, namely 'Jew' (rather than 'New Christian'), was freely and successfully used to incite the masses." Openly condemning his subjects for their brutality, King Manuel restored the New Christians' right to leave the kingdom.

So began a trickle of departures that would continue, though with frequent restrictions, over the next 250 years (Roth 1941: 196). The first to leave made their way north to Antwerp, a major trading port, or east to lands around the Mediterranean, where they joined earlier settlements of Spanish Jews, together forming the outposts of the Sephardic diaspora (Benbassa and Rodrigue 2000).[4] Others boarded ships bound for Africa, India, and Brazil, for this was the height of Portugal's "Age of Discoveries" (Hespanha 1997). As a result, today there are people throughout the world who trace their ancestry to the fleeing forced converts and their descendants.

The great majority of sixteenth-century New Christians remained in Portugal, however, where they could continue to practice some semblance of Judaism at home provided they were not discovered. In 1512, the king added fifteen more years to the two-decade ban on investigating their adherence to Catholicism. Without texts, rabbis, public gatherings, or religious paraphernalia, Portuguese Judaism became a stripped-down, secretive shadow of what it had been. As the situation became increasingly dangerous, even core elements like circumcision and dietary laws were abandoned (Gitlitz 1996). Over time many New Christians assimilated entirely into the Catholicism mainstream, but others secretly persisted in maintaining whatever Jewish practices they could. As word of their tenacity and perilous survival spread beyond Portugal's borders, these crypto-Jews took on legendary status as a symbol of Jewish resistance. Today, Jews around the world remember the Portuguese Marranos as heroes and martyrs: heroes, because they kept their religious identity alive despite grave danger; martyrs, because their trials did not end with the forced conversions. In 1536, facing rumors of widespread secret Judaism in his realm, Manuel's son and successor, King João III—grandson of Spain's Ferdinand and Isabella—summoned the Inquisition to Portugal.

THE INQUISITION: JEWS EVERYWHERE— OR NONE AT ALL

Once again we encounter a perceptible shift in the boundaries and content of the categories "Christian" and "Jew." Whereas the Massacre of 1506 showed clearly that the Portuguese people and their priests still considered the New Christians "Jews," with the Inquisition's advent thirty years later the church declared them to be, above all, "Catholics." Why? Like its infamous Spanish counterpart, the Portuguese Inquisition was an ecclesiastical court charged with rooting out heresy among Catholics. As such, it had no jurisdiction over Jews. In Portugal, of course, there were no longer any Jews, only baptized Catholics, so no one escaped scrutiny. According to the Inquisition's logic, a New Christian who practiced Judaism in secret was not a Jew; he or she was a *judaizante* (Judaizer), a heretical Catholic performing Jewish rituals. Here the existing categories were applied in reverse: no longer were the former Jews classified as fundamentally Jewish but suspected of pretending to be Catholic; instead, they were now fundamentally Catholic but accused of acting like Jews. Hence the Holy Office, as the Inquisition was known, began its work by compiling and disseminating a list of dozens of practices said to indicate Judaizing, from thoroughly cleaning house on Fridays to bathing the dead before burial.[5] Priests read the list to their parishioners and instructed them, under threat of excommunication, to denounce anyone they suspected of having participated in such activities. "By this means," notes historian Cecil Roth (1941: 100), "the whole population became enlisted as accomplices of the Holy Office in its task of eradicating heresy."

The Inquisition's hallmarks were the requirement of confession and the use of torture to secure it. According to a seventeenth-century procedural code, "the confessions of those accused of heresy are their only hope to merit merciful treatment, and they are the Holy Office's invaluable source for names of new suspects" (quoted in Saraiva 2001: 52). From the moment of arrest, the accused were presumed guilty. Imprisoned at the nearest tribunal, their assets seized, they would be required to provide a genealogy including all relatives, living or dead, and indicating which, if any, had been tried by the Inquisition in the past. If the individual denied all wrongdoing or did not confess to the Inquisitor's satisfaction, he or she would be tortured, sometimes for many months. Once having confessed, the accused would have to name other "heretics," again under threat of torture; the more denunciations, the greater the mercy promised. Anyone named would in turn be interrogated, and so the process continued, making everyone a potential denouncer of neighbors, friends, and family. No one of New Christian descent was immune, from the largest coastal cities to the tiniest mountain villages. Some forty thousand extant trial records, most preserved in the Portuguese National Archives, document the cases of adults and children, men and women, aristocrats and servants, university students and farmers, housewives and chambermaids.

Because the entire process was designed to extract confession, it was paradoxically admission of guilt, rather than innocence, that would save one's life. Those who demonstrated sufficient repentance—by confessing to all alleged heresy and swearing to accept Catholicism entirely—were "reconciled" to the church and sentenced to public whipping, banishment, forced labor, or permanent incarceration. The harshest punishment was reserved for "unrepentant Judaizers," individuals who either steadfastly refused to confess any wrongdoing or unapologetically declared themselves followers of the Law of Moses. Their sentence was death by garroting or burning at the stake. In a grotesque ceremony known as the *auto-da-fé* (act of faith), hundreds of prisoners would be paraded through the streets to a public square, where an audience of thousands awaited them. After a fiery sermon—in which those to be punished were referred to explicitly as *Jews* (Saraiva 2001: 108)—a priest would read each judgment aloud, enumerating the offenses in detail, and then turn the prisoners over to civil authorities for punishment or immediate execution. According to eyewitness accounts, those burned at the stake died agonizingly slowly, taunted by a jeering crowd.[6]

While in Portugal, I heard about the Inquisition constantly from Jewish heritage tourists and outreach workers, whose reading and research in preparation for the trip had immersed them in its terrible history. Among the urban Marranos, it was a far less frequent topic of conversation. The Inquisition may have been the constitutive fact of their presumed Jewish ancestry, long lost and now regained, but it was not the focus of their attention. As we will see, this disjuncture came to the fore at various points, with varying degrees of impact, in interactions between urban Marranos and their foreign visitors. For Jewish travelers, the Inquisition, forced conversions, and Marranos themselves fit into a global Jewish heritage of repeated persecution, destruction, and survival—much like the Holocaust and its survivors—and consequently merited solemn attention and commemoration.

Of course, it is impossible to know from Inquisition records whether the thousands upon thousands convicted were in fact practicing a form of Judaism in secret, nor whether they would have considered themselves *judeus* at all. Because the trial format rendered any distinction between "accused" and "convicted" inconsequential, the Inquisition has left a legacy of suggestion and suspicion but little certainty. Indeed, revisionist historians question the "Jewishness" of the New Christians, noting that the trial records cannot reliably tell us what practices people followed; they can only be taken as transcripts of what the accused told the Inquisitors, whose use of torture effectively guaranteed confession and unfounded denunciations. Moreover, they argue, the Catholic Church benefited richly from the confiscation of assets accompanying each conviction and so would logically have sought to perpetuate the specter of hidden Judaism indefinitely (Salomon 1998; Saraiva 2001). Nonetheless, the majority of historians agree that some level of Jewish identification and practice must have persisted throughout the sixteenth and seventeenth centuries, because there is ample documentation of New Christians leaving Portugal for Belgium, Holland, France, Italy, and England and once there "returning" to their ancestral religion (Lipiner 1985; Melammed 2004).

Although by now generations removed from normative Judaism, upon arriving in a safe locale many New Christians sought to join a Jewish community or even created their own from scratch. The most influential of these *sui generis* communities was in Amsterdam. Founded by New Christians at the turn of the seventeenth century, in just fifty years its membership grew from two hundred to nearly three thousand. Sephardic rabbis traveled from as far as Venice and Salonika to guide the congregation's leaders, who had no prior experience living in a Jewish community (Melammed 2004: 73). Continually replenished with newcomers from Portugal, Amsterdam's community became the primary site for Marranos and other New Christians to learn about normative Judaism, including many who subsequently moved on to distant lands. These "returnees" to Judaism were among the earliest settlers of Holland's New World colonies, where they founded the first synagogues in North and South America: Tsur Israel in Recife, Dutch Brazil (1638), and New York's Shearith Israel (1654), known to this day as "the Spanish and Portuguese Synagogue." Together with New Christians arriving directly from Portugal and from Portuguese Brazil, they also launched new congregations throughout the Caribbean. In 1699, descendants of the Portuguese Jews founded London's venerable Bevis Marks, known colloquially as "the Spanish and Portuguese congregation." Now the oldest synagogue in Great Britain, until the 1800s its religious services and community meetings were still conducted in Portuguese (Carvalho 1999: 82). At the turn of the twenty-first century, my fieldwork brought me into contact with dozens of descendants of these emigrant communities who traveled to Portugal as roots-seekers and activists for the contemporary Marrano cause. Hundreds more participated in internet discussion groups like Nostálgia, creating a global community of memory that included urban Marranos in Porto and Lisbon as well.

Historical records suggest that many New Christians remained in Portugal and continued to Judaize well into the seventeenth and eighteenth centuries. By this time, however, their practices bore little relation to normative Judaism, having become an amalgam of fragmentary rituals, Catholic-tinged prayers, and literal interpretation of the Old Testament (Gitlitz 1996). Oddly, Inquisition trial proceedings reveal that some would-be Judaizers learned their practices from the Holy Office itself. In one city's records, for example, "there are references to young men who used to attend autos-da-fé so as to learn the prayers mentioned in the sentences of the condemned, because in their hometowns there was nobody still alive who knew them" (Rowland 2001: 137). Ironically, then, the Inquisition may have perpetuated a Jewish identity among the very people whose souls it sought to reclaim. By identifying and terrorizing them as a suspect class in Portuguese society for more than two hundred years, by reading aloud the details of alleged Jewish practices and prayers during autos-da-fé, and by referring to the convicted explicitly as "Jews," the Inquisition could only have increased New Christian self-awareness as a distinct population defined by Jewish ancestry. Intermittently enforced "purity of blood" laws, barring anyone with even the smallest fraction of New Christian descent from specified jobs, universities, and trade guilds, surely heightened the effect (Saraiva 2001: 116–22; Yerushalmi 1982: 12–16). And because New Christian status was ascribed on a hypodescent ("one-drop") basis, demographic projections based on likely rates of intermarriage indicate that as much as a third of the Portuguese population would have been classified as New Christian by the mid-eighteenth century (Rowland 2001: 144).

Thus in the seventeenth and eighteenth centuries Portugal was simultaneously utterly absent of Jews and overflowing with their presence. Judaism as an organized religion had ceased to exist, and with it the social category it had defined. There were no synagogues, no cemeteries, no *judiarias,* no rabbis, no public ceremonies. Those who continued their fragmentary Jewish practices did so in hiding; otherwise they donned the mask of a faithful Catholic. To anyone looking for a religious community, Portugal was indeed devoid of Jews. But for those who based their understanding of Jewishness on descent, there were Jews everywhere. A fundamental premise of the Inquisition was that "the desire to 'Judaize' . . . was an ethnic phenomenon, transmitted by blood" (Saraiva 2001: 75, 137–38). From this perspective, an enormous percentage of the population was *latently* Jewish. Moreover, the Inquisition's extraordinary activity—some 750 autos-da-fé in 250 years—

suggested to the rest of the world that Portugal had a severe "Jewish problem." Indeed, no less a luminary than Erasmus is said to have referred dismissively to the Portuguese as "a race of Jews" (Sachar 1994: 180), and Spanish anthropologist Julio Caro Baroja (1961: 341) notes that similar attributions were made throughout the next three centuries: "Even in the nineteenth century, the idea that Portugal was absolutely saturated with Jewish elements was widely held. An English sojourner in Spain, stopping over for a few days in Lisbon, ... speaks of the Portuguese as a 'half-Jewish race' and of the 'Jewish fat and sensual faces' of the women of Lisbon."

No Jews, many Jews. This vacillation between absence and presence, oblivion and memory, still defines Portugal's Jewish imaginary. Like an optical illusion card that shows a different picture when tilted this way and that, the Portuguese landscape seems to shift continuously: now empty of Jews, now full, now empty again. Everything depends upon the angle of vision and where the light is cast.

ANCESTORS AND IMMIGRANTS

In the early modern era, the category "Jews" became still more complicated. The last auto-da-fé to include a conviction of Judaizing took place in 1765. Shortly thereafter the prime minister, the Marquis of Pombal, introduced a far-reaching program of social and economic reforms that drastically curtailed the Inquisition's activities (Birmingham 1993: 79–95). For our purposes, the most important reform was the abolition of all distinctions between Old and New Christians. Official registers of New Christian family lines were destroyed; the very act of identifying another person as a *cristão-novo* became a crime punishable by public flogging and even banishment (Saraiva 2001: 226–28; Bethencourt 1903: 253–54). As the still-circulating legend that opens this chapter indicates, however, the prohibition against naming New Christians has never been particularly well enforced; indeed, in the synagogue caretaker's narrative, Pombal names even himself. Tellingly, the term *cristão-novo,* though rarely used in reference to the present, retains its meaning to this day.

The legend of the three yellow hats reflects a curious effect of Pombal's reforms: if there was no longer any way to document definitively who was or was not of Jewish origin, *anyone* could be. In Portugal today, popular wisdom has it that all Portuguese could easily have "New Christian" or "Jewish" ancestors. While in the field, I encountered dozens of people who saw themselves as neither Jewish nor Marrano but, upon hearing about my research, immediately volunteered that they probably had "Jewish" ancestry themselves. Some were eager to explain why they were certain it was so. Other scholars report encountering similar claims (Siporin 1993).[7]

But saying one has Jewish or New Christian ancestry is very different from saying that one is a Marrano or a Jew. Rare in Portugal even today, in the aftermath of the Inquisition it was unthinkable. From the end of Inquisitorial persecution in the 1760s to the overthrow of the monarchy in 1910, we have only a handful of reports of native Portuguese identifying themselves as *judeus,* usually upon encountering a foreign Jewish traveler. The early nineteenth-century establishment of an immigrant Jewish community in Lisbon seems to have prompted occasional contact as well. One day in 1819, for example, two men from the rural interior reportedly appeared at services to ask the calendar date of Yom Kippur that year (Mea and Steinhardt 1997: 58 n. 10). Throughout the later nineteenth and early twentieth century, village clergy and amateur ethnographers published several reports of surviving crypto-Jewish enclaves in the rural Trás-os-Montes and Beira provinces (e.g., Alves 1925); foreign travelers, too, began to publish breathless accounts of unexpectedly encountering Marranos.[8]

While the image of these rural Marranos continues to dominate foreign Jewish imaginings of what might be meant by "Portuguese Jews," in Portugal *judeus portugueses* has come to refer to an altogether different population: the nineteenth- and twentieth-century immigrant Jewish community and its descendants. This disparity in reference generates considerable confusion for visiting Jews, who typically have heard little if anything about the latter group. The earliest Jewish immigrants arrived in the late eighteenth century, primarily from North Africa. They were Sephardic Jews, hailing from a traditional Orthodox milieu. Most settled in Lisbon. Their arrival coincided with a period of rapid social change, from Pombal's reforms in the 1770s to the abolition of the Inquisition in 1821 and, five years later, declaration of freedom of religion for foreign nationals (Martins 2006: vol. 2). That freedom came with the stipulation that religious meeting spaces could not have "the outward form of places of worship" (Bethencourt 1903: 266). In 1834 citizens, too, were allowed "the right to follow any religion, provided that they did not show disrespect for the state religion, Catholicism, duly limiting [their] practice . . . to the privacy of their home" (Mea and Steinhardt 1997: 36 n. 28). It is in deference to these laws that Lisbon's stately Shaaré Tikvá synagogue, inaugurated in 1904, stands well back from the street, hidden behind a high wall.

Ashkenazi Jews, too, came in increasing numbers at the turn of the twentieth century, fleeing pogroms in Eastern Europe and, later, the Nazis (Mucznik 1999). Initially many formed small congregations of their own, meeting in private homes and rented apartments, as they preferred the familiar melodies, pronunciation, and traditions of Ashkenazi Judaism to the Moroccan Sephardic rite followed at Shaaré Tikvá. The immigrant Jewish population grew quickly, culminating during World War II, when tens of thousands of refugees crossed into Portugal and found assistance in Lisbon (Milgram 2011). Although the vast majority ultimately settled elsewhere, those who remained became integrated into the existing Jewish community. By 1950 most of the area's mainstream Jews attended Shaaré Tikvá, now evenly divided between Sephardic and Ashkenazi congregants.

These, then, are the primary "Portuguese Jews" of the twentieth century, defined by their foreignness and their normative Jewish practice. But what of those who came before—the *cristãos-novos,* the Inquisition-era *marranos,* and their descendants—all of whom have long been considered "Portuguese Jews" by foreigners and, at different historical moments, by the Portuguese as well? In the early 1900s the two groups' paths converged, in an encounter that produced an internationally circulated tale of isolation, discovery, and revival whose echoes reverberate to this day. Indeed, the early twentieth-century history of Portugal's Marranos, and above all their relationship with Jews in Portugal and abroad, prefigures important aspects of the urban Marrano movement at the turn of the twenty-first century. As we will see in chapters 3, 4, and 5, this is a story of foreign fascination with the *idea* of Portugal's hidden Jews, a fascination that has not abated for over a century. In the past, as in the present, it involves direct intervention by organizations and individuals seeking to bring the Marranos to normative Judaism, provide them with religious educational resources, and welcome them into "the Jewish people" of the present day.

THE LAST MARRANOS

The early twentieth century was a period of significant political and social change in Portugal. In October 1910 a republican revolution overthrew the monarchy and installed the nation's first liberal, secular regime. For the first time, total separation of church and state was imposed by law. In keeping with a contemporaneous trend toward anticlericalism, the revolutionary government took dramatic measures to ensure that the church would have no hold over the new society: religious orders were expelled, marriage was made "exclusively civil," divorce became legal, and religious rites could no longer be held in state institutions (Costa Pinto 2003: 8–9). Given the rapid relaxation of Catholicism's formerly dominant role, coupled with a general climate of secularization and growing popular interest in Freemasonry and other esoteric traditions, it should not surprise us that it was precisely during this period that glimmerings of long-hidden Jewish identity and practice surfaced in rural areas. As was the case for the fleeing Marranos and New Christians in seventeenth-century Amsterdam, in the early twentieth century foreign Jews again played a crucial outreach role.

The new chapter began with Samuel Schwarz (1880–1953), an Ashkenazi immigrant living in Lisbon. A mining engineer and amateur historian, Schwarz is remembered chiefly for having stumbled upon a village of crypto-Jews, high in the mountains along the border with Spain, in 1917. While we have his firsthand account of that encounter and its aftermath, published in both Portuguese and English (Schwarz 1925, 1926), his dramatic story has had far more impact as unattributed lore—endlessly told and retold, in popular and scholarly histories, rabbinic sermons, tourist guidebooks, documentary films, on package tours, and by word of mouth. Although details frequently change in the telling, the story generally runs as follows.

Schwarz was traveling through Beira Baixa, a remote province along the eastern border with Spain. At the time—so the story goes—no one believed there were any surviving indigenous Jews anywhere in Portugal. But when Schwarz arrived in Belmonte, a hilltop village with a few thousand residents, and inquired where he could purchase supplies for his mining operation, a villager shocked him by warning him away from a particular shopkeeper, saying, "It's enough for me to tell you he's a Jew!" Stunned, Schwarz pressed for more information. He learned he had stumbled upon something truly extraordinary: a community that survived the Inquisition with its "Jewish" identity intact, not only in its own eyes, but in the eyes of its neighbors. Although he would find that their rituals—always practiced in secret—were only distantly related to normative Judaism, in local terms members of this community were called *judeus*—Jews.

Schwarz befriended the shopkeeper against whom he had been warned, who in turn introduced him to many other families. He learned that the religious leaders were elderly women, rather than men; it was they who intoned the old "Jewish" prayers during community observances. But he could not convince anyone to tell him these prayers, because they did not recognize him as a fellow *judeu:* "Jew" was a social category that, for them, had an exceedingly narrow definition. Finally, one old woman challenged Schwarz to recite any prayer he knew, to prove he truly was Jewish. He had little hope of success, since they had been disconnected from normative Judaism for centuries and seemed completely unaware of the existence of Hebrew. Nonetheless, he began to say the *Shema,* Judaism's basic affirmation of faith. When he came to *Adonai,* "Lord," the women standing around him gasped and covered their eyes, as observant Jews do when reciting the prayer. "He is a Jew," the old woman proclaimed, "for he knows the name of *Adonai.*" It was the only word of Hebrew they had retained.

In most popular accounts the story ends here, for the moment of discovery of what the Jewish world knows as "Marranos"—secret Jews—is its high point. There is considerably more to be told, however; Schwarz's subsequent research and writing, though now largely forgotten, stoked international Jewish imaginings and engagement with the Portuguese Marrano cause and had a similarly important effect on local perceptions of native Jewishness within his adopted country. He was also a central figure in an internationally funded effort to reach Marranos throughout the country and bring them to normative Judaism, to which I return below. Through his conversations with Marranos in Belmonte, Schwarz discovered that there were at least a dozen similar communities scattered throughout Portugal's remote border regions. Fascinated, he pursued all leads, documenting prayers and customs and adding them to the collection he had begun in Belmonte. He published them first in a Portuguese-language volume titled *Os cristãos-novos em Portugal no século XX* (New Christians in Portugal in the twentieth century) and then in English as an article for *Menorah,* an international Jewish studies journal.[9] In each he sketches a general history of the Portuguese Jews and New Christians, characterizes the physiognomy of the twentieth-century Marranos ("pure Sephardi"), and lists common surnames. He also offers an estimate of the number of Marranos in Portugal, based on "popular reckoning" by villagers in the areas he visited:

> I naturally include only those Maranos [*sic*] who have remained conscious of their Jewish origin, for the number of completely assimilated families is beyond conjecture. It is safest to say that there exists a scattering of Maranos throughout the land, and a rather greater proportion in the provinces of the Beira-Baixa and Trás-os-Montes.... [In some areas] many villages are considered to be inhabited exclusively by Maranos.... Awaiting the

day when a statistical survey will be made, one can estimate that altogether at least ten thousand Marano families still survive throughout Portugal. (1926: 146)

Schwarz's assessment has had lasting influence in two respects. First, he greatly extends the meaning of the word *Marrano*. Where previously it had been used by Jews abroad as a social category based on *behavior,* that is, secretly practicing Judaism after converting to another religion, in Schwarz's writing it becomes *racial.* Hence he notes that he will initially estimate "only those Maranos who have remained conscious of their Jewish origin," as there are far too many "Maranos [who have] completely assimilated" to hazard a guess. Here *Marrano* and *New Christian* are interchangeable terms, both defined primarily by descent.[10] Second, his estimate of ten thousand surviving Marrano families, equaling perhaps sixty thousand people, is based on the "reckoning" of villagers who were not necessarily Marranos themselves; some likely provided estimates based on the presumed or imputed descent of their neighbors. As we do not know what term Schwarz used to inquire in Portuguese, nor precisely what the social category *judeu* or *cristão-novo* meant in each of the villages at that particular moment, it is difficult to know what to make of his numbers. Nevertheless, his ten-thousand-family estimate made a tremendous impression on the Jewish world at the time and has generated awe and wonder ever since. Schwarz thus profoundly influenced the thinking of foreign Jews who would work on behalf of a Marrano revival, both in his own time and at the turn of the twenty-first century.

Each of Schwarz's publications includes a detailed account of his stunning discovery in Belmonte. These have served as the source for dozens of published retellings, many of them far more widely read than Schwarz's own. Some have obviously been embellished for heightened effect; very few mention that Schwarz found Marrano communities anywhere other than Belmonte. Continually rediscovered by would-be tourists and outreach workers around the world, the story of Belmonte's revelation retains its immediacy and romance. If anything, it has gained drama in the retelling, and its continual redissemination has prompted a steady stream of international visitors over the past hundred years—most believing they are among a select few to have made the long journey to meet "the last Marranos."

The hallmark of the Belmonte story, particularly in its more dramatic, popular forms, is its emphasis on the community's isolation and insularity. According to most accounts, "these isolated Portuguese villagers had believed themselves the last Jews on earth" (Sachar 1994: 182). It is this detail in particular that fires the imagination and emotions of those who imagine them from afar. Yet Schwarz's account suggests that this detail, though compelling, is inaccurate. In fact, he gained the community's trust not during his first visit, nor even in Belmonte itself, but in a far more cosmopolitan locale— over two hundred miles away. Walking on a Lisbon street, he saw the shopkeeper he had been warned against in Belmonte. Writes Schwarz, "I began to ply him with questions; and in order to inspire him with confidence induced him to come with me to the [Shaaré Tikvá] synagogue. There he confessed his Jewish descent and that of his family, who ... still persisted in secretly practicing Judaism" (1926: 142). Clearly, some of the Belmonte villagers had had prior encounters with normative Judaism and were not nearly so isolated as popular lore would have it. Otherwise a brief visit to Lisbon's synagogue— an ornate three-story building, as opposed to the private homes or fields where *judeus* gathered in Belmonte; men intoning prayers, rather than elderly women; and an unfamiliar liturgy in an unknown language—could hardly have inspired confidence. As with so many "first contact" narratives—from the reputed discovery of isolated "Stone Age" tribes by anthropologists to tropes of travel writing on primitivist tours (Stasch 2011)—the desire to find an untouched remnant of the past has profoundly shaped the retelling.

HIDDEN WITHIN, PART I: PORTUGUESE
MARRANOS AND FOREIGN JEWS

The discovery in Belmonte was not an isolated event, despite its singularity in the imaginings of many. While Schwarz was collecting Marrano prayers and rituals, a Porto-based man launched a Marrano outreach and community-building effort of his own. In this case, however, the individual in question was a native-born Portuguese, a decorated military officer who identified as Jewish by descent. Artur Barros Basto (1887–1961) was not from a rural village like Belmonte, nor was he raised in a crypto-Jewish environment. As with retellings of Schwarz's discovery, popular sources that Jewish travelers encounter before arriving in Portugal greatly simplify and embellish details of Barros Basto's life and work. A meticulously researched biography, written by Portuguese scholars, is widely available in Portugal (Mea and Steinhardt 1997), but because the majority of foreign tourists and outreach workers cannot read Portuguese Barros Basto and his movement are remembered to very different effect in Portugal than outside that country. For urban Marranos, I found, the twists and turns of Barros Basto's life story offered a model and a cautionary tale of building a Marrano-based Jewish community from scratch and securing foreign support to that end. Abroad, he was largely imagined as a crypto-Jewish leader who had learned secret prayers from his elders as a child and gathered other Marranos around him in adulthood, only to be brought down by an anti-Semitic government. Barros Basto himself was cognizant of the difference mainstream Jews saw between those who were merely of New Christian descent and those who had been raised with secret Jewish rituals and whispered revelations. Over time he progressively changed details of his family history, apparently to ensure the foreign support he needed for his movement to succeed.

Although he knew from childhood that he had paternal New Christian ancestry, Barros Basto was raised in Porto by his mother, a strict Catholic. He rejected Catholicism as a teenager and read voraciously about other faiths, at one point thinking he might want to become a Muslim. He explored ancient Judaism through the Old Testament but thought it was a dead religion; it was not until he was seventeen that he learned there was a Jewish community in Lisbon. Two years later, upon entering Lisbon's military academy, he attended services at Shaaré Tikvá, befriended members of the congregation, and soon came to think of himself as Jewish. In the eyes of Lisbon's mainstream Jews, of course, Barros Basto's declared New Christian ancestry and adoption of Judaism did not make him a Jew, no matter how earnestly he might wish it. The community's leaders refused as a matter of policy to assist would-be Jews in pursuing conversion, fearing charges of proselytism, and Barros Basto ultimately had to complete the process before a rabbinic court in Morocco. He then returned to Porto and set about creating a Jewish community of his own, gathering the few Ashkenazi immigrants who had settled in the area. Together they founded Porto's first synagogue since the fifteenth century, meeting in a rented apartment and using a Torah scroll donated by Jews in Lisbon.

This was in 1923, precisely when Schwarz was beginning to disseminate news of his dramatic discovery in Belmonte. Believing that there must be thousands of people throughout the rural north who, like him, were aware of their New Christian ancestry and intrigued by Judaism, Barros Basto decided he would be their leader, offering them his own Jewish community as a place where they would be accepted as Jews "with open arms, even without the official blessing of a rabbinic court" (Mea and Steinhardt 1997: 56).

His opportunity arose unexpectedly. The Lisbon Jewish community, seeking funds to establish a religious school for their children, seized on Schwarz's discovery as a way of generating international support for their project. In a letter published in London's *Jewish Chronicle* in 1925, the community's leaders requested donations to build a boarding school for Marrano children. It would be situated in Lisbon, so that the Jewish community's own children could also be educated there (Mea and Steinhardt 1997: 62). The international response was swift and enthusiastic. Wrote an observer at the time, "The appeal evoked historic memories to which no Jew could be insensible. It was all the more impressive because few Jews outside Portugal and Spain were aware that any descendants of Marranos, who played so conspicuous and romantic a part in the Jewish history of the sixteenth and seventeenth centuries, had survived.... [T]hese valiant Marranos—though sorely maimed and decimated—kept the flag of Judaism flying to the end. European and American Jewry owe much to their gallant example" (Wolf 1926: 3, 7).

Two venerable international Jewish philanthropic and educational institutions, the Alliance Israélite Universelle and the Anglo-Jewish Association, sent a delegate, Lucien Wolf, on a monthlong investigative mission. Wolf traveled the country with Schwarz and Barros Basto as his guides, then met with the Portuguese president, prime minister, and leaders of the Lisbon congregation. In the end Wolf did not recommend locating the boarding school in Lisbon, deeming Porto a more appropriate site due to its proximity to the regions of greatest Marrano concentration, the energy and enthusiasm of the community's leader, Barros Basto, and "the fact that, given that he defined himself as a Marrano, [Barros Basto] apparently knew better than anyone the psychology of the Marranos" (Mea and Steinhardt 1997: 67).

Although Wolf supported Barros Basto and Schwarz in their desire to bring the "Marranos" into contact with the mainstream Jewish world, he was cautious in projecting how many would likely be reached. In his formal report, submitted in 1926, he approvingly cited Schwarz's estimate of thousands of Marranos in the Trás-os-Montes and Beira regions (Portuguese Marranos Committee 1938; Schwarz 1926: 146). But he made a point of distinguishing between "Marranos properly so-called" and "semi-Marranos," meaning those who were merely conscious of their ancestry and perhaps interested in learning about Judaism. On the basis of that distinction, he emphasized that Schwarz's estimate of ten thousand Marrano families was either too high or too low. If intended solely to indicate those who still practiced crypto-Judaism, the estimate was far too high. But if outreach was to be directed toward anyone conscious of Jewish origin who was "beginning to manifest an intelligent interest in Judaism," the estimate was far too low (Wolf 1926: 12).[11] He also cautioned that very few Marranos had explicitly requested assistance, whether from Lisbon's established Jewish community or from the international organizations that stood ready to help. "In spite of the Jewish interest which has been aroused among them," he wrote, "not more than three or four have manifested the slightest desire to re-enter the Synagogue." The reasons were twofold, in his view. First, among those who were truly Marranos (i.e., hidden Jews), there was a widespread feeling that "their crude secret Judaism [was] the only Judaism." Second, for the educated "semi-Marranos," many of them intellectuals who maintained consciousness of Jewish ancestry but no secret practices, there were social pressures against making the drastic life changes necessitated by abandoning Catholicism for Judaism—not to mention "the dislike of adult circumcision" and the simple fact that no mechanism for conversion existed in Portugal (1926: 14–15).

As word of Schwarz's remarkable discovery spread, however, Wolf's attempts to clarify the terms and populations involved were generally ignored in favor of the simpler but far more dramatic image of thousands upon thousands of frightened secret Jews awaiting outreach and assistance. An extraordinary outpouring of international support followed, with two overarching organizations created to raise funds and guide the movement. These were the Portuguese Marranos Committee, based in London's Bevis Marks Synagogue, and the Nederlandsch Marranen Comité, made up of Sephardic Jews in Amsterdam (Mea and Steinhardt 1997: 99)—each, not coincidentally, a community founded by Marranos centuries earlier. With their underwriting, Barros Basto launched what he called the *obra do resgate,* "work of redemption," making outreach missions to rural "Marrano" communities in an effort to bring them to mainstream Judaism. Accompanied by members of his Porto congregation, which now included Marranos who had sought him out personally, he traveled throughout the east and northeast of the country, bringing with him educational materials, enthusiasm, and the conviction that there was no longer any need to be afraid to declare oneself a Jew in Portugal. With his guidance, small synagogues formed in numerous mountain villages and towns.

Although his foreign supporters believed that his efforts focused solely on reaching "true Marranos," meaning crypto-Jews like those Schwarz found in Belmonte, Barros Basto's project quickly took on shades of proselytism. Like Schwarz, and contra Wolf, he used the term *Marrano* to refer to anyone of

New Christian descent; thus, like Barros Basto himself, many of the people who became involved in the movement had not previously practiced Jewish rituals in *any* form—syncretic, fragmentary, or otherwise. Fearing political fallout, the Lisbon Jewish community openly distanced itself, criticizing Barros Basto to the project's supporters in Portugal and abroad. Undiscouraged, and still enjoying the full support of the London Marranos Committee, B'nai Brith, and other international Jewish organizations, in 1929 Barros Basto launched the Marrano boarding school. As it offered a free general education at the high school level, in addition to classes in Hebrew and Judaism, it quickly attracted students with no known New Christian ancestry.

Barros Basto also founded a newsletter, *Halapid* (Heb.; The Torch), to give Marranos throughout the northern provinces a sense of connection to Jewish history and to teach them about Jewish religion and culture (Mea 1998). As his reach expanded, copies of *Halapid* made their way to communities all over Portugal and then to Jewish communities around the world. It soon became a tool for international publicity and fundraising. In addition to reporting his own activities, Barros Basto translated and reprinted articles published in other countries about his movement. The newsletter generated a stream of visitors from abroad, including rabbis, educators, and tourists. To them he made a point of grounding his movement in Portugal's pre-Inquisition Jewish history, particularly the medieval era, taking them on walking tours of the former sites of Porto's *judiarias* and embellishing stories about his background to make himself more authentically "Marrano" (Mea and Steinhardt 1997: 26, 79). Through his efforts, the "redemption" of Portugal's lost Jews, widely celebrated as a historical miracle, attracted enthusiastic support from all corners of the world.

Having reached many hundreds of people throughout northeastern Portugal, Barros Basto chafed at using a rented apartment as a synagogue. He believed that even from afar Marranos would feel more pride if they had an imposing synagogue to represent their movement, a "Jewish cathedral" on par with Portugal's largest churches. His appeals to Jewish communities in the United States, England, Europe, and farther afield were remarkably successful. The largest donation came from Sir Ely Kadoorie, a Sephardic philanthropist living in Shanghai, whose wife was of Portuguese Jewish origin. Construction began in the late 1920s. But even before the great synagogue was completed, serious problems plagued the project. Emissaries from the international agencies and foreign Jewish communities criticized Barros

Basto for not moving quickly enough to introduce normative Judaism, allowing his acolytes to develop new syncretic Catholic-Jewish rituals instead. At the same time, both the Lisbon Jewish community and the Ashkenazi Jews in his own congregation openly questioned his leadership. An avowed republican, Barros Basto walked a dangerous path in publicly encouraging Jewish practice in the mid-1920s: a 1926 military coup paved the way for a strongly Catholic-aligned, far-right regime that would retain power for fifty years, headed by the fascist dictator António Salazar (Costa Pinto 2003; Machado 1991). The public's unfamiliarity with Judaism, coupled with lack of support both within the Jewish community and without, left Barros Basto vulnerable to an easy avenue of attack: for performing circumcisions at the boarding school in observance of Jewish law, he was arrested and charged with molestation. Even after a thorough investigation and acquittal, he was brought before a military court, convicted of improper conduct, and stripped of his military rank and benefits. An outspoken critic of Salazar's dictatorship, he was investigated by the secret police repeatedly over the ensuing decades.[12]

Although the enormous synagogue was completed and inaugurated to much fanfare in 1938, with dozens of international dignitaries and hundreds of people in attendance,[13] it never had a real congregation. By 1940 the entire project had come to an end. The causes for its failure were many. Despite the brief window of opportunity offered by the openness of the First Republic, anti-Semitism was still pervasive (Martins 2006: 3:123–58). In some towns, Catholic residents boycotted businesses owned by the new Jews; many Marranos lost their jobs. Barros Basto found himself challenged on all sides. With the dramatic events of World War II and its aftermath, Jewish communities abroad found their financial support urgently needed elsewhere. The hundreds of Marranos Barros Basto had found in the Trás-os-Montes and Beira provinces melted away; one by one, the synagogues closed. In the end, the expected 15,000 to 20,000 Marrano "returnees" to Judaism did not materialize. For decades Barros Basto's great synagogue stood empty, the key passed down among a small network of people, until a group of expatriates organized a new Jewish community and reopened the doors in the early 1980s.

From the perspective of Schwarz, Barros Basto, and international supporters of the *obra do resgate,* early twentieth-century Portugal was home to tens of thousands of Marranos awaiting identification and encouragement: they saw a landscape filled with (potential) Jews. That image, oddly enough, also surfaced in anti-Semitic screeds by Portuguese far-right nationalists, who argued that an overwhelming percentage of their country's population was of Jewish descent—particularly those of the opposite political persuasion—and thus could not be trusted (e.g., Saa 1925). Writes historian David Canelo,

> If in 1925 the reactionary [nationalist] Mario Saa, surely one of the foremost Portuguese anti-Semites since the Inquisition, envisioned Judaism in every corner of Portuguese society, that vision was no different in essence from that of the Jews [abroad] who imagined the Trás-os-Montes and Beira Interior provinces to be crowded with crypto-Jews. For them, there was hardly a single remote corner in the mountain ranges that—perhaps understandably, given their enthusiastic illusions—was not the hiding place of secret Jewish culture, the heritage of centuries past. (2004: 160)

The nationalist paranoia may have dwindled away, but the echo of Schwarz's discovery reverberates into the present. Firmly planted in the imaginative lexicon of the Jewish people, there the Portuguese Marranos have remained ever since: an object of reverence and wonder.

In concrete terms, however, with the failure of the "work of redemption" the image of a countryside teeming with hidden Jews soon faded. For decades thereafter, beyond Lisbon's established community Portugal was once again a country without Jews. Like the forced converts before them, Barros Basto's neophytes and their descendants remained in place but were effectively invisible to outsiders. Only Belmonte continued to be identified with "Marranos" or "Jews" in the public eye, both within and outside Portugal. For decades Barros Basto's movement was little more than a footnote in Jewish history, completely overshadowed by the dramatic tale of Schwarz's discovery. Nearly every foreign visitor I encountered identified Belmonte as the site they had heard most about, the anticipated highlight of their journey to "Jewish Portugal."

PORTUGUESE (CRYPTO-)JEWS TO THE WORLD

In the decades following the failure of the *obra do resgate,* little was heard from the crypto-Jews in Belmonte, although travelers' reports continued to appear periodically in the Jewish press (e.g., Novinsky and Paulo 1967). The situation changed dramatically after the 1974 Revolution, which ended Salazar's fascist dictatorship, and with Portugal's accession to the European Economic Community in 1986. The return to a policy of religious freedom in 1974, together with a rising trend toward cultural and religious pluralism, seems to have emboldened some of the Belmonte community's younger members to seek contact with the Jewish Community of Lisbon and the Israeli embassy in the early 1980s (Canelo 1990, 2004; Garcia 1993, 1999). Word soon spread; as had their predecessors nearly a century earlier, Jewish educators from abroad made their way to Belmonte, hoping to help the community out of hiding and into the light of normative Jewish practice. Scholars, journalists, and tourists were not far behind.[14]

Within a few years the Belmonte crypto-Jews were once again an international sensation. The primary catalyst was a documentary film, *The Last Marranos* (1990), by the French Jewish filmmaker Frederic Brenner. Brenner visited the village repeatedly over a five-year period, slowly gaining the community's trust. One family allowed him to film a carefully guarded secret ceremony, a greatly altered version of Passover. It is a remarkable sequence in the film, the family dressed entirely in white, baking matzo on hot tiles in a darkened room, intoning prayers under their breath. Others consented to be interviewed, and more rituals were committed to film. Although Brenner reportedly told participants that his footage was for educational purposes (Canelo 2004: 201–3), the resulting feature-length film was released commercially. It appeared first on the international Jewish film festival circuit, then on public television stations throughout France, Spain, the United States, and, ultimately, worldwide. A great majority of tourists and outreach workers I met had seen it before their trip, many enthusiastically recounting what they saw as bizarre and moving rituals. It eventually appeared on Portuguese national television. Abroad and within their own country, the crypto-Jews became a subject of discussion and fascination. Stories about them appeared widely in the Portuguese media, as well as in the *New York Times* and leading papers in other countries.

Ironically, just as they became famous for their survival in secrecy, many sought a "return" to normative Judaism (Garcia 1993, 1999). On request, the Israeli embassy located a Portuguese-language source of religious educational materials, then arranged for a rabbi to be sent for a few years with funding from the Jewish Agency, the Israeli government's outreach arm to Jews worldwide. The selected rabbi happened to be Orthodox; as he was their first teacher, the community developed and still maintains a strict commitment to Orthodox Judaism. Because none could prove unbroken Jewish descent since the forced conversions five hundred years earlier, the *judeus* of Belmonte were told they had to undergo formal conversion to be recognized as Jews. In the first few years of the 1990s approximately half the community, by then numbering some two hundred people in fifty nuclear families, underwent Orthodox conversion. Others chose to continue in the secretive, syncretic religion in which they had been raised (Garcia 1999; Mea 2005).

In their quest to join the Jewish world, Belmonte's crypto-Jews received a flood of international support. Volunteer educators, rabbis, and donors flocked to guide and underwrite the community's transition to normative Judaism—a major religious and cultural change (Garcia 1999), like their ancestors' transformation from Jews to Catholics—and help them finance construction of a synagogue. Most of the funds came from a single donor, Salomon Azoulay, a French Sephardic businessman. The 1993 cornerstone laying was an internationally publicized event, attended not only by the synagogue's underwriter but also the president of the Israeli Knesset, the Israeli ambassador, and representatives of the Sephardic communities of France, Switzerland, Israel, and Morocco. The synagogue's inauguration was held three years later, on December 4, 1996, the five hundredth anniversary of Portugal's Edict of Expulsion. Among the hundreds of people in attendance were representatives of the Portuguese government and Jewish dignitaries from Europe, North America, South America, and North Africa, as well as Israeli political and religious leaders (Garcia 1999: 170–72). Press releases, speeches, even the printed invitation explicitly linked the synagogue's inauguration to the Expulsion and Inquisition, indelibly underscoring the village's standing as a symbol of Jewish resistance and survival.

The Orthodox conversion of a large percentage of the Belmonte community, coupled with the peculiar rituals captured in Brenner's film, has created a curious role for its members. Far from being "hidden Jews," this community of small shopkeepers and farmers has for decades been subject to continuous international fascination and scrutiny. Not only is Belmonte a fixture on the Jewish heritage tourism circuit, receiving hundreds of independent travelers and package-tour participants annually, but the community features in at least four documentary films and numerous scholarly publications. Dozens of journalists write about the "hidden" Jews each year. Yet the community's public face is the synagogue leadership—precisely those who have embraced "mainstream" Orthodox Judaism. When package-tour groups come to meet "members of the Belmonte crypto-Jewish community" they are received in the synagogue, a freestanding, three-story building fronted by an enormous metal menorah, where religious services are much like Orthodox rites anywhere. Ironically, the very fact that one can visit and pray with the world's most famous "Marranos" or "crypto-Jews" means that they are no longer either. Despite the remote location of their mountain village and their notorious reticence with strangers, they are now among the most easily found and widely known signs of Jewish presence, past or present, in the country.

Foreign interest in assisting the Portuguese Marranos did not lessen after the Orthodox conversion in Belmonte. In part, this is because news of their entry into normative Judaism has not caught up with the impact of Brenner's film, with its extraordinary footage of rural villagers performing barely recognizable "Jewish" rituals. Abroad, relatively few people know that most have abandoned their parents' and grandparents' syncretic crypto-Judaism (Canelo 2004; Garcia 1999). At the same time, throughout my fieldwork those few who were aware expressed grave concern over the lack of Jewish educators or even a permanent rabbi to guide the next generation. This was the stance of international organizations like Shavei Israel and Kulanu, among others, which in recent years have sent ritual objects, educational materials, and short-term educators to Belmonte. One outreach group underwrote rabbinic training for a local youth in Jerusalem, hoping he would someday return to lead his community.

Over time, Shavei Israel extended its activities beyond Belmonte. Having placed a rabbi there for one year beginning in 2003, the organization then expanded his remit to include the emerging urban Marrano community in Porto, a four-hour bus trip away. He relocated to Porto in 2004, returning to Belmonte for life-cycle rituals and other rabbinic duties. His new home was the small, never-inhabited rabbi's apartment in Barros Basto's great synagogue. There he self-consciously resumed the "work of redemption," using the media to invite "Marranos" throughout northern Portugal to attend his Introduction to Judaism classes and frequently making reference to Barros Basto's movement in his sermons, interviews, and public appearances. Shavei Israel's executive director, too, drew upon that rhetoric. In a recent interview, he could have been quoting Barros Basto or Schwarz when he proclaimed, "There are tens of thousands of B'nai Anusim [i.e., descendants of forced converts] throughout Portugal who are conscious of their special historical connection to the Jewish people. We owe it to them and to their ancestors to reach out to them, embrace them, and welcome them back home."[15]

We have come full circle, for once again an international outreach organization saw a Portuguese landscape filled with hidden Jews awaiting discovery and assistance. Turning their gaze to cities as well as to the rural northeast, organizations like Shavei Israel and individual activists like Nostálgia's

Graciana Mayer believed that Portugal harbored large numbers of descend-ants of Jews who still identified as such, and they posted much to that effect online. Whether their motivation was to hasten the Ingathering of the Exiles, to reach out to "lost brethren" and offer educational support, or merely to make contact with people for whom they felt a deep if abstract affinity, the result was the same: the urban Marranos in Porto and Lisbon, like the Belmonte crypto-Jews before them, became both a social cause and an object of wonder, the target of efforts to complete Barros Basto's work of redemption.

Despite the many differences between them, the urban Marranos and Belmonte's *judeus* were of a piece in the foreign Jewish imagination, colored as it was by Brenner's film and by mass media, fiction, and folklore. Travelers arrived in Portugal expecting to hear stories of peasant grandmothers light-ing candles on Friday night with the shades drawn, of mumbled prayers whose meaning had been forgotten, and of secrecy above all. For what was a Marrano, if not a hidden Jew? The widespread coverage surrounding revela-tions of crypto-Judaism in the American Southwest in the 1990s offered a host of additional images:[16] deathbed confessions of Jewish ancestry, child-hood instruction in secret rituals, methods of slaughter, and avoidance of certain foods passed down over generations. All this they brought to their encounters with the urban Marranos, in addition to the weight of centuries of Jewish imaginings of the Marrano as a heroic figure of resistance, faith, and survival.

HIDDEN WITHIN, PART II: JEWISHNESS AS PORTUGUESE HERITAGE

In Portugal today the existence of a Jewish religious community is no secret. Though largely ignorant of its rituals and beliefs, most among the Catholic majority are aware that Judaism exists in their country, like Islam, Hinduism, and other minority faiths found in the largest cities. The official community organ of Lisbon's Jews, the Comunidade Israelita de Lisboa (CIL; Jewish Community of Lisbon), provides the public face of Jewishness in Portugal. It administers the Shaaré Tikvá synagogue, in addition to other community and public-relations programs, and its leaders are regularly contacted by the media for comment on matters related to religion and politics. By 2000 the vast majority of CIL's membership were native-born Portuguese citizens.

Nonetheless, Portuguese Jewishness—the religion and its adherents— was still widely seen by the Portuguese as something particular to a small community of urbanites, descendants of immigrants who had imported the religion from somewhere else.

But there is yet another twist in the social distinction between Portuguese Catholics and Portuguese Jews. Along with the normative Jewish community and the former crypto-Jews, today a third group in Portugal is widely understood to embody a form of Jewishness: the Portuguese people themselves. Whereas the Portuguese government's first public apologies for the Inquisition were addressed to "the Jews" as a distinct Other, over the past twenty years the discourse around Portugal's Jewish history has gradually shifted to invocations of shared multiethnic descent that position all Portuguese as heirs to the Jewish past. In the following pages I briefly sketch this discursive transition.

On March 17, 1989, President Mário Soares made a nationally televised request for forgiveness from the Jewish people for their suffering during the Inquisition (Yerushalmi 1992: 42–43).[17] Standing in the well-preserved *judiaria* of Castelo de Vide, a medieval village in the Alentejo province, he addressed an invited audience that included the Israeli ambassador and representatives from CIL. He spoke of the essential role Jews had played in Portuguese history since the nation's founding and stressed that the Inquisition had run directly counter to the traditional Portuguese ideals of universalism and tolerance, whose origin he located in the Middle Ages, during the golden age of social integration of Jews and Christians. It was this tradition of tolerance and coexistence, he said, that was finally recovered with the 1974 Revolution. With this speech, Soares launched a discourse of democratic multiculturalism that would become the hallmark of subsequent governmental statements on the Jewish place in Portugal's national "heritage."[18] This discourse appears as well in tourism materials and popular histories, which present the Edict of Expulsion as having been forced upon an unwilling, fundamentally tolerant King Manuel and his subjects by the fanatical Spanish crown.

President Soares's remarks were echoed emphatically on December 5, 1996, in a session of the Portuguese Parliament commemorating the quincentennial of the Edict of Expulsion. The culmination of a national, weeklong program of events, it began with speeches by leaders of the Portuguese political parties "highlighting the atrocities of that epoch [and] expressing regret at the terrible events of the past" (Pinto n.d.: 18). The Parliament then voted unanimously to reaffirm the 1821 repeal of the edict.[19] The session closed with speeches by the president of the Israeli Knesset and the Portuguese president, Jorge Sampaio, who called the edict an "iniquitous act with deep and disastrous consequences" for his country. Four years later, during an international interfaith conference, José Policarpo, patriarch of Lisbon and head of Portugal's Catholic Church, stood at the site of Lisbon's Palace of the Inquisition and formally apologized for the Inquisition's "intolerable acts of violence against the Hebrew people."[20]

Throughout the 1990s, a series of high-profile museum exhibitions, films, historical novels, and other commemorative projects reflected a growing interest in the country's "lost" Jewish history. Lisbon's Universidade Nova released a facsimile edition of Samuel Schwarz's 1925 book, exhibition catalogs included dense texts by academic historians (e.g., Borges 1999; dos Santos 1994), and a series of widely publicized conferences examined different periods of Portuguese Jewish history. By 2002 Jewish studies centers had been established at two major universities. Well before that, beginning in the late 1980s but with rapid growth from 2000, the Portuguese National Tourist Office and municipalities nationwide launched campaigns to develop an international market for Jewish heritage tourism, marking medieval *judiarias,* printing brochures and maps, sponsoring archaeological and historical research, and underwriting multilingual books about Jewish settlements in various parts of the country, to be sold in local tourism offices (e.g., Monteiro 1997).

Excluding academic publications, the bulk of this commemorative activity focused on the period prior to the Inquisition. Mention of the modern era, if any, was limited to the arrival of Jewish immigrants in the nineteenth and twentieth centuries and to brief notice of Belmonte's emergence in the 1990s, the latter invariably celebrated as an indication of Portuguese democracy and pluralism in the aftermath of the 1974 Revolution. A major international traveling exhibition, *Signs of Judaism in Portugal,* emphasized the distant past, granting Barros Basto's *obra do resgate* just four sentences in the catalog and displaying no objects related to his work. Similarly, a commemorative stamp set celebrating Portugal's Jewish heritage, issued by the national postal service (CTT Correios) in 2004, portrays only illuminated manuscripts and other art related to Portugal's medieval Jews. A single stamp displays the interior of Shaaré Tikvá, in a nod to Lisbon's current Jewish community, but there is no indication that anything related to Jews occurred between 1496 and the modern era. The accompanying coffee-table book, written by the celebrated historian Maria José Ferro Tavares, begins in the fifth century and ends with the forced conversions and onset of the Inquisition.[21]

Thus at the level of officially endorsed national memory, Portugal's Jewish heritage effectively begins before the nation's founding and ends at an unspecified moment during the Inquisition when the majority of New Christians ceased to identify as *religiously* Jewish. However, this is not a simple case of "imperialist nostalgia" (Rosaldo 1989), where the conqueror mourns the passing of what he himself has destroyed. It is precisely those who today construct and commemorate the official version of Portugal's "lost" Jewish heritage that are most likely to say that all Portuguese probably have Jewish ancestry or that Portuguese culture is permeated with an underlying Jewishness. Discursively, these individuals position themselves and the nation as a whole as the cultural and even genetic heirs of Portugal's "lost" Jews—heirs, that is, not of the Jews who escaped to other countries, nor of the Marranos who persisted in their faith in rural mountain villages, but of the one-third of the population classified as New Christian by the Inquisition's end.

From "them" to "us": the discursive shift at work here incorporates a "lost" Jewishness into the very essence of the Portuguese people. Popular histories and museum catalogs, both those intended for international consumption and those written for a Portuguese audience, gesture explicitly toward this reorientation. In her introduction to the *Signs of Judaism* catalog, Maria Helena dos Santos writes:

> The Portuguese . . . believe themselves to be a mixture of many races and after a number of centuries have opened the doors of their country to the Jews. This openness, which has always been seen in Portugal in times of freedom, is very much in agreement with the ingrained intuition of our collective memory. . . . Nowadays, with a relaxed shrug of the shoulders and a wry smile, we Portuguese acknowledge that somewhere along the line, we all have a drop of Jewish blood running in our veins. (In Cabral 1999: 17)

Although relatively recent in public discourse, the model of a Portugueseness grounded in shared, mixed ethnicity that contains "a drop of Jewish blood," among others, has a long history in Portuguese ethnological description (Leal 2000a; Sobral 2004). Today, erudite works and popular texts, elementary school lessons and tourist guidebooks, depict the contemporary Portuguese people as arising from a mixture of historical populations that includes Lusitanians,

Phoenicians, Carthaginians, Suevi, Visigoths, Romans, "Moors," and Jews. For Jorge Dias, a leading mid-twentieth-century Portuguese anthropologist, it was precisely that hybrid ethnogenealogy that gave his people their unique national character: "The psycho-social personality of the Portuguese people ... carries within it profound contradictions that can be explained by the different tendencies of the populations that formed the country" (1990[1950]: 142). More recently, in the preface to the Jewish heritage coffee-table book released by CTT Correios, its director writes, "It is almost a cliché to affirm that we are a people in whose 'genetic code' is inscribed a stew [*caldo*] of cultures and civilizations, long-disappeared but still reflected in our unique identity" (Costa 2004).

The suggestion that centuries of Jewish presence directly shaped Portuguese culture surfaces regularly in popular texts and in serious works of scholarship. Sociologist Moisés Espírito Santo, for example, argues that centuries of Jewish and crypto-Jewish presence have profoundly influenced popular Catholicism in Portugal. In one essay, he offers a Jewish cultural explanation for many seemingly innocuous aspects of popular religious practice, then concludes with the overarching Portuguese "messianic mentality":

> Portuguese messianism is a genuinely Jewish product: ... aside from Judaism, the messianism which has always animated the Portuguese mentality has no equal in the history of humanity. ... We might say that our very cultural identity is that we are *old Jews and new Christians,* Jews pretending to be Catholics. (Espírito Santo 1993: xxi–xxii)

Similarly, in a bilingual historical study of Jews in Viseu, a city in central Portugal, published by the city's regional tourism office, the author provides a survey of pre-Inquisition Jewish cultural life and then concludes,

> All of us are heirs of that [Jewish] Culture. This culture is part of our way of being, our knowledge, our everyday life. And there is no need to work out in detail the explanations for that. Within each one of us there is a Jewish heritage. (Monteiro 1997: 145)

Is every Portuguese person, then, a little bit Jewish? Where does that Jewishness reside? At the level of the nation, at least, the rhetoric cited here suggests that as "heritage" it resides in the body, mentality, and daily practices of each and every Portuguese. As a collective inheritance, Portuguese Jewishness is both a present absence and an absent presence, a lost people and culture that has, through the peculiar mechanism of their loss, become a pervasive, constituent component of the nation as a whole.

Exploring how the social category "Portuguese Jews"—and the modifier "Jewish"—has been understood and applied over time reveals a curious bifurcation. Since the time of the forced conversions, in Portugal the category has operated on two distinct registers—religious practice and genealogical descent—that seem to rise and fall independently. Nowhere is this clearer than in the present. As a religion, that is, normative Judaism, Jewishness is limited to a very small percentage of the Portuguese population, and those who view it as "foreign" are correct in that it was reintroduced by immigrants in the early nineteenth century. According to widely circulated figures, the number of Jews in the entire country—where "Jews" refers to members of the organized Jewish community or Jewish foreign nationals—hovers around five hundred. And yet a surprisingly large number of Portuguese people evidently consider themselves "Jewish." In the 1981 national census, for example, nearly 6,000 individuals chose that designation (Bastos and Bastos 1999: 157–60). The number dropped to 3,500 in 1991, where it remains today[22]—a change that Portuguese scholars argue may be a response to a contemporaneous wave of European anti-Semitism, rather than a major shift in self-identification, especially given that the demographics of the areas in question did not noticeably change in the 1990s (Bastos and Bastos 1999: 159).

In fact, Jewish self-identification remains remarkably widespread, as mapped by the regional breakdown of the national census in both 2001 and 2011: throughout the country, but especially in the Trás-os-Montes and Beira regions, in literally dozens of townships a handful of residents elected to classify their religion as "Jewish." While in most areas just one or two people identified themselves in this way, in some towns as many as two dozen did.[23] Importantly, then, individuals who call themselves Jewish are not concentrated solely in areas populated by Jewish immigrants, their descendants, and expatriates. These are ethnic Portuguese, many of them in rural areas, perhaps the children and grandchildren of people involved in Barros Basto's movement. In her study of Jewish history in Covilhã, the city nearest Belmonte, Maria Antonieta Garcia describes the nebulous way such individuals understand themselves to be Jews:

> In Covilhã the memory of Jewish descent survives, in some cases accompanied by an affirmation of identity. There are people throughout the region whose claim to being Jewish remains in an epistemological penumbra: some

are practicing Catholics, who call themselves Jews! To call oneself Jewish is a personal choice.... Being a Jew, as Edgar Morin wrote, has become an adjective that permits different degrees and tonalities. (2001: 182–83)

In Covilhã, as in Portugal as a whole, to identify oneself as Jewish by descent is an acceptable option, a personal choice, carrying a wide range of potential meanings.

More widespread still is the construction of collective Jewish heritage as shared ancestry and national "mentality," imagined to be no less pervasive for its invisibility and widely presumed by Portuguese intellectuals and a surprising percentage of the ordinary population to be carried within their bodies as well as in their culture. Nonetheless, the dozens who told me they probably had Jewish ancestry would likely not have checked "Jewish" on a census form; most articulated feeling a profound connection to the Portuguese Jewish people—those of the distant past, rather than immigrant-origin Jews of the present—without quite being "Jewish" themselves. The distinction here is important. As the next chapter demonstrates, urban Marranos felt strongly that they were Jews themselves, as individuals, not merely of Jewish descent or "Jewish" in the diffuse sense afforded by being Portuguese. The difference here lies not in ancestry, nor in faith; it is a question of one's innermost sense of self and the imagined community with which one identifies most.

In turn-of-the-millennium Portugal, then, one could by one's own description be "of Jewish descent"—or even just "Jewish," depending on the speaker—without being Jewish in the religious sense, without considering oneself a Jew, and without having any relationship at all with the community known as Portuguese Jews. Consider Leonor Mendes, a medical student whom I met at a dinner party in Lisbon in 2004. Her Star of David pendant immediately caught my eye. She explained that some of her ancestors were Jewish, so she wore it to honor them; on other days, in honor of her Catholic ancestors, she wore a cross. As for her own faith, she was Catholic, like her mother before her—a woman who, it bears noting, had published several articles in genealogical magazines about the family's Jewish origins. Then there was Jorge, a fifty-year-old tourism professional in a coastal resort town near Lisbon. He told me that his cousin, a jeweler, had made him a half-inch silver Star of David superimposed by a crucifix, in recognition of his feeling that he was Jewish by descent and Catholic by faith. And Xénia Brindes, a doctoral student in Portuguese history, explained that preliminary research on an unrelated topic had led her to *cristãos-novos* and then to Inquisition records, which described practices that sounded remarkably like things she remembered from childhood. She did not think of herself as Jewish, but expressed interest in attending an evening service at Shaaré Tikvá ("just to learn") and had joined the Nostálgia forum. She volunteered that she now believes she has Jewish ancestors—and that everyone else in Portugal does, too. While each of these individuals felt connected to the Portuguese Jews of the past, none described himself or herself as Jewish in the sense of personal affiliation. It was family history, long lost.

Hence we are left with three distinct ways of imagining Jewishness in the Portuguese present, based on three configurations of overlapping criteria. First, for most Jewish tourists and others who envision Portugal from afar, the category "Portuguese Jews" is firmly anchored to history—the forced converts and their descendants, the original Marranos—and hence closely associated with hidden Judaism, past and present. Second, for many contemporary Portuguese, "Portuguese Jews" refers to a population of foreign origin, their religion imported via nineteenth- and twentieth-century immigrants from North Africa and Eastern Europe and their rabbis speaking heavily accented Portuguese, even today, in media appearances; at the same time, for many Portuguese, the entire nation shares an inherent Jewishness as heritage, hidden within, as collective descent and/or cultural traits transmitted over many generations. And third, for the urban Marranos whose story forms the heart of this book, Portuguese Jewishness is a rare inheritance, hidden deeply within the individual self. It inheres neither in lived community affiliation nor in religious practice, neither collective descent nor shared cultural traits, but in presumed direct ancestry and the very stuff of the spirit.

Are Portuguese Jews a thing of the past or the present? Are they defined by descent or religion? Does the term refer to indigenous Portuguese or the descendants of immigrants? The extent to which the category "Jews" and the subjects to whom it might be applied remain blurry indeed was reflected in a 2008 newspaper headline about Lisbon's urban Marranos. Above the masthead, advertising the feature story in the paper's weekend magazine was a teaser line: *Um shabat entre judeus portugueses que estão a estudar para ser judeus*—"A Shabbat with Portuguese Jews who are studying to be Jews."[24]

Essentially Jewish

BODY, SOUL, SELF

Perhaps instead of talking about identities, inherited or acquired, it would be more in keeping with the realities of the globalising world to speak of *identification,* a never-ending, always incomplete, unfinished and open-ended activity in which we all, by necessity or by choice, are engaged.

ZYGMUNT BAUMAN
"Identity in the Globalising World"

ON A COOL JUNE MORNING, still so early that the vast paved square of the Praça do Comércio was not yet awash in Lisbon's blinding summer sun, twenty-four tour participants clambered off a blue and white tour bus. This was the final stop on the 2002 Nostálgia Conference-Tour, created expressly for descendants of Portugal's Inquisition-era crypto-Jews, now scattered throughout the Portuguese diaspora, and Jews hoping to understand their experience (Leite 2005). Gathered by Graciana Mayer, the Portuguese South African founder of Nostálgia, we had come from nine different countries to "walk in the footsteps of our ancestors," as the tour materials put it, on a quest for lost Jewish roots. Over the preceding week our guides had shown us hints of medieval Jewish presence in one town after another: sites of long-vanished *judiarias,* buildings that may have been used as synagogues, hollowed-out spaces in stone doorways where a *mezuzah* might once have been mounted.[1] We also paused at public squares in several cities where autos-da-fé were held, honoring the Inquisition's dead with the traditional Jewish mourner's prayer. The crypto-Jewish-descendant participants felt their ancestors' suffering keenly, and some moments were startlingly emotionally raw. But visits to the dead and forgotten were leavened by contact with the living, in informal meetings Graciana had arranged with "Marranos" (or "crypto-Jews" or "Anusim," depending on the speaker) at various stops along the itinerary. While other tour participants were eager to meet them, this was my first immersive fieldwork and I found myself tongue-tied, much too shy and uncertain to talk to them myself, even missing a scheduled early morning gathering in Porto with the excuse of writing up field notes in my hotel room instead.

This June morning, the final day of the tour, promised one last opportunity to meet Portuguese Marranos. Our destination was a nondescript auditorium in one of the eighteenth-century buildings that line three sides of the Praça do Comércio, the fourth side opening onto the brilliant blue of the Tejo River. The day's focus was a conference with presentations by tour participants, some of them academics, all of them knowledgeable in the history of Portuguese crypto-Judaism. Graciana had publicized the event on the Nostálgia forum and invited local academics and members of HaShalom, the Lisbon Marrano association, to join the audience. When we arrived there were at least twenty people present, most seated toward the back of the room. I craned my neck to see them from my spot in the second row. Which were the Marranos? It was impossible to tell. Earlier in the tour we had had dinner with former crypto-Jews in Belmonte, and perhaps because I had seen *The Last Marranos,* the 1990 documentary featuring several of our hosts, still easily recognizable, or perhaps because they were unpretentious, rural people in a largely insular world, they had been exactly as I expected. Here, I saw only fashionably dressed Lisbonites who would be indistinguishable from anyone else on the city's streets or its university campuses. Throughout the tour Graciana had cautioned us that many Anusim, as she called them, were still nervous and even frightened about revealing themselves, and she warned us not to push too hard, not to ask too many questions. From participating in Nostálgia and other internet forums I knew that descendants worldwide were highly conscious of their ancestors' lifesaving emphasis on secrecy, to the point of replicating it themselves (cf. Jacobs 2002; Kunin 2009). But no one in the auditorium looked particularly nervous or even self-conscious. They sat in clusters, chatting, some of the younger attendees in a group talking and laughing among themselves.

Late that afternoon, the conference over, the bus trundled back up the leafy Avenida da Liberdade to deposit us at our hotel. In the lobby I was surprised to see half a dozen young adults from the conference awaiting us. Within moments Graciana introduced me to Catarina Queirós, the first "Marrano" with whom I would have an extended conversation. She was the furthest thing I could imagine from the typical image of a Marrano, that storied elderly peasant woman in a black kerchief, furtively lighting candles in a darkened room with the curtains tightly drawn. The people I had met briefly in Belmonte seemed wary, taciturn, even standoffish, but Catarina's lively, urbane demeanor was something altogether different. Dressed in high-heeled boots and fashionable jeans, with pitch-perfect English and an unending store of witty, irreverent asides, she was every inch the cosmopolitan graduate student. Within a few minutes she was telling me funny anecdotes of her life as a student in several countries, describing the doctoral research she had abandoned to take on a different subject, and recounting how her life had changed since she joined the Nostálgia forum. She was not only perfectly willing to answer my questions, she had obviously given her identity a great deal of thought and wanted to share her story. There was no sign of fear, no indication that she was breaking a familial legacy of silence, nothing of the kind. Instead, she wanted to tell me how she realized she was Jewish and about the repercussions of that discovery.

As my research progressed over the next four years and I met dozens of other self-identified Marranos, I found that Catarina was not unusual. Most were happy to share their personal histories and, like Catarina, had gone through an intensive process of introspection and study—indeed, of self-cultivation—that led to and continued throughout their involvement in the Marrano associations. To my surprise, I learned that the vast majority had not been raised as crypto-Jews, not even those who learned as children that they had Jewish ancestry, and most were unique in their natal family for pursuing it. Their identity as Marranos was thus not something passively received from previous generations, transmitted through syncretic rituals and secrecy. It was a development in young adulthood, the outcome of a striking degree of self-awareness through which they discovered their (ancestral) Jewishness and recognized it as an essential component of their innermost self. Only later did they come to think of themselves as "Marranos." Moreover, their common association under that banner obscured wide variation in their paths toward a Jewish identity, as well as the source of their knowledge that they had Jewish ancestry and even their relative comfort with the word *Marrano* itself.

In this chapter and the next, I explore the processes through which people *become* Marranos in contemporary urban Portugal and the practices through which the Jewish and Marrano self is constituted and expressed. To say that a sense of oneself as a Jew or Marrano emerges at a particular moment in time and through a particular set of circumstances is not to minimize its experiential truth. Like other groups who develop a radically new sense of self in adulthood (Grünewald 2001; Kessell 2000; Sturm 2010), the urban Marranos provide a dramatic but not unusual example of how social and personal identities are ever-emergent, continuously created and negotiated in diverse engagements with a fluid array of people, things, and ideas. "When we consider the temporal flow of experience," writes anthropologist Katherine Ewing, "we can observe that individuals are continuously reconstituting themselves into new selves in response to internal and external stimuli" (1990: 258). By highlighting *becoming,* a process, rather than approaching identity as a unified, timeless essence, we can explore how senses of self are made and remade, sometimes consciously but more often unconsciously, via the adoption and performance of practices, attitudes, values, and ways of conceiving of one's relationship to oneself and to others. As social beings, each of us is a composite of multiple allegiances and self-understandings that may be communicated or called upon in one situation but not in another (Campbell and Rew 1999; Kondo 1990). Nonetheless, most people experience their innermost sense of self, their identity, as if it were fixed, whole, and essential; this is certainly true of how urban Marranos articulated their Jewishness, even as they explained that they had not always thought of themselves as Jews.

My analytical focus in this chapter is thus not (only) identity, but *identification,* an active, often emotionally charged process of seeing oneself as a particular kind of person and intentionally cultivating the qualities and practices proper to it. I examine the variety and contingency of urban Marranos' modes of self-identification as Jews and tease apart the Portuguese cultural logics of race, nation, descent, and the self that make their articulation of a Jewish self coherent, both to themselves and to others. As we will see, identification, a core component of self-making, is a dialogical process: it is through our interactions with others, whether face-to-face or imagined, that we become self-aware and develop, reflect upon, and refine our sense of ourselves (Mead 1934; Cohen 1994; Holland et al. 1998: 19–46). Indeed, encounters with foreign Jewish tourists and outreach workers, Portuguese Jews, and other self-identified Marranos played a crucial role in shaping urban Marranos' understanding of who they were at the core and of how they might best go about *becoming*—recognizing, enacting, living as—that truest self.

THE ESSENTIAL JEWISH SELF

Early in my fieldwork, I came upon a photocopy of an article in a popular magazine about Portugal's Jewish history, written in 1994.[2] It began with a remarkable line: "Ana Gonçalves never dreamed she was Jewish." According to the author, Ana was not baptized and never understood why, until "by pure chance, when she was twenty-four she discovered everything." She stopped by the public library and, in a rush, picked a book at random. When she got home she realized it was a historical novel about the founding of the State of Israel. Reading it, she was overcome with a desire to live and work on an Israeli kibbutz. When she told her mother, the reply was simply, "Do you know why you feel that way? Because you, too, are a Jew." Suddenly Ana's entire life made sense. It had been strewn with clues all along, the author tells us, but she hadn't had the key to decode them. Left unexplained here is the relationship between the selection of the book, the desire to live on a kibbutz, and Ana's unknown Jewishness, let alone what her mother meant by "You, too, are a Jew."

I have never met Ana, but her story is familiar. Underpinning the portrait of unrecognized clues, inexplicable desires, and mysterious coincidences is a set of mystical assumptions about ancestry and personal traits, practice and meaning, and body and spirit that I found common to the life stories of many urban Marranos. Once Ana knows who she "really" is, she can finally recognize and interpret the clues that lead to just one possible conclusion. For those familiar with Portuguese logics of the relationship between ancestry and the self, the obvious implication is that Ana's mother has revealed that she has Jewish *ancestry;* it is her ancestry that makes Ana have feelings that are apparently those of a Jewish person. Like all life history narratives, this one makes implicit causal connections between past and present, event and outcome, that must be intuitively understood by both teller and listener for the narrative to be coherent (Linde 1993). That these connections would be coherent to a Portuguese readership is reflected in the author's lack of explanation for the mother's claim that her daughter is a Jew and for the "clues" that reinforce it.

While its causal logic may be specific to the immediate cultural context, the story of Ana Gonçalves reflects a widespread Western understanding of "identity" as the self's core truth, not necessarily fully realized in one's social persona but always there, nonetheless, available for expression (Battaglia 1995: 2–3). Her story gives the impression that one's sense of self can change overnight, that a single moment of discovery can cause an awakening of who one "really" is inside. But however abrupt the discovery, the process of acquiring a new social identity is slow, uneven, evolving over time and developed in interaction. As her story demonstrates, part of that process involves retrospectively connecting unrelated experiences in narrative, seeing them as premonitions of one's current identity or position (Linde 1993). Just as middle-class Americans often begin the narrative of their career choice with childhood traits and hobbies, in explaining how they developed a Jewish identity urban Marranos recounted a series of personal and familial clues that became meaningful to them only in retrospect.

Like identities, life stories evolve over time, even from one telling to the next, affected by contextual factors like audience, mood, cross-linguistic competence, available time, and shared background knowledge. Which details seem important, what counts as a significant turning point or revelation, whether shifts in identity seem in retrospect to have been sudden or gradual—all are subject to change and consequently alter how the story is told (Peacock and Holland 1993). In this section, I approach participants' self-narratives primarily as factual sources, that is, as *life histories* (Frank 1995), distilling from them three different paths by which urban Marranos came to see themselves as Jews. In compiling these "paths," I draw on presentations of self from casual café conversations to local and national meetings, from their discussions with foreign Jewish visitors to interviews some gave the Portuguese media, and from accounts they wrote at the request of rabbis and Jewish outreach groups to formal interviews I conducted during my fieldwork.[3] These diverse discourse units are as important for understanding the lives recorded as a single full telling (Linde 1993: 21). I return to the act of narration—the consolidation and telling of full *life stories*—in chapter 3. It is important to note that the articulations of Jewish identity explored in this chapter and the next were recorded at a very specific time and place, the urban Portugal of early 2004 to mid-2005. The same individuals subsequently had intensive interactions with foreign Jewish outreach organizations that generated significant changes in the nature and articulation of their identity, transformations that I explore in the second half of the book.

The three trajectories I delineate here, presented through the life histories of seven representative individuals, have certain features in common. In each case, experimentation with a Jewish identity began in the teens or early twenties, often following a lengthy—in some cases, lifelong—interest in Jews and Jewishness. This was true regardless of the individual's age, which in 2005 ranged from twenty-three to fifty-six. While all felt that they had Jewish ancestors, they based that belief on different kinds of evidence, with varying levels of certainty. Their degree of engagement with religious observance varied as well, but all articulated some connection to Judaism, the religion, as well as to Jewish ancestry. Most mentioned social ties and emotional bonds with Jews from other countries or with fellow Portuguese who identified with Jewish ancestry as playing an important role. Finally, despite not being Jewish according to Jewish law or even by religious or cultural upbringing, all felt strongly that they had *already* been Jewish in some fundamental way, all along. Identifying with Jewishness was thus less a matter of embracing something new than giving name to a preexisting facet of the self.

From a Jewish Family History to a Jewish Self

I first met António Silva Abreu at a board meeting of Menorá, Porto's Marrano association, on what turned out to be his twenty-fifth birthday. He was a tall, gregarious graduate student, always neatly dressed, with an impish sense of humor and a penchant for quoting Nietzsche and other philosophers in the midst of casual conversation. An only child, he was born in Brazil to a Portuguese father and an Arab Brazilian mother. When he was still very young his parents separated. He and his father returned to Portugal and settled in Porto, where his paternal grandparents lived. It was there, as a small child, that he remembers his grandmother taking him one afternoon to see Porto's grand synagogue. "There's something we want you to understand," she told him. "We have Jewish ancestry." Her family had been part of the *obra do resgate,* the Marrano revival movement of the 1930s, and she spoke to him of meeting Barros Basto and seeing the enormous synagogue he had built for the Marranos. But that afternoon was António's only memory of any Jewish-related activity in his childhood. Although he recalls his grandmother mentioning practices she learned as a child, she no longer adhered to any of them. She died prematurely, and so it fell to his father, who did not identify strongly with their Jewish origins, to answer António's questions. He did not discourage António's curiosity but could offer little information. For António, "Jewish" was thus something the family had once been, a matter of history, a defining memory transmitted "by word of mouth, from my grandmother, to my father, to me [*de boca a boca, por avó, para o pai, para mim*]."

When he was eighteen, out of the blue he received a mailed invitation from the synagogue's administration to attend a concert there. This was in the late 1990s, when the synagogue was run by expatriates from Israel, the United States, and Britain, and concerts and other cultural events were occasionally held in the synagogue sanctuary. He never learned why he received the invitation; perhaps, he thought, his grandmother had asked years earlier for his name to be added once he turned eighteen. Out of curiosity he decided to go. Thereafter he began to attend services, hoping to understand his family history better. At that point, he told me, "I didn't have a clue about what it means to be a Jew, or even a Muslim or a Christian! I really knew nothing." There was no rabbi, and most of the community members ignored his presence, but he kept going, reading whatever he could find on his own to learn more.

Eventually he realized that there were other outsiders attending services at the synagogue, and they all had similar stories. For António, that was a critical moment. There was, in his words, "something real here," a group whose shared background of Jewish ancestors from villages in the northeast suggested there was "sort of a *people,* a minority population in Portugal" that persisted into the present. They became friends, studied Judaism and Portuguese Jewish history together, and collectively reinforced one another's growing identification with and cultivation of an ancestrally Jewish sense of self. Several of them formed the kernel of Menorá, in which António would become deeply involved.

Although he later came to think of his Jewishness in more spiritual, individual, and overtly religious terms, at this early point it was framed as a quasi-ethnic legacy, a kind of birthright whose content became clearer the more he learned and exchanged ideas with the others. Porto's synagogue had been built *for them,* he would tell anyone listening, the descendants of the Inquisition-era forced converts who were now gathering together. By virtue of descent, there was something already present in his body, heart, and soul that not only connected him to the Jewish people, but somehow mystically made him Jewish, as well. "This Jewish way of being, it's in our hearts already," he told me in 2004. "When I see a Jew, I feel an immediate affinity. I'm struck by the sense that we're the same." Embracing the Jewish religion seemed to him a natural and necessary next step.

Like António, Joaquim Torres Martins remembered his grandmother telling him about the family's Jewish origins when he was a little boy in Lisbon, nearly fifty years ago. Now a gregarious, bookish schoolteacher, by the early 2000s Joaquim had joined virtually every Jewish-related organization in Lisbon: the Portuguese Association for Jewish Studies, the Portugal-Israel Friendship Association, and HaShalom, Lisbon's Marrano association. He traced his earliest feelings of connection to Jewishness to his grandmother. When she told him stories of her childhood on the Spanish island of Majorca, she would emphasize that her family were *chuetas,* "little Jews," a still-significant Majorcan social category denoting descendants of

Inquisition-era converts to Catholicism (Moore 1976). Although she spoke proudly of her ancestry, like most *chuetas* she was a practicing Catholic and knew nothing of the Jewish religion, nor did she feel a need for connection with a Jewish community. The same was true of her daughter, Joaquim's mother, though the latter had an anticlerical streak and did nothing to discourage Joaquim when he began to explore his roots.

From the moment he was old enough to understand what it meant to be of *chueta* origin, Joaquim felt that he was linked with the Jewish people, past and present, and even as a child he always felt a "predilection" for Jews. But at that point he considered himself *chueta,* not Jewish, the latter quality being one he then understood primarily in religious terms. In fact, he felt absolutely no personal tie to any religion. Catholicism held no appeal for him. As it happened, his childhood home was near Lisbon's Shaaré Tikvá synagogue. In his early teens he often saw the rabbi with his long beard and dark suit coming and going through the high gates, but he had no idea who he was, nor what was housed in the building. When he learned that it was a synagogue he was fascinated and felt an urge, even a calling (*apelo*), to go inside. Although he was just fourteen, he went in alone and had a lengthy conversation with the rabbi, who invited him to return any time he wished. At that time, the mid-1960s, the synagogue's doors were open to the public, and over the next three years Joaquim attended services sporadically. Initially it was simply to learn more about the religion of his ancestors, but he continued for reasons that were not entirely clear even to himself. His attendance waned when he entered college, then took a job in another city. When he moved back to Lisbon the rabbi he knew had retired, replaced by a series of far less welcoming religious leaders, and he did not attend the synagogue regularly again.

Yet over the course of his twenties and thirties he came to identify with his Jewish ancestry more and more, perhaps because he was increasingly friendly with members of the Lisbon Jewish community who were his age, perhaps because a series of coincidences led him to become deeply involved with others of Jewish descent in archaeological projects related to Portugal's medieval Jews. He began to suspect that his Portuguese forebears, like his grandmother's family in Majorca, had Jewish roots; his maternal grandfather and both paternal grandparents, all Portuguese, carried surnames that were common among families from their region who fled to Amsterdam during the Inquisition. In his early thirties he decided to openly wear a Star of David pendant. It was just something he wanted to do; it felt right. It was an outward indication of his emerging Jewish identity, which continued to deepen over the following two decades. "At that point," he told me, "it was as if it was on my skin. Now it is inside me. It's not just on the skin, it's passed through my skin, it's become my flesh, it's become my blood."

By the time I met him, in 2004, at fifty-four years of age Joaquim was seriously considering going through a formal program of religious study in order to be considered Jewish according to halakhah. When I asked if he thought of it as conversion, however, he said no, it was a *return* to something he already was: "For me, it's a return, because I left but I returned [*eu sai mas voltei*]." "You left?" I asked. "Well, I didn't leave, but my grandparents did, my great-great-great-great-grandparents did, they were forced to leave, therefore I did." In framing his Jewishness as an ancestrally transmitted aspect of the self that had been lost by force, to be regained bit by bit in the present, Joaquim voiced a common feeling among urban Marranos. As I discuss below and in chapter 5, they took great exception to the word *conversion* in reference to their situation, arguing that they could not be converted to something they already were. Said Joaquim,

> For me it is return. They can call it what they want, but for me it is a return. If they want to call it conversion, let them call it conversion, but for me it is return. I don't feel that it's conversion from one thing—to something that cannot be changed. I already am, therefore—Whatever, mentally, I already am. Regardless of whether I practice the rituals, you understand? If I don't practice the rituals, it's because I still don't know how.

For Joaquim, Jewishness was intrinsic to himself, whether or not he had mastered the basics of Judaism. Still, he hoped to become more observant in the near future; like António, he felt religious practice was the missing piece. With it his Jewish self would be fully realized.

Both Joaquim and António experienced a fairly direct progression from awareness of Jewish ancestry, to attending a synagogue out of curiosity and then increasingly pursuing "things Jewish," to developing a personal Jewish identity, and ultimately to engaging actively with the Jewish religion. While the broad outlines of this trajectory were common among members of the Marrano associations, for some the route did not lead directly to Jewish religious observance. Pedro Alves Sequeira, for example, spent considerable time exploring Buddhism and other Eastern religions before deciding on liberal Judaism as the best fit for his belief in free will, personal responsibility, and full engagement with the modern world. A broad-shouldered young man with a piercing gaze, Pedro was born in Lisbon and grew up knowing that he descended from "Jewish" families on both sides. Although all his living relatives were Catholic or agnostic, his parents and grandparents made no secret of their origins. However, Pedro felt no particular connection to his Jewish ancestry until the early 2000s. He was an undergraduate at the time, and as it happened Hebrew was one of the optional courses for his degree. It seemed natural to choose it—why not, given his family background?—and the language came easily to him. The other students struggled, but "it seemed like it was already inside me," he said. "Maybe things like that are carried in our genes, just like dogs have it in their genes to bark when someone knocks at the door. It's something like that."

His curiosity piqued, he turned to the internet. He discovered sites listing surnames from Inquisition records and found four of his family's names there. He read avidly about Portuguese Jewish history and found it compelling, but the religion itself did not attract him; at that point he was aware only of Orthodox Judaism, and it seemed too strict, too focused on praying. All the while he continued studying Buddhism, with which he identified strongly. He thought of himself as Buddhist by religion, Jewish by blood (*judeu de sangue*). But when he was twenty-six, a chance encounter resulted in a fundamental change of course. He was in a music store, looking at jazz CDs, when he overheard a couple his age speaking Hebrew. Intrigued, he approached them and learned that they were Israelis living in Lisbon. They chatted in English, exchanged contact information, and soon became good friends. A year later Anat laughed affectionately as she told me about their first meeting. "He felt Jewish, but he didn't really know what it meant," she said. "Most of what he knew was folklore, like he had heard that having attached earlobes meant that someone was Jewish." She and her husband encouraged him to talk about his background with the rabbi at Shaaré Tikvá. Although he did not attend services, he did call the rabbi, a Shavei Israel emissary who had just arrived in Portugal. A week later he attended a session of the rabbi's Introduction to Judaism class, where he met others with similar family stories and discovered that there was an association made up of people like himself. He soon became an active member of HaShalom. The more he participated, the less he felt that he could limit his Jewish identity to blood alone: "I started asking myself, how can I be Buddhist and Jewish at the same time?" He began to read about the various branches of Judaism and found that the religion's emphasis on critical thought appealed to him philosophically, as did the concept of Jewish peoplehood.

As was the case for António and Joaquim, Pedro's path led to a Jewish identity grounded fundamentally in family history, first pursued independently and then embraced through involvement with a broader community. But whereas some participants, like António and Joaquim, found religious practice an important part of realizing that identity, for Pedro and others like him it was not essential. Several told me that while they were intrigued by Jewish rituals and would pursue Judaism were they to practice any religion at all, they were motivated primarily by a desire to reclaim their ancestral connection to Jewishness and to the Jewish world, to be part of the Jewish people. As Pedro put it, "I feel the call of the blood [*o apelo do sangue*] more than that of the religion." What was crucial to him was a growing sense of self as an *ethnic* Jew, understood in terms of ancestry ("blood"), history, culture, and even, in his words, tribalism. Thus he felt strongly that he needed to be part of a Jewish community, find a Jewish spouse, and raise children with a Jewish ethnic identity, desires that were shared by many members of Menorá and HaShalom.

Those whose lives took this path typically learned as children that their family was "Jewish," referring not only to pre-Inquisition ancestry, but to the intentional cross-generational transmission of collective identity as "a Jewish family," indexing a now-lost legacy of hidden religious practice. However, while several recalled an older relative explicitly telling them about their family's history, no religious practices were taught in connection with the revelation. If there was a memory of secret rituals having been preserved into the modern era, whether Jewish or syncretic, that memory also included the rituals' loss after the great-grandparents' or grandparents' generation. The family's Jewishness was thus in relation to the past, perpetuated only through collective affiliation with the word *Jewish* itself. For these individuals, the path to a *personal* Jewish identity progressed from passive awareness of family history to active curiosity and exploration in the teenage years, followed by the formation of key relationships with Jews of immigrant origin or other Portuguese who embraced Jewish ancestry. These relationships proved pivotal in the transition from seeing oneself as having a Jewish family history to seeing oneself as Jewish in the present.

From Fascination to Revelation

Paula Rocha Mendes was a foreign language instructor whose passion for things Jewish stretched back more than twenty years, to the early 1980s, when her schoolteacher assigned *The Diary of Anne Frank*. The story stirred something in the eleven-year-old girl. From then on, but especially in her teens, she kept an eye out for TV programs and movies related to Jews and read every relevant book she could find. When she was old enough to travel on her own, she selected international destinations with Jewish historical significance—Amsterdam, New York, Jerusalem, Vienna—and made a point of visiting Jewish sites, even attending synagogue services where she would try to meet local Jewish people. When I asked why she was so drawn to the subject, she replied that it was a matter of innate taste: "It's the same reason I like chocolate so much. That's just the way it is. It's hard to explain. Like why I love tea, and don't like coffee." When she began research for her master's degree in comparative literature, in 1994, she chose "of course" to pursue a topic involving Jews. In retrospect, she phrased this as if it were a foregone conclusion. What else would she study?

When we met, Paula was in her mid-thirties. A quiet, solitary woman with a dry wit and striking features, she told me that she had only recently begun attending services and classes at the Porto synagogue and participating in Menorá's meetings and events. But her feeling of connection to the Jewish people—indeed, of being Jewish herself—began years earlier, in solitude and then through correspondence with Jews she met when traveling abroad, alone. Although she was baptized Catholic, her parents never went to church and she had no religious upbringing. No one in the family discouraged her obvious interest in Jews, but none shared it, either. In her early twenties, she decided that she wanted as much as possible to live a Jewish life. Seeking more information on Jewish religious customs and finding nothing available in Portugal, in 1992 she ordered a series of books from the United States. On her own, bit by bit, she began to follow the religious prohibitions and did her best to keep the Sabbath: "I started learning, and it was, 'From now on, I won't do this, I won't do that.' For instance, to me, it's completely absurd now to even consider going shopping on a Saturday [the Jewish Sabbath]." Over time she came to think of herself as Jewish and the Jewish people as *her* people, though she knew the feeling was not likely to be reciprocated. To explain, she told me, "You know the song by Amália [Rodrigues, a renowned Portuguese *fado* singer] called 'Povo que lavas no rio' [People Who Wash in the River]? In the middle, it says, 'People, people, I belong to you.' Even if—Whether they accept me or not."

Then, in the mid-1990s, a neighbor in her parents' hometown told her that her family had New Christian ancestors on both sides. Her maternal aunt corroborated the story. Her immediate reaction was, "I knew it. I've always known. Of course." While for Paula the personal, spiritual aspect of her Jewishness was more important than her ancestry, revelation of the latter lent credence and authenticity to her intuitive sense of self. Indeed, after months of classes on ritual minutiae with an Orthodox rabbi sent by Shavei Israel, she confided, "I was more Jewish before all these foreigners came here to teach me how to be Jewish. I was on my own. I never had to prove anything to anyone." Then, to underscore the point, she added, *"Mais vale sê-lo que parecê-lo"* [better to be it than to seem it]—a Portuguese proverb meaning that it is preferable to be something, through and through, than merely to appear it on the surface. To Paula's mind, Jewishness was inherent to herself, in her spiritual allegiance and her ancestry, not in adherence to imposed requirements of ritual practice.

Where Paula's path proceeded gradually, through solitary study and then quiet confirmation, Dulce Oliveira's route was far more dramatic. In fact, much about Dulce was dramatic: emotionally volatile, with a taste for fashionably logoed T-shirts and jeans that made her appear much younger than her fifty-six years, the petite but fiery woman was a longtime leader in the struggle for Marrano acceptance at Portugal's synagogues. For several years she had been a key figure at HaShalom, and over time she had learned not to mince words when portraying the Marrano predicament. When a high-level Israeli religious leader came to Portugal to investigate the situation and asked each HaShalom member how long they had been waiting to "return" to Judaism, Dulce looked him in the eye and, thinking of her ancestors, said flatly, "Five hundred years."

Like Paula, Dulce did not learn that she had Jewish ancestry until she was in her twenties. Still, for as long as she could remember she had been drawn to anything related to Jews. Growing up in 1950s colonial Mozambique, she attended a Catholic elementary school and frequently got into trouble for questioning basic principles of Catholic doctrine. Neither her parents nor her grandparents were religious; in fact, she was not baptized until she was four years old, and even then only because it was necessary for admission to the Catholic school. Her father often expressed affection and admiration for the Jewish people. As a small child Dulce was fascinated by the idea that Jesus was a Jew and felt crushed upon learning that the language the priest spoke during her school's mass was not the Hebrew she imagined Jesus speaking, but Latin. She recalls wanting to learn more about Jews, continually asking questions and reading what few books she could find. She even wondered if she might somehow be Jewish herself, especially after one of her schoolteachers, a Brazilian immigrant, commented, "You know, you have a Jewish profile, a Jewish nose, even the way you look at things [*a maneira de olhar*] is Jewish." Stranger still, when she was a young teenager her mother warned her that if she ever met her estranged grandmother, who lived in Portugal, she must never mention Jews in her presence. Why, her mother didn't know; she could only say that it was a forbidden subject.

When she was sixteen Dulce's parents sent her to a high school in Lourenço Marques, the colonial capital. She lodged at a residence run by nuns, but did everything she could to avoid attending Mass. The service held no interest for her, and she saw no reason for confession to a priest. She found herself drawn instead to the city's sole synagogue, located by chance on her daily route from the residence to the high school:

> Every day on my way to school I had to pass right in front of the synagogue doors. Whenever I saw that they were open, I would go in and sit for a while. It made me so happy [*contentinha*] just sitting there quietly, touching the prayer books, ta-ta-ta, and the guard saw that I never took anything, so he would always let me come in.

She also formed an important bond during her years in the capital. An old friend of her father lived there, and as it happened he had married a South African Jewish woman. Dulce often left the nuns' residence to spend weekends in their home, a time she remembered with great fondness. The woman was not religiously observant; from their conversations Dulce learned that Jews did not eat pork and that boys must be circumcised, but little more. Still, the relationship left a lasting impression. It was her first contact with a Jewish person, and one with whom she had a particularly warm friendship.

Several years later, in 1972, Dulce traveled to Portugal for the first time. By then she was in her twenties, married, with a toddler daughter and another child on the way. She had continued to pursue her interest in Judaism—contrary to her husband's wishes—and even insisted on giving her daughter a Hebrew name, Talia. But she was utterly unprepared for the revelation that came when she visited her mother's family in the north of Portugal:

> I was talking with my uncle alone. I don't remember what it was that we were talking about, but he said, "Oh, man, you really are Jewish" [*Eh pá, és mesmo judia*]. And I said, "*What?* Why?" And he said, "That's just so Jewish, you're Jewish just like your grandmother." I don't remember what the conversation was about. I don't remember. But my aunt came running into the room and

said, "Why on earth are you telling her this now?" It's true. My mother's whole family knew, and they never said anything. And then my uncle said only, "What, after all these years it's still a secret?"

Dulce was elated. Although her uncle did not elaborate, in her understanding having a "Jewish" grandmother meant that she, too, was Jewish after all. A few years later Mozambique won its independence and Dulce, now a single mother, moved permanently to Portugal, settling with her daughters in Lisbon. Over the next three decades she tracked down every possible clue to her ancestors' identity and religious practices. She read widely on Judaism and the history of the forced conversions and the Inquisition. She began to suspect that some of her family's peculiar traditions were Jewish practices whose origin had been forgotten, such as avoidance of pork and the use of different sets of dishes for different categories of foods. Hoping to learn more, beginning in the early 1980s she attended weekly services whenever possible at Shaaré Tikvá. Although she understood little and no one ever spoke to her, she felt deeply that she was Jewish and that all she needed in order to fully realize that identity was to learn how to live as a Jew.

Despite learning about their ancestry only in adulthood, Dulce, Paula, and others whose lives took this path understood themselves as inherently Jewish from birth. This self-understanding operated on two levels, sequentially and then simultaneously: first, in spirit, as a result of a seemingly innate, lifelong attraction to both the people and the religion, even in the absence of concrete information about Judaism or contact with "mainstream" Jews; and second, in body, as a biological descendant of Jews who were forcibly converted to Catholicism hundreds of years earlier. These two levels of identification became so intertwined that they too framed their adoption of Jewish identity as a "return." Nonetheless, their personal Jewish identity had seemed to emerge gradually from within, as a matter of individual inclination; the subsequent revelation of "Jewish blood" served to provide an explanation for their childhood fascination with Jews and Judaism, making it seem, in retrospect, a kind of biological predestination. As one young man in Porto put it, "We were born like this. Something inside us calls."

Diagnosis: The "Jewish Gene," a Jewish Soul

Whereas the first two paths to a Jewish identity combine awareness of ancestry with independent spiritual or philosophical inclination, in varying degrees and at different points in the life course, the third path has a more overtly mystical character. Here, individuals first came to the conclusion that they were intrinsically Jewish, at the level of the soul, and then retroactively determined—based on a variety of clues, with more accumulating over time—that they had Jewish ancestry. Although some vaguely remembered an older relative saying the family had Jewish origins, others told me there had never been any mention of it at all. For many, the greatest clue was the very feeling of being compelled to pursue a Jewish identity; this they interpreted as a sign of Jewish descent, for reasons I discuss below. The experience was thus initially neither one of reconnecting with lost familial heritage nor of exploring a new religion, but instead of realizing a hitherto unrecognized aspect of the self. As Catarina, the graduate student whom I met in the hotel lobby, bluntly put it, "It's like being a transsexual." When I asked her to elaborate, she said,

> OK, so it's like being a female transsexual; that is, you're a woman in a man's body and you live in a world of men only. And you've felt different, and bizarre, and out of place all your life. And then you go to this place where you find [gasps] women! And all of a sudden you realize, I didn't have a problem with men in general, I just had a problem with the fact that I wasn't a man, I'm a woman.

She continued:

> When you think about how we all describe it, there comes—Either it's a sentence that's said, or something that was seen, and it just—It all sort of crystallizes. And then you realize that you were not a freak after all, you were just Jewish! [laughs] And then you think, "What the hell is this Jewish thing?" Because we don't know! It makes sense, but on an intuitive level. It's not really something that you can explain or analyze or make sense of. I mean, rationally. You really have to turn mystical at some point, because how else can you explain all these people being diagnosed with their—um—Jewishness?

For Catarina, Jewishness was a condition transmitted across generations, remaining dormant or undiagnosed in the individual until a series of events—or even a single revelatory moment—forced its recognition.

Like most Portuguese Catarina was baptized Catholic, but her parents were deeply suspicious of the church given its open collaboration with Portugal's fifty-year dictatorship, and they raised her with no religion at all. From her early teen years she was intrigued by Jewish history, particularly German Jewry and the Holocaust, but she never thought of her interest as anything more than intellectual curiosity. In 1989 the Lisbon native went to Germany as a high-school exchange student, choosing that country specifically because she had met a group of very friendly, left-wing Germans at a scouting camp and she wanted "to understand how the Holocaust was possible." Around the same time news broke of the reemergence of Belmonte's crypto-Jews, and Catarina was fascinated. The story took on added meaning a few years later, in college, when she fell in love with a classmate whose family originated in a village near Belmonte and who spoke proudly of having Jewish ancestors on both sides. They took Hebrew classes at the university together with his aunt, who enrolled as an auditor, and even went to Israel on an extended vacation. When the time came to choose a research site for her senior thesis in the social sciences, she decided to spend a semester on an Israeli kibbutz.

Still, contrary to the experiences of Paula, Dulce, and others like them, none of this added up to a significant aspect of Catarina's identity at the time; none of it made her suspect that she was in some way Jewish herself, nor was she particularly affected when her aunt made an offhand reference to Jewish ancestry in their own family: "I was a teenager when she said it, it was at dinner one night, and I thought, 'Oh, cool,' you know. And that was it. Then I totally forgot about it." It only became significant in retrospect. In 2006, telling me her full life story, she listed that and a series of other suggestive details—people giving her Jewish-related gifts for no particular reason, her lifelong distaste for Catholicism, the ancestrally Jewish boyfriend, her desire to understand the Holocaust, her choice of the kibbutz as a field site, even a childhood penchant for writing in her notebooks from back to front, as is the case with Hebrew texts—and she said, "Now I look back and it seems like the universe was adamant about it, like, 'I will make you become aware of it if it kills you!' It's like there was a gene or something inside me screaming to be expressed."

The turning point came while she was living in Israel. Although she quickly fell in love with the country, initially she did not experience it through the eyes of someone who felt Jewish, nor, for that matter, did she feel any ethnic or religious connection there. Indeed, she recounted going to the Western Wall in Jerusalem early in her stay and feeling absolutely nothing:

> I saw all those people praying, I thought, why are they, [laughs] you know, *davening*[4] in front of a wall? [laughs] It's a wall! It's stone, for God's sake, what are they doing? And I just couldn't feel it. I mean, I knew the explanation for it, but I couldn't feel it.

Several months later she returned to the Wall, but this time everything was different. She had spent the evening at a lively Jerusalem café with two friends her age from the kibbutz, an American woman and a half-Israeli, half-British man, both struggling with the decision whether to remain permanently in Israel. The three talked for hours about identity, politics, and religion in the heady way of young adults with all the time in the world. Suddenly, she told me, something "clicked," and in a flash she understood how it all fit together—her lifelong interest in Jews and Jewish history, her desire to live on the kibbutz, her feeling of being at home in Israel, and, at the root of it all, her aunt's comment that the family had Jewish ancestry. It was simple: *she was a Portuguese Jew.* She was overcome by an urge to go to the Western Wall, "because I knew then *what the Wall was.* Whereas before, it had just been puzzling."

It was late at night, but she convinced her friends to go with her. When they arrived at the Wall she felt inexplicably compelled to stand alongside the scattered Orthodox women, their long skirts swaying as they whispered their prayers to the stones.

> I remember that I—I touched the stone, I touched the Wall, and I—just put my forehead against it. I was there for just a little while, I thought, but my friends told me that I was there for close to an hour. It was amazing because I remember, while I was there, I had my eyes closed and I could hear these women praying in Hebrew beside me. And then I got the whole Wall thing, you know—I mean, you were there as Jews *had* been there for thousands of years, and as, God willing, Jews *will* be there for thousands of years, and it was just—It was being a link in a chain, and I realized that's what being Jewish is, it's being a link in a chain, and *I* was part of that chain. So then I went home and I called my parents, I rang them at 3 A.M. and announced, *"I'm Jewish!"*

Her parents' response to this unexpected declaration was neither to encourage nor to discourage her. Like many urban, educated Portuguese they were wary of any apparent religious fanaticism; when she returned to Lisbon they expressed concern that she might be joining some sort of cult. Once satisfied that nothing of the sort was happening, they left her to her exploration.

When Catarina first told me, shortly after we met, what had happened to her at the Western Wall, I thought it sounded like a conversionary experience. But when I asked if she would describe it as a religious or spiritual awakening, she replied that those terms didn't quite capture the feeling: "No,

I'd call it a *diagnosis*. Because when I realized I was Jewish, it all fit together, it all made sense." Conversion, she said, was absolutely the wrong conceptual framework. Speaking on behalf of herself and the other members of HaShalom, she said, "There would be nothing wrong with calling it that if we didn't already feel Jewish, if we didn't feel like we have *always* been Jewish and it was taken from us. But there's this whole weight of ancestry and of righting five hundred years of wrongs, see? In this situation it's not something you've just found. It's something that you've lost in a dramatic way, and you want it back." Note that here Catarina is referring to the historical loss of Jewish identity and not to the Jewish religion, per se. For her, religious observance was less important than heeding the call of what she half-jokingly called "the Jewish gene," the feeling of a bodily, even "cellular" connection to Jewishness that demanded expression as a social identity in everyday life.

Tiago Mascarenhas, on the other hand, was one of the "self-diagnosed" members of the Marrano associations for whom Judaism, the religion, was paramount. A wiry, energetic man in his late thirties, Tiago had experimented with religion since childhood. Born and raised in northeastern Brazil, he was exposed to far greater religious diversity as a child than other participants in my research, and his encounters with other faiths peppered the life history he recounted to me. Although born into a devoutly Catholic family, he never found Catholicism compelling, and in his early teens a close friend introduced him to evangelical Christianity. The Old Testament in particular intrigued him, with its stories of the ancient Israelites, and he began to feel a powerful attraction to Judaism and to the idea of the Jewish people. A few years later, still in Brazil, he became friendly with a Jehovah's Witness who was studying Hebrew. When his new friend showed him a Hebrew-language newspaper, Tiago found it strangely, hauntingly beautiful:

> I never forgot that newspaper. It was one of those things, one of those little things, that for me were very important. It was like that Hebrew newspaper—it was something I had never seen before, but I thought it was incredibly beautiful.
>
> Oh, man, I don't know how to explain it. You understand? I mean, at that point I didn't—I still had no idea of—of what I wanted, of what I was, of what I knew, of what I aspired to [*do que eu queria, do que eu era, do que eu sabia, do que eu pretendia*], but everything that was related to Judaism, to Jews, to Israel, I immediately sat up and took notice. Without anyone telling me anything. That's what's so strange.

There were no Jews in his hometown. When he was eighteen he left the evangelical church for a liberal Anabaptist community, but he continued to have doubts about Christianity. He confessed to one of the church leaders that he was fascinated with Jews and Judaism and that he sometimes even wished he were Jewish. To his surprise the church leader told him that he suspected his own ancestors were Jews. Far from discouraging Tiago's interest, he talked openly with him about Jews, the Inquisition, and the large Jewish community in São Paulo.

Later that year, Tiago traveled to São Paulo on church business and seized the chance to visit Bom Retiro, the city's Jewish neighborhood. He went in search of a Judaica shop and bought himself a yarmulke, then put it on and walked down the street, feeling what it would be like to be taken for a Jew by passersby. It was a peak moment, for, as he later explained using Catarina's analogy of the transsexual, "I feel that I'm a Jew, but that I didn't have the good fortune to be physically born a Jew." A few years later, in his early twenties, Tiago emigrated to Portugal, the country his father's family had left centuries earlier. His Lisbon apartment was near Shaaré Tikvá and he wanted to attend services, but couldn't muster the courage. It was nearly a decade before he felt ready to identify openly as Jewish. In the interim he read whatever he could find, searching on the internet for information, and participated in an international Jewish chat room where he met others struggling with identity issues of their own. Eventually he found his way to HaShalom.

Over time, Tiago became increasingly convinced that he had Jewish ancestors. It was, he felt, the only rational explanation for why he would have had such a strong interest in Jews and Judaism without ever having any exposure to them:

> I don't see any other explanation. How else would a child who was never exposed to anything—nothing at all, not on television, not by people, not in books—a child who was never exposed to anything related to Judaism, why would that child always want to get involved with it [*se aproximar*]? Look, if you're a kid and you have a friend at school who's Jewish, and he has a bar mitzvah, and invites you—You'd go to the synagogue, it's very nice, and all that. Maybe you'd want to be Jewish. But no. I lived in a city in the Northeast of Brazil, where there were absolutely *no Jews,* there was no synagogue, there was absolutely nothing, nothing, nothing. And I, as a kid and ever since, I wanted to be Jewish. Why?

By the time we met, in 2004, he had amassed a range of other clues, including the timing of his ancestors' departure from Portugal hundreds of years earlier, his family's strict Catholicism (which he interpreted as a long-forgotten technique for hiding Jewish ancestry), ancestral surnames found among Sephardic Jews, and even such physical characteristics as the shape of his nose.

Yet Tiago's greatest source of certainty arose from the longings of his own soul, which he felt had come home, as it were, through his process of "returning" to Judaism. Drawing upon the kabbalistic concept of the *neshamah* (Heb., pl. *neshamot*), the Jewish soul bestowed by God, he told me that he believed that anyone who wishes to become a Jew is *already* Jewish: "It's my opinion that no *goy* (Yid.; non-Jew) ever converts. If a *goy* converts and becomes a Jew, it wasn't a *goy* who converted, for me it was a Jew who returned to Judaism." He continued:

> I think it's the Hasidim who explain it like this. Everyone who converts has a *neshamah,* a Jewish soul. When the Torah was delivered at Sinai, it was delivered, as it is written, for the Jewish people of the present, of the past, and of the future. All those *neshamot* were there, were present, at Sinai. You understand? All those Jews who would come in the future, and all those who would enter Judaism. And for some reason, some of them were physically taken away from Judaism, but their *neshamah* was there. I see it in this mystical way. I'm really mystical, aren't I! [laughs] So it's more or less like that. First there are souls, and then there are people, right? And those people are Jews. They were born Jews, they always were Jews. Take the people in HaShalom. The souls of those people were at Sinai. Those souls already had their destiny. But those people, for whatever reason, they became distanced from Judaism. Whether by the Inquisition, or—whatever. But they had their *neshamah* waiting to return.[5]

Tiago believed that the urban Marranos' souls had always been Jewish; it had simply taken them time to realize it. This interpretation was not posed in contradiction to ancestral claims, but instead offered corroboration on a different plane. For Tiago, as for several other of the more religiously inclined participants at HaShalom and Menorá, to embrace a Jewish identity was to make a *double* return: on behalf of his ancestors and on behalf of his own (Jewish) soul.

ESSENCE AND CHOICE

Each of the foregoing paths to a Jewish identity involves a complex series of connections between ancestry, spirit, body, desire, and the self. In adopting an identity different from the one with which they were raised, the people among whom I conducted my research clearly made a choice about what kind of person they wanted to be in the world. At the same time, they articulated that choice in terms of things that could not, in their eyes, be chosen or changed at all: the soul, the body, the past. Lynn Davidman's work on the conversion narratives of secular American Jewish women who become Orthodox Jews provides an indication of what is at stake here. Davidman (1991: 82–90) identifies two distinct rhetorics through which participants articulated their relationship with their newly adopted identity: a rhetoric of *choice* and a rhetoric of *compulsion*. The rhetoric of choice she found to predominate among women who pursued modern Orthodoxy. In speaking of their spiritual lives, these women presented themselves as rational actors who had weighed their religious options freely. Although none were raised in an Orthodox home, they spoke of Orthodox Judaism as inherently "their own" on the basis of their Jewish birth; and yet, paradoxically, they made it clear that they had adopted that version of Judaism entirely of their own accord. The women who became Lubavitch Hasidic Jews, on the other hand, were much more likely to utilize a rhetoric of compulsion. They described their entry into Orthodoxy as predestined, guided by God, a matter of abruptly realizing their "true path" and having "no option" but to follow it (Davidman 1991: 87).

The presumption of divine intervention is perhaps not surprising in the case of the women who chose Lubavitch Hasidism, an ultra-Orthodox sect. Indeed, the only explanation Davidman offers is that both belief in predestination and the women's narratives conveying it arise as part of the socialization process, in that Lubavitch rabbis emphasize that God controls one's fate and encourage newcomers to internalize that view. It is the modern Orthodox women's emphasis on self-determination, on their freedom to *choose* a fundamentalist approach to Judaism, that she finds worthy of analysis. Drawing on the work of Robert Bellah and his colleagues, Davidman traces the women's attitude to the widespread middle-class American view that "the self is constructed by picking and choosing from available options" and, moreover, that "individuals are free to define their own selves, choose their own values, and thus become their 'own persons'" (1991: 84, citing Bellah et al. 1985: 82). According to this model, neither God nor the social identity of one's forebears determines one's choices, even if one places great value on either or both: beyond potential constraints of race, gender, economic mobility, and the like, the individual stands before a religious and cultural smorgasbord, free to select at will.

Globalization provides unprecedented fuel for the free-flowing type of self-making described by Bellah and colleagues, as Wade Roof (1999) notes in his study of American religiosity at the end of the twentieth century. More and more people are routinely exposed to unfamiliar religious philosophies in the media, bookstores, fitness regimes, self-help courses, and even their neighbors' homes, Roof argues, a change accompanied by heightened attention to the self as the ultimate arbiter of spiritual fulfillment. Increasingly, he suggests, individuals look within themselves, rather than to received doctrine, for answers to religious questions. Thus in the American "spiritual marketplace," individuals readily leave the church of their childhood and evaluate religions on the basis of how personally resonant they are, experimenting with different sects or even entirely different faiths until they find the one that seems best suited. Within certain constraints, ethnic and cultural heritage have become a matter of choice, as well, and not only for the "white" Euro-Americans who have long had freedom to choose from among multiple European "ethnic options" (Waters 1990). Indigenous peoples and other ethnic minorities increasingly *elect* to be "traditional," "not [by] hanging onto a heritage acquired by birth but, like the rest of us, buying it in the heritage hypermarket" (Lowenthal 1998: 224). Similar processes are at work in places around the world. An ever-expanding array of social practices, art forms, musical styles, foodways, beliefs, and images have come unmoored from their original cultural and geographical contexts in a process known as "cultural deterritorialization," providing rich resources for new ways of imagining the self (Appadurai 1996; Mathews 2000).

Indeed, according to sociologist Zygmunt Bauman, the opportunity for and necessity of autonomous self-making is a central characteristic of modern life. He points to a global trend toward "individualization," which he defines as "the emancipation of the individual from his or her ascribed, inherited, and inborn determination of social character: a departure rightly seen as a most conspicuous and seminal feature of [the] modern condition. . . . To put it in a nutshell, 'individualization' consists in transforming human 'identity' from a 'given' into a 'task', and charging the actors with the responsibility for performing that task" (Bauman 2001: 124). Identity has become a "task," according to Bauman's formulation, because our global cultural moment is characterized by the repeated disembedding of individuals from ascribed and even achieved social positions: the roles that earlier generations were born into or struggled to attain are no longer permanent or even stable. One must consequently engage in a continuous project of self-making, for "needing to *become* what one *is* is the feature of modern living.... Modernity replaces the *determination* of social standing with a compulsive and obligatory self-determination" (2001: 124).

While the Portuguese class structure continues to exert powerful influence over social standing, belying Bauman's claim that all is now open to change, his emphasis on the obligatory nature of constructing and performing a *personal* identity is apt. In fact, other than the persistent (though weakening) class hierarchy, over the past forty years Portugal has seen extraordinary upheaval in its systems of social categorization. Progressive loosening of religious and social strictures in the post-Salazar era, rapid modernization following the country's accession to the European Economic Community in 1986 and the European Union in 1993, and a dramatic influx of ethnic and cultural diversity in the form of migrants from the former colonies, Eastern Europe, China, and long-standing Portuguese communities abroad, not to mention a burgeoning tourism industry, have created an environment in which urban young adults are exposed to a far greater variety of social worlds, with an attendant array of possible social identities, than were their parents.

Although Portugal is not yet marked by the prevalent "spiritual quest culture" that Roof (1999) identifies in America, there are indications pointing in that direction. A 2011 study by the Catholic University in Lisbon, for example, found that 10 percent of the Portuguese population had made a major religious change at some point in adulthood and that the fastest-growing religious groups were "believers without a religion" (4.6 percent) and Protestants (2.4 percent). Among the former, the primary reason given for eschewing Portugal's organized religions was personal conviction. These statistical data correspond to qualitative changes I observed during my research. Vastly more information about religious, spiritual, and cultural alternatives could be found in the public sphere as I prepared to leave Portugal in 2006 than when I first visited that country a decade earlier, and discussions of spirituality and personal fulfillment were becoming commonplace. Consider, for example, that as recently as the late 1990s most chain bookstore shelves labeled "Religion" contained only books on Catholicism. By the mid-2000s, many stores had expanded their "Religion" category to include a sizable subsection titled "Esoterism," with introductory texts on world religions like Islam, Buddhism, and Judaism alongside primers on meditation, crystals, numerology, Rosicrucianism, Kabbalah, and Sufism.[6] In major urban areas one can now find Zen centers and ashrams offering meditation classes; alternative healing clinics promoting herbal medicine, Reiki massage, and acupuncture; and community centers providing courses on the practices and underlying philosophies of yoga, qi gong, and tai chi. Hundreds of evangelical Christian congregations have formed in recent years, supported by denominational bookstores and reading rooms for the curious. It may be limited to the largest cities and all but invisible unless one is actively looking, but the "spiritual marketplace" is slowly opening up in Portugal.

How prevalent, then, is a rhetoric of religious or spiritual choice? The vast majority of the Portuguese population is culturally Catholic. While church attendance among self-professed Catholics is low, hovering around 20 percent, Catholicism is still assumed in public discourse, in national holidays, and in cultural traditions.[7] Nonetheless, I often heard Portuguese young adults speak of weighing religious options in language much like the Americans interviewed by Roof and Davidman. Among the circle of college-educated urbanites with whom I regularly socialized, even those not involved in Marrano associations seemed seriously interested in spiritual self-realization. They spoke of attending seminars, reading books, taking classes, learning from friends and coworkers. One of my Porto housemates, a technical writer in her thirties, described in detail why the neopagan Wicca movement resonated spiritually for her. In Lisbon, an art teacher in his late twenties talked for hours about his interest in New Age rituals and his belief in past lives. Even practicing Catholics talked about independent exploration. One friend, a biologist in his early thirties, followed up our frequent discussions about his spiritual journey by offering me the Portuguese translation of *Conversations with God,* a 1995 American best-seller that presents a mystical Christian perspective on the relationship between God and humanity. The book's eclectic combination of insights from Protestantism, Buddhism, and Hinduism had proved helpful in his personal search for meaning as a Catholic. Another longtime friend and his girlfriend spoke to me of their joint spiritual exploration, from religious reading groups to Catholic youth organizations, leading to their decision to volunteer for Catholic charities abroad as a means of deepening their connection with the divine. In each of these cases, highlights and turning points in their stories were linked to independent thought and individual choice.

When we turn to the urban Marranos, the situation looks rather different. Each of the individuals whose story I have recounted thus far was the sole person in his or her family to pursue a Jewish identity in the present, and each arrived at that identity both consciously and autonomously at a particular moment in young adulthood. Yet not one of them felt that he or she had *chosen* to be Jewish, nor did any describe their experience as one of conversion, of becoming something new existentially, religiously, or in any other sense. Although some used a rhetoric of choice when describing their decision to pursue Judaism as a religion, that choice was expressed as arising from the foundation of already being Jewish, in body or spirit or some combination of the two. Like the modern Orthodox women in Davidman's study, they felt that Judaism was "theirs" from birth; becoming religiously observant might be optional, as might be the selection of one branch of Judaism over another, but whether to be Jewish was not. In their stories, highlights and turning points were linked not to independent thought and individual choice, but instead to moments of discovery, revelation, and recognition. Tellingly, the term they used for adopting a Jewish identity was not *escolher,* to choose, or *tornar-se,* to become, but *assumir(-se),* to assume, to take on, to claim, to reveal, to declare—the same verb used for "coming out" as gay or lesbian.

The underlying discursive structure here is what I call a rhetoric of *essence.* Urban Marrano narratives of becoming Jewish are neither of intentional self-transformation nor of divine intervention, but instead of discovering, naming, and giving voice to something preexistent at the core of their being. Even the claim of having a Jewish soul did not seem to suggest involvement of an external entity; in fact, references to God were exceedingly rare. Those who felt compelled to be religiously observant articulated their desire as an incontestable drive coming *from within.* Raquel Gouveia, a thirty-one-year-old teacher in Lisbon, lived in Israel with her labor-migrant parents as a teenager. She put it this way:

> I lived in Israel for many years. I started going to the synagogue there. My family descends from Jews, and I *need* to go to a synagogue, I need it like I need to drink water every day. It's here inside me [pointing repeatedly to her chest], do you understand? It's a need inside me.

Similarly, José Barata, a college student who regularly attended services at the Porto synagogue, said of his initial attraction to Jewishness, "It was more of an internal call, not from my mind. It came from inside me—from the gut. It wasn't intellectual." Catarina, on the other hand, used explicitly biological terms like "genes" and posited that there could be something like "cellular memory" passed down from one generation to the next:

> You know, anyone who feels drawn to Judaism must have had, at some point, some deep cellular connection to it. I think we are driven by body cues and

smells and things that we're not aware of to a really, really great extent. And it doesn't make any sense otherwise, because OK, so you can go the psychological route and say, "These people all had deep yearnings, and they were only able to, I don't know, satisfy them through Judaism." But that's—There's too much of a pattern for that to be so, because it wouldn't have to be Judaism, and everyone is really precise in the way that we say that it's Judaism or nothing. So I think that maybe there *is* a cellular memory that we're not aware of.

Others were still more literal in specifying biogenetic substance as the origin of their Jewishness. Pedro argued that it was no more possible for a non-Jew to choose to be Jewish than a phenotypically white person could choose to be black. "Either you are by blood, by birth, or you're not," he said. "It's corporeal."

Whether cast in the language of internal drives, cellular memory, or concrete corporeal substances like blood and genes, the rhetoric of essence tied the urban Marranos' embodied Jewishness to an ancestral source. However, implicit in their talk was the belief that this ancestry need not be present on all sides of the family, nor must it derive from any particular type or degree of ancestor. Indeed, just one might be enough. This runs counter to the typical Euro-American model of genealogical distance, according to which the number of intervening generations between an individual and his or her ancestor translates to "a measure of the magnitude of the biological component" shared between them, and hence directly affects the strength of connection felt (Schneider 1984: 173). As anthropologist Circe Sturm found in her study of white Americans who embrace an ancestral Cherokee identity in adulthood, these "new" Cherokees—and, I argue, urban Marranos—hold a conception of ancestral substance as "racial homeopathy": the presence of a single ancestor is apparently sufficient to pass the defining essence down through the generations (Sturm 2010: 42). Although superficially similar to the "one-drop" standard of racist social categorization known as hypodescent, according to which individuals with any amount of stigmatized ancestry are automatically assigned to that category, this differs in two significant respects. First, the assumption of ancestral Jewishness—whether articulated as blood, genes, or any other bodily metaphor—is so widespread as to be socially neutral in Portugal (see chapter 1). Second, and more importantly, here, as with Sturm's white-to-Cherokee "race-shifters," the social category in question is entirely self-ascribed.

In grounding their Jewishness in descent and therefore in biology—the "code of the body," "what we now understand as really-real" (Zoloth 2003:

130)—urban Marranos drew upon long-standing Western discourses of bio-logical determinism that granted irrefutability and necessity to their sense of self. David Lowenthal (1998: 196) dubs this mode of identity assertion "the lineage mystique," wherein "we attribute what we are to *being,* which cannot be changed, rather than *doing,* which can." This perspective came up when-ever a visitor inopportunely implied that urban Marranos had a choice in whether or not to be Jewish. One summer evening in 2005, for example, an American visitor had just finished teaching a large group at HaShalom about Jewish dietary laws. Energized by their obvious commitment to Jewish learn-ing, she remarked enthusiastically, "It's wonderful, so moving, to be here with you! It's not a good time to be Jewish in Europe, and yet I hear you saying, sincerely, 'We want to be Jews!'" To her dismay, many were offended. Dulce, Catarina, Pedro, and several others spoke at once, their voices thick with frustration at having to explain themselves yet again: "We don't *want* to be Jewish, we *are* Jewish!" Added Catarina, under her breath, "We want to be *recognized* as Jews. We already are Jewish. What we lack is knowledge."

There is a semi-racialized model of Jewishness at work here, one that clearly diverges from the strictly genealogical way that halakhah ascribes Jewish identity to a Jewish woman's offspring. It more closely resembles the widespread American conception of Jewishness, including among many secular and Reform Jews, as something essential and embodied rather than chosen and intellectual, carried "in the blood" and transmissible by either parent (Glenn 2002); but here, too, there are significant differences. Although urban Marranos articulated their Jewishness as something transmitted through biogenetic substance(s), received from unspecified progenitors, and directly connected to their desire to live a Jewish life, they did not ascribe Jewishness equally to their parents and siblings, who presumably had the same "blood"; nor did they assume that each and every person in Portugal who had a Jewish ancestor was "Jewish" in the same way that they were. Moreover, their life histories clearly indicate that in their own eyes ancestry alone did not make them Jewish. While it provided the ground for their expressions of Jewish identity, equally prominent in their stories were distinc-tive details about their personalities and interests that they considered indica-tive of an essential Jewish self. These included a lifelong interest in Jewish things, ideas, history, and practices, as we saw in the cases of Paula, Dulce, Tiago, and Catarina; unexpected aptitudes or behaviors, such as Pedro's evi-dent knack for Hebrew or Catarina's penchant for writing in her notebooks from back to front; an overwhelming urge to attend a synagogue or a sense of being "at home" among Jews, as Joaquim, Raquel, and António described; and, in all cases, a powerful desire to join the Jewish people and/or the Jewish religion. Thus descent was, from their perspective, necessary but not sufficient to make one "Jewish" on an individual level. It was the combination of ancestry and indicative characteristics that signaled the presence of an innately Jewish self or, to use Tiago's language, a *neshamah,* a Jewish soul.

If not everyone of Jewish descent has a Jewish self, then where does that seemingly innate self come from? Returning to Catarina's rhetoric of "a gene that gets activated," it may be helpful to think in terms of a hereditary but *recessive* genetic condition: in the implicit logic of their stories, the urban Marranos' inherited Jewishness is much like a rare, recessive allele, whose expression from one generation to the next is unpredictable and erratic. It surfaces only in certain offspring, not as a physical condition but instead intellectually, emotionally, and/or spiritually, as a cluster of desires, interests, aptitudes, and longings. António, whose grandmother had been part of Barros Basto's movement in the 1930s, put it this way:

> I wouldn't say I chose it. Sometimes we don't really know why we do things. There must be something guiding us. Because generation after generation, everyone thinks, "Well, it's going to end. There's no more Judaism in Portugal." And generation after generation, there's always *someone* in the family that says, "No. Wait a minute. This calls to me."

Here we see the rhetorical merging of collective ancestry and individual attraction that so often appears in urban Marrano life histories. Recall that some Marranos indicated they knew about their Jewish ancestry from childhood but felt a calling only later, while others seemed always drawn to the subject of Jews and Judaism, only to discover their ancestry in adulthood. Still others, like Tiago, took the calling itself to be a sign of Jewish descent. Regardless of the timing and the degree of certainty in any given case, it is the combination of ancestry and attraction, and the perception that the two are linked, that defines the particular construction of the Jewish self at work here.

A final crucial aspect of the essential Jewish self, as understood by urban Marranos, is that it is not immediately apparent to the person who possesses it, or to anyone else. It is a "true" self, but by definition invisible, hidden even from the conscious self and revealed only in subtle but telltale signs. Though understood to be both innate and hereditary, this true self requires recognition, attention, and cultivation if it is to be fully realized as a personal and social identity. There is always a "coming out" process, first to oneself and then to others. Thus the individuals among whom I conducted my research had to make a conscious effort, to paraphrase Bauman (2001: 124), in order to *become* what they already were. In this sense, in Bauman's terms, the urban Marranos were quintessentially modern subjects.

Therein lies the paradox of the urban Marranos' form of Jewish identity. They articulated their experience of self-fashioning as Jews—in the final analysis, a voluntary, self-ascribed identity—as being utterly outside the realm of choice. And yet the fact that such a self-ascribed identity was conceivable in the first place was due to recent transformations in Portuguese society that have made space for self-identification and spiritual self-determination—space, that is, for choice. As Bauman (2001: 122, 124) suggests, modernity replaces the idea of predestination with that of the "life project": no longer bound by ascribed or inherited determinations of social character, each individual is responsible for deciding who he or she wants to be and then working to become that person. Ironically, in the case of the urban Marranos, the "true self" many identified and hoped to become was based precisely upon the presumption of predestination and essential (inherited) identity. Faced with the obligatory task of self-determination, these modern subjects elected to see themselves as already determined.

HERITABLE IDENTITIES AND THE LOGIC OF GENEALOGICAL CAUSALITY

In seeing themselves as already determined—whether by direct biological ancestry or by diffuse spiritual inheritance—urban Marranos drew upon Portuguese cultural models of the relationship between descent and the self. In this section, I sketch a series of ways that social identities are *heritable* in contemporary Portugal. Some of these identities are primarily a matter of inherited social position, like class, but others are taken to bear a causal relation to who one is as a person, individually, in terms of behavior, character traits, desires, and personal proclivities. Taken together, these heritable identities reflect an underlying model of the self that is always, in one way or another, potentially shaped by past generations. It is this same cultural model that underpins and motivates the claims about the essential Jewish self explored in this chapter. Cultural models, "presupposed, taken-for-granted models of the world that are widely shared (although not necessarily to the exclusion of other, alternative models) by members of a society and that play an enormous role in their understanding of that world and their behavior in it," are resources for sense-making, rather than a structure determining thought (Holland and Quinn 1987: 4). Revealed in talk and reflected in action, they play a crucial, though generally unconscious, role in reasoning on a daily basis. Such models invariably coexist in tension with other models, even when they are blatantly contradictory. Thus modern Portuguese subjects like the Marranos seem to have no difficulty maintaining a view of themselves as free to act at will, to choose their own path, even while understanding themselves to be shaped at a fundamental level by the identity of their ancestors.

One sweltering August afternoon, Catarina and I sat in her sixth-floor Lisbon flat, watching TV and drinking can after ice-cold can of soda. Every hour, a public service announcement warned that the temperature was dangerously high and that the elderly, small children, and people with certain illnesses should not go outside. With or without the warning, I would have found it unthinkable to leave the shade of the apartment; even with the blinds lowered, it was 95°F inside and approaching 110°F on the street in full sun. Lisbon's is a searing, dry heat, and in Catarina's condominium-block neighborhood there were broad expanses of asphalt, with few trees. I was miserable. Catarina, on the other hand, was perfectly content. "It's because I'm from the Alentejo," she said, referring to the country's hottest, driest province. "I love the heat." She stretched out her limbs lazily. I pointed out that she was born in Lisbon and that she'd never said anything about living anywhere else in Portugal. "No, no," she laughed. "My mother's *family* is from the Alentejo." Later in the conversation, she commented that she was always happier in dry, dusty places, again because of her family origins. I found her logic curious, but when I asked other Portuguese friends about it only one thought it odd, and not for the reason I expected. "Catarina's not from the Alentejo," scoffed Manuel Teixeira, a fellow member of HaShalom. "They're so slow there. I worked with a guy from the Alentejo, and he was the slowest, dumbest person I've ever met. Catarina is really quick and high-strung [*nervosa*], like people in the north. Didn't she say her father was from Valença?" Catarina had indeed mentioned that her father's family was from Valença, a town in Portugal's northernmost (and, ironically, wettest and coldest) coastal province, the Minho. "You see?" said Manuel. "That makes a lot more sense. She's a northerner!"

Here we see that where one is "from" is transmitted by genealogical descent, and it carries with it certain expected behavioral and psychological traits.

Whether these traits are thought to be transmitted biologically or culturally was never clear to me, but the fact of their transmission was never in doubt. According to this logic, Lisbon-born Catarina was "a northerner" or "from the Alentejo" not by residence or place of birth but by *descent*, which also accounted for her love of warm weather and high-strung personality. I encountered similar claims throughout my fieldwork. Early on it was a source of much confusion, as members of the Marrano associations would frequently tell me that they were "from" a particular village or region in Trás-os-Montes or Beira Alta, provinces where hidden Jews sought shelter during the Inquisition. Upon further questioning I would learn that it was their grandparents or even great-grandparents who had last lived there; the individuals themselves were invariably born in an urban center or even on a different continent, in one of the former colonies. Few had ever visited the ancestral village. In an extreme, perhaps tongue-in-cheek case, friends even extended an ancestral geographical identity to me: despite my great-grandfather's birth in central Portugal, and although the Portuguese side of my family has lived in Lisbon for more than a century, upon learning that my great-great-grandfather and all known generations preceding him lived in Ovar, a coastal town in the north, I was deemed a northerner (particularly by northerners themselves). A number of them went so far as to explain how they could readily recognize me as a northerner, based on my light skin and summer freckles, my anxious personality, and my tendency to speak very quickly.

Whether intended in jest or not, such comments reflected a deeper, long-standing practice of claiming and attributing geographical ties on the basis of past generations. The commonly heard phrase *a minha terra*—"my land," "my place of origin"—carries with it both a prosaic sense of origin and an ineffable feeling of belonging, nostalgia, and allegiance. Indeed, as Brazilian anthropologist Maria Beatriz Rocha-Trindade (1987) puts it, Portugal is a country of mini-homelands (*micro-pátrias*); local residents and their descendants, even those born in an urban center or abroad, strongly identify with ancestral villages and surrounding regions as "sons" or "daughters" of that land (*filhos da terra*). These local attachments nest within a broader sense of being a northerner or a southerner, a deeply ingrained social distinction that has figured prominently in the Portuguese imaginary for more than two centuries and still surfaces routinely in everyday conversation. There is a lingering undercurrent of "race-thinking" in this distinction. A number of nineteenth-century ethnologists, still widely read, argued that the two regions were racially distinct, settled and seeded by groups they referred to variously as Germanic tribes, Aryans, or Celto-Iberians, in the north, and Mediterraneans or Semites, including Moors, in the south (Bastos 2000; Sobral 2004). The racial characteristics attributed to those founding populations persist in stereotypes about northerners and southerners today, although the two regions' differences are typically expressed in cultural and psychological terms rather than in the determinative idiom of race.[8]

Portugueseness itself has long been understood in "ethnogenealogical" terms. Whether in the writings of nineteenth-century intellectuals or in present-day popular discourse, to be Portuguese is to belong to a "community of descent" whose members share a unique constellation of traits by virtue of their common ancestry (Leal 2000a, 2000b). This widely held model of national identity "locates the source and meaning of cultural differences in the 'bloods' of different human populations" (Williams 1993: 162). Here "blood" serves as a generic symbol for both relatedness and belonging: it is this "blood" that transmits the nation's unique cultural characteristics from one generation to the next. By circular logic, those characteristics, once identified as constituting a primordial folk culture, serve in turn as evidence of the people's shared ancestral origins. Thus, for example, *fado,* the achingly sad musical genre known as Portugal's national song (Gray 2007; Leal 2000b), and *saudade,* an emotion approximating longing or nostalgia that is said to be uniquely Portuguese (Bouquet 1993; Leal 2000a, 2000b), are popularly identified as manifestations of an innate Portuguese fatalism and melancholia. Colloquially, *português de raça,* "thoroughbred Portuguese," refers to a person who perfectly embodies the nation's stereotypical psychological and behavioral qualities.[9] Whether consciously believed or not, the implication here is that pure Portuguese ancestry confers uniquely Portuguese cultural and psychological qualities, and vice versa.

As in other European countries, then, Portuguese national identity finds expression in the deterministic language of primordial populations, descent, and blood. But the ancestral framing of Portuguese regional identity—of ties to the land, to one's *terra*—is subtly different. Here, identification is more potential than essential or absolute: if one's parents or grandparents come from two different regions of the country, for example, one might feel such a strong tie to just one ancestral zone and perhaps see in oneself traits particular to that region, as Catarina suggested of her comfort in extremely hot and dry landscapes. Other offspring may more obviously "belong" to a different ancestral region. The language of *terra* is not that of blood or genes, but of belonging, identification, and "natural" tendencies in one's own character whose cross-generational transmission is assumed but not precisely explained (cf. Pina-Cabral 1997). Both are drawn into what Diane Austin-Broos (1994) calls "a discourse of heritable identity." Writing of Jamaican ethnic and class identities across generations, she identifies two models, biological and environmental, by which social positions and characteristics are inherited. Whereas the biological model takes social standing and certain personal qualities to be fixed, transmitted by descent and so defined at birth, the second looks to the cumulative influence of sociocultural context and individual behavior over generations. But in Portugal, as in Jamaica, the two are not so distinct as they initially seem: "environmental inheritance ... can itself be naturalized through the view that environmental [i.e., sociocultural] effect in fact becomes internalized" and hence passed on to the next generation (Austin-Broos 1994: 230). Thus a Portuguese individual is not only "from" a particular region by virtue of descent, but, as a *filho da terra,* through some mechanism that is neither purely biological nor purely environmental (or cultural), may also bear the qualities of one born and raised there.

Social class, too, is determined by descent in Portugal. The class system is a central aspect of all social interaction, encoded in accent, forms of address, gesture, dress, and consumption patterns, but less readily legible by profession or educational level. There are three distinct social classes: *classe alta* (upper class; also *os ricos,* "the rich," or, idiomatically, *pessoas finas,* "fine folk"); *classe media* (middle class); and *classe baixa* (lower class, "working class" in North American and British terms; also *os pobres,* "the poor"). While it is increasingly possible to move upward within the middle class, primarily via higher education, the boundaries between *os pobres* and the middle class and between the middle class and *os ricos* remain fairly rigid. Throughout my research, I was struck by a pervasive fatalism among my working-class friends, who explained that nothing they did could change the fact of their lower birth (however much they might rail against it), and by a subtle air of entitlement among my friends who were born into the middle and upper classes. Across the spectrum, all appeared to view their inherited position as "just the way it is"—natural, enduring, and constitutive of important aspects of their social persona.

Underlying each of these heritable identities is a basic Portuguese cultural model: the self is constituted by ancestry, not only physically, but socially and behaviorally. Whether the determination of self is absolute (e.g., Portugueseness or, typically, social class) or potential (e.g., geographical identities), something of past generations always carries into the present, in a phenomenon João de Pina-Cabral (1997) calls "continued identities."[10] For a concrete demonstration of this principle we need look no further than Portuguese naming conventions. While a name sets the individual apart as a unique person, it simultaneously encodes familial relationships and inserts the individual into a particular corporate group (Pina-Cabral and Veigas 2007). In Portugal, names are especially socially significant for their crystal-lization of cross-generational ties (Bouquet 1993; Pina-Cabral 1997). Everyone bears at a minimum the mother's father's surname and the father's father's surname. A daughter, Isabel, born to Maria Antunes Cravo and Manuel Trindade Neves, for example, would typically be known as Isabel Cravo Neves. At the parents' discretion, however, a child's legal name could include three or even all four surnames. The Portuguese civil code permits mainte-nance of up to six surnames, but because some prestigious surname pairs are treated as one, a single individual could carry the surnames of as many as twelve ancestors, reaching back four or more generations. Generally, the longer the chain of names, the higher the social standing of the family. Ancestry and even the characteristics it carries are thus fixed and imprinted upon the individual in the most personal and yet public form: the name by which he or she is known.

As heritable identities, both social class and the familial prestige indicated by one's surnames are primarily a matter of social position. Other heritable identities, like geographical belonging, affect not only social positioning but also aspects of one's personality. Catarina believed there was a causal connec-tion between her mother's birth in the Alentejo province and her own love of dry heat and dusty landscapes, whereas her friend Manuel argued that her high-strung personality came from her ancestors in the north. Similarly, other friends told me that their ancestors must have been among the Celts who first settled in the north, because they felt melancholy when they heard bagpipe music; or that they were certain they descended from the Moors, because their families were incredibly tough and hardworking, a stereotype presumably held over from when Portugal's medieval Muslim population was enslaved (Cutileiro 1971: 206–7); or, most commonly of all, that their ancestors must have been Jews, based on a series of indicators like those named in the life histories earlier in this chapter.

There is a fundamental principle at work here, a corollary to the Portuguese cultural model of the self that I call *genealogical causality:* by virtue of descent, the individual shares psychological, emotional, and behavioral characteristics with his or her forebears, and, consequently, one may infer ancestry from such characteristics. This is different from pure biological determinism, because genealogical causality, like heritable identities, does not require a specific, biogenetic mechanism of transmission, nor does either parental line take precedence over the other.[11] Indeed, as I have stressed throughout this chapter, its very ambiguity and unpredictability is an essential part of the model: we need only reflect, once again, on the case of regional identities and attributes.

Cultural models are so powerful in part because they operate at a level below conscious thought. In arguing that a single cultural model underpins Portuguese attributions of inherited geographical identity, nationality, and social class, and that this model also underpins the construction of Jewishness explored in this chapter, I do not mean that urban Marranos intentionally utilized an existing framework to explain their feeling of being Jewish. Rather, I suggest that the underlying model and its logical entailments fundamentally shaped their reasoning about who they were and how they came to be that way. If ancestry can confer a range of social identities, then it stands to reason that having a Jewish ancestor—even just one—would allow one to be Jewish in the present. Similarly, if the identity of one's ancestors is reflected in the self via a recognizable set of desires, interests, preferences, and behaviors, then one could logically infer, as did many of the people whose stories I have told in this chapter, that "lost" or neglected Jewish ancestry was in some way responsible for their fascination with "things Jewish," their unexpected aptitude for learning Hebrew or aesthetic thrill at seeing a Hebrew newspaper, their lifelong distaste for Catholicism, their sense of being at home among Jews, and, above all, their desire to join the Jewish people and/or practice the Jewish religion. This is the logic of genealogical causality at work.

But there is an aspect of their construction of Jewishness that goes well beyond genealogical causality, for some urban Marranos did more than think of themselves as having received traits from past generations: they also hoped to act on their ancestors' behalf, even stand in for them to, as Catarina put it, "right five hundred years of wrongs," referring not to a desire for social recognition or apologies, but to an intimate act of "reclaiming" an identity that was forcibly denied. Often, their language suggested that they felt they carried within them some significant aspect of their ancestors—whether biogenetically or spiritually—that could prompt specific feelings and desires, as in the concept of cellular memory. Recall that in describing their entry into the Jewish community and their adoption of Judaism, they spoke of *returning*. As Joaquim said,

For me, it's a return, because I left [Judaism] but I returned. . . . Well, I didn't leave, but my grandparents did, my great-great-great-great-grandparents did, they were forced to leave, therefore I did.

Or, again, as Catarina put it,

In this situation it's not something you've just found. It's something that you've lost in a dramatic way, and you want it back.

Recall, too, Dulce's answer to the question of how long she had waited for her situation to be resolved: "Five hundred years."

Statements like these suggest a "mutuality of being" across generations similar to that implied by the "kinship 'I,'" a phenomenon first noted among the Maori by anthropologists in the 1950s and since documented on at least three continents (though not yet, to my knowledge, in the Western world). In these cases, individuals use "I," the first-person pronoun—rather than "we" or "they"—in speaking of the actions and experiences of kin, suggesting that things that have befallen one's relatives somehow also transfer to oneself (Sahlins 2013): "I left Judaism but I returned." The implication of such "mystical influence" explains why the "sins of the father descend on the sons, daughters, and other kinsmen, who then must suffer the effects" (Sahlins 2013: 46, 49). Among urban Marranos, however, this kinship "I" appeared only when speaking of presumed direct ancestors, rather than all forebears; more specifically, only those whom they believed to have been Jewish; and more specifically still, only in the context of suffering, loss, survival, and recovery of identity.

While more limited than the kinship "I," then, this usage mirrors its assumption that experience can be shared transpersonally among kin, across generations. Combining the urban Marranos' selective conflation of ancestors and self and the generation-skipping logic of genealogical causality, this is a model quite similar to that held by the Sadah, a descent group that was for centuries the source of leaders of the Yemeni Imamate (vom Bruck 2005). The Sadah trace their origins to the prophet Mohammed, and, as such, they are "privileged vessels of divine and legal knowledge by the very fact of their ancestry" (Bloch 1996: 219). Each holds a special potential for studying the Qur'an, transmitted by descent from the Prophet, though not all will manifest it; mastering Islamic law comes easily, "since it is being implanted in ground which already awaits it" (Bloch 1996: 221). "In such a system," writes Maurice Bloch, "birth transmits essential and immutable qualities and gives

potentialities that, if only given the right environment, will develop of themselves. This implies ... that each individual is a replacement of his forebears
or the vessel in which the eternal element is given a temporary incarnation"
(1996: 224; see also vom Bruck 2005: 102–27). For the Sadah, then, some
ancestrally transmitted traits are potential rather than absolute; like the
urban Marranos' Jewishness, the Prophet's qualities can skip generations and
do not surface in every member of a family, as if caused by a recessive gene.

A similar phenomenon exists among "white" Americans who come to
identify as Cherokee (Sturm 2010). While they are often the only person in
their family to embrace an indigenous identity, they believe that "their
Cherokee ancestors maintain an active presence in their lives" (Sturm 2010:
72). Indeed, "many even insist that their ancestors are literally embodied
within them—as an essential, biogenetic, cultural, and racial substance—
and, if listened to, will guide them toward their true path and identity.....
From the moment of birth, ancestral memories and culture are lurking
beneath the surface of their own consciousness, even though they may not
recognize this until later in life when there is a moment of racial awakening"
(Sturm 2010: 41–42). In all three of these cases, once the inherited potential-
ity is awakened the individual brings that "eternal element"—an ineffable
thread of existential continuity with one's forebears—into the present. It is
this augmented model of genealogical causality that enabled urban Marranos
to speak of *returning*.

TRUTHS IN TENSION

When describing my research to American friends, I was often asked if the
urban Marranos were "really" Jewish. From an anthropological perspective,
I would reply, given that Jewishness is defined differently in different cultural
contexts, there is no single way to answer that question; much more interest-
ing, to my mind, is whether urban Marranos believed that their own stated
criteria proved their Jewishness. I pondered this often during my fieldwork.
While members of the Marrano associations were largely well-educated individuals whose everyday interactions were carried out in a rational mode that
I found entirely intelligible, there was just this one point, their invocation of
emotional or behavioral clues as evidence of Jewish ancestry, that was difficult to square. Did Dulce sincerely *believe* that her childhood rejection of
Catholicism was caused by her then-unknown Jewish ancestry? Could Tiago

have been speaking literally when he told me that having Jewish ancestors—which his parents denied—was a logical explanation for his otherwise sui generis interest in Judaism as a boy? Was Catarina, a graduate student in the life sciences, using terms like "cellular memory" metaphorically, or did she truly believe that biogenetic substance could carry emotions and preferences along with other heritable traits? How much of what I was hearing, I wondered, remained at a discursive level—an extension of the cultural models of heritable identities and genealogical causality, on the basis of which they might unconsciously reason but would not characterize as true if questioned—and how much of it reflected sincerely held belief?

Anthropologists have long struggled with how to handle questions of belief (Carlisle and Simon 2012; Lindquist and Coleman 2008; Mair 2013). Given that beliefs can be documented only indirectly, on the basis of behavior or speech, how are we to know the content of another's mind? Consider, for example, the difficulty of determining whether a statement someone makes *about* their beliefs reflects their beliefs-in-practice, the implicit truths about the world as they experience it that shape their actions in the everyday. Can we assume that people are always able and willing to articulate what they take to be true? What of mutually contradictory beliefs, self-delusion, lying? Nonetheless, the question of whether the urban Marranos believed in the possibility of bio-genetically induced genealogical causality strikes me as worth pursuing, not least because the foreign Jewish visitors who traveled long distances to interact with them seemed to find their statements about ancestry and the self coherent as well. Whether this was due to visitors' estimation of their hosts' sincerity or because those statements resonated with mystical models of Jewishness that they, as Jews, may or may not have "believed" is difficult to know.

These are important questions for understanding the urban Marranos' emergent sense of self and the dynamics of their encounters with visitors, but they cannot be answered in a straightforward yes-or-no manner. This chapter presents my best approximation of the emotions, experiences, and cultural logics that led participants to articulate their sense of self as they did, while recognizing that they, too, were "working through the relationships between self and truth" (Carlisle and Simon 2012: 224). Whatever culturally inflected criteria they used to explain it, their feeling of an essential, embodied Jewishness was a constant and consistent theme. In our discussions, some volunteered that they grappled with what and how to think about that feeling. Several indicated that they held the mystical, ancestral explanation to be "true"—but in a qualified sense. Catarina explained it this way:

It really isn't something you can make sense of rationally. You can't analyze it. I can't seriously consider genetic memory, because, as a scientist, that's crazy. But at the same time it's not just a metaphor, not in the sense that we experience it. That's why it's so uncomfortable.

Tiago, too, stressed that he took a mystical perspective on his belief that he could unknowingly be influenced by forgotten Jewish ancestors.

The only explanation I have is—either I'm crazy, or there has to be a logical explanation. Look, I see things from two angles [*por dois prismas*]. One is a mystical angle, OK? An angle that's based in believing—I'm a bit Hasidic in this, I believe a little bit in reincarnation. I don't believe in spirits, but I believe there's something that connects us, there are lives that are interconnected, there are things that you can't explain that influence your life. I don't know, I can see things from this perspective, and then I can see them from the other side. It's hard to explain [*Não dá para explicar*]. It's unexplainable.

Catarina, Tiago, and others who understood their Jewishness through a similarly mystical lens articulated propositions about the world that seemed mutually contradictory, even to themselves. Their understanding of their inherent Jewishness was based on subjective experience and emotion, directly countering what they considered scientific facts. Yet they seemed able to hold these two distinct registers of "truth" in tension: there was the truth of the everyday, the material world wherein they moved as bounded bodies, weighed concrete evidence, and made decisions based on demonstrable cause and effect, and the truth of the spirit with its own logic, ineffable and unverifiable, where their certainty of their Jewishness lay.

THE SELF WITHIN

In 1997, the *Washington Post* revealed that then–Secretary of State Madeleine Albright's family was secretly Jewish, prompting an emotional debate over whether she should embrace that identity publicly. Her parents, Czech wartime refugees whose own parents had died in concentration camps, chose after escaping to become Catholic and raised Albright with no knowledge of her Jewish background. At issue in the ensuing controversy were, as historian Susan Glenn (2002) puts it, questions of "descent and consent, blood and belief"—or, in the terms used in this book, of *essence* and *choice*. While many pundits suggested that in this age of ethnic options Albright should be allowed the latitude to define herself as she saw fit, Glenn offers a bald assessment that rings true in the American context: "only if we ignore the centrality of blood logic to modern Jewish identity narratives" (2002: 139). Describing a long-standing practice among secular American Jews of proudly "naming and claiming" others as Jewish solely on the basis of ancestry—including "Who's Who"–type encyclopedic volumes (and now websites) listing public figures of known or surmised Jewish parentage—Glenn argues that it is clearly not Orthodoxy that has kept "blood logic" alive in the Jewish world. "It is one of the ironies of modern Jewish history," she writes, "that concepts of tribalism based on blood and race have persisted not only in spite of but also because of the experience of assimilation" (2002: 140).

This American "blood logic" is a racial conception of Jewishness, not genealogical causality, and we must be careful to distinguish the two. While the urban Marranos felt that their Jewishness was fixed, essential, and ancestrally transmitted, they did not see it as racially determined in the manner Glenn describes. Theirs was not a tribal, population-based sense of belonging—*We who share this ancestry (or blood, or DNA) are Jews*—at all, but a hybrid of mysticism and embodiment—*We who are Jews have received our Jewishness from the past and carry it in our bodies and our souls.* Far from automatic and rarely ascribed to them by others, Jewishness was a core but hitherto unknown aspect of their being, something they had to discover before they could live it in practice. Already present within, the Jewish self was not a matter of choice; and yet to identify it and identify with it was, returning to Glenn's terms, to *consent* to the immutability of *descent*—of a mystical, generation-skipping, "recessive" kind.

The intertwining of body and spirit, genealogical descent and mystical inheritance, was a common thread in my conversations with members of Menorá and HaShalom. Initially, as they moved along their solitary paths toward "rejoining" the Jewish world, they encountered little that shook their faith in their essential Jewishness. On the contrary, their sense of self was largely coherent with Portuguese cultural models of how the individual is shaped by descent. In chapter 1, I discussed the frequency with which one hears Portuguese from many walks of life say that they "might be Jewish," meaning that they could have Jewish ancestry; as such, Jewishness would seem to be just one more heritable identity of the potential rather than determinative kind, as available for self-attribution as being "from the Alentejo." It was only upon attempting to enter Portugal's normative Jewish community, in most cases by entering a synagogue in Lisbon or Porto, that the people I call urban Marranos discovered that their conception of essential Jewishness would not necessarily be accepted by everyone, and indeed that the local Jewish community had no category for "returning" ancestral Jews. Their encounters with Jewish community representatives, their discovery of one another, and the profound transformations to their individual and collective identities that followed—through which they became "Marranos"—is the subject of the next chapter.

THREE

Outsider, In-Between

BECOMING MARRANOS

> People tell others who they are, but even more important, they
> tell themselves and then try to act as though they are who they
> say they are. . . . Identities are lived in and through activity and so
> must be conceptualized as they develop in social practice.
>
> DOROTHY HOLLAND ET AL.
> *Identity and Agency in Cultural Worlds*

MENORÁ MADE ITS HEADQUARTERS in a fifteen- by twenty-foot rented room in a century-old office building in the heart of the Porto's historic center. A small sign by the office door read, *Menorá: Associação de Cultura Hebraica do Porto* (Menorah: Jewish Cultural Association of Porto). Inside, the room was spare. Though its parquet floors and freshly painted walls gleamed and its wood-framed windows looked down onto a tidy back garden, what little furniture there was had been gathered at random, secondhand. Along the north wall was a pair of mismatched tables, end to end, with folding chairs and space for eight to sit boardroom-style; across the room was a sitting nook, with two worn, mismatched couches, a rug, and a wicker shelving unit containing bottles of wine—some kosher, some not—and books in several languages. Near the back windows stood a desk piled high with books and papers, a twelve-inch menorah precariously perched on one corner. Posters of Israeli monuments and landscapes adorned the walls, alongside others announcing university lectures and museum exhibitions on Jewish topics.

According to its by-laws, Menorá was founded in 2002 to promote and preserve Jewish culture and heritage in Portugal. Its leadership and founding members were drawn from two venues: several met in a Jewish studies class taught at a local adult school by Ricardo Carvalho, the shipping clerk and autodidact who became the association's first president; others met at Porto's synagogue. Initially, the association's membership was diverse: among its founders were a member of Porto's normative Jewish community of mixed Ashkenazi Jewish and Portuguese Catholic ancestry; a handful of Portuguese of no known Jewish origin, pursuing Jewish studies out of intellectual interest; and a larger number of individuals who identified as ancestrally Jewish and wanted to develop a connection with the Jewish world at large. Early on, the group's leaders contacted the Israeli embassy in Lisbon to volunteer their help in bringing embassy-sponsored cultural events to Porto, two hundred miles to the north, and requested support from the cultural attaché for their activities. Over the next two years they collaborated with embassy staff on several public events, including an art exhibition, a concert of classical music, and a Jewish holiday dinner, open to the public, catered by a Yemeni Israeli chef. They also met to discuss Jewish topics, studied Jewish history and theology together, delved into the saga of Portuguese Jews and crypto-Judaism, and occasionally celebrated Jewish holidays in their office. Those who had been studying for several years taught those with little knowledge, though none was by any means expert.

In July 2004, when I began research in Porto, the forty-member association had been in operation for more than two years and its core participants had become close friends. Each Saturday afternoon they gathered at a café near the office, had an espresso, and caught one another up on gossip about the organized Jewish community. Often there would be news from Menorá's sister association in Lisbon, HaShalom; the two had been "twinned" for more than a year, and their leaders were in regular contact. By four o'clock, when a half dozen or so people had arrived, they would walk together to the office building, nod to the doorman, climb the worn granite stairs to the second floor, and officially begin the meeting. Seated around the makeshift conference table, they typically started with current business, ranging from coproducing a special issue of a local historical journal on Portuguese Jews and Marranos to planning the Porto run of an international Jewish film series.

Inevitably, however, the meetings veered off course, into heated debate over the pressing issues many members faced: how to become integrated into Porto's Jewish community, how to join the broader Jewish world, whether conversion should be necessary for their acceptance as Jews, and which branch of Judaism—Orthodox, Conservative/Masorti, Reform, Renewal—would be most willing and appropriate to assist them. For although the association began primarily as a cultural one, as more and more people joined in search of a place of Jewish belonging, those who had come purely out of intellectual interest dropped away. The remaining members became increasingly focused on the history of Jews in Porto, particularly Barros Basto's failed early twentieth-century Marrano revival—for which the city's grand synagogue had been built—and they began to view themselves as heirs to his work. By the early months of 2004, Menorá had become entirely and explicitly an association of *Marranos*.

In order to understand the confluence of factors that led to that point, we need first to venture out of Menorá's humble office and attend Friday evening services at Barros Basto's great synagogue, as I did many times during my fieldwork. The following excerpt from my fieldnotes, written two weeks after I arrived, captures the atmosphere at that time. This particular evening was my first service at the synagogue, though I had visited it several times while participating in package Jewish heritage/outreach tours. On this occasion I went at the invitation of Antonieta Pereira, whom I had met at a Menorá meeting the previous Saturday.

July 16: At around eleven this morning, Antonieta called to invite me to services at the synagogue. She said she was bringing her sons and that several others from Menorá were going. We agreed to meet at the café near the office at 7:00 P.M. and take a cab. When I arrived, though, she suggested we sit and have an espresso. I wasn't sure how long we'd be there or even when services started, but she didn't seem to be in any hurry. Her sons—aged 10 and 14— sat patiently while we talked. . . . I told her I wouldn't necessarily have any idea what was happening at the synagogue, since I've only been a few times in my life, and I'd need her help. "That's OK," she said, "I've been going for eight years." Eight years! And she still feels like an outsider.

Eventually it was time to go. . . . As we were pulling up in front of the synagogue she said she didn't know whether the outer gates would be open or if we'd be able to go in at all. She was surprised to see them propped wide open. The caretaker (who I later learned lives in the building and isn't Jewish) and a portly older man I didn't recognize were standing on the steps. There didn't seem to be anyone else around, even though she said we were right on time.

Once we were inside Antonieta walked a bit hesitantly through the foyer and peered into the enormous sanctuary. There was no one there. She sighed and said there might not be services tonight. We'd have to wait and see. She gestured for me to follow her to the right, into a little side room. *"Outra vez, o salão da tristeza"* [again, the hall of sorrow], she muttered under her breath. Inside there were framed portraits of serious-faced men on the walls, heavy drapes, and a long, dark, wooden table. The lights were on, but it seemed dimly lit.

At the table's head sat Ori Safer [community president, a Moroccan Israeli expatriate], looking very much at home. On his right was a sinister-looking middle-aged man with a dour expression. There was no one else there. After an awkward pause in the doorway, we went in and sat at the table with them. Ori smiled at me and nodded impassively to Antonieta. I sat to the right of the sinister man, who Antonieta later explained is Ori's bodyguard, plus the security guard when the synagogue is open. Antonieta sat at the foot of the table, seemingly as far from Ori as she could get. Her sons sat to her right, across the table from me. They were absolutely silent. So was the sinister man.

As soon as I sat down, Antonieta introduced me to Ori: "You've already met, yes?" "Ah, yes," he said, looking at me, "When you were here with the tour group earlier this year, we talked outside." He turned to Antonieta and started questioning her about the rabbi Shavei Israel sent to Belmonte last year. He was strangely aggressive. Did she know that the Belmonte community had not renewed the rabbi's contract? She did, because the rabbi has been coming on Sundays to teach her and the others Hebrew and basic Judaism and they know he's hoping to move to the Porto synagogue, but she acted as if she knew nothing. I stayed quiet. The atmosphere was oddly combative. Ori abruptly turned to me and asked what I thought about the candidates for the upcoming U.S. presidential election. I gave my honest opinion. He just nodded.

Then the awkward silence began. It dragged on, and on, and on. No one said anything. The tension was painfully thick. Antonieta whispered that we were waiting to see whether enough people would come to hold services. I asked audibly, to the table at large, how long they usually wait. A few minutes more, said Ori. We waited about half an hour.

Suddenly two tourists came in, escorted by the portly man from the front steps. Ori jumped up and greeted them warmly, introducing himself as community president. They were a Spanish couple, both Jewish, and since Ori speaks Spanish he affably offered to give them a tour of the building. I wanted to see how he'd interact with tourists and asked if I could go along. He said it was fine, so I went, leaving Antonieta and her sons alone at the long table with the silent security guard, waiting. . . .

When we came back from our tour more people had straggled in. Manuel, António, and Octávio from Menorá were in the foyer, talking quietly, waiting. After about an hour there were maybe twelve people there, but apparently Ori and the Spanish tourist were the only male Jews according to halakhah. Since Ori is Orthodox, that was that. The others didn't count. No services tonight. . . .

When Antonieta and I left, it was 9:30 and Ori was still talking animatedly with the tourists. They were exchanging business cards, chatting about people they knew in common. In the cab on the way to dinner, Antonieta said everything went the way it usually does.

Everything went the way it usually did: sometimes there was a *minyan* (Heb.; quorum) and the full evening service could be held, but more often than not there wasn't. When there wasn't, according to his mood the president might decide to lead those portions of the prayer service that can be performed without a *minyan;* at other times he would not, closing the synagogue without explanation.[1] Sometimes Menorá's members were ignored, watching quietly as Jewish tourists were warmly welcomed; at other times they sat in the "hall of sorrow," drawn into stilted conversation while waiting for "real" Jews to arrive. Sometimes the security guard would refuse to let them through the gates, for no apparent reason; at other times the gates were locked and no effort spent ringing the buzzer would bring someone to open them. Without a rabbi and with just a handful of individuals carrying the key—chief among them Ori and his brother, titular heads of the congregation—there was no guarantee from week to week that the doors would be open, especially during the summer months. Typically there were many more "non-Jews" than Jews present for Shabbat services. Indeed, even counting the Jewish tourists who appeared nearly every week, only rarely did the fifteen to twenty people in attendance meet the requirements for a *minyan.*

Under these circumstances, newcomers understandably felt frustrated, singled out, or rejected, particularly those entirely new to Judaism. Even Antonieta, who had been attending for eight years, felt she was an outsider. The feeling did not lessen on those occasions when services were held. Whether by accident or by design, once inside the synagogue's richly decorated sanctuary the people I soon learned to think of as *dos nossos* (Pt.; literally, "of ours," meaning "one of us") remained clustered together, spatially and socially segregated from the Jewish community's leaders and those few local Jews who attended. During services, from my perch in the women's gallery alongside Antonieta and two or three others from Menorá I could easily see distinct seating areas on the main floor below. Gathered in one corner were the ten or so men *dos nossos,* recognizable by their hesitation about when to sit or stand during the services, then a gap of several rows, and then a smaller cluster of community members, who rarely interacted with them. We in the upper gallery, too, seemed to be invisible to the few women from the community who came now and then. They sat in a different section and appeared to notice our presence only when one of us made some sort of gaffe, usually from lack of familiarity with the service, which invariably prompted a disapproving look.

Despite the clear spatial segregation, it is noteworthy that two Portuguese men who identified as ancestrally Jewish were on the synagogue board, and both sat with the community leaders during services. In addition, one member of Menorá had been a dues-paying synagogue member for nearly a decade and was on friendly terms with both Ori and his brother. Nevertheless, he sat apart, alongside those who felt like outsiders. Thus the spatial mapping of inclusion and exclusion, whether perceived or actual, was not a simple case of prejudice against those who were not Jews according to halakhah. Certainly the Jewish community members did not go out of their way to welcome ethnic Portuguese newcomers, whom they assumed were non-Jews, and typically barely acknowledged their presence; but the newcomers' shyness and reluctance to explain themselves may have been equally at cause. Both parties saw the lack of communication as an affront.

Of greater concern than the matter of spatial separation, though, was that of the *minyan*. From the perspective of those who felt they were Jewish-in-essence, in a way that could be neither chosen nor changed, the fact that they could not be counted stood in direct contradiction to their sense of self. For the men, it was an explicit denial of their identity; in this Orthodox setting, the women experienced it vicariously but no less powerfully. In Lisbon, too, the congregation rarely mustered a *minyan* without the presence of tourists, despite the regular attendance of two or three members of HaShalom. In both synagogues, they were continuously reminded that they were, in the words of HaShalom leader Dulce Oliveira, *os não-contáveis*—those who cannot be counted. They were non-Jews.

In the previous chapter, we saw three primary paths by which participants came to think of themselves as essentially Jewish. There, the informing social contexts were the family of origin and the nation; their self-understanding was shaped primarily by family stories, personal inclinations, and Portuguese cultural models of the relationship between ancestry and the self. For the most part, their journeys were solitary. Although childhood and young adult friendships with "mainstream" Jews figure significantly in many of their life histories, only two or three had any idea that there were other (possible) descendants of Portuguese Jews who felt as they did. Prior to the widespread media coverage of the Belmonte community in the 1980s, they were also largely unaware of Portuguese crypto-Judaism. Most, however, had a cursory understanding of the Inquisition and forced conversions, and all were aware from childhood that it was possible for Portuguese people to have Jewish ancestry. Thus until they made contact with the organized Jewish community their sense of having a Jewish self was formed primarily through introspection and emotion, rather than social interaction. To think of oneself in isolation as Jewish on the basis of ancestry and personal proclivities is one thing; to attempt to proclaim and enact—to *be*—that self among others who identify as Jews but on an entirely different basis is quite another.

Social identities do not develop in a vacuum, nor are they static. Whether in internal dialogue or direct encounters, urban Marranos—like all humans, everywhere—expressed, reflected upon, and refined their sense of self in continuous interaction with others. Having come to understand themselves as intrinsically Jewish, they sought ways of externalizing and experiencing that Jewishness in their everyday lives and, most importantly, of finding a community in which to do so. As I noted in the previous chapter, most were alone among their parents and siblings in self-identifying as Jews, and their families demonstrated little interest in the matter beyond the occasional comment about having Jewish ancestry. Consequently, the desire to find a space of Jewish belonging was a driving factor in their attempts to enter Portugal's Jewish communities, alongside their need to learn from others what being Jewish entailed. As individuals embracing a new identity, they were concerned with behaving in a manner consistent with who they felt they were and increasingly professed to be, and they were sensitive to how others judged their efforts.

This chapter explores the transformations that occurred once they attempted to enter the world of Portugal's organized Jewish communities, which rejected them as non-Jews, and when they subsequently discovered other "outsiders" like themselves. It provides an ethnographic portrait of the processes through which they *became* Marranos, the existing social category that seemed closest to who they felt they were, and of the distinctive practices and dispositions through which that new facet of the self was constituted and expressed. I give particular attention to how they learned to recognize and narrate the ways in which they were ancestrally or otherwise essentially Jewish, in dialogue with foreign visitors. For as we will see, interacting with Jewish tourists, volunteer educators, and outreach workers played an extraordinarily important role in shaping urban Marranos' sense of self, both in relation to their presumed ancestral Jewish past and in relation to the Jewish people of the present.

THE FIGURED WORLD OF PORTUGUESE JEWS

When urban Marranos ventured into the orbit of the organized Jewish communities, they encountered a new cultural world, one with its own assumptions, implicit rules, and social categories. Dorothy Holland and colleagues (1998) coined the term *figured worlds* to denote the multiple coherent social formations through which we move on a daily basis and, in some cases, to which we consider ourselves to "belong." These worlds—constellations of roles, actors, activities, attitudes, meanings, and norms, aspects of which have been studied variously as "subcultures," "fields" (Bourdieu 1993), and "communities of practice" (Lave and Wenger 1991)—are porous and open-ended, but behaviorally demarcated. That is, one moves in and out of them, adjusting consciously or unconsciously to the norms and assumptions involved, just as one learns the rules of a game and, while within the frame of the game, attributes appropriate meaning to objects and actions inherent to it. Examples include the workplace, criminal networks, the art world, the Boy Scouts, Alcoholics Anonymous, medicine, academia—any social formation, consciously apprehended or not, in which we participate, whose norms we learn, and through which we interact with diverse actors.

The idea of figured worlds is a powerful one for understanding how people come to understand themselves and their relationships to others in culturally patterned ways. Figured worlds are conceptual structures, frameworks through which we recognize the roles of others, interpret actions, and make decisions. As Holland and colleagues (1998: 60) explain, a figured world is "a landscape of objectified . . . meanings, joint activities, and structures of privilege and influence—all partly contingent upon and partly independent of other figured worlds, the interconnections among figured worlds, and larger societal and trans-societal forces. Figured worlds . . . supply the contexts for meaning for actions, cultural productions, performances, disputes, for the understandings that people come to make of themselves, and for the capabilities that people develop to direct their own behavior in these worlds."

Most importantly for our purposes, figured worlds "provide the contexts of meaning and action in which social positions and social relationships are named and conducted. They also provide the loci in which people fashion senses of self—that is, develop identities" (Holland et al. 1998: 60). To enter a new figured world is to learn a new set of rules of behavior and vocabulary; to discover implicit structures of power and prestige, as well as explicit hierarchies; to become familiar with the array of activities proper to the figured world; to engage in practices that both inculcate and reinforce particular orientations and dispositions; and to position oneself and be positioned according to that world's available categories and relationships. The more emotional engagement one feels with a figured world, the more fully that positioning will be adopted and lived as a coherent, pervasive identity.

To depict the figured world of Portuguese Jews, then, is to identify the constellation of activities, roles, assumptions, and norms encountered, held, challenged, and embraced by those who interact within the social field constituted by Portugal's several Jewish communities, their institutions, their members, and their boundaries. During my fieldwork, for example, within this figured world it was general knowledge that each of the formally constituted Jewish communities—in Lisbon, Porto, Belmonte, and Faro[2]—had recognized leaders and, in some cases, a paid administrator; a synagogue or other space for prayer and holiday observance, with its own implicit and explicit hierarchies; community activities such as holiday celebrations and cultural events, which might or might not be held at the synagogue; a category of associates, or *members,* who were also called *Jews;* and a category of select *non-members,* associates who participated in community activities but were not called *Jews.* In addition, it was assumed that there could be people called *Jews* who never attended activities and were not affiliated with any Jewish community. Leaders of the local Jewish communities were expected to be in contact with each other and invite one another to major events, reflecting a sense of interconnection nationwide, and on the national and international stage all were represented collectively by the Comunidade Israelita de Lisboa (CIL). Also part of this figured world were several ancillary institutions, such as the Portugal-Israel Friendship Association and the Portuguese Association for Jewish Studies, whose membership could overlap with that of the Jewish communities but might also include people who were neither called nor self-identified as *Jews.*

The distinction between *Jews* and *non-Jews* was highly socially significant to actors within this figured world, as was the distinction between those who were religiously observant and those who were not.[3] These are two different distinctions. One could be quite Jewish without being religiously observant; one could also be quite religiously observant without being Jewish. Whether religiously observant or not, within this world "Jews" were assumed to be of a certain financial and educational level, typically upper or upper-middle class and university educated. In addition to Jews and non-Jews, there were two other recognized categories of actors: *potential converts* and *Marranos,* like those in Belmonte, who maintained a communal identity as Jews over centuries. I will have more to say about these categories below.

Among the named roles in this figured world were community president, vice president, treasurer, and so forth; board member; *rabi* (Pt.; rabbi), a scholar and teacher of Jewish law; and *hazzan* (Heb.; cantor), the person who leads a synagogue service. While a *hazzan* is necessary for communal prayer services, a rabbi is not. In fact, until Shavei Israel sent a full-time rabbi in 2004, Porto had not had one since the Inquisition, and Lisbon's Shaaré Tikvá synagogue often went extended periods without hiring one. In both synagogues a community member typically served as *hazzan*. Even if sent by an external agency, a rabbi was understood to be employed by his congregation, who could choose to retain or dismiss him, and he had very little power, explicit or implicit, to set policy or determine the religious or social character of the community. That role was reserved for community leaders. The Israeli ambassador and embassy staff also intersected with this world through their support of cultural events and their appearance at major community functions. They did not, however, participate in the religious life of any of the formally constituted Jewish communities.

Most of the people who ultimately joined an urban Marrano association discovered the assumptions and norms of this new cultural world by coming into direct conceptual conflict with them. Let us take the fundamental question of who is or is not a Jew. We have seen that these individuals felt they were Jewish on the basis of deep attraction, emotional resonance, and presumed descent. But they quickly learned that they would not be recognized as Jews on that basis at the synagogues: not only would they not be counted for the *minyan,* but in Lisbon a community leader explicitly forbade them from donning a prayer shawl during services—a practice that was, he told them, reserved for "Jews." Nor would they be invited to read aloud from the Torah during a service, an honor routinely granted to tourists, whose Jewish credentials were never checked.

I found this obvious disparity perplexing. Why were the urban Marranos immediately designated non-Jews, seemingly on sight, while foreign visitors—especially tourists—were readily accepted? When I posed the question at a Menorá meeting early in my research, everyone looked at me incredulously. How could I not understand? It all went back to the forced conversions and the Inquisition, which wiped out any likelihood of unbroken maternal Jewish descent. Even if a group of hidden Jews had managed to remain endogamous—marrying only among themselves—all those centuries, they told me, there would be no way to document it. Thus, they had learned, it was impossible for someone who was 100 percent Portuguese to be Jewish, at least if one followed the logic of halakhah—as did the leaders of Portugal's normative Jewish communities. Being able to read from the Torah, having substantial religious knowledge, or feeling Jewish-in-essence were irrelevant. "Look," exclaimed Ricardo, Menorá's president, "in Portugal, to be recognized as a Jew, you have to have a foreign-sounding last name. It can be an Arab name, even a Muslim name. A person who has an Arab name, or a Polish or German name, is automatically assumed to be a Jew, but I can't be Jewish because my last name is Portuguese." He continued:

> We're all from the provinces, from villages that are no different from any other Portuguese provinces or villages. We come from those old stone houses, village houses that are no different from any other houses. We speak the same Portuguese, say the same village sayings that village people say. We all have Portuguese surnames. And we want all that to be absolutely different! This is our dilemma: we are sure we are different [i.e., Jewish], we want to show proof that we are different, and the only thing we can show is that we are 100 percent Portuguese.

In a country where surnames carry great social significance (Bouquet 1993; Pina-Cabral 1986), Ricardo's observations had the ring of truth. Looking at member rolls of the organized Jewish communities, I was struck by the relative rarity of Portuguese family names. Virtually everyone bore at least one obviously foreign surname, either North African (Sephardic) or German (Ashkenazi), such as Assayag, Abecassis, Assor, Bensaúde, Goldschmidt, Grossman, or Weinberg. Because Portuguese naming practices preserve both maternal and paternal surnames, and even the grandparents' if desired, these identifiably Jewish names were retained even in cases of intermarriage. Thus the absence of such a name was as socially significant as its presence: bearing only Portuguese surnames, presumably indicating unbroken Portuguese ancestry, a person would be unlikely indeed to be recognized as a Jew.

The newcomers also quickly realized that most Jews in Lisbon and Porto did not attend services at the synagogues. The primary locus of Jewish activity, they concluded, must be elsewhere, perhaps in CIL's lavish Jewish community center, the Maccabi Country Club, whose activities and events were regularly documented on the CIL website. Located in a wealthy suburb— and boasting an opulent clubhouse, tennis courts, a vast garden with lagoons, a swimming pool, and a soccer field—its well-attended Jewish holidays, lectures, classes, choral groups, summer camps, and young adult events were utterly inaccessible to anyone not associated with the community. Similarly, the far smaller Porto community held invitation-only events in hotels or rented halls. Ironically, then, while the synagogues seemed the obvious point of entry for self-ascribed ancestral Jews, those buildings were all but empty. Orthodox religious practice was tangential to everyday life for most members of the normative Jewish community, who were evidently more engaged with social and cultural aspects of being Jews.

This last point was among the most frustrating for the newcomers. They adopted the shorthand *judeus de carteirinha*—"card-carrying Jews" or "Jews with a (membership) card"—for those who were accepted as Jews by the normative community, whether by maternal descent or Orthodox conversion. The primary right that came with the *carteirinha,* from their point of view, was freedom from practicing Judaism. Of CIL's two hundred member families, fewer than ten or fifteen people came regularly to the synagogue. Among those, none were the people whose faces appeared in the media as community representatives. Both the rabbis and the urban Marranos complained about the low level of observance, whether in Lisbon or in Porto: community members drove on the Sabbath, ate shellfish and pork, intermarried with Portuguese Catholics. But those "non-Jews" who wished to be recognized by the community, whether Marranos or would-be converts, had to demonstrate familiarity with and adherence to the very religion that Portugal's "real" Jews seemed to have little time for.[4] Initially unaware of the many ways Jews observe Judaism in the home—whether weekly Shabbat dinners or holidays like Hanukkah or Sukkot, typically celebrated with family and friends—the newcomers saw only hypocrisy. They, the ones who were willing to do whatever it took to *be* who they felt they were inside, were designated "non-Jews," while the ones with a *carteirinha* could break the rules and continue being "Jews" with impunity.

They noticed, too, that in the world they were entering it was widely assumed that Jews would be of a higher social class and educational level and would have national and international ties with other Jews, whether familial, social, or professional.[5] Observing the treatment of tourists, they noted that community members routinely engaged visitors in conversation, with both parties attempting to find other Jews they knew in common. There seemed to be an entire interconnected world, reaching far beyond the local community, to which the Portuguese Jews belonged and assumed other Jews belonged, and to which urban Marranos by definition had no access. The latter all came from working- or middle-class backgrounds, and in Portugal's profoundly class-conscious society they were sharply aware of social distinctions between the community's most visible members, who were relatively wealthy, and themselves. Meetings of the Marrano associations were peppered with comments about how they would never be high-class enough to be accepted. After a HaShalom meeting one night, Nuno Sanches and his wife, Luisa, offered to give several of us a ride home. We had just gone to dinner together and everyone was in a jovial mood, cracking jokes and playfully poking fun at each other. As we approached the car, everyone was surprised to see a BMW rather than Nuno's Hyundai. It was his boss's car, he explained; he had borrowed it for a business trip. "Just imagine if I drove up to Shaaré Tikvá in this," he said wryly, to the knowing laughter of his passengers. "*Olha, melhor parecê-lo que sê-lo!* [Hey, better to seem it than to be it!]" By reversing the terms of the familiar proverb *mais vale sê-lo que parecê-lo,* "better to be it than to seem it," Nuno implied that the appearance of wealth would go further in opening the community's doors than any deep commitment to Judaism.

Nuno's comment may have been motivated by the case of two young men active at CIL, Carlos Bensaúde and Jaime Saruya Reis, who were often invoked as an example of the kind of people welcomed into the Lisbon community despite being non-Jews according to halakhah. Both were regular participants in activities at the Maccabi Country Club and, although still studying for conversion, were leaders in CIL's young-adult group. Like the urban Marranos, they were making a "return" on the basis of Jewish ancestry. But their Jewish antecedents were much more recent: each carried a surname that community members readily recognized as indicating immigrant Jewish descent. In addition, they came from quite wealthy backgrounds and had preexisting social and familial ties to leading members of CIL. Whether because of their ancestral connection to nineteenth-century Portuguese Jewish families or their social standing vis-à-vis the normative community, or both, the two were treated very differently from the individuals with whom I spent my time. "It's a closed club everywhere," sighed Ricardo, explaining the reasons members of the Marrano associations would never be accepted. Speaking to a tour group, he ticked them off one by one: they were far from upper class, they did not have foreign names, they were not raised in a Jewish context, and they had no social or professional ties to that world. As such, Ricardo saw no way that they would ever be considered "real" Jews in Portugal.

Why did they care so much? the less tactful tourists asked. Why did they want acceptance from the normative community? Did they think it would give them higher social status? They took offense at that, protesting that they wanted to be accepted only to have a context in which to *learn.* They were, as one put it, "Christians without faith, Jews without knowledge," trapped in a no-man's land, *a terra de ninguém,* between their culturally Catholic upbringing and the Jewish identity they wanted to live out in daily life. If the community's doors were closed to them, where could they go to gain the necessary religious and cultural knowledge? Beginning in 2004, Orthodox rabbis placed in Lisbon and Porto by Shavei Israel offered classes on Judaism, covering Hebrew, the Jewish calendar, basic prayers, and so forth. But while sympathetic, the rabbis were unable to offer a concrete program of "return" or conversion because that would require a rabbinic court (Heb., *beit din*) of three—a major obstacle in a country with just two rabbis, neither of whom had his congregation's support for such activity. In the past, rabbis had come from France to convene a *beit din* for community members' spouses and other relatives, but that was at the behest of synagogue leadership and at great expense. Lacking the financial means to fly to Israel or New York for weeks or even months of study on-site, as some did, in preparation for a *beit din* acceptable to Portugal's nominally Orthodox congregations, and without a community that would accept them and convey the practical knowledge they sought, all their study remained theoretical.

They also cared because they were deeply humiliated by their continual exclusion. Not being counted for a *minyan* was only one of the ways this occurred. There were the thousand tiny cuts of exclusionary gestures—a hand extended for a handshake, ignored; a sidelong glance of disapproval when they stood or sat at the wrong time during services; the customary after-service greetings to others, but not to them; spatial segregation in the synagogues; lack of access to many community activities, whether due to location, exclusivity, or cost; and exorbitant fees to attend events that were free for members and at which, having paid, they were largely ignored. The deepest cut was explicit rejection, in the form of literal gatekeeping. Both synagogues were surrounded by high fences with a single gate, and each had an individual acting as security guard for services and community events. These guards thoroughly questioned non-members, even those whom they recognized from previous attendance, and at their discretion turned people away. While urban Marranos and other Portuguese were sometimes denied entry, I neither saw nor heard of any foreigner who professed to be Jewish being refused, nor were those of us from abroad questioned after our first attendance.

The worst gatekeeping occurred in Lisbon, where a community member who often conducted security checks would grill newcomers so intensely that many expatriate Jews I met, including staff at the Israeli embassy, felt unwelcome and did not return. Questions he asked me and others, whether foreigners or Portuguese, included the following: Are you Jewish? (If yes) Where do you usually attend synagogue? (If no) Why are you here? What do you know about Judaism? (To all) What is your full name? Do you have government-issued identification? Where are you from? What do you do for a living? Why do you want to see how they pray here? Do you have any knives or guns with you? Does anyone else know that you are here? Who? Are they Jewish?

As might be imagined, some of these questions were not easy for urban Marranos to answer, beginning with the seemingly straightforward "Are you Jewish?" How were they to respond? At times the security volunteer let them in without incident; at other times he seemed to single them out for harassment. One October evening in 2004 he stopped Tiago Mascarenhas. A slight, unassuming man, Tiago had attended services at least half a dozen times. After the usual questioning the volunteer commanded him to stand spread-eagled for a pat-down search. Acting as if he felt something unusual, he ordered Tiago to remove his jacket and empty his pockets, then searched him again. This transpired on the sidewalk in front of the synagogue gate, on a chilly, rainy night, while passersby stopped to stare. Shivering and near tears but determined not to let anyone see that he was humiliated, Tiago withstood the search in the hope of being admitted. Finally the rabbi's wife saw what was happening and found a CIL staff member to stop "the craziness," as she put it, and let him pass. I was unable to obtain a satisfying explanation for Tiago's treatment that evening. He had been turned away in the past, but then spent time with the newly installed rabbi and his wife, attended services, and was known by sight to the volunteer guard and other community members. It is hard to imagine that he was seriously considered a threat. Perhaps he was deemed unwelcome by certain community leaders who were rumored to have blacklisted others; perhaps the security volunteer was, as some suspected, simply mean-spirited. Whatever the case, despite being the most peculiar and explicit case of exclusion during my time in Portugal, Tiago's painful story captures the powerlessness and rejection many felt. Indeed, the story became something of a rallying cry.

Thus there was one more social category in this figured world, an unspoken catchall whose existence urban Marranos discovered only slowly: outsiders. Not just "non-Jews," but literally *outsiders,* those trapped just beyond the normative community's boundaries, their presence nonetheless known to those within. This, they realized, was the category to which they belonged. Potential converts did not, for only people who had already been accepted into the community socially were taken seriously as potential converts. Former crypto-Jews like those in Belmonte did belong among the outsiders, for they too failed to meet the community's norms but bumped up against its edges. One by one, throughout the late 1990s and early 2000s, newcomers discovered that there were others like themselves who felt equally rejected. Some met for the first time at one of the synagogues, like the group that created Menorá; others found each other at meetings of the Portugal-Israel Friendship Association; still others met at the rabbis' classes. As connections mounted, additional newcomers were absorbed into the network without first experiencing rejection from the normative community. They heard stories from those who had, though, and over time came to identify with that experience, recognizing that they were all in the same situation. By mid-2004 Menorá and HaShalom were in full swing, each with around forty dues-paying members and a core group that met regularly. Unfailingly, conversation at their meetings cycled back to frustration at being unable to join the Jewish world and live as Jews. Given their profound emotional attachment to being Jewish, it should come as no surprise that they internalized the position of outsider and began to live it, intensely: within the figured world of Portuguese Jews, that was the sole social category open to them, and the one into which many were explicitly placed, over and over, in face-to-face interaction.

CATEGORICAL OUTSIDERS: THE MARRANO BOX

Until she reached her forties, Dulce Oliveira had never heard the words *marrano* or *b'nei anussim*. Nor, for that matter, did she have much knowledge about the Inquisition or Iberian Jewish history. After years of sporadically attending services at Shaaré Tikvá, where she sat alone and understood little, in 1998 she saw on the evening news that a Sephardic studies program had been created at the University of Lisbon. As part of its mission it would offer mini-courses for the general public; the first, on Portuguese Jewish history, had just opened for enrollment.

Seven years later she still had the course binder to show me, its syllabus, handouts, and photocopied readings neatly arranged. It had been a life-changing experience, not only for what she learned—a historical and religious context that made her family's odd behaviors and silences intelligible—but because of two people she met there. One was an older Ashkenazi man, Senhor Isaac, who listened thoughtfully to her story and encouraged her to contact a dear friend, "a Marrano," he said. The friend lived in Porto, where Dulce's grandparents had lived. Perhaps this friend knew her family or could help her track down clues about her Jewish ancestry. She was thrilled at the prospect. At the course she also met Francisco, a college student from Belmonte. He was raised in a crypto-Jewish milieu, still a child when his family converted to Orthodox Judaism along with much of his community. He and Dulce chatted after class and he, too, listened carefully to her story. Although he attended services at Shaaré Tikvá, he understood her sense of exclusion. There was another synagogue in Lisbon, he told her, called Anshei Emet, where "Marranos" (his word) regularly gathered. He gave her a contact number and suggested she arrange to meet them.

From the course materials and conversations with her new friends, Dulce soon learned the history of Portugal's Marranos over the past five centuries, the extraordinary survival of crypto-Judaism in Belmonte, and the rise and fall of Barros Basto's twentieth-century revival movement. Armed with a stack of newly published books on twentieth-century Marranos, she read avidly. Her understanding of herself, of the possibilities for who she might be, began to change: previously she knew only that she was "Jewish" but an outsider vis-à-vis the Jewish community. Now she realized that her grandparents and great-grandparents might have been Marranos, actual hidden Jews, for they lived in the same area and perhaps even moved in the same circles as people whose descendants she was to meet at this other synagogue.

Although she did not discover family ties at Anshei Emet, she did meet several others there who understood themselves to be Jewish by descent, all of them frustrated at the impossibility of integrating into Lisbon's Jewish community. Each had found Anshei Emet through word of mouth: while the address was listed in the telephone directory, it was invisible from the street. There was no sign above the door, no indication that on the second floor of a crumbling apartment building in a modest residential neighborhood there was a decades-old synagogue, complete with a sanctuary, kitchen, meeting rooms, and a cabinet (the *aron kodesh*) containing several Torah scrolls. Founded in the early twentieth century by Ashkenazi immigrants, the congregation had dwindled to just a few families in the past fifty years. The distinction between Sephardic and Ashkenazi had become increasingly socially insignificant; younger generations thought of themselves simply as "Portuguese Jews" (Steinhardt 2003) and left to join the much larger Shaaré Tikvá. By the 1990s the synagogue had long lain in disuse. Two families maintained the electricity, water, and phone accounts, and one or two older men would unlock the door every Saturday morning and sit inside, in case a Jew came by, looking to attend services.

Why keep the doors open? Why did the older men not join everyone else at the main synagogue? Some years earlier, there had been a struggle between two would-be leaders at Shaaré Tikvá. The smaller faction, which happened to be largely Ashkenazi, was forced out and joined the declining congregation at Anshei Emet. Because the majority were not religiously observant they did not hold Shabbat services, but they gathered for the most important holidays—Rosh Hashanah, Yom Kippur, Passover. In between there were only the two older men, both of Polish Jewish descent, whose weekly presence kept the deteriorating synagogue alive. For Dulce, the fact that these men had found welcome at Anshei Emet after being rejected by the primary Jewish community was crucially important, for she felt it made them sympathetic to people like her. "Look," she told me,

> I think I can compare the Poles' [*polacos*] attitude to ours, the Anusim. The Poles made their synagogue there because they weren't able to stay integrated in CIL. You see? We have to keep Anshei Emet alive. Some of the new people [in HaShalom] weren't there, they don't understand, because they didn't have to go through that phase—when Alexandre [a HaShalom leader] first knocked at the door and the Pole opened it for him, he opened it for all of us. There it is: Anshei Emet served as a place of welcome *once again* for those who were not accepted by the other side.

Thus the Marranos, rural or urban, were not the only ones to occupy the category *outsider* in the figured world of Portuguese Jews. Here was another group, members of the barely surviving Ashkenazi synagogue, who stood alongside them outside the primary community's walls.

With guidance from members of Anshei Emet, urban Marranos began meeting regularly at the synagogue to study Jewish history and religion and to learn basic prayers. When they looked into formalizing their activities as a legally constituted *associação,* they discovered there was already one attached to the synagogue: HaShalom, a cultural association active from the 1930s to the 1980s, founded under CIL's umbrella but now registered at Anshei Emet's address. The faction that left Shaaré Tikvá included members of HaShalom's final board of directors, who effectively took it with them. These older men collaborated closely with the young newcomers to resurrect it as an entirely new association.

The 1999 Statutes of the HaShalom Jewish Association mark an important step in the constitution of urban Marrano consciousness in Portugal. In addition to advocating for human rights, as mandated by Jewish tradition, and disseminating knowledge of Jewish culture, the mission statement emphasized two additional spheres of activity: (1) assisting any Jewish immigrants in becoming settled in Portugal; and (2) continuing the *obra do resgate,* "work of redemption"—Barros Basto's term for identifying Marranos and supporting their "return." With these two emphases, the reconstituted HaShalom declared itself an institution devoted to welcoming outsiders. Barros Basto's earlier efforts also influenced the classification of members:

1. The following will be considered *Full Members:* all Jews and Redeemed Ones [*resgatados*] age 14 or older.
2. The following will be designated *Redeemed Ones:* all crypto-Jews [*cripto-judeus*] and Marranos, as well as all Righteous Proselytes.
3. The following will be considered *Auxiliary Members:* all individuals or entities who wish to be affiliated with HaShalom and respect its mission, and do not fit into one of the other member categories.

By explicitly linking HaShalom with the *obra do resgate,* by using "Marranos" and "crypto-Jews" to mean different things, and by lumping crypto-Jews, Marranos, and "Righteous Proselytes" (the rabbinic term for Gentile converts) together in the category *resgatados,* HaShalom's founders staked out a series of social distinctions and categorical groupings that would have profound implications for its present and future members.

Jews, Marranos, crypto-Jews, Gentile converts: four categories eligible for full membership. For the statutes' authors, as for Barros Basto before them, "Marrano" meant anyone of pre-Inquisition Jewish descent who sought connection with the Jewish world. Crypto-Jews were those who, like Dulce's new friend from Belmonte, were raised from childhood with syncretic practices and consciousness of belonging to a community of hidden Jews. Although Gentile converts were distinct from Marranos because they lacked Jewish ancestry, they, too, were included among the people to be assisted through the "work of redemption." Curiously, however, the association's membership form required applicants to select from just two categories. After a section requiring basic identifying information there was another section, "Religious Situation" (*situação religiosa*), with two choices:

JEWISH ☐   MARRANO ☐

OTHER—SPECIFY _____

The form implies that there are just two targeted categories of members, in two "situations," Jewish and Marrano. The applicant must choose one or the other, or specify an exception. As at Shaaré Tikvá's gate, here the ancestral Jew had to answer an inherently difficult question: are you Jewish? In this case, however, there was an alternative beyond a simple "no": Marrano. Faced with these two options and by now familiar with the term's meaning in Barros Basto's time, many would-be members checked the Marrano box.

But what did it mean, exactly, to check the Marrano box? Certainly it meant the new member was *not* (yet) Jewish, for the two were presented as distinct options; it also meant *not* a convert, for to be a convert would be to be a Gentile, an absolute non-Jew, a category with which these individuals emphatically and explicitly did not identify. And yet in my conversations with members, I learned that none would have used the term *Marrano* in self-reference prior to joining HaShalom or talking with one of its leaders. This is a matter of categorical boundaries, of named identities as containers whose contents are neither fixed nor necessarily clear (Barth 1969). For those who checked the box, to be a Marrano was to be neither one thing nor the other, neither a Jew according to halakhah nor a convert; it was to be an outsider; it was to be connected historically to a social category that was always in-between. The category "Marrano" only makes sense in opposition to two other categories, Jew and Christian, and as we saw in chapter 1 the terms of that opposition have shifted continuously over time and from different perspectives. Thus the *content* of Marrano-ness was something the group had to create in practice, together; it did not already exist. Because each came to Menorá or HaShalom without having previously been part of a self-conscious "Marrano" community, their participation entailed collectively creating a set of practices and dispositions that constituted being—*becoming*—a Marrano. I address this process in the next two sections of this chapter.

There is more to say about the Marrano box, however. Not everyone who identified as an ancestral Jew checked it, and among those who did, several were ambivalent. Tomás Silveira, for example, grew up with a number of syncretic practices, though he did not realize what they were until he was an adult. When he joined HaShalom, he checked the Jewish box. Asked why, he explained,

> I had an argument with Dulce about that. I told her that they shouldn't put the word *Marrano* on the form. It's an insult. It's an offensive term. And they said, no, it's not. Look, I know, over at Shaaré Tikvá, I'm Anusim, OK? But

I am a Jew. You, me, we are Jews. I don't identify with the words *Marrano* and *B'nai Anusim*. I am a Jew, in my own way [*Sou judeu, à minha maneira*].

Pedro Sequeira, too, was uncomfortable with the word, though for a different reason:

I don't feel I'm a Marrano. I've never had to hide anything, no one ever transmitted that identity to me, and no one ever made me do anything against my will. I wasn't raised with a hidden identity. I never refused to eat pork and then had to eat pork against my will. I never refused to go to Mass and then had to go to Mass. I say that I'm B'nai Anusim, because that's the only thing people understand. But I feel that I'm a Jew. Ethnically, I'm a Jew. But if I say I'm a Jew, people *definitely* will never understand. And I won't say I'm a convert. I'll never say that. I'm not a convert. If I say I am a convert, then my family history will be lost. So I say Marrano, or B'nai Anusim.

Both Tomás and Pedro emphasized that "Marrano" did not quite capture who they felt they were. Yet despite their discomfort with the word in *self-description*—discomfort shared by a surprising number of participants in my research—Tomás, Pedro, and the others seemed to have no qualms about referring to each other or to the entire group as "Marranos." Particularly in self-mocking banter, but also in serious discussions about their position vis-à-vis the mainstream synagogues, members of HaShalom and Menorá routinely used the term in its collective form. HaShalom members also phrased it in the diminutive, a common Portuguese way of expressing affection, informality, or sympathy, as in *nós, os marranitos* (we, the little Marranos).

The logic behind this collective designation was grounded as much in history as in individual ancestry. The more participants delved into the saga of Barros Basto's earlier Marrano revival, the more they came to feel that their collective structural position relative to the Jewish community—that of the rejected outsider, indigenous Portuguese of presumed Jewish descent, not accepted by (descendants of) immigrant Jews—was identical to the position occupied by Barros Basto and the people he sought to bring into the Jewish world. His story, painstakingly detailed in the new biography nearly all had read (Mea and Steinhardt 1997), suggested the word could be used proudly: *Marrano* was a term of honor, celebrating ancestral resistance and survival. As an example of how the term could be embraced collectively, even if some would not have described themselves that way individually, consider the following.

One October evening in Porto, just before midnight, a group of friends was urging me not to leave. The small, homey restaurant showed no sign of closing and there were still several open bottles of wine on the table. Everyone wanted to continue Antonieta's fiftieth birthday celebration on into the night. The ten of us had been attending Menorá meetings every weekend of late, usually followed by dinner or drinks, and we knew each other fairly well by now. It had been a long evening, conversation flowing loose and easy. I was exhausted from hours of rapid-fire Portuguese, with ever more ribald jokes coming from all sides, and the last thing I wanted was to stay out later. I protested that I was tired, that I needed to go home and write up the day's field notes.

"But you're *our* anthropologist!" cried Octávio. "You can't leave! You're the Marranos' anthropologist! You have to stay with us!" There was a chorus of agreement, followed by general ribbing at the American who wanted to call it a night so early. Didn't I understand that the Portuguese don't really get going until midnight? I agreed to stay and the conversation flowed on.

Soon I was nodding off at the table. It was time for bed. As I got up to leave, Antonieta made one last try, invoking a rumor shared at the previous week's meeting: "Wait, wait, I have an idea. Let's all go see the Russian stripper we've been hearing about, the Jewish one. Let's go! A whole gang [*malta*] of Marranos, we Sephardim going to see the Ashkenazi stripper!"

Manuel, a bespectacled poet in his early forties, chimed in: "It's true, you need to see what we Marranos do late at night! You know we like to *marrar . . .*" Everyone laughed uproariously, appreciating Manuel's clever pun linking *marrano* and *marrar,* a verb meaning "to butt," as in the head-butting thrust of fighting rams—a not-so-subtle sexual metaphor. Laughing along with them, I backed out of the restaurant, waving, and went off into the unseasonably warm night to find a cab.

The Menorá members who sat around the table that night used the term *Marrano* playfully, in a way that expressed both their recognition that I was primarily interested in them *as* Marranos and their sense of being a cohesive group. So, too, did their highly self-conscious usage reflect its relatively recent adoption; here, again, "Marrano" is in effect an empty container, a named but newly acquired identity defined primarily in opposition to other possible identities. Antonieta, in particular, used it in a sense that jokingly conveyed the group's sincere feelings of difference. With the phrase "a whole gang of Marranos, we Sephardim going to see the Ashkenazi stripper," she made explicit their shared Iberian Jewish ancestry while simultaneously stressing their cohesion as a "gang" in contrast to the immigrant (here, Ashkenazi) Jewish Other. In Porto, it is important to note, urban Marranos identified strongly as Sephardic, but in the narrow sense of indigenous Iberian Jews as opposed to the immigrants and expatriates who ran Barros Basto's great synagogue. As such, they felt they had greater claim to the designation "Portuguese Jews" and indeed to the synagogue itself. They used the term *Marranos* earnestly in their activism for historical and religious recognition, even joining forces with supporters in the mid-2000s to create an organization called American Friends of Marranos. Yet not one of them was raised a hidden Jew, and only a few would have chosen "Marrano" in individual self-reference.

Writing of the perpetual tension between collective and individual identities, Anthony Cohen (1994: 17) notes that however varied individual interpretations of shared symbols and practices may be, "at the very least, there will be a feeling among the members that they do share a modicum of agreement. This sentiment may be regarded as a *sine qua non* of the group's very existence, suggesting that however little the members may actually share with each other, it must be more than they share with members of what they recognize as other groups." Whether in Porto or in Lisbon, each group's sense of *collective* belonging under the rubric "Marranos"—an extraordinarily powerful historical symbol—overrode individual variation in their interpretation of the term and in their personal self-designation: collectively, they were not exactly Jews, certainly not vis-à-vis the normative Jewish communities; nor were they collectively converts, per se, for the vast majority felt strongly that they had Jewish ancestors. What brought them together and cemented their connection to one another was a shared sense of being *outsiders* in the figured world of Portuguese Jews, set apart by their belief that they were essentially Jewish on the basis of both ancestry and attraction. In this sense, they were structurally and historically similar to the rural (former) crypto-Jews, the *marranos,* who were also marginal to the normative Portuguese Jewish community. Hence "Marrano" was the most appropriate existing category, the one whose meaning would be immediately understood by those around them—however much the subtleties of their individual life histories might diverge.

If its meaning as a historically distinct social category was clear, however, the *content* of urban Marrano-ness was far less so. Whether they chose to call themselves Marranos, Anusim, or B'nai Anusim, each of those terms framed their sense of self in relation to a particular history of being unable to be who one really is, due to social forces beyond one's control. As such, the *absence* of Jewish knowledge and upbringing was encoded in the very term they used to describe themselves. But if to be an urban Marrano or B'nai Anusim was to live with an empty space where Jewishness should be, how could one fill it? For Catarina Queirós, the sardonic graduate student always ready with a startling analogy, it required becoming *bionic*. "We're like bionic Jews," she said frankly during one of our first conversations. "We have to build our Jewishness from foreign materials. You get a mezuzah, that's like one finger. We even have to learn Jewish humor from outside, because we don't know it. We have to create appendages that aren't there yet."

BECOMING A MARRANO

Let us begin with the basic problem of feeling "Jewish" but having no idea how to go about living as a Jew. Visiting the closest synagogue offered little concrete information, nor were other resources readily available. Until the mid-2000s there was no Portuguese publisher of books on contemporary Jewish religious or cultural practices, very few publications on Jewish history, and none at all on how to *become* Jewish. The easiest source of books was via direct order from Brazil, a Portuguese-speaking country with a far larger Jewish population; those with sufficient language skills shopped online from other countries. Some traveled or lived abroad for a time and brought books back when they returned. However they came by them, each home I visited had at least one full Jewish-themed bookcase. Some collected books about Jews in other countries; others collected fiction with Jewish characters; still others, theological texts. A few bought anything they could find. One man mentioned to me offhand that he had twenty-five boxes of Jewish books in his home; another had a wall of bookcases custom-built to house his personal library. They read voraciously.

They also absorbed a great deal from mass-media imagery of Jews in New York, Jerusalem, London, São Paulo, and elsewhere. By the late 1990s it was common for Portuguese homes to have cable television, including a diverse range of foreign channels. American movies and TV shows, many with overtly Jewish characters, were ubiquitous. Although it initially took me by surprise, I grew accustomed to participants' frequent references to Jewish-themed movies and characters—*Seinfeld, The Big Lebowski, Yentl*—to illustrate a point or convey their feelings. While dependence on popular media sometimes distorted their perceptions of Jewish life elsewhere, it also fueled their efforts to imagine a different kind of Jewishness for themselves than they saw locally.

The internet, too, was a crucial resource. There they learned about Jewish theology, religious diversity, cultural traditions, and ritual practice; heard recordings of Hebrew prayers; ordered books, music, and videos; and met Jews in other countries through chat rooms, bulletin boards, and other social media. Some joined discussion groups, like Nostálgia, that focused on Portuguese and Jewish history and genealogy. Many first encountered the terms *crypto-Jews* and *B'nai Anusim* online and found them useful for understanding their ancestors and themselves. Some even learned about Menorá or HaShalom through an online conversation with someone in another country. For the most part, however, this online activity did not generate face-to-face contact; it was a venue for learning *about* Jewishness rather than a means of engaging with it directly.

When the Shavei Israel rabbis arrived and began offering weekly courses on Judaism, it seemed an opportunity for hands-on learning had finally come. Each spoke passable Portuguese and was personally committed to Marrano outreach. But some urban Marranos found their emphasis on ultra-Orthodox adherence to Jewish law off-putting. One afternoon in Porto, for example, the rabbi began a lesson on care of the self. He was a warm, gentle man, only a few years older than many of his students, and the atmosphere was relaxed. Sitting at the head of a long wooden table in the synagogue's dining room, he started with care of the soul. He spoke of the importance of taking time for meditation and reflection, particularly on Shabbat. His students diligently took notes, nodding. But when he turned to minutiae about caring for the body and mentioned that women should wear elbow-covering sleeves and long skirts, people looked at each other in disbelief. And then: "You must never, never drop fingernail or toenail cuttings on the floor," said the rabbi. "They must be cared for as part of the human body. Put them carefully in a tissue and burn them. If you have to put them in the trash, OK. Better to burn them than put them in the trash, but you must never, never let them touch the floor." Such arcane details of ultra-Orthodox observance were both frustrating and a source of incredulous amusement to participants, who sought much more concrete instruction on the broad contours of living a Jewish life in the modern world, ideally in contact with other Jews, than the rabbis were prepared to offer.

While classes, books, websites, and films are sources of knowledge, they do not provide a living social context to put that knowledge into practice and deepen it through social interaction. Writing of learning as a culturally and historically situated phenomenon, Jean Lave (1991: 65) suggests that we view it "not as a process of . . . internalization of knowledge by individuals, but as a process of becoming a member of a sustained community of practice." People learn, she argues, through "legitimate peripheral participation" as newcomers in existing informal communities, to which they are drawn due to shared interest in a given issue. First as peripheral observers, then as partial participants, and ultimately as full "practitioners," individuals become adept at the skills, attitudes, and knowledge that define the group they have joined. While most obvious in trade apprenticeships—for example, to become a butcher or a midwife—Lave argues that this is equally true of organizations like Alcoholics Anonymous, where participants learn over time to behave, speak, and think of themselves in characteristic ways. Thus, she writes (1991:65), "developing an identity as a member of a community and becoming knowledgeably skillful are part of the same process, with the former motivating, shaping, and giving meaning to the latter, which it subsumes."

Lave's analysis of the crucial role of social context in learning helps to elucidate the situation in Portugal. Denied full access to the normative Jewish communities—communities of practice in which their would-be "peripheral participation" was continuously marked as *il*legitimate—the ancestral Jews' learning could only go so far. As much as they gleaned from books, courses, and other sources, it was difficult to work such disparate bits of information into a lived identity. In their attempts to align their external person with their internal sense of self, many modified their daily lives and, in some cases, their bodies. Some attempted strict adherence to Jewish dietary laws, but found it excessively difficult. Others limited their activity on Friday evenings and Saturdays, staying home in an attempt to observe the Sabbath. In the greatest show of commitment, some men managed to find doctors to perform circumcision, no small feat in a country where the procedure is undertaken only as a remedy for serious medical conditions. (Newborn circumcisions are performed for the Jewish community nationwide by a urologist member of Shaaré Tikvá.) When I expressed surprise that they had taken such a drastic step, each said he had felt it necessary in order to feel fully Jewish. But to what extent could these independent steps help them become "knowledgeably skillful," to use Lave's terminology? And how can one develop an identity as a member of a community—here, the Jewish world at large—when there is no face-to-face manifestation of that community to join and from which to learn?

Menorá and HaShalom offered a way to sidestep these problems, providing those who felt they were Jewish-in-essence with an alternative community of practice. Unlike the cases Lave describes, here *all* began as peripheral participants and slowly became adepts, learning together and in the process developing a more or less encompassing identity as a member of the group. However, I suggest that by participating in the associations, where they studied Judaism and engaged in various aspects of Jewish cultural and religious practice, these individuals did not learn to be Jews, per se. They learned, instead, to be *Marranos,* for whom one of the definitive practices *was learning itself.* A central component of being a Marrano, that is, was learning to be Jewish, newly adopting the material and behavioral qualities of what they understood Jewishness to be—thus becoming, in Catarina's words, "bionic Jews." Over time, they collectively developed a set of practices and dispositions that, combined with the pursuit of learning, became constitutive characteristics of being a Marrano. As we will see, some of these were substantially different from those of normative Jewishness, in any of the many ways it could be defined. From possession and use of Jewish material culture to adopting Hebrew names, from exploring forms of religious observance to learning to articulate their personal journey in a common narrative structure, these new practices were vitally important in externalizing and expressing what had previously been an internal, private identity, and together forging a sense of belonging.

Materializing Identity

Until nearly a year into my fieldwork, when I rented my own apartment in Lisbon, I often stayed at Catarina's flat during my biweekly trips from Porto to attend meetings, classes, and events with members of HaShalom. She and I were the same age and had become close friends, so she gave me a key and free run of her apartment. One morning I decided to look more closely at her collection of Jewish books. A title on one of the overstuffed shelves stood out: *Choosing Judaism.* The slim American paperback struck me as incongruous, not because it was a guide to becoming Jewish, but because its title explicitly engaged the language of choice to which Catarina and others took such exception. I flipped through the pages. With chapter titles like "But I Don't Feel Jewish!" and "Your Jewish Spouse," coupled with assurances that joining a synagogue was the best way to make Jewish friends and find a supportive community, it was clearly intended for a radically different situation than the one in which the urban Marranos found themselves. But one passage caught my eye:

> It is very important to establish a Jewish environment in your home. If you don't already have Shabbat candlesticks, buy some. . . . Buy a mezuzah if you don't already have one. . . . Buy a Jewish calendar. . . . Locate a bookstore that specializes in Jewish books.[6]

By intentionally surrounding oneself with the external trappings of Jewishness, the author implies, one will feel more Jewish internally. This is a proposal for an act of overt self-authorship, in which one consciously brings one's material surroundings into alignment with the new self one hopes to become—or, in the case of urban Marranos, the "true" self they hoped to reveal.

I glanced around, taking in the apartment anew. Yes, Catarina had indeed established a "Jewish environment," one in keeping with her quirky young-adult aesthetic. Amongst the living room's bright pop-art touches—a Warholesque series of photos of Catarina in a devil costume, a lime-green bean bag chair, hot-pink throw pillows, a fluffy imitation-fur area rug—were indications of a Jewish identity. On a side table, behind a vase of shocking-blue and hot-pink silk roses, stood an eight-branched brass candelabra; nearby was a framed black-and-white photograph of a soldier leaning his forehead against the Western Wall in prayer. More items were scattered throughout the apartment: a smaller menorah on a nightstand; a stack of Jewish-themed fiction by the front door; a small tapestry with embroidered Hebrew letters tacked over a vent; even a modernist wooden mezuzah affixed to the outer door frame. Other homes, I recalled, had similarly been made "Jewish," some with more religious overtones. Raquel Gouveia, who grew up in Israel in a labor migrant family, decorated her Lisbon apartment almost exclusively with Judaica: prints of Hebrew calligraphic art and depictions of holy sites in Israel adorned the walls, a menorah and two large pairs of candlesticks stood on a sideboard, and a challah platter and seder plate rested on display mounts. Men, too, created a "Jewish environment." When Joaquim Martins invited me for dinner and gave me a brief tour of his home, I counted eleven menorahs of varying sizes dispersed throughout the apartment. Some were three-dimensional, others were depicted in paintings or photographs, and one adorned the front of a greeting card propped on a bookshelf. It was the winter holiday season, and combined with the mezuzah on the doorjamb and a large bookcase of Jewish-themed volumes, the repeated menorah motif sat in uneasy juxtaposition with the Christmas tree placed prominently in the living room by Joaquim's mother, who lived with him. When I asked if she minded the apartment's overwhelming emphasis on Judaica, however, she reminded me that she was of *chueta* origin herself. She found no contradiction in the simultaneous expression of her own cultural Catholicism and her adult son's Jewish identity.

The objects with which people decorate their homes, anthropologist Daniel Miller (2008) suggests, offer us "access to an authentic other voice" that supplements what they tell us about themselves. The things they put on display, whether photographs, purchases, or gifts, reveal a great deal about their lives, their relationships, and their sense of self. Writes Miller (2008: 2), "The person in [a] living-room gives an account of themselves by responding to questions. But every object in that room is equally a form by which they have chosen to express themselves. They put up ornaments; they laid down carpets.... Some things may be objects or gifts retained from the past, but they have decided to live with them.... These things are not a random collection." Material things—the items we buy, collect, move among, adorn ourselves with—are always embedded in social systems of meaning and value. For the urban Marranos, each item of Judaica no doubt had its own personal significance and associations; as an assemblage, however, the objects were an essential component of their emergent sense of being Jewish. Objects and people are mutually constitutive: just as we make things meaningful by using them, exchanging them, valuing them, and displaying them, they simultaneously make us who and what we are. By surrounding themselves with Jewish things—as the author of *Choosing Jewish* suggests anyone beginning a Jewish life should do—urban Marranos created a material world in which they continuously expressed and were reminded of who they felt they were inside. These objects were initially unfamiliar to them, however; in Catarina's terms, they were "foreign parts." Ironically, then, by expressing themselves through Jewish material culture they did so in a foreign tongue.

The Portuguese home is a private space, reserved for oneself, family, and close friends. Typically social gatherings take place in restaurants, so the objects one selects for display at home make a far less public statement than the clothing or jewelry one wears. Although they dressed like any other Portuguese of similar socioeconomic standing, the urban Marranos developed a number of practices involving self-adornment as a means of expressing their emergent Jewish identity. In the previous chapter I described how Joaquim Martins began wearing a Star of David pendant in his early thirties, as a sign of his increasing identification with Jewishness. He was not the only one. Over time the Star of David became a shared symbol of belonging, with resonance unique to the Marrano associations.

To see this resonance in action, consider a photograph taken at a Menorá board meeting in late 2004. Seated around the makeshift conference table, everyone—including the anthropologist—is looking up at the camera, laughing. The photographer, a member of Menorá who lived in Canada but stayed in Porto for months at a time, stood on a chair to capture us all in one shot. Just as he was about to take the photo, Antonieta called out, "We should all take out our Stars of David!" "Stars of David out!" commanded Ricardo, laughing. "Show 'em! [*À mostra!*]" With that he unbuttoned his collar to reveal a small gold star and with a mock flourish several others drew pendants out from under their shirts as well. I had noticed that Antonieta always wore a Star of David—a necklace, a tiny star dangling from a hoop earring, a pair of star-shaped studs—but this was the first time I realized that nearly everyone, men included, wore one. A year later, as HaShalom members gathered to meet a lawyer at his downtown Lisbon office to discuss legal aspects of starting their own Jewish community (see chapter 5), Dulce made the connection explicit. She looked appraisingly at each person, smiled knowingly, and said to me, "Look, everyone's wearing their star! I knew they would." She paused dramatically for effect. "Could it be that I'm wearing one? [*Será que tenho?*]" Another dramatic pause. "Of course I have one, but I left it at home." She shrugged ruefully, as if it had been an obvious oversight.

In the symbolic universe of the Marrano movement, Dulce may well have felt that something was missing. The vast majority of members of HaShalom and Menorá owned, and often wore, a Star of David pendant. They were especially likely to wear them when together; the more important the function, the more pendants appeared. Curiously, however, I never saw anyone in the normative Jewish community in Lisbon or Porto wearing a visible Star of David. There are three likely reasons for the pendant's pervasive appearance among urban Marranos. First, in Portugal, as in other Catholic countries, it is not uncommon to see women or men wearing a crucifix pendant. For women, crucifixes come in diverse styles and a range of sizes, whereas men tend to prefer a discreet gold cross about a quarter inch in length. With their Stars of David, urban Marranos mirrored precisely this gendered variation in style, size, and visibility. It was thus initially the Catholic social context, and not a Jewish one, that the Marranos engaged with their adoption of the pendant. Whether intentionally or not, the Star of David served as a small gesture, in a widely intelligible symbolic language, indicating that its wearer identified as Jewish and not Catholic.[7] Second, the star served to remind the individual, perhaps even more than those around him or her, of his or her emergent sense of self. Third, of course, it became recognized within the group as a common Marrano possession, rather than a generically Jewish one.

Unlike the pendant, whose symbolic weight as a marker of identification, difference, and belonging was fairly straightforward, other "Jewish" items with which urban Marranos adorned their bodies carried ambiguous messages or operated within a more circumscribed symbolic domain. Several of the men purchased prayer shawls from abroad, for example, but rarely used them because they had no venue in which to do so. The Jewish prayer shawl, or *tallit* (Heb.), is worn during individual morning prayers at home, which most had not learned, and in morning services at a synagogue. In Lisbon, these men had been explicitly forbidden from wearing one during services; in Porto, where the community did not hold morning services, men from Menorá were able to use their *tallit* only once a year, during the High Holidays. A few of the women also bought prayer shawls, but because the synagogues were Orthodox and thus only men could wear them, they were kept as treasured possessions. Hence, like that most private of Jewish markers, circumcision, their ownership of a prayer shawl was something few people knew about, but it made them feel more Jewish simply for having been accomplished.

The men also became accustomed to wearing a *kipá* (Heb.; skullcap, yarmulke) when attending synagogue services or reading sacred texts. They did not wear it every day, nor at ordinary meetings at Menorá or HaShalom. These are standard patterns of usage for Reform or Conservative Jews, as Jewish law stipulates that a man's head must be covered during prayer or sacred study (Orthodox men typically wear one at all times; see Boyarin and Boyarin 1995). However, together the men generated a new practice: they wore one whenever they held an especially important meeting or attended an important event together as "Jews." All of them wore a *kipá* at HaShalom's meeting with the (non-Jewish) lawyer about starting a new Jewish community, for example, as did every man in attendance at the 2004 national meeting of Marranos/Anusim, held in a generic municipal meeting hall. They also wore one whenever a rabbi came to meet with them collectively, even if only to talk informally about their backgrounds. There was no discussion about it beforehand. It had become the unspoken norm in these contexts, and newcomers quickly learned by example to do the same. In each case, the message of this unconventional usage was straightforward: collectively and individually, we identify as—are—Jews, and so we wear this element of Jewish dress.

Other "Jewish" items of self-adornment were used much like their non-Jewish analogues, offering a more subtle gesture of identification. Members occasionally wore T-shirts bearing Jewish-themed logos or images, such as the Hebrew University seal; others collected similar clothing but, as in the case of the prayer shawls, never wore it. Most, whether male or female, carried a key-ring charm related to Jews or Judaism. A few had a simple metallic fob adorned with a Star of David, but a brightly enameled, Israeli-made style was most common. Purchased in Judaica shops abroad or received as gifts, these key rings took the form of a *hamsa,* the traditional hand-shaped Middle Eastern amulet to ward off the Evil Eye. On the reverse was a prayer for safety while traveling, engraved in Hebrew script. Although most were unaware of what the hand represented, they recognized the key rings as a generic sign of Jewishness and carried them accordingly.

Writing of patterns of acquisition and display of Judaica among observant and secular Jews in America, sociologist Samuel Heilman (1988) notes that the quantity of Jewish objects one owns—whether overtly related to ritual (Hanukkah menorah, Shabbat candlesticks, prayer shawl) or not (Star of David pendant, challah platter, *hamsa* key ring)—is not indicative of religiosity or institutional affiliation. On the contrary, he argues, whatever the ritual context for which they were made, in many homes these items serve a largely decorative function. Moreover, what is often most important for Jews who own them is not their original ritual context, but their significance as a marker of identification with the Jewish world at large:

> There is a sense across the board of Jewish life that some objects are the *sine qua non* of being an identified Jew. Whether one buys or possesses a mezuzah for hanging on the doorpost in line with Jewish law or simply to express a symbolic attachment to being a Jew ... that mezuzah serves to link one with all others who have one. The same might be said about menorahs, haggadahs, wine goblets. . . . For the Jew who acquires, keeps, and attends to Judaica does so, albeit at various levels of meaning and in a variety of contexts, to reaffirm some attachment to Jewish life. (Heilman 1988: 277)

In this sense, the urban Marranos' decorative use of Jewish ritual objects and their self-adornment with Jewish items as a statement of identification were entirely consistent with the behavior of secular American Jews. What made the Marranos different was the literal foreignness of the things they chose to acquire, display, wear, and treasure as items of self-expression. While objects and people are always linked in a relationship of mutual constitution, the

Marranos' purposeful selection of these items as a central component of *re*making themselves throws into relief the powerful role material culture can play in the shaping of identity.

Names, too, provide a means of externalizing and supporting an emergent identity, and are connected in myriad ways to feelings of identification, inclusion, and belonging. After I had been in Porto about two months, I received a text from Paula Mendes, a Menorá member, outlining plans for dinner that Friday. I recognized all but one name. "Who's Aviva?" I asked Miguel Santos, Menorá's vice president, with whom I was having lunch. "She's going to dinner with us this week. Have I met her?" Miguel laughed. "That's Antonieta! It's her Hebrew name." Miguel, I learned, also had a Hebrew name. In fact, nearly everyone at Menorá and HaShalom did, and they used them among themselves in emails and texts. I was now included in an inner circle of naming. Over time, these names became increasingly public. Some introduced themselves by the Hebrew name when interacting with new members and with foreign Jewish visitors, in addition to within the group: Joaquim became Shimon; Dulce went by Dina; Miguel, a published author, wrote a weekly newspaper column as Meir Raziel. Some of these names caught on within the group more readily than others. Foreign Jewish visitors, on the other hand, unquestioningly accepted the Hebrew name as the one to use. But some urban Marranos never brought their Hebrew name into conversation; for them, it was private, held close—like the prayer shawl—and used only online with strangers, if at all.

Names are essential to the constitution of social beings (Bodenhorn and vom Bruck 2006). To be named is to be tied into a network of social relations and meanings; whether given names, nicknames, or pseudonyms, names fix the named within a system of categories (gender, ethnicity, class, kinship), relationships, and perceived personal characteristics. Around the world, changes in kin relations, social standing, or ritual status all contribute to transformations of the self that are acknowledged and furthered by naming practices. For urban Marranos, adoption of a Hebrew name was clearly tied to the development and cultivation of a Jewish sense of self. However, Judaism makes no requirement that one have a Hebrew name for everyday interaction. While Jews receive a Hebrew name at birth or upon conversion, it is used only in ritual contexts such as life-cycle transitions or during synagogue services, when one is called to read from the Torah. The urban Marranos, on the other hand, used the Hebrew name more like an alter ego: a nom de plume when writing, a username for social networking sites, a personal name at a workshop with a visiting rabbi. Like the *kipá,* their use of Hebrew names was contextually distinct from that of the normative Jewish community, functioning above all as a marker of their identification as Jews. Like the Star of David, the *kipá,* and other material items, it served as a mode of performing and constituting the Jewish self: because I am Jewish, I have a Jewish name, therefore I am a Jew.

Where did they get these names? Some had studied modern Hebrew at one of the synagogues or a university and, as is typical in language courses, selected a Hebrew name for classroom use. Others chose a name as part of their solo exploration of Jewishness, prior to finding Menorá or HaShalom; still others took a Hebrew name only after joining. They used diverse criteria: a direct translation of their given name; a name starting with the same letter, with the same number of syllables; or a name whose meaning they found appropriate, as in the poignant case of a Porto man whose lifelong feeling of never belonging anywhere led him to select Gershom, a biblical name meaning "stranger" or "(in) exile." Regardless of how they came by the name—and some changed theirs over time, having found a better fit—most used it only within a tightly circumscribed set of social contexts, the "Jewish" or anonymous parts of their lives. Those were the moments in which they could express this facet of their identity most freely.

"We Have to Be More Catholic than the Pope"

One warm Saturday evening, nine Menorá members and I sat in a restaurant, looking over the menu. We had just finished a lengthy meeting, as usual debating what could be done about the situation at the synagogue, and I was famished. The waiter took our orders—everyone declined the evening's special, pork loin—and I waited impatiently for the small plates of appetizers that would appear at any moment. In Portugal, the familiar bread and butter provided at the beginning of a restaurant meal are supplemented with an array of morsels to share—olives, cheeses, octopus salad—that are charged to the table only if consumed. Soon the waiter arrived with the first set of small plates. *Presunto,* thinly sliced cured pork. A current of tension rippled around the table. No one moved to put any on their plate. I wanted to take a piece, but it was still early in my fieldwork and I didn't want to offend. What if they kept kosher? The next plates arrived. Mussels, served on the half shell and topped with a garlicky vinaigrette. My stomach growling, I lifted my hand to reach for the plate nearest me, but paused: this, too, was *trefah* (Heb.; not kosher). Again, no one moved to take any. When our entrées came, I saw that everyone had ordered a simple dish of grilled or stewed beef, lamb, chicken, or fish. Could it be that they all avoided shellfish, pork, and combinations of meat and milk so assiduously? Throughout the meal I kept on eye on those tempting small plates, left untouched, until a passing waiter took them away.

Jewish dietary laws (Heb.; *kashrut*) presented a conundrum for members of the Marrano associations.[8] In Portugal, pork and shellfish are dietary staples, particularly at celebratory meals; refusing to eat them among family and friends would mean overtly rejecting an aspect of Portuguese belonging, drawing a distinction between self and loved ones that few participants were willing to make. Wishing to be accepted as Jews, they avoided pork, shellfish, and other blatantly non-kosher foods when around Jews or when eating together, many of them quietly returning to their ordinary habits at other times. In the restaurant that night, I was certainly part of the reason they were all so careful; at that early stage, they had no way of knowing that I was not raised in a Jewish community and that I did not follow the Jewish dietary laws, but they did know I was observing them. To be sure, several members sincerely attempted to keep kosher at all times, as they were committed to pursuing a stricter form of Judaism. They were in the minority. For the most part, avoiding certain foods became, like the *kipá* and the Hebrew name, a shared Marrano practice, something they did in the "Jewish" parts of their lives, in ways that differed from the normative Jewish community.

Their situation was complicated by the great variation in dietary observance across the different branches of Judaism. One afternoon after I had been in Portugal about six months, Ricardo called me from Lisbon. He and several HaShalom members were at a gallery opening, featuring paintings by a prominent Israeli expatriate. Leading members of CIL were there, as were Israeli embassy staff. On seeing the elaborate, catered spread of unmistakably *trefah* foods—*presunto* alongside artisanal cheeses, seafood salad, and the like—he and Catarina were struck by the incongruity of their gatekeepers openly flouting Jewish law. "It's absurd," Ricardo said, laughing incredulously. "All these people from CIL are here eating *presunto,* like it's nothing!" He and Catarina had both lived abroad, and they knew that it was common for liberal Jews and those who identify primarily with Jewish ethnicity, more than religion, to choose not to follow *kashrut*. But they also knew they would never be granted that latitude, despite their preference for less stringent forms of Judaism. Lacking the *carteirinha* of birth to a Jewish mother, their only way to be accepted as Jews was to convert; and to convert meant taking on the Jewish religion—which, in Portugal's synagogues, meant Orthodoxy. Regardless of the branch one follows, Judaism is not primarily a religion of faith or belief; it is a religion of practice. Adherence to the Commandments, however interpreted by one's religious community, is generally considered more important than what one thinks or believes. Required to display their Jewishness through their actions, the urban Marranos were trapped, as they put it, having to be *mais católico do que o Papa,* "more Catholic than the Pope," held to a higher standard of observance than the gatekeepers required of themselves.

This is not to say that urban Marranos were disinterested in religious observance. Many devoted a great deal of time to exploring the differing perspectives and norms of Judaism's several branches and experimenting with aspects of Jewish practice in their daily lives. Indeed, part of becoming a Marrano involved cultivating an attentiveness to learning about Judaism and studying its underpinnings, and details of religious practice were often discussed at meetings. Their interest in becoming knowledgeable and skillful in those components of the religion that were meaningful to them was absolutely sincere. But relatively few were drawn to becoming Orthodox or even to being rigorously observant in a more liberal branch. Instead, because their identification with Judaism stemmed from a sense of being *already* Jewish in some essential way, many wanted to live a Jewish life of the kind exhibited by "born" Jews in Portugal's normative communities, by tourists they had met, and in American popular culture. That would mean living a Jewish life just as the majority of Portuguese lived a Catholic one: culturally. They did not want to be considered "fanatics" (*fanáticos*).

Their predicament became clear to me during an educator's visit to HaShalom in December 2005. Chaya Kaplan and her husband, Ezra, a leading Conservative rabbi, had been flying to Lisbon from New York regularly over the previous four months, teaching HaShalom members the basics of religious practice according to Conservative Judaism and helping them form a Jewish community of their own, in preparation for going before a *beit din* for a "return" ceremony (see chapter 5). Chaya had been explaining the dietary laws, which Conservative Jews follow in modified form, and the group was discussing the problem of eating with people who do not keep kosher. Seated around the worn meeting table at Anshei Emet, they spoke in a mixture of English and Portuguese.

CHAYA: You'll have to tell people that you're Jewish, and there are things you can't eat.

ROSA: What if we don't want to tell people we're Jewish? I have a client who told me a few days ago about someone he said was very strange, he didn't like him, he said, "Let me tell you, he's very weird, he's Jewish." I don't want to lose a client.

CHAYA: Really? This is very serious. Is it a problem here in Lisbon to say you are Jewish?

ROSA: Yes.

CHAYA: So how will you identify yourselves as Jews? After you go before the *beit din,* who will know that you are a Jew?

ROSA: My friends and family will know.

PEDRO: The problem is not being Jewish, though. In Portugal, it's strange to be religious at all. People who go to Mass every Sunday are seen as really old-fashioned.

. . .

CHAYA: What about the Jewish holidays? Will you be able to miss work to observe them?

NUNO: Yes, there's a new law, Article 14, that allows us to miss work because we're members of a religion that requires staying home that day. We just have to prove that we really are in that religion. I have my Article 14 letter ready already, the rabbi signed it, to show my boss so I can miss work on Jewish holidays.

CHAYA: Will there be repercussions for doing this?

NUNO: Yes, but not for being Jewish. The repercussions will be for being religious and using that as an excuse for not working.

Others chimed in, commenting on their discomfort with telling people that they could not do this or that because they were following Jewish law. Chaya sighed and said,

I think of how the Jews in this country practiced in secret for hundreds of years. It cannot be secret in 2005! If it is, we will have accomplished nothing by coming here to work with you. . . . Last time, we said we could not believe that anyone—in the year 2005, in Europe—would choose to be a Jew. And the answer you gave us was, "We *are* Jews, and we want to return, in our hearts." And that really affected us. But we worry about you. Will you be Jews in secret? It seems so ironic that after all this hiding, after five hundred years, you can't just open up!

But Chaya had misunderstood. The problem was not one of keeping their Jewish identity secret, as it had been for the original Marranos; it was the awkwardness of making one's Jewishness known specifically by adhering to religious restrictions in a largely secular country. Most urban Marranos didn't mind telling people that they were Jewish in a cultural sense, but like many Portuguese they mistrusted fanaticism and felt the appropriate place for religion was a house of worship or their own home.

Nevertheless, they were not ignorant of Jewish law. As my experience dining with Menorá members made clear, they were well aware of the dietary restrictions and made a concerted effort to follow them when they were together and especially with foreign Jews. Part of being an urban Marrano, I learned, was to be continually self-conscious, ever aware that one's Jewishness was in question, that at any moment one could be rejected, that there were gatekeepers at every turn. Although they might joke together about the exigencies of strict observance—on one occasion, for example, Nuno, who with his wife kept strictly kosher, laughingly told me in English that *kashrut* was an appropriate term because kosher food was so expensive in Portugal that it was actually *CASHrut,* and at meetings participants routinely teased one another about whether the snacks they had brought were kosher—they took their ambiguous position vis-à-vis the Jewish world quite seriously. Because they were conscious of being in a marginal category, not-quite-Jews but not-quite-Gentiles, they attempted to meet the perceived requirements of whoever their interlocutor might be at any given moment. Insecure as to whether their Jewishness would be recognized by others but certain of its reality for themselves, they vacillated between the degree of observance necessitated by their marginal position and that which seemed to them most feasible and authentic in their everyday lives.

Menorá and HaShalom offered a relatively safe context in which to explore Jewish religious practices and consider what level of observance they wanted to pursue. From taking turns blowing the *shofar,* the trumpet-like ram's horn used in synagogues to herald the entrance of the Jewish New Year, to gathering on Saturday evenings to perform Havdalah, a relaxed ritual usually conducted at home to mark the close of the Sabbath, together they stumbled through prayers, learned traditional Jewish songs, laughed over mistakes, and felt their way into Jewish ritual practice. In both associations, members who had mastered basic Hebrew offered formal classes for the others, and at HaShalom one man led a Saturday afternoon discussion group on Jewish texts and ritual practice. But they also attended Jewish-related concerts, exhibits, and films together; shared recommendations for Jewish music and movies they enjoyed; and swapped stories of travels to Jewish places abroad. In doing so, they helped each other develop a sense of connection to the Jewish world at large that both encompassed and transcended religion.

Despite the general air of camaraderie and even intimacy at HaShalom and Menorá, participants rarely shared their stories at meetings. When I began my fieldwork among them I had expected to find something like an American-style support group, as the Nostálgia internet community often seemed to be. There, newcomers from around the world posted lengthy accounts of how they learned they descended from hidden Jews and discussed subsequent transformations to their identity, invariably prompting posts of appreciation and encouragement from others. I imagined that in Portugal, too, newcomers might introduce themselves at meetings with their stories, or perhaps they would discuss issues that had arisen with their loved ones since they began to identify openly as Jews, as I had observed among crypto-Jews from the American Southwest at the Society for Crypto-Judaic Studies annual meetings (Kunin 2009). Nothing of the sort happened. Eventually I learned that most explained their background to just one or two of the associations' leaders upon applying for membership.

Nonetheless, participating in the group had a profound effect on the way members understood their personal and familial Jewish history—the way, that is, that they *knew who they were*—and consequently how they narrated it to others. As we saw in the previous chapter, most came to the associations with a strong attraction to Judaism and/or Jewishness and, in most cases, a family story of long-ago Jewish ancestors. But that was all. Their leaders frequently alluded to Barros Basto's earlier movement when discussing their collective position as outsiders, and they recommended his biography to newcomers. Several members were avidly studying the history of the Inquisition-era Marranos, and they photocopied academic articles to distribute at meetings. With this continually reinforced connection to the past, participants began to see their own family history in a much larger, more fleshed-out historical context. Having learned about *marranos*—crypto-Jews—past and present, they searched their memories for clues of hidden or syncretic Jewish practices in their parents' and grandparents' homes. As one man in Lisbon frankly told me, "You read all this stuff, and you start to think it's about you. It just makes sense."

Thus another part of becoming a Marrano entailed learning to discern details of family history that suggested Jewish roots and engaging in the project of looking for them. Although they already knew in their hearts that they were Jewish-in-essence, this practice of historical and genealogical excavation revealed additional layers of evidence. One of the first things participants pointed to was surnames. In Portugal, popular belief has it that surnames naming trees (e.g., Oliveira, "olive"; Carvalho, "oak"; Pereira, "pear") or suggesting extreme piety (e.g., Espírito Santo, "Holy Spirit"; Santos, "saints"; Cruz, "cross") were adopted by New Christians upon baptism and thus indicate Jewish ancestry (cf. Siporin 1993). Members of the Marrano associations were familiar with this folklore long before they made their way to HaShalom or Menorá, but most actively looked into the surnames of earlier generations only after joining. From time to time at a meeting someone would mention that they had just discovered a "New Christian" surname in the family tree, but far more exciting was finding that one's surname was widespread in the Sephardic world (e.g., Mendes, Pinto, Fonseca) or that it appeared on a list of people tried by the Inquisition. Long lists of Sephardic names and of surnames culled from Inquisition records are easily found online, and participants routinely consulted them. Again, in Portugal names are potent markers of social identity; hence a name connecting one's family to Jews, however tenuously, could be a treasured clue.

From historical texts, documentary films, and conversations with one another they also learned about practices identified during the Inquisition as signs of crypto-Judaism, such as changing linens on Fridays, sweeping toward the center of a room rather than out the door, avoiding pork, lighting candles on Friday evenings, avoiding Catholic Mass, burying the dead in a shroud, and slaughtering chickens by quickly cutting the throat and draining all blood before butchering. It was the last of these that proved most salient for many participants, as it recalled childhood memories of visiting grandparents in the countryside; some recognized and remembered other indicative practices as well. What is most significant for our purposes, however, is the practice of looking for such clues in the first place, a practice that I argue was itself constitutive of being a Marrano.

They also sought corroboration in the location of their ancestral villages, a subject that came up often. Their common interest in Portuguese Jewish history meant that all were familiar with the settlement patterns of Inquisition-era hidden Jews in the Trás-os-Montes and Beira provinces, in Portugal's far northeastern corner and mountainous eastern border region, respectively; they soon learned, too, that Barros Basto had focused his outreach efforts there. Thus being able to say that one's family was "from Trás-os-Montes" provided instant credibility; being "from Beira Alta" was slightly less impressive, but the strongest impact came from being able to say that one came from

Belmonte or a nearby town. One woman, telling me about a friend who was interested in joining HaShalom, responded to my question about whether she had Jewish ancestors by exclaiming, "Suffice it to say that she [i.e., her grandparents] is from Belmonte!" Reading ancestral place of origin as a sign of Jewish descent was a marked tendency in both associations.

There is a mode of reasoning at work here that Stephan Palmié (2007) calls "divinatory logic," or "abduction." An observed circumstance is explained in terms of one plausible cause, despite the existence of several plausible explanations. Medical diagnosis works this way, he notes, as do detective work and divination. Imagine that I see a friend on the street with wet hair. It is entirely plausible that she has just taken a shower, and I might reasonably conclude that she has, but she could equally plausibly have just gone swimming. Abduction gains force through corroboration: just as in solving a crime, the more suggestive clues that can be traced to a single plausible cause, the more persuasive the explanation becomes. Having ancestral origins in a province where some of the population may descend from Jews is not in itself an indication of Jewish ancestry, but place of origin combined with indicative cultural practices, surnames widely considered "Jewish," and oral history of Jewish descent—and all of this together with an apparently genealogically induced predilection for things Jewish—creates a convincing case indeed. One derives cause from consequence; circumstantial evidence points toward an inferred explanation.[9]

To identify the use of divinatory logic is not to question its findings. Given the complex history of Portuguese conversion and intermarriage, there is no way to know with certainty whether or not a given individual has Jewish ancestry, nor is it an anthropologist's place to pronounce a verdict. A more useful approach is to accept their claims as social facts (cf. Carroll 2002; Kunin 2009; Seeman 2009; Sturm 2010) and look instead at how, through their participation in the Marrano associations, these individuals came to build a particular self-conception and then share that self-conception with others. How did they learn to recognize clues and fashion them into a coherent account of lost ancestry and ultimate self-recognition? While they did not tell their stories to one another at meetings, they were called upon to explain their background by a continual stream of interlocutors—rabbis, outreach workers, tourists—over and over again. They were expected to have an intelligible narrative, one that explained their interest in Judaism and, crucially, provided evidence that their ancestors were Jewish. Lacking such a story, an individual was not a Marrano but an ordinary convert. Given that they felt they were *already* Jewish, this they most emphatically did not want to be.

A life story is more than a factual narrative about oneself told to others. It is also a medium through which identities are fashioned and expressed. How we organize information about our lives, select details to convey, trace causal relations, and draw conclusions all shape our understanding of ourselves as much as they shape others' understandings of us (Holland et al. 1998; cf. Kunin 2009: 197–99). These are also culturally patterned phenomena, in that narrative sequencing, assumptions about individual agency and fate, and criteria for causal coherence are consistent within cultural groups but often vary from one to the next (Frank 1995; Linde 1993). In the Marrano associations, participants implicitly learned to filter their life experiences in such a way as to draw new causal connections and highlight new details, creating a coherent narrative of memories, events, and turning points that buttressed their emotional certainty of being Jewish. Indicative surnames, mysterious practices, location of ancestral villages, family rumors of Jewish ancestry, and attraction to Jews and Jewishness came together in varying combinations as components of a roughly standardized life story that I came to think of as "the Marrano story." This life story was elicited via sequential questioning during interactions between urban Marranos and foreign visitors, or narrated fully in response to a single question about their Jewish background. Much like the material culture with which they surrounded and adorned themselves, their Hebrew names, and the new religious behaviors they explored together, the act of self-narration was a central component in the twin processes of becoming and being a Marrano.[10]

TELLING THE MARRANO STORY

The person as a character is not separate from its life experiences, but the plot allows for a re-organization of the events which provide the ground for the experiences of the person/character. . . . [I]t is the identity of the plot that grants the character his identity. One proposes one's identity in the form of a narrative in which one can re-arrange, re-interpret, the events of one's life . . . to take care both of permanence and change, [and] to satisfy the wish to make events concordant in spite of the inevitable discordances likely to shake the basis of identity.

DENIS-CONSTANT MARTIN
"The Choices of Identity"

Learning to fit one's own life experiences into a shared narrative structure can be a powerful element of identity acquisition, as anthropological studies of religious conversion and socialization into groups like Alcoholics Anonymous (AA) have shown.[11] In the case of AA and evangelical Christianity, one learns this narrative structure not through explicit instruction but by hearing the stories of others. Personal stories are an essential part of each AA meeting, and "as the AA member learns the AA story model, and learns to place the events and experiences of his own life into the model, he learns to tell and to understand his own life as an AA life, and himself as an AA alcoholic" (Cain 1991: 215). By reinterpreting his or her past in terms of a generalized pattern, the story model, the individual begins to identify with the generic type of person referenced by that model—*I am a born-again Christian, an alcoholic, a Marrano*—as well as to identify with other individuals who describe their lives in that way.

In the case of urban Marranos, the shared narrative pattern I call the Marrano story was not nearly so formulaic as the AA personal story or the Christian conversion narrative, nor was it learned solely or even primarily by listening to others. Instead, it was shaped largely through social interaction—with tourists, outreach workers, and rabbis. During my fieldwork I observed as new members arrived and over time became adept at telling their story, for it was elicited in virtually every interaction they had with foreign visitors. When I asked Dulce how many times she had told her story to people from abroad, for example, she sighed, "Oh, Naomi, I really have no idea." "Ten times? Twenty?" I asked. "At least forty," she replied, and then started counting them: at least eleven visiting rabbis, including the chief Sephardic rabbi from Israel, who had come to evaluate their situation; the several package tour groups that had visited HaShalom in recent years; dozens of individual tourists, whom she met at HaShalom or at services at Shaaré Tikva; and six or seven Jewish outreach workers. In Porto, Menorá received fewer visitors due to its distance from Lisbon, Portugal's primary tourist destination. Nonetheless, there, too, a series of rabbis and tour groups had passed through. Most such visits were scheduled informally, online, through mutual contacts. Individual tourists also found their way to HaShalom and Menorá through word of mouth, web searches, or meeting a member at Shaaré Tikvá or the Porto synagogue and subsequently visiting the group as a whole.

The precise context in which Dulce and the others told their stories varied with the visitor. Some foreign rabbis elected to speak with each member individually in a side room, interviewing them as if gauging their sincerity as potential converts. Others elicited a brief narrative from each in the presence of all, going around the table one by one. Tour group visits were far less formal; at both HaShalom and Menorá there was typically a period of standing around and mingling, in which tourists would ask Marranos bluntly about their background: "Did your grandmother say special prayers?" "Did your parents tell you that you were Jewish? How old were you?" "Are you circumcised?" Or even just, "Tell me your story!" Outreach workers generally addressed questions to the group as a whole, expecting, some later confided with a tinge of disappointment, to hear more about grandmothers lighting candles without knowing why or doing such-and-such a thing mysteriously on Friday nights.

When Rabbi Ezra and Chaya Kaplan met with HaShalom members for the first time, Chaya did not hesitate. "Now," she began heartily, smiling encouragingly at the twelve people seated around the long meeting table, "tell us about yourselves. We want to know. Do you have crypto-Jewish families?"

She turned to her right, where Tiago sat. He answered, "Since childhood, I've wanted to be a Jew. I don't have a story of my family having been Jewish, but I have suspicions. I asked my father about it before he died, and he laughed. That's all."

After a pause, Chaya turned to Pedro, who been involved with HaShalom less than a year. "What about you?"

"My grandmother was I guess what you could call a *schochet* [Yid.; a ritual slaughterer, following *kashrut*]. When I went to her house as a child, I saw that she would kill chickens in a hidden place in the yard and she'd mumble something. She didn't want me to see."

Chaya took a notebook from her purse and began writing, then said, "And she did it quickly, I imagine." (Here Chaya was referring to a tenet of kosher slaughter, the requisite speed of the single cut that must sever all major arteries, veins, and nerves in the neck at once.) "How old were you?"

PEDRO: I think I was six or seven at the time.

CHAYA: What else did she do?"

PEDRO: Ahh—there were no lights on in her house on Saturday.

CHAYA: Mmmmm. Does your family say they are Jews?

PEDRO: They say they are Jews, but also that they are Christians.

CHAYA: What about holidays? Was there anything about Hanukkah?

Pedro paused, pursed his lips, and exhaled, thinking. Another pause.

> CHAYA: The big holiday for crypto-Jews, we hear, is Pesach [Heb.; Passover]. Was there anything about that, around Easter? Using different dishes, maybe?
>
> PEDRO: No, nothing like that.
>
> CHAYA: Did they sing any songs?
>
> PEDRO: No.
>
> CHAYA: So they say they are Jews, and they also say they are Christians.
>
> PEDRO: Only my father's brothers and my grandmother said, "We are Jews."
>
> CHAYA: And what did it mean to you, when you were a boy, to know that you are a Jew?
>
> PEDRO: It was not very important. I was not brought up a religious person.

Chaya's questions clearly led Pedro down certain paths of inquiry: grand-parental practices, syncretic holiday rituals, cross-generational transmission of identity as Jews. But beyond the grandmother slaughtering chickens in a particular way (the most common practice by far in the life stories I heard), Pedro was unable to provide a coherent Marrano narrative. At that point, he had explained his background just a few times. It was only months later, after interactions with a series of different interlocutors, that I heard him deliver a detailed, coherent, chronologically ordered version of his life story. Dulce, on the other hand, was able to respond to Chaya's request immediately with a lengthy, well-structured, compelling narrative, as she had already been doing for years.

Opportunities to share the Marrano story with an appreciative audience offered a powerful validation of the teller's emergent sense of self. One summer evening three men from HaShalom managed to enter Shaaré Tikvá for the Shabbat service. As they waited for it to begin, they noticed a large, clearly international tour group in attendance. A synagogue member who was sympathetic to the urban Marranos brought the Israeli tour director over, telling him, "You might like to meet these men; they are B'nai Anusim." The tour director became very excited. "This is history, right in front of us!" he exclaimed. After the service he invited them to join the tour group for dinner at the hotel, suggesting they could share their stories with everyone afterward. As Tiago subsequently described it,

He was really, really curious. It was like a little boy seeing a bear in the zoo for the first time, you know? He asked Tomás, then Paulo, then me to talk, to tell our stories. I didn't want to go, because you know I'm really shy. But he insisted. He said, "Please, please!" So we went.

We were in front of the room. We each stood up in front of everyone. And there I told my story yet another time. . . . First Tomás told his story. He cried and cried—Tomás, when he remembers his grandmother, "the rabbi" [of her village], he cries and cries and cries. Tomás was the hit of the day. The tourists were absolutely enchanted by him. They'd never seen a Marrano. And more than that, a Marrano who talked about how he remembered his grandmother who taught him prayers and all that. And who cried woefully. I mean, they'd never seen anything like that.

So then Paulo told his story, and I told mine. They were very moved. The tour director asked us to come back the next day, because he wanted to interview us and tape it. He had a little video camera. He wanted to show the video when he gives lectures about Marranos.

Although the tour group did not ask any questions, instead allowing the men to narrate their stories in full, their emotional response was obvious and, for Tiago, unforgettable. He found potent validation in the tourists' reaction, not to mention the tour director's desire to use his story to teach others about Portuguese Marranos. After their negative interactions with the mainstream Jewish community, Tiago and the others were never sure that their Jewishness would be recognized. In this light, sharing their stories was, as Catarina put it, a way of "staking a claim":

> You take people who have a claim, and the claim is, "We're Jewish." And for the most part, we have nothing to show for it. Some can tell stories about, I don't know, deformed rituals that have been passed on and sometimes are beyond recognition. But some of us don't even have that. So it's a way of staking your claim, really, and to make yourself more Jewish and more admissible. Because the truth is, we're always expecting someone to tell us, "You're not really Jewish." Always. That's why we're so grateful every time someone visits. They visit, and they listen to us, and they leave us feeling that yes, we're worthy of something.

Given their sensitivity to visitors' responses, it is not surprising that over time their narratives began to resemble each other in both structure and highlighted details, subtly influenced by their interlocutors' questions and reactions, as well as by hearing one another's stories and reflecting on their own memories in light of what they were learning about crypto-Judaism.

Such subtle convergence of self-narratives is very common among populations united by acquiring or newly expressing a second identity. As I noted in the previous chapter, each telling of a life story is shaped by context, audience, mood, and the like, and decisions about which details to include change over time. From gay and lesbian coming-out stories to the "personal journey" narratives of secular Jews who become Orthodox, from illness narratives of fibromyalgia sufferers to transgender narratives of self-recognition, numerous studies have shown that each of these story models, too, has a standard structure, with implicitly codified turning points and a common narrative arc.[12] Over time, as newcomers are socialized into the group, the structure and emphasis of their narratives shift and become more alike. In the case of the Marrano story, this convergence was primarily around types of indicative clues and the narrative arc of fascination and (self-)discovery, hinging on a pivotal flash of recognition.

By the time I concluded my research in 2006, most members' life stories contained the following elements:

1) a long-standing interest in Jews and "things Jewish";

2) family origins in villages in Trás-os-Montes or Beira Alta;

3) familial oral history of having Jewish ancestry;

4) in most cases, familial or individual antipathy to the Catholic Church; less frequently, children not baptized or baptized quite late; parents and/or grandparents not married in the church; and/or a familial preference for the Old Testament;

5) memories involving the grandparents' generation; grandmothers identified as central actors who revealed the family's hidden Jewish past, preserved crypto-Jewish practices, or provided the conduit of Jewish descent;

6) a pivotal revelation or climactic moment of recognition, where learning about a particular Jewish practice or ritual object abruptly made previously unexplained family behaviors or possessions intelligible as signs of Jewish origin: the "diagnosis," as Catarina called it;

7) listing of specific practices and objects from childhood now seen to be remnants of Judaism, for example, lights not turned on in the home on Saturdays, newly recognized as observance of Shabbat; a fine, white fringed shawl, passed down over generations, reinterpreted as a prayer shawl; a rural grandmother's method of killing chickens, now identified as the ancient practice of kosher slaughter;

8) discovery of entire branches of "New Christian" surnames (names of trees, etc.) in the family and, in some stories, family lines in which everyone married only within the immediate community or extended family;

9) feeling attracted to and inexplicably at home with Judaism and/or the Jewish people;

10) a strong desire to "return," to be recognized as a Jew and to find belonging among the Jewish people, and frustration with not being able to do so in Portugal.

This common structure and content arose organically in response to interpersonal reinforcement and implicit direction from listeners' lines of questioning, apparent interest or disinterest, and expressions of emotion, all of which tended to be fairly consistent. Life stories are an inherently dialogical medium, and an overwhelming majority of foreign Jews were remarkably sympathetic interlocutors. In a happy confluence of cultural models, they too found it plausible that the desire to be Jewish could arise from ancestral and mystical causes. On hearing that a few members of the Marrano associations weren't sure they had Jewish ancestry, some visitors charitably suggested that of course they must, and because of the forced conversions they just didn't know it; that would explain why they felt as they did. Many more commented that the urban Marranos exemplified the *pintele yid* (Yid.; little Jewish dot)—the essential spark of Jewishness said to reside within all Jews, even those unaware of their Jewish origins, that unexpectedly awakens and leads one to want to live as a Jew. And Porto's Shavei Israel rabbi taught that Jewish souls recognize the Hebrew prayers; when a Catholic individual attended services and was moved, he said, he knew they had a Jewish soul that had somehow been misdirected into a non-Jewish body. From casual tourists to Orthodox rabbis to secular outreach activists, a wide range of foreign Jews found the urban Marranos' stories of self-discovery and essential Jewishness entirely coherent.[13]

Sometimes the visitors' role in reinforcing the Marrano story was more overt. In late 2005, for example, the Shavei Israel rabbi in Porto suggested that participants write out, refine, and practice their stories in anticipation of sharing them with foreign visitors and, eventually, a *beit din* that might recognize their "return." Anshel Rappaport, a Canadian outreach activist who visited both associations several times, particularly emphasized the importance of emotion, asking for well-crafted, heartrending personal narratives that he could circulate to raise material, educational, and moral support from North American Jews. During a meeting at HaShalom, he urged the group's leaders to make it a priority:

> We need crypto-Jews all over the world to be in touch and telling their story. We need poetry, plays, music to tell the story of the agony of your ancestors. We haven't found a way to get your story on the radar over there [in North America]. We need to put Portugal on the map! The Society for Crypto-Judaic Studies has a newsletter, but you need to write articles! Tell your stories! Write moving stories about how you found your ancestors. You need to tell your stories, even if not as individuals, then as organizations.

Thus, filtering their familial and personal history into the format of the Marrano story was not only a fundamental part of the process through which participants developed an individual and collective identity as Marranos. As an element of their hoped-for appearance before a *beit din* and a means of generating attention, connection, and support from abroad, the Marrano story was also instrumental.

FLEXIBLE CATEGORIES AND TRANSIENT STATES

In the previous chapter, I described how urban Marranos developed a sense of themselves as essentially Jewish, more or less in isolation, based on cognition and emotion and articulated in terms of ancestral and mystical causality. In this chapter, we have seen how they came to view themselves not only as essential Jews but as *Marranos* through interaction with others. This intersubjective constitution of self operated both on a local level, as a matter of belonging—"We are Marranos"—and in conversation with foreign visitors, who asked, "Are you Marranos?" and wanted very much to hear a positive answer. By adopting a new set of behaviors and attitudes in dialogue with other ancestral Jews and with tourists and outreach workers, as well as with the mainstream communities in absentia, they came to understand themselves as members of a coherent group of like individuals.

Recall that at the time of their founding both Menorá and HaShalom counted among their members people with no known Jewish ancestry but a general interest in Judaism, others who identified as descendants of Inquisition-era Jews, people who felt that they had a Jewish soul but knew of no Jewish family background, and a few who were already Jewish according to halakhah. While the several dozen who were interested in Judaism solely as an intellectual matter eventually dropped away, the two associations never lost their otherwise heterogeneous character. As stated in HaShalom's 1999 statutes, membership was to be extended to "all Jews and *resgatados* [redeemed ones]," where *resgatados* included "crypto-Jews, Marranos, [and] all Righteous Proselytes"—that is, Gentile converts. Yet both associations developed an identity as "Marrano" institutions, eliding entirely the variety and complexity of their members' individual paths to an essential Jewish identity.

We have returned to the issue of self-classification, specifically what the category "Marranos" might signify under these conditions and why individual members continued to use divergent terms in reference to themselves. In both groups, the most vocal and visible members described themselves interchangeably as Marranos—descendants of long-ago forced converts, following Barros Basto's broad application of the word—or B'nai Anusim, depending on their audience. *Marrano* was most commonly used among themselves or when speaking with Portuguese friends who were not involved; *B'nai Anusim,* the rabbinic term for forced converts, they used among themselves or when interacting with foreign visitors, unless the visitor used *Marrano* first. Most learned to call themselves B'nai Anusim from foreign Jews, typically online or in encounters with Orthodox outreach workers like the Shavei Israel rabbis. As a term of individual self-reference, some preferred B'nai Anusim, or simply Anusim, because it emphasized the role of their ancestors' suffering and gave a Hebrew name to their experience. Others preferred to call themselves Marranos, proudly marking their identification with an ancestral Jewish resistance specific to the Portuguese context. Whatever term they chose, these most vocal members felt strongly that their ancestors were Jewish before 1497 and had suffered for their faith. As founders and leaders, they gave the associations their profile. Faced with just two options for self-designation—"Jewish" or "Marrano"—on HaShalom's membership form, most newcomers chose the latter, despite any misgivings they may have had. But not all did so, and indeed not all assumed that their ancestors had been Jewish prior to the Inquisition. In light of the participation of individuals who simply wanted to convert to Judaism, as well as a few whom most Jews would recognize as undeniably Jewish according to halakhah, how do we make sense of the continuing use of *Marranos,* or the affectionate *marranitos,* as a catchall for the entire group? Three cases help to clarify the matter.

Nuno and Luisa were a young married couple who joined HaShalom together. A few years earlier, after an extended period of religious exploration,

Nuno had decided that he wanted to convert to Judaism. His decision was based solely on what he could learn from the internet and books he ordered online. Eventually Luisa decided that she too would like to convert. Neither entered HaShalom with any suspicion that they might have Jewish ancestry, nor did they articulate their identity in those terms. They simply wanted to convert, and they made no secret of it. Many things about the religion attracted them. Each had been raised in a minimally culturally Catholic home; their families were supportive of their decision to become Jews. Nuno first encountered HaShalom members at the Shavei Israel rabbi's classes on Judaism, and they invited him to a meeting at Anshei Emet. When I asked why he joined a Marrano association, rather than pursuing conversion at Shaaré Tikvá, he explained that he shared the members' experience of rejection:

> I really didn't know what *Marrano* or *B'nai Anusim* meant. I didn't know what I was going to find there. But what's important is that I really identified with that group, because they were people that—It was a much more friendly, familial environment. That was something I didn't find at all when I tried to go to Shaaré Tikvá, where the atmosphere was much colder. So I identified with the group, not in the sense of having Jewish ancestors, because as far as I know I don't, but I identified with them because of the rejection, *rejection*. They had all been stopped at the gate, and all that. And that happened to me, too. So I identified with them because of that. We all had a kind of stigma.

Although they knew nothing about Marranos and had never heard of the forced conversions, Nuno and his wife were immediately accepted at HaShalom on the basis of their shared sense of stigma and rejection by the mainstream community. As a working-class couple with no social ties to Portugal's Jewish world, they had no clear means of entry, and they had not felt welcome at the synagogue. They claimed neither to be crypto-Jews like the people of Belmonte nor to be B'nai Anusim like most of the group's members, but they too were *outsiders,* and hence they were welcomed. While they were not exactly Marranos in the same sense as the others, they were considered *marranitos,* counted among the group's core members by virtue of their common rejection.

Cécile Rodrigues, too, encountered rejection at the mainstream synagogue. But unlike any other member of either association, Cécile was neither Portuguese nor a descendant of Inquisition-era hidden Jews. A soft-spoken, always elegantly dressed poet in her fifties, Cécile was born in Paris to

Austrian Jewish parents. They were Holocaust survivors who hid their Judaism during the war, in order to avoid deportation, and then never reclaimed it. Cécile discovered in adulthood that they were Jews and set about learning what it meant. She had married a Portuguese immigrant in Paris in the 1980s and raised a family with him there; after his premature death, she relocated to Lisbon, where she attempted to attend services at Shaaré Tikvá. She was asked to prove that she was Jewish, something she could not do, as her parents had left no trace of their prewar Jewish life. When she consulted the newly arrived Shavei Israel rabbi, he explained that if she wanted to be recognized as a Jew she would have to convert.[14] He suggested that she attend his classes, where she met Dulce and other HaShalom members. She soon realized that they had spiritual and emotional experiences in common. "There are two kinds of crypto-Judaism," she told me. "Historical and individual. In my family it was individual; for the people at HaShalom it was historical." Cécile may not have been a Portuguese Marrano, but with her "lost" Jewish ancestry the association's leaders immediately saw her as one of them.

For the third case, consider the anthropologist. As I noted in the introduction, I was raised with a family story that my father's Portuguese ancestors had long ago been Jewish. I shared this story with leaders of HaShalom and Menorá when I requested permission to study them. Some months later, when asked to fill in the HaShalom membership form, I checked the Marrano box—I had already learned that they were using it in the expanded sense of "pre-Inquisition Jewish descent"—and wrote "on my father's side" (*do lado do pai*) in the margin. I also checked the Jewish box, despite not having been raised religiously Jewish, and added "on my mother's side" (*do lado da mãe*), because my mother is of Ashkenazi origin. They asked me no further questions, and I was readily welcomed into the group as a participant-researcher. Toward the end of my fieldwork, however, the criteria for full participation began to narrow. In late 2005, with the help of Rabbi Ezra and Chaya Kaplan, HaShalom members set about creating an independent Jewish community (see chapter 5). At a series of contentious meetings, the group's leaders came to the decision that only "Marranos" (or "Anusim") and people pursuing conversion could be founding members. And so, Catarina told me apologetically, I could not be counted among them. Cécile would be, however. I was confused and yet fascinated by how the lines of inclusion and exclusion were drawn. Clearly it was not simply a matter of ancestry. Neither Cécile's parents' unbroken Austrian Jewish descent nor my own family lore of Portuguese ancestors who lost their Jewishness seemed to be relevant. On what basis was Cécile eligible to be a founding member, when I was not? The reply: my mother was Jewish, by origin if not by affiliation, and her Jewishness was never in doubt. Whatever my own sense of self might be, to the group I was a *judia de carteirinha* and could in principle find acceptance at Shaaré Tikvá. Cécile, on the other hand, could not prove her Jewishness, so she was included.[15]

These three cases suggest that "Marrano" was a flexible and porous category for people who defined themselves in those terms. Sometimes they used it in a narrow historical sense, referring to people who maintained hidden religious practices, that is, crypto-Jews, as in Belmonte. More often, it carried a quasi-racial meaning: anyone of pre-Inquisition Jewish ancestry. Finally, there was its categorical usage, defining members of the two associations on the basis of experience: collectively, the Marranos (or *marranitos*) were those who felt that they were Jewish-in-essence, but were rejected by the mainstream communities on the basis of not being sufficiently Jewish. They were those who had been refused entry, who had been told they could not wear a prayer shawl, who were not counted for a *minyan*. Hence to be included among the *marranitos* was not necessarily a matter of ancestry or hidden religious practice at all. It was, instead, no more and no less than to have had one's claim to an essential Jewish identity—whether ancestral or spiritual—denied.

Thus, not all Marranos (or *marranitos*) were B'nai Anusim, where the latter was understood to mean descendants of Portuguese forced converts, and not all B'nai Anusim were Marranos. Several other individuals who occasionally came to lectures and other events hosted by the associations believed they had pre-Inquisition Jewish ancestry, but were not interested in becoming Jews—however defined—in the present. Members of HaShalom and Menorá did not consider them Marranos, nor would these individuals have called themselves that. They were, however, recognized as fellow B'nai Anusim. Tellingly, when planning a national meeting in 2004 the leaders of HaShalom and Menorá went back and forth about how to describe the event for publicity. Should it be the National Meeting of Portuguese Jewish Associations? That was too broad, as the Jewish communities of Lisbon and Porto might well consider it their purview and take it over. What about the National Meeting of Marranos? That wasn't quite what they had in mind, as people would likely mistake it as referring to crypto-Jews like those in Belmonte, which might discourage the intended participants from coming. In the end, they decided to call it the National Meeting of Portuguese Anusim, the most inclusive and yet specific term for the people they hoped to attract.

Nonetheless, throughout the meeting speaker after speaker referred to the associations' members individually and collectively as *Marranos*. That was the term that described their common predicament.

MAKING MARRANOS?

The social category "Marrano" has long had a clear referent in the Jewish world, meaning one who practices Judaism in secret after having converted to another religion (Roth 1941). Although less widely used in Portugal, there, too, it has had a fairly stable meaning, referring since the time of Barros Basto either to crypto-Jews or to their descendants, defined in a quasi-ethnic sense (Carvalho 1999). The material I have presented in this chapter suggests that in early twenty-first-century Portugal, *Marrano* carried yet another meaning. It named a *status,* a relative social position, rather than an essentialized ethnic or religious category. To be a Marrano was to be an outsider who felt that he or she had a valid claim to Jewishness that had been denied by the country's normative Jewish communities, gatekeepers to the Jewish world. As *marranitos,* HaShalom and Menorá members understood themselves to be hovering betwixt and between—not between Catholicism and Judaism, as the historical definition of *Marrano* would have it, but between realizing they were Jewish within and being accepted on that basis among the Jewish people. Despite the many stumbling blocks they faced, most believed that somehow, someday, they would leave their "Marrano" status behind. Tomás, whose grandmother taught him secret prayers as a child, explained it simply: "After I make my return I will be a Jew, not a Marrano. Because Marrano, Anusim, those are words I didn't know when I was a child. I was just Jewish."

Shifting our focus from the usual ontological question—*What is a Marrano?*—to a phenomenological one—*What is it to be a Marrano?*—enables us to recognize that, as with all social categories, urban Marranos are socially and culturally produced, not born. As I have argued throughout this chapter, the Marrano self was a formation that developed at a particular moment in each of these people's lives, the outcome of an identifiable set of historical and social circumstances. So who, in the end, were these twenty-first-century "Marranos"? Simply put, they were a heterogeneous group of people who shared a set of longings and experiences. They wanted to be able to be Jewish in a way that would be acceptable to and recognized by the Jewish world. They wanted to feel they belonged. They wanted to learn about

Judaism, to determine for themselves what kind of Jewishness they would embrace in their daily lives. They wanted contact with Jews who could help them externalize the sense of self they had nurtured within. They wanted "papers," some official indication that they had been accepted as Jews by some Jewish authority. And they were individuals, each with a distinct life history, who found their way to each other because of a shared desire to pursue a Jewish identity and a common experience of rejection. What they were not was the storied crypto-Jews immediately imagined by would-be visitors upon hearing that there were Marranos in Lisbon and Porto. They were not the Marranos of the rural interior. There was nothing hidden about them.

Despite their disparate paths to a Jewish identity, together members of the Marrano associations developed a set of defining practices, dispositions, and opportunities for learning that nurtured their emerging sense of self and provided a place of belonging, however socially separate from other parts of their lives. Recent ethnographies of adult identity transitions, such as Sturm's (2010) analysis of white Americans who embrace Cherokee ancestry, similarly find that social connections with other newcomers, whether institutionalized or ad hoc, play a pivotal role in processes of socialization and solidarity building. In cases like the Cherokee race-shifters and urban Marranos, who adopt a social identity into which others are born, newcomers often find themselves positioned in ways other than they expect: as inauthentic, as "non-Jews," or, in the Cherokee case, as "wannabes." Even when their outsider classification is expected, as in Sarah Benor's (2012) study of non-Orthodox Jews who adopt Orthodox Judaism, connections with other "aspirants" provide safe spaces in which to navigate the transition. Among the Orthodox, social differentiation persists between individuals who were born Orthodox and those who entered as adults (known as BTs, *ba'alei teshuva*), with the latter remaining "in a state of in-betweenness, a cultural borderland" (Benor 2012: 17). Like the urban Marranos, they consciously and unconsciously acknowledge their difference through hybrid behavioral and linguistic practices. And, in all three cases, such hybrid practices become a norm into which subsequent newcomers are socialized.

Taking on a new identity does not necessarily mean discarding who one was before. Different facets of the self are called forth in different social settings, reinforced by choices about dress, behavior, even the name by which one introduces oneself. The contexts in which this occurs are not neutral: as anthropologist Dorinne Kondo (1990: 43) reminds us, we must ask "how selves *in the plural* are constructed variously in various situations, how these constructions can be complicated and enlivened by multiplicity and ambiguity, and how they shape, and are shaped by, relations of power." In this chapter I have traced a series of situations through which this diverse group of individuals came together under the ambiguous banner of "Marranos." They adopted the term following a specific historical precedent, Barros Basto and his movement, within a structurally similar system of power relations. Like Barros Basto, they were born into neither a mainstream Jewish milieu nor a crypto-Jewish one, but they felt strongly that they were Jews and should be accepted as such. It was the tension between their internal sense of self and their treatment by others that led them to conceive of themselves as Marranos. Indeed, as my return to the United States drew near, some participants privately told me that they thought the entire discourse of "Marranos" would not have arisen were it not for their continuous rejection, as individuals, from the mainstream communities. Without Portugal's myriad forms of social hierarchy and exclusion, from social class to closed networks, there would have been no need to tell their Marrano story. Said one longtime participant,

> People are trying to legitimate their very valid spiritual aspirations with the past. So they present themselves this way, and Jews think, "Oh, they're trying to follow and honor their ancestors, they're people of such valor, doing this."
>
> We cannot deny the past in Portugal. It's a given fact, the past, what happened here [to the Jews] in Portugal. And so here we are, always digging, digging, digging into the past to legitimate why we knock at the doors of the synagogues. I know sometimes people are lying to themselves, they don't have any clues at all, but what can we do? Because if they just knock at the door and say, "Oh, I want to convert," it would be probably worse than it is to knock at the door and say, "Oh, I have this ancestry." Well, it's easier to explain this way.
>
> Now we have a situation in Portugal where it's the only way people can try to get into the synagogues. Because right away, it's "Why? Why? Why?" I know the tradition is, you need to knock at the door three times, and the rabbi should refuse you three times, that's the tradition, challenging the convert to be sure he really wants to be a Jew, because being a Jew is not belonging to a country club, you know all that.
>
> But in Portugal, it's exacerbated. The initial refusals are exacerbated. So people try to have—And it's easier, it's very common, in Portugal, "Oh! I have Jewish ancestors! My surname is the name of a tree, so I'm a Jew!" Of course. It's much easier.
>
> So we think, "Hmm. Well, he's not a Marrano, but OK. He's with me. He makes another member in the army." Because we need each other. But it was

created by them! Refusing, refusing, confronting us, ridiculing us, treating us badly, all that produced this situation, and it's just never going to end.

While few would suggest so openly that others might be lying to themselves or exaggerating their ancestral claims, several members said they suspected the politicized emphasis on being a collectivity of "Marranos" who wished to "return," rather than individuals of putative Jewish descent seeking conversion, had arisen as a way of attracting attention and bringing help to their cause. For however much they may have valued the experiences of their ancestors, most did not want to remain defined as "Marranos" at all; they hoped to find a way out of that in-between state and live as what, by their own definition, they had been all along: Jews. It is to their efforts to engage foreign Jews to that end, thus shifting from the Portuguese social space to a global one, that we now turn.

FOUR

"My Lost Brothers and Sisters!"

TOURISM AND CULTURAL LOGICS OF KINSHIP

IN 1926, THE BRITISH JOURNALIST Lucien Wolf submitted his report on the Marrano situation to the Alliance Israélite Universelle and the Anglo-Jewish Association. As recounted in chapter 1, he had spent a month traveling through Portugal's northeastern hinterland, guided by Samuel Schwarz and Artur Barros Basto, to assess whether and how Jewish organizations could help Marrano villagers return to the Jewish world. His recommendations were measured, but about one thing he was emphatic: the Jewish people had an obligation to lend their support, for reasons of historical debt and, equally importantly, of kinship.

> From time to time we have waxed enthusiastic over other more or less dubious off-shoots from Jewry, such as the Chinese Jews of Kai-feng-fu, the Falashas of Abyssinia, the Black Jews of Cochin and the Daggatoun of Timbuctu. But these Marranos are much nearer to us. They are part and parcel of European Jewish history, the near kindred of all our Sephardi congregations in Western Europe and America, and the descendants of men and women who for two and a half centuries waged an heroic fight in defense of Judaism for which their co-religionists can never sufficiently testify their admiration and their gratitude. They have a claim upon us which we cannot put aside. If we may not be able to satisfy it to the full, we should, at any rate, not spare the effort to do so. (Wolf 1926: 19)

The outpouring of funds that followed, not to mention the ensuing stream of curious travelers, suggests that Wolf was not alone in his assessment. Although their numbers have waxed and waned, Jewish tourists and outreach activists have traveled to Belmonte and other Marrano-identified sites for nearly a century, generating an ongoing foreign presence no less conspicuous today than it was in the 1920s. For nearly as long, these same travelers have visited and attended services at the synagogues in Lisbon and Porto. As anthropologist Laurence Loeb (1989) observed, whatever their degree of religious affiliation, Jews often become "avid anthropologists" of Jewish life when abroad (cf. Loewe and Hoffman 2002). This touristic openness to learning about local life was not lost on those who would ultimately create Menorá and HaShalom. In the mid-1990s, Dulce Oliveira, Ricardo Carvalho, and others began to notice that after services independent travelers frequently approached synagogue-goers with questions. To their surprise, quite unlike the dubious reaction of the local Jewish community, tourists assumed that they descended from Inquisition-era Marranos and were eager to hear their stories. Over time, as I discuss below, they became more deliberate in seeking contact with foreign visitors, who stood to provide the Jewish knowledge and encouragement they lacked.

It was during this period, the mid-1990s, that the first commercial package tours of "Jewish Portugal" began. Following a thematic marketing campaign by the Portuguese National Tourist Office, large providers like Elderhostel (now Road Scholar) and several small, private tour companies in the United States, Israel, France, and England began offering bus tours on what quickly became a standard circuit through the countryside (Leite 2007). In addition to a scheduled opportunity for participants to meet "the last Marranos" in Belmonte—"the climax of the trip," a British tour organizer told me in 2002—arrangements were made in Lisbon and Porto for participants to attend synagogue services en masse. This too Menorá and HaShalom's future leaders noted, and they soon realized that tour groups did more than attend services: itineraries typically included a tour of each synagogue and an informal meeting with community representatives. As the Marrano associations grew and their reception in the synagogues worsened, their leaders sought to arrange similar visits.

The standard, scheduled meeting between Jewish heritage package tourists and members of local Jewish communities is a peculiar institution. It is predicated upon touristic assumptions of mutual relatedness, mutual curiosity, and mutual intelligibility, assumptions that are not always warranted. Framed by tour providers as an opportunity for genuine interaction, a once-in-a-lifetime opportunity to speak informally with "the Jews of_____," the meeting may be a rote performance for those local community members who have already met several tour groups and will likely meet many more; after the third or fourth time, the groups tend to blur into one another. Sometimes the local community receives an institutional donation for their trouble, folded into the package tour price or given spontaneously by individual tourists. On other occasions, there is no monetary benefit. Why local community members would take time out of their daily lives to meet a busload of tourists is rarely a question tourists consider. A visit with "members of the community" is listed on the itinerary, and given that the tourists are curious about them, surely they are curious about the tourists as well. Underlying this attitude is the still more pervasive presumption that it is good for Jews everywhere to be in touch with one another, even if only fleetingly. It is this presumption of Jewish *peoplehood,* with its attendant imagery of interconnection and mutual dependence for survival, that lends poignancy and force to the idea of traveling to meet "lost" or "isolated" Jews—Wolf's "off-shoots from Jewry"—in far-off lands.

In the Jewish imagination, Marranos are nothing if not "lost," revered for carrying their Jewish identity secretly, in isolation, for centuries. As we saw in chapter 1, they have long served as a touchstone, a potent symbol of Jewish survival despite terrible odds. For many Jews, they are proof positive of *netsach yisrael* (Heb.; [the] eternal people Israel), the indomitable spark of the Jewish spirit over generations. The opportunity to meet an actual community of "Marranos," widely understood to mean crypto-Jews, is invariably an emotionally weighty experience. In accompanying nearly a dozen groups of tourists to Belmonte, I watched as men and women from numerous countries reached out to touch the arm or hand of a representative of the community, their voices cracking with emotion, exclaiming that the person in front of them was living proof that the Inquisition did not succeed. That the community is located in a high mountain village more than four hours from Lisbon adds to the impact of the visit: one must travel a long way to find them. They are country people, their elderly women still dressed in the traditional widow's black blouse and skirt, kerchief tied under the chin. It is easy, though patently erroneous, to imagine that one's tour group must be the first to have made the journey. The profound language barrier means that the nature of their relationship with tourism—it funds their synagogue, as they routinely offer a home-cooked dinner with community members for a fee that tour providers quietly fold into the package tour price—is obscured. Instead, the visit appears to be hosted entirely out of local desire for connection with the Jewish world—which, of course, it may also be.

During my fieldwork, Menorá and HaShalom were not yet standard components of the Jewish heritage tour itinerary, certainly not in the way Belmonte had already been for over a decade. Between 2002 and 2005, four large package-tour groups visited HaShalom and two visited Menorá, in each case because there was a personal connection between one of the tour leaders and the Marrano associations. But both associations also attracted a steady stream of independent travelers, among them Jewish heritage tourists, seekers of Jewish roots from the Portuguese diaspora, outreach workers, and rabbis. As on a package tour, the independent traveler would typically expect—and receive—an opportunity to meet informally, one-on-one, with their members. These visits were arranged in advance, via email, or impromptu after a chance encounter at one of the synagogues. Although few urban Marranos spoke fluent English, the touristic lingua franca, they were otherwise superficially intelligible to their visitors. Like most of the tourists who came to meet them, they were urban, apparently middle class, educated, and relatively fashionably dressed. Their most exotic characteristics were the aura of mystery and ancestral dignity that surrounded them collectively as Marranos (or "B'nai Anusim"), and the life stories they told. Still, for the most part tourists treated them only slightly less reverentially than they did the people of Belmonte.

For urban Marranos, foreign Jews, too, were both superficially intelligible and slightly exotic. As de facto representatives of the Jewish world, their brief appearances in Portugal offered glimpses into a life the Marranos found tantalizingly unfamiliar and yet hoped somehow to embrace as their own. Just as the travelers had a long-held image of "the Marrano" that they brought with them to the encounter, so too had the local people long imagined, and in many cases idealized, "the Jews" beyond Portugal's borders. But unlike their visitors, who generally came to Portugal once and did not return, over time the urban Marranos had dozens of encounters with foreign Jewish travelers and their imaginings and reactions to them began to change.

In this chapter and the next, I examine the context, texture, and overall character of their face-to-face interactions, including change over time. Here, I focus in particular on the desires and conceptual frameworks that led them to each other and through which they made sense of each other's presence and actions. Most forms of direct tourist-toured interaction studied by anthropologists occur within highly mediated contexts that emphasize difference, such as ethnic crafts markets or formal cultural performances (Bruner 2005; Causey 2003; Little 2004). Among Marranos and their foreign visitors, on the other hand, there was a shared assumption of fundamental commonality, communicative transparency, and goodwill that resulted in surprisingly informal exchanges. However, beneath the appearance of mutual understanding and even emotional intimacy, culturally distinct structures of reasoning led to continual partial misunderstanding, or *communicative slippage,* both in the moment of encounter and after. And yet far from causing discord, it was precisely that slippage that enabled their interactions to work smoothly.

MEETING MARRANOS

Without two key individuals, Elsa Cruz and Graciana Mayer, it is unlikely that the urban Marranos would have become an object of sustained international attention. Told from childhood that she descended from Jews, Elsa was among the earliest members of HaShalom. In 1997, a year or two after she became involved in the group, the thirty-five-year-old mother of four obtained a tour-guide license and began collaborating with a local agency to offer three- to five-day Jewish heritage itineraries. At that point there was relatively little infrastructure for Jewish heritage tourism in Portugal, and initially her itineraries were designed for couples or families traveling in private cars. Thanks to the Portuguese National Tourist Office's efforts, interest grew quickly, and by 2002 she had expanded to package tours. Nonetheless, she charged very little. Her motivation, she said, was to bring Jews from abroad into contact with urban Marranos, or "crypto-Jews," as she called them. Her English-language website explained:

> Some think that three hundred years of Inquisition have left permanent marks in the lives of those whose ancestors were severely persecuted and that this fear can only be overcome by contact with other Jewish lives. If our tours enable further crypto-Jews to step forward ... we believe it is a privilege for those who choose to come.

Accordingly, her itineraries emphasized opportunities for informal contact with "crypto-Jewish" communities. In Porto she arranged visits to Menorá's headquarters, often followed by a member-led walking tour of the *judiaria;* in Lisbon she provided a brief reception with HaShalom members at Anshei Emet; and in Belmonte she offered the opportunity to meet former crypto-Jews, now Orthodox, and attend services at their synagogue. These face-to-face meetings were interspersed with stops at medieval Jewish sites throughout the country. Her itineraries thus presented the people visited in Porto, Lisbon, and Belmonte as collectively of a piece, described interchangeably as "crypto-Jews,"

"Marranos," or "Anusim" and implicitly linked to the medieval synagogues and *judiarias* along the way. Their very different histories were elided entirely.

Elsa's efforts were aided by Graciana Mayer, the Portuguese-South African founder of Nostálgia, the online forum for people exploring lost crypto-Jewish ancestry. Having made her own "return" decades earlier, Graciana sought to support anyone of Portuguese descent interested in ancestral Jewish religious and cultural roots—particularly her *primos* (Pt.; cousins), as she called them, still in Portugal. The two women met online in the mid-1990s. Thereafter, Graciana routinely sent potential clients to Elsa, mostly individuals who stumbled upon the Nostálgia website while planning a trip to Portugal and emailed her for travel advice. In turn, Elsa organized Graciana's two special-audience Conference-Tours. Graciana also frequently referred travelers to Menorá's president, who spoke adequate English. Between them, Elsa and Graciana were responsible for perhaps 50 percent of foreign visits to Menorá and HaShalom during my fieldwork.

As an activist working worldwide to connect descendants of Portuguese crypto-Jews with one another and provide information about Judaism, Graciana also collaborated with international organizations launching outreach to "Marranos," "crypto-Jews," or "Anusim." (Each organization used different terms in reference to the same population.) In her writing and public speaking, she too presented the urban Marranos as historically of a piece with Belmonte's crypto-Jewish community. Jewish outreach organizations followed her lead. Shavei Israel, in particular, produced a stream of press releases about their efforts among "the Marranos of Portugal," generating numerous reports in *Haaretz,* the *Jerusalem Post,* and Jewish newspapers worldwide.

The tours Elsa and Graciana created, the Nostálgia website and discussion forum, and Graciana's efforts to attract assistance from Jewish organizations had a domino effect. Tourists, activists, and educators passed through the doors of Menorá and HaShalom, seeking to meet, commune with, and assist these storied remnants of the Inquisition; thereafter, they posted travelogues, spoke to their social clubs and synagogues, and told friends about the trip. Informal publicity snowballed. HaShalom and Menorá enhanced their web presence, realizing there were Jews beyond Portugal's borders who appeared genuinely interested in their plight. Online, both associations used "Marranos," "B'nai Anusim," and "crypto-Jews" interchangeably in reference to their members, as did travelers who wrote or spoke publicly about meeting them. Consequently, the people of Menorá and HaShalom seemed a homogeneous group to would-be visitors, their individual paths to a Jewish identity obscured by the terms used to describe them as a collectivity.

No traveler arrives at his or her destination a blank slate. As Edward Bruner (2005: 22) puts it, "Tourists begin each trip with some preconceptions about the destination—a pretour narrative," that is, a composite, relatively consistent image of place and people based on information transmitted via popular culture, media reports, tourism marketing, and so forth. This information intersects with broader conceptual frameworks, *metanarratives* or *imaginaries,* that tourists carry about the nature of self and other, modernity and the exotic, home and away, assistance and the needy (Bruner 2005; Leite 2014; Selwyn 1996). While in Bruner's analysis the "pretour narrative" seems to be acquired passively, I found that many tourists actively sought information before traveling—via the internet, documentary films, historical texts, novels, public lectures, and any other source that would help them make the most of their journey. Indeed, for many the trip was the culmination of a lengthy engagement with the topic of Portuguese Jews and Marranos. Even those Jewish tourists who had no prior expectation of meeting Marranos were aware of their existence, whether through the vague consciousness of the Inquisition and its aftermath so common among Jews worldwide or, more prosaically, by having read the few lines about Portugal's "crypto-Jews" provided in popular guidebooks like *Lonely Planet, Frommer's,* and *The Rough Guide.* When they encountered self-identified Marranos or B'nai Anusim by happenstance at one of the synagogues, they were often as emotionally affected as those who had long planned for such a moment. Regardless of the circumstances that brought them to the urban Marranos, then, these foreign visitors already had a conceptual structure in place that provided a general frame and script for their face-to-face interactions.

Such preconceptualization of the touristic encounter was nowhere more apparent than among outreach activists and Portuguese-Jewish roots tourists, both of whom made their journeys with great anticipation and seriousness of purpose. Graciana Mayer's Conference-Tours brought the two types together, along with a few scholars of crypto-Judaism, past and present. In organizing the two tours, which attracted a combined total of fifty-two participants from ten countries, her goal was to provide an opportunity for learning and exchange between self-identified descendants of Portuguese crypto-Jews from abroad, "Anusim" in Portugal, and Jewish educators and activists who sought to help them all. Long before the tours began, participants anticipated the personal connections they would make and the kinds of encounters they would have. For those who traced their ancestry to Portugal's pre-Inquisition Jews, it would be a rare opportunity to meet people both on and off the bus who shared their experience of discovering and embracing lost Portuguese Jewish roots. For volunteer outreach activists, on the other hand, Graciana's status as self-styled "conduit to the Anusim" meant unique access to a group of "lost" Jews with whom they could forge personal bonds and assess logistical and educational needs. Both roots tourists and outreach activists articulated a clear sense of what they expected to find and why they cared so much: the people they would meet were long-lost *kin,* whether understood in concrete genealogical terms as fellow descendants of Portuguese Jewry, and hence "cousins," or in more diffuse terms as bearers of the common lineage that binds all Jewish people, making them fundamentally related to one another as a "family." Thus their face-to-face encounters with the Marranos would—did—have all the affective display of a family reunion.

Let us join such an encounter as it unfolds.[1] It is April 2004, and the Nostálgia Conference-Tour is in its second day. The group has just left the opulent Shaaré Tikvá synagogue, where they've had a strained interaction with a community representative. When asked about the community's treatment of Marranos, he claimed that there are just a few in Lisbon, all from Belmonte, and they attend Shaaré Tikvá. Several people disputed that, because we've already been told that there are Marranos gathering elsewhere in Lisbon. They're listed prominently on the itinerary, just after Shaaré Tikva:

> *April 18 (Lisbon):* Visit to the Shaaré Tikvá synagogue, still under restoration for the Centenary celebrations. The tour proceeds to Anshei Emet, originally the Ashkenazi synagogue but now the "home" of the Lisbon Crypto-Jewish community where we will be welcomed and have the opportunity of meeting members of this community.

The conversation at Shaaré Tikvá has ended in an impasse, with Graciana doing her best to smooth any ruffled feathers as we leave. Now we are back on the tour bus, twenty-six passengers on blue plush seats, luggage stowed in the hold below in anticipation of our departure from Lisbon and out into "Jewish Portugal." But first, as we make the short trip across town, Elsa, our guide, takes the bus microphone.

> We are on our way to Anshei Emet now. The synagogue was founded in 1925. It served the Ashkenazi community, and over time it had less and less

members, and it was closed down. But the key was passed down until it came to one man who decided to open up the synagogue again. He went there on Shabbat, alone or with one or two other Jews. Eventually he decided to open it to the Marranos, for he saw that it was difficult for us to be accepted at Shaaré Tikvá. We wanted to learn Hebrew and the prayers, and he gathered us and gave us a place to go.

Anshei Emet, "home" of the Lisbon Marranos! This is a moment many have eagerly awaited, the first of several encounters we will have with Portuguese Marranos over the coming week. An air of excitement rises as the bus pulls up to the curb and pauses, idling, for us to disembark. But where is the synagogue? All we can see is the decaying facade of a nondescript nineteenth-century row house, one in a series stretching down the block. Its paint is pocked and dusty, and the cracked sign for a long-closed mechanic's garage hangs above the entrance.

We follow Elsa and Graciana off the bus and onto the sidewalk, waiting while they push open the wooden door. There is no handle, only a hole where one used to be. We crush into the tiny foyer. It is dimly lit, dilapidated; above us, ancient pale green paint peels from walls buckling with water damage, revealing chunks of crumbling plaster. A layer of dust covers empty tenant mailboxes lining one wall. Tour participants exchange glances: where are we, exactly? Up the dark, narrow, rickety stairs we go, holding tight to the banister, which feels on the verge of coming loose. The stairs are slippery, well-worn wood, and Graciana jokes that if anyone stops paying attention, even for an instant, they might fall and break their neck. Up, around a corner, another worn flight of stairs—and we've arrived.

A small landing, no more than six by four feet, cream-colored walls freshly painted, with three doors left, right, and straight ahead. The door to our left is open, and from within spill out voices, light, a hubbub of activity. This is the synagogue, a converted flat, and the first room we squeeze into is packed with more than twenty people, mostly young adults. A cry of recognition: a young woman sees Graciana, throws her arms around her neck, and gives her *beijinhos,* the Portuguese greeting of a kiss on each cheek. A clamor of introductions and greetings follow as we all try to fit into the ten- by twelve-foot room, spilling over into a second room to the side. Everyone is smiling; with the bustle and crowding and excitement at first it is difficult to distinguish tourists from hosts. A table in the center of the room is covered with food— cookies, little cakes, potato chips, drinks. More awaits in a kitchenette off this room. It's time to mingle freely, and participants approach Marranos individually, introduce themselves, and ask questions, enthusiastically expressing their support. They have already seen and heard how dismissive people at Shaaré Tikvá can be. The outreach workers want to show a more welcoming face of the Jewish people; the roots tourists see people with whom they share a forgotten family history, and they anticipate an instant bond.

Almost immediately Martha, a middle-aged American who volunteers doing outreach work with "lost" Jewish communities in Africa, is deep in conversation with Catarina. Martha is smiling broadly, eyes wide, nodding at every word. She is asking Catarina about her Jewish background, family names, unusual traditions. She stands very close to her. Meanwhile, Graciana puts her arm around Jaime, a student in his early twenties. As we pass she says he is her "nephew"—whom she met online six years ago. They both laugh and she squeezes him tighter. He calls her *tia,* "aunt." In a corner Jeannie, a Cuban American tourist and genealogist who recently discovered that her ancestors originated on the Portuguese-Spanish border, many with surnames suggesting Jewish roots, is gesturing enthusiastically, talking to Dulce. She is comparing names and saying they might actually be cousins, *primas*! Dulce smiles slowly, gravely, replying simply, "Yes, yes." Nearby, Jeff, a Portuguese American who recently converted to Judaism, is telling his own story of spiritual and genealogical discovery to Tiago, who nods in recognition at the feelings he describes. And Yaniv and Rita, Israeli grandparents who volunteer to assist members of "isolated" Jewish groups once they have resettled in Israel, are listening intently as Tomás tells them about his grandmother, who taught him secret prayers, her fear of being known as a Marrano, and his own commitment to being Jewish in the present. They are patient with his broken English, sympathetic to his desire for acceptance, touched by his story. Rita pats his arm. Yaniv leans in to hear better. The energy in the room is high, conversation rising in an exuberant din that sounds more like a party than a meeting of strangers.

And then, after only an hour, just as suddenly as we arrived, it's time to leave. Tour participants and HaShalom members exchange email addresses, promise to write, give *beijinhos,* hug, wave—and then out the door we go, back down the rickety stairs, faster this time, clutching the banister, out onto the sidewalk and into our seats on the waiting bus. We're off to the next stop on the tour.

What is a fleeting encounter like this about? First and foremost, it fulfills a desire for direct contact, putting face and flesh to the abstract image of "the Marrano"; as a near second, it is about emotion and interpersonal connection, however briefly expressed. For many visitors these meetings offered a heady emotional mixture, combining an effervescent feeling of bonding, or *communitas* (Turner 1974), with—if we are to be honest—a discernible degree of exoticization. While the vast majority of visitors embraced the Marranos as part of "the Jewish people," and although foreign crypto-Jewish descendants viewed them as bearing a shared "family" history, they were nonetheless unmistakably Other. They were Portuguese, disconnected from the Jewish world both locally and abroad, descendants of the forced converts who stayed behind. Some, like Tomás, had extraordinary stories. The dilapidated synagogue, situated in what was literally a condemned building, added to the romance. Occasionally visitors would be given an impromptu tour, including a sanctuary that was no longer used. A few years earlier the upstairs neighbor's pipes developed a leak, undetected until the ceiling caved in, bringing down a washing machine in a rain of plaster and splintered wood. Although the wreckage had been removed, the furniture was gone and the air smelled of dust and mildew. The hole in the ceiling gaped. The upstairs unit had long since been vacated, as had most of the building, by order of the city. The group used one of the apartment's remaining two rooms as a makeshift sanctuary; at barely twelve by twelve feet, the pews were so close together that it was difficult to move between them. Overall the space was clean and tidy, but the baseboards and moldings were badly chipped, the furniture old, the pipes loud and the electricity erratic.

Coupled with the physical disintegration of the building, the energy and warmth visitors found inside fit squarely within the metanarrative of destruction and near-miraculous survival: Portugal's Jews had been wiped out by the Inquisition, and yet here were signs of life, a vibrant community that was undergoing, as one Italian tourist said with a catch in her voice, "a beautiful rebirth." This was the point visitors repeated most often in their conversations with me and in travelogues after the fact: an extraordinary revival of Jewish identity was occurring in urban Portugal, involving energetic, proud young adults. Visitors were especially affected by the most dramatic Marrano stories they heard, later generalizing them to the entire group. Most of all, they were moved simply by occupying the same space and interacting with the local people. Their exchanges ran the gamut from merely smiling to sharing stories of travels to Jewish communities elsewhere, from talking about their own identity issues to asking them detailed questions. Energized and heartened— or, as most put it, "moved"—by the encounter, visitor after visitor promised to stay in touch, to send books and other educational materials, to lobby their rabbi and their community to support the urban Marranos' efforts to be recognized as Jews through some kind of "return" process. And yet remarkably few followed through. Although some volunteer outreach activists publicized their findings upon returning home, little came of it beyond visits from still more curious travelers and occasional proposals for conversion and educational programs that stalled in the earliest planning stage.

Studies of tourist experience provide a possible explanation for the disparity between visitors' earnest expressions of support, even affection, during the moment of encounter and their silence after returning home. First, whether undertaken purely for recreation or as an expression of deeply held commitments, all modes of leisure travel represent a temporal and experiential break in the routine of everyday life, one that is necessarily marked by a series of contrasts from the ordinary: home/away, work/play, mundane/extraordinary (Graburn 1989, 2001). In this liminal "time out of time" period, tourists often show an openness to experience that they would not manifest at home (Picard 2012); they are in search of peak moments, of new discoveries and new connections, of things they cannot do or find in their everyday lives (Harrison 2003; Hom Cary 2004; Whittaker 2012). It should not surprise us that visitors' promises to stay in touch, made in an intense moment of interpersonal connection, could upon returning home be forgotten or abandoned, the encounter sealed off within the temporal confines of the journey—now transformed into memory, a narrative of the extraordinary to be recounted in the everyday.

However, the way visitors talked about the people they met suggested a deeper conceptual bond than their failure to remain in contact would imply. Before, during, and after their encounters, many spoke of the Marranos in the vocabulary of kinship: "part of the (Jewish) family," "brothers and sisters," "our people," "our cousins." During one Conference-Tour, an Ashkenazi American retiree told me that she had brought a small piece of art from her late parents' home, intending to give it to one of the Marrano communities along the way. She explained her desire to do so in terms of sharing with kin: "It's not about making a donation; that would be leaving a thousand dollars or something. It's about *sharing*. They're *part of the family*." At the word *family* she traced a circle in the air in front of her, two hands arcing from top to bottom as if drawing a globe, a sphere of relatedness. "Because we can't trace my family back farther than my grandfather on my father's side, we don't know—It's very possible that we come from the Iberian Peninsula. And if that's the case, then they're even *more* part of the family. And if not, we're all part of the larger family." After the Conference-Tour ended, I asked

Anshel Rappaport, the eighty-year-old Ashkenazi Canadian who had been a Jewish educator and outreach volunteer his entire adult life, why he had decided to come. He replied without hesitation, as if it were self-evident: *"Because! My lost brothers and sisters!"*

As Anshel's response suggests, the language these travelers used reflected the metanarrative that prompted most of them to make the journey: as Jews, they belonged to the Jewish "family," as did the Marranos. The latter represented a "lost" or "isolated" branch of the family, who needed contact and bonding with other Jews to be brought back into the circle of kin. This the travelers intended to provide. Similarly, those travelers who traced their own ancestry to pre-Inquisition Portuguese Jews typically spoke of the urban Marranos as their "cousins," reflecting a second metanarrative of the genealogical quest and discovery of long-lost relations. In both cases family reunification, as it were, seemed an end in itself. I address the consequences of these framings of the situation below, but first let us look at how the urban Marranos approached their encounters with foreign visitors.

MEETING FOREIGN JEWS

Like Elsa Cruz, Ricardo Carvalho, founding president of Menorá, felt strongly that the urban Marranos needed to have face-to-face contact with Jews from abroad. Given the scarcity of materials about Judaism and Jewish culture in Portugal, he saw foreign visitors as vital sources of information. "You know how we all collect Jewish books?" he asked me. "We also collect Jewish people. Every time someone new comes to talk with us, we learn more about what it means to be Jewish." Both he and his counterparts at HaShalom argued that only through intervention from abroad would they ever be accepted into the Jewish world. This could be through a "return" or conversion process facilitated by a foreign organization, or by creating their own Jewish community with outside support. The logistical specifics were less important than the possibility of resolution to their perpetually liminal state. They put great stock in the warmth and acceptance showered upon them by foreign visitors. In contrast to their outright rejection by Portugal's normative Jewish communities, each positive interaction offered hope of a different future.

For the goal of learning about Jewishness, any contact with Jews was helpful and so they were not picky. If a group or individual made contact, the associations' leaders were ready to arrange a gathering. Consequently a wide swath of contemporary Jewish life passed through their doors: secular Israeli couples on holiday; black-hatted emissaries from Chabad, barely out of their teens; a Yemeni Israeli photographer of "exotic" Jews, seeking a photo shoot; six French-Jewish young adults passing through on a pan-European cycling tour; a busload of retirees from a Masorti synagogue in England; a stream of rabbis from around the world, male and female, young and old, representing every imaginable offshoot of every branch of Judaism. All were welcomed equally, though rabbinic visits were a source of greater anticipation and stress. Relatively few rabbis and outreach activists came in a strictly professional capacity, however; they usually scheduled the visit during a vacation in Portugal, out of curiosity and, often, to offer moral support. As a result, the urban Marranos made few distinctions among their visitors. All were *pessoas de fora,* "people from outside," "foreigners," Jewish tourists who might one day become "friends." Each encounter held out the possibility of categorical recognition or rejection, empathy or indifference. Would they be accepted as Jews or not? How would their stories be received?

Let us now join HaShalom's members as they prepare for a visit. It is April 2005, and this time it is a group of Italian Jews, twenty or so, on the last leg of a Jewish heritage tour of Portugal. A few days ago Dulce got word that they would like to join HaShalom for Havdalah, the brief, informal ceremony marking the close of Shabbat on Saturday evening, and she immediately sent out her usual notice:

> This Saturday we will have Havdalah around 7:45 P.M., and ☺ we will have a visit from a group of Italian Jews who would like to meet us [*desejam conhecer-nos*]. Reasons enough to show up!

In recent weeks members have been observing Havdalah together every Saturday, followed by an hour-long Hebrew lesson taught by Tomás, so we can expect that most of the gang (*a malta*) will come. Dulce arrives a few hours early to prepare for the visit. She sweeps the meeting room and kitchen, straightens the chairs, brushes crumbs from the table, puts away books and papers left out after last week's Hebrew class. After a while Nuno and Luisa arrive to help, and she sends them out to buy snacks for the guests. Tidying done, she leans against a doorjamb and taps her foot nervously. Suddenly Catarina bursts through the door, a bundle of nerves and distraction. "Who's coming, again?" she asks. Dulce tells her what little she knows—it's a group of Italian Jews; there are about twenty; Ricardo sent them after they visited Menorá a few days ago—and the two sit down to wait. Catarina chews a fingernail and crosses one leg over the other, swinging her foot. She wonders aloud what this visit will be like. There's always the chance that someone will say, "Come on, you're not really Jews!" Dulce shrugs, and just then Nuno and Luisa return with crackers, vegetables, dip, soft drinks. They give the receipt to Dulce. She sets everything out on the table, just so. A clatter on the stairs: Tomás, Pedro, and Manuel have arrived. Soon we are all present, and the air in the room begins to buzz with conversation and anticipation.

Then, abruptly, the room goes quiet: there are voices coming from the entryway downstairs. They're here! The voices get louder as the Italians come up the stairs and then they're inside, a sea of new faces and voices, all smiling, elderly and well dressed, talking, a rush of people crushing into the little meeting room. On their heels up the stairs comes João Trausch, a young man whose grandfather was among Anshei Emet's founders. Dulce is visibly relieved to see him, the group's only *judeu de carteirinha,* because he is always more comfortable in these situations. She asks him to tell the visitors the history of the synagogue. But immediately there is a problem: none of the Italians speak Portuguese, only two speak English, and just one speaks French. Their Portuguese-speaking guide has not accompanied them. And so begins a laborious chain of translation, with João's Portuguese translated into French by another HaShalom member, then from French into Italian by one of the visitors. Questions go back the other way, Italian into French, French into Portuguese. When the French-speaking tourist tires of her role, an English-speaking member of HaShalom and an English-speaking visitor step forward.

It takes about twenty minutes to tell the synagogue's relatively simple history this way. Then, at a loss for what to do next, Dulce offers in her halting English to show them the space, and a few local people tag along in case she needs help with translation. Down the hall we go, past the doorway to the little kitchen, past the bathroom with its exposed pipes that hiss and sigh, through the curtain that masks the entrance to the former sanctuary. The tourists are shocked at the gaping hole in the ceiling, dismayed at the degradation of the large room, which is dark and ghostly quiet and covered in a light layer of dust. They talk amongst themselves. Then suddenly they are handing Dulce Euro notes, piles of them. They want to support HaShalom, to contribute to the synagogue's restoration. Dulce pulls the official receipt book from her bag; as HaShalom's president and an Anshei Emet board member, she always brings it when visitors come. Silvia, an Italian in her sixties, leans over and whispers in my ear that when she heard about "these

Marranos" she knew immediately that she *must* come, to show—here she pauses, not knowing the English word, then says in Italian—*solidaritá.*

Now the usual mingling begins. Verbal communication continues to be a challenge, though there is a great deal of smiling and physical contact, and some exchanging of family names. "*Parenti!*" (Ital.; relatives), says one older woman, clearly delighted, gesturing to herself and then to Manuel. She is Sephardic, and her maiden name is di Castro; Manuel's mother's maiden name, she has learned, is Castro too. She takes Manuel's hand and squeezes it. He smiles broadly, feeling for the moment that they are indeed related, that he actually belongs among Jewish kin. It is a rare and affecting experience for him, one he will describe to me afterward. In a corner of the make-shift sanctuary, squeezed between the pews, Tomás is telling his story. As usual he becomes teary-eyed when he speaks of his grandmother, and as usual a group has gathered around him. Again there is need for translation. The visitors have many questions. They want to know if it would be helpful for them to share what they have learned here back home. "Of course!" cries Tomás. Listening, local people suspect that mistakes and even exaggerations are made as the chain of translation moves back and forth, but what is to be done? "It doesn't really matter," whispers Catarina. She too is soon "mobbed," as she later puts it, and tells her story to at least four different people in twenty minutes. By the end of the hour the faces have blurred together, and she confesses she can't remember a single name. Within two months she'll have forgotten what country they were from. So many come; so many are curious.

It is time for Havdalah. We push the pews to the sides to gather in the makeshift sanctuary, standing tightly in a circle. No one remembered to buy wine for the blessing, but beer is a permitted alternative, and someone remembers there's a can in the refrigerator. It is hastily poured into a plastic cup and moments later we are ready to begin. First raising the cup of beer, then passing around a box of spices for all to smell, then holding up a braided, multi-wick candle that he has lit, João Trausch reads the blessing for each step of the ritual from a photocopied sheet, hands trembling. He is shy and unaccustomed to reading prayers before strangers, and he stumbles over the Hebrew. The plastic cup, the substituted beer, and João's tentative perform-ance conspire to make this an informal, even intimate moment. As is custom-ary, after the blessings the lights are turned off and we stand together in the dark, the candle's dancing light illuminating faces around the circle. Here there is no spatial separation between hosts and guests, almost-Jews and Jews.

Quietly now, one of the Italians begins to sing "Eliahu Hanavi," the slow, mournfully pitched song that traditionally closes the brief ceremony. One by one tourists join in, and then so do the few members of HaShalom who know it. It is a simple melody, very repetitive, just a few words, and within moments nearly everyone has lifted their voice. Later several local people will tell me it was a magical moment. "For the first time in one of these visits, for the first time, I was truly moved," Manuel will say. "Suddenly I had the feeling that beyond all the cultural differences—You know, these are the things that make you Jewish, these songs, these prayers, because these are things you can share with somebody from a different country, even a totally different continent." For that brief moment, others will say, standing in the circle, they felt they belonged there.

The candle flame is extinguished, the lights come back on, and there's a quick rush to take photos together. Then there are handshakes and hugs and *beijinhos* and promises to spread the word and they must go. Taxis have come to take them to dinner; they have a reservation waiting. They are gone. Exhausted, Catarina, Nuno, and Dulce collapse into pews; Luisa leans against the doorjamb and sighs. It has been just over an hour of smiling at strangers, talking about themselves, straining to understand across substantial linguistic barriers. The "whirlwind," as Catarina calls it, has left the building. Now it's time to debrief and clean up before heading home. Everyone is worn out and oversaturated, but happy. They've answered questions about their background, their family names, their ancestry— they've told their Marrano stories—and although they know the majority of their visitors don't mean to imply anything with their endless questions, sometimes it feels like they have to prove themselves as Jews. This time they've all felt accepted, even welcomed. But what will come of it?

For urban Marranos, encounters with foreign visitors were at once intense, emotionally taxing, and uplifting. Intense and taxing, because it took a great deal of emotional stamina to make it through the encounter, given the insecurity most felt about how they would be received. Many were fairly shy people, and they would not under other circumstances have chosen to discuss such a vulnerable part of themselves at such length, particularly not with strangers. In addition to the reactions they received as individuals, there was always the possibility of collective rejection, an uncomfortable experience that did on occasion arise. In August 2004, for example, a pair of young Chabad emissaries arrived from Israel, tasked with finding non-observant Jews across southern Europe and encouraging them to strengthen their connection with Judaism. Having heard there was a Jewish cultural organization in Porto, they contacted Miguel Santos, the group's vice president, to arrange a meeting. Miguel gathered several members at Menorá's office, inviting me along to translate if needed. The visitors were warm and encouraging as they listened to Miguel describe the group's cultural activities. Then one began a lengthy sermon on the importance of religious practice over cultural events. After two hours, having finally asked about their hosts' Jewish upbringing and realizing they were not Jews according to halakhah, the visitors' warm demeanor evaporated and they made a quick exit. On their way down the stairs they suggested that the group contact the Israeli Chief Rabbinate about Orthodox conversion. As for the two of them, they were polite but firm: their mandate did not include assistance to Gentiles, educational or otherwise.

That kind of categorical rejection was rare, however. For the most part, visits from foreigners, whether tourists, sympathetic rabbis, or outreach workers, were profoundly uplifting, because they offered precisely the sense of Jewish belonging—however briefly—that was impossible to achieve in the Portuguese context. The mere fact that there were Jews, any Jews, who were interested in spending time with them offered a momentary antidote to their isolation. As they slowly realized, most tourists and secular outreach activists were not concerned with matters of halakhah; they had come to meet Marranos, and consequently arrived primed to embrace them. Their attitude was warm, attentive, friendly, sometimes reverent, sometimes effusive, on occasion even loving. It was this general atmosphere of acceptance that many members of HaShalom and Menorá sought from tourist visits, in addition to whatever information about Jewish life they could glean during their encounters—such as learning to sing "Eliahu Hanavi" alongside their Italian visitors.

They also had more pragmatic concerns. They hoped that somehow, through some connection they might make during one of the visits, assistance in dealing with the local impasse would materialize. Unlike their visitors, they did not use kin terms when speaking categorically about foreign visitors; instead, they differentiated between *turistas* (tourists) and *amigos* (friends). "If they come once and we never hear from them again, they're tourists," Ricardo explained. "If they come back, they're friends." They sincerely hoped that such "friendships" would form and attended closely to the dynamics of each encounter, dissecting visits together afterward. Thus there were simultaneously emotional and instrumental aspects to their collective engagement with visitors from abroad. Stymied by their inability to be recognized as Jews or to pursue a process of "return" locally, they felt the only solution lay in forging connections with *pessoas de fora*. They also had emotional reasons for wanting to form lasting bonds with their visitors, for they lacked an enduring sense of Jewish belonging that only such relationships could provide. Thus, for urban Marranos, just as for their visitors, these brief encounters were primarily about personal contact, emotion, and connection, but with an added dimension: a desire for that connection to continue long beyond the visit.

FRAMING RELATIONS

While both urban Marranos and their foreign visitors conceived of their interactions in terms of relatedness, connection, and belonging, generally speaking they did so at different levels of abstraction and according to different conceptual frameworks, or *cultural logics*. As a result, they had markedly divergent expectations of what the outcome of their encounters should be. In this section I sketch the structures of reasoning that generated these different expectations, looking at the cultural lens through which each group made sense of each other's presence and behavior. My particular interest is in how the visitors' use of kin terms and open demonstrations of affect shaped the dynamics of the encounter and its aftermath. For although both the foreign visitors and their local hosts understood these things to convey positive emotional engagement in the moment, they triggered different *cultural schemas* regarding the kind of relationship being formed and the mutual responsibilities and obligations that came with it. The use of kin terms, as Janet Carsten (2004) argues in her analysis of conceptual blurring between the family and the nation, can never be "just" metaphorical (cf. Schneider 1977, 1980; Herzfeld 2005). Metaphors structure our thought, suggesting a particular framing of the situation in which they are employed; they have logical entailments that guide our reasoning and motivate our actions; and they cannot help but be culturally inflected (Kovecses 2006; Lakoff and Johnson 1980). In this case, metaphors of *family, cousins, brothers and sisters, relatives,* and *our people,* though superficially mutually intelligible, carried different associations for tourists and outreach workers than they did for the urban Marranos, and they prompted different paths of reasoning.[2]

Primos and Am Yisrael

Let us begin with visitors who found their way to HaShalom and Menorá through Graciana Mayer. Many were members of the Nostálgia forum and learned there of the urban Marranos' existence. Members often prefaced their posts with "Dear *primos*" (cousins) or, if replying to a particular individual, with the singular form, "Dear *prima* Graciana." Those who employed the kin term were people of Portuguese descent, typically non–Portuguese speaking, who had recently discovered that they might have Portuguese Jewish ancestry. Jewish participants with no Portuguese background often followed suit. But very few of the Portuguese nationals who subscribed used *primo* in their posts. Luciano Borges, one of Menorá's founding members, made a point of asking about it when he joined Nostálgia. The ensuing correspondence is revealing, particularly as the responses came from Portuguese Americans who had posted previously about traveling to Portugal as Jewish heritage tourists. Responding to a post by a forum member whose ancestors came from Madeira, Luciano wrote:

> It's funny to read "primo" in the mails here. Where I live (on the coast in northern Portugal), only the fishermen community uses this term. Is it a Madeiran tradition too?

A responding post explained that *primo* was used metaphorically to indicate a feeling of "great affinity," based on its use as a form of address in small Portuguese villages where everyone is related. It was appropriate, the individual wrote, because Nostálgia members felt intimately linked to each other via their shared connection to the Jewish people:

> Dear Primo Luciano Borges,
>
> For one thing, I couldn't confirm if it is a Madeiran tradition to address as "primo," since I only know Madeira from a tourist's point of view. But Madeira being a small community, I think they do.
>
> As for Nostálgia, when I joined it I found that a number of participants were already addressing each other as "primo/prima" as is the habit in small, closed communities in Portugal as far as I know, namely in small hamlets and villages where most people really have family ties. I never asked, but would venture to say that the usage of "primo/prima" here is most appropriate, since most participants seem to have a great affinity: they are Jews, Crypto-Jews, Anusim or have great admiration and respect for the People of Israel.

A second subscriber agreed, signing his post "AdeusShalom," an invention of Nostálgia members that merged the Portuguese *adeus* (good-bye) with the Hebrew *shalom:*

> Dear Primo Andre,
> I couldn't agree with you more.
>   The use of "primo/prima" in this newsgroup is very appropriate indeed, for the reasons you mentioned.
> AdeusShalom, Jeff

A third post suggested that *primo* felt right because it just might be accurate: "Maybe it's because we may all be related."

Small wonder, then, that when longtime Nostálgia members made their way to Portugal on Graciana's Conference-Tours they repeatedly made comments like "We're all *primos* here!" or "It's so good to meet my *primos,*" both to each other and to urban Marranos. Because all believed their forebears had been persecuted by the Inquisition, the term indexed an emotional connection on the basis of shared ancestral experience. It also gestured toward the possibility that they were all literally *ethnic* kin, descendants of the "lost" Portuguese Jews, who were, Nostálgia members knew, a distinct ethnic category at the time of the mass forced conversions, marrying only among themselves. Experientially, ancestrally, ethnically, or religiously, *primo* implied that they were all somehow "related." In addition, they used the term one-on-one upon discovering a shared surname: "You're a Mendes, too? We must be *primas!*" Here, the term combined the more general sense of relatedness with the possibility of actual genealogical connection—though, as Graciana said of having enthusiastically embraced a woman in Belmonte after learning that they shared a family name and announcing that they were *primas,* "Oh, it's just a loving thing. I don't think we're actually related."

What, then, did it mean to call someone *primo* in this context? Nothing in the behavior or affect of the people who used the term in their encounters with urban Marranos suggested anything beyond a stance of receptiveness, a general openness to discussing their feelings, to describing their personal journey, and to offering emotional support—in short, a generalized, if intensely felt, sense of commonality and solidarity. Notably, most used the word in Portuguese despite the fact that very few spoke the language beyond a few phrases. In rare instances some translated it into English, calling the local people and each other "cousin," but only on discovering shared surnames. Thus tourists used what was for them a foreign term, one that did not call up the conceptual framework of "cousins" conveyed in their native language, whether English, French, Dutch, Hebrew, or Afrikaans. From their perspective, *primo* meant simply "a person who shares some aspect of my experience in the domain of Jewish ancestry and who presumably feels an emotional connection to me on that basis, to whom I feel an emotional connection, and who could conceivably be a distant genealogical relative." This framing of the relationship suggested no mutual obligation, no responsibility beyond expressing a sense of belonging, and even affection, in the moment of encounter. As we will see, *primo* has a very different set of entailments for those who speak Portuguese as a native language.

Jewish tourists and outreach workers used a greater variety of kin terms. The most common was simply "family," often in the context of expressing dismay that the Marranos were not accepted locally. As one outreach volunteer exclaimed upon hearing about Menorá members' rejection at the Porto synagogue, "You're part of the Jewish family, and it's shameful that you're not being welcomed back with open arms!" He later explained,

> Look, they're my family. They're part of the Jewish family. They're *ethnic Jews,* and we should carry them on a silver platter, because for five hundred years they remained what they remained, with the little knowledge that they had.

Others spoke of "brothers and sisters," "relatives," and "our people," whether in conversation with urban Marranos or speaking about them before or after the fact. Some articulated their feelings in the broadest categorical sense of "being related." After meeting HaShalom members and hearing of their difficulties, Ruth Tapper, an Ashkenazi American historian, said simply, "I have a cosmopolitan view of Jewry. I really believe you're a Jew if you say you're a Jew, and it doesn't matter where you're from, we're all related." This "familial" framing was invariably accompanied by physically affectionate behavior—touching an arm lightly during conversation, squeezing a hand, putting an arm around the shoulders or even hugging, and of course smiling broadly—whether or not they could communicate verbally. A great deal of interpersonal warmth came from the visitors' end of these encounters.

The generative metaphor at work here appears to be that of "the Jewish people," a foundational concept in Judaism rooted in the Torah. As "descendants" of the original patriarchs Abraham, Isaac, and Jacob and the matriarchs Sarah, Rachel, and Leah, Jews are from a ritual perspective all related to one another; Judaism is transmitted by birth, and those who convert into the faith are, as I discuss in the next chapter, given a new ritual lineage as *ben Avraham Aveinu* or *bat Sarah Imenu*—"son of Abraham the father" or "daughter of Sarah the mother." This is a remarkably clear case of the conflation of kinship, religion, and nation in a single domain (Schneider 1977). The overall conceptual framework of a global Jewish family—according to which all Jews are "sons" and "daughters" of the same distant ancestors—allows in turn the utilization of "brothers and sisters," "our kin," and "our people" in conversation between Jews of radically different national and cultural backgrounds. Not only was this conception of face-to-face relatedness widely assumed among traveling Jews I encountered in Portugal, it is an essential principle of Judaism, known as *am yisrael* (Heb.; the Jewish people, Jewish peoplehood): "The bonds of Jewish peoplehood have stood at the heart of Jewish group definition since the days of Abraham and Sarah. Judaism is more than a religion; it demands identification with the Jewish people as a whole, a familial closeness with Jews of all kinds everywhere" (Elazar n.d.; see also Roth 2007: 12–17). Interestingly, during tourist encounters I found the language of kinship used most frequently and most freely by secular and even openly atheist Jews. This suggests that the concept of *am yisrael* far outstrips its grounding in Jewish religious texts and has become a basic component of Jewish cultural identification, at least in the United States, Canada, Australia, Israel, England, and France, where most secular travelers I met originated. The more religiously observant visitors tended to see the urban Marranos as proto- or semi-Jews, remnants of an important part of Jewish history who could not be included in "the Jewish people" until they had converted according to halakhah. For the time being they remained, as Shavei Israel's publicity put it, "our lost brethren," who needed to be brought back to the family fold via ritual reincorporation.

Despite its emphasis on mutual identification, the concept of *am yisrael* does not appear to carry with it an inherent sense of mutual obligation or responsibility. It was good enough, it seemed from my observations and conversations in the field, to recognize and care about one another as "kin," to feel a "familial" connection that some experienced as immediate and others, distant. Even the most passionate outreach activists saw their role primarily as one of connecting people with each other—the "lost Jews" with "the Jewish world"—and, if the local people wished, sending educational materials and assisting them in gaining halakhic status as Jews through a program of conversion. Some tourists would make a monetary contribution, as they routinely did when visiting synagogues on vacation. Above all, however, the primary logical entailment of the framing of all Jews as "family" was that *they should love and care about one another in the abstract,* even sight unseen. This was the sense in which Anshel, the Canadian outreach activist, articulated his feelings:

> I came to connect, to bond, to leave them with a feeling that I'm—that I'm family, that they're family to me. And that I want to bond with them, and that they should bond with outsiders, they shouldn't feel isolated, they shouldn't *be* isolated! I want to say, "You're one of us, and we're coming because you *are* us, and we are you."

As we saw with the roots-seeking tourists who came in search of *primos,* Jewish tourists and outreach workers appeared to hold a concept of *family* in which, as David Schneider wrote of the American kinship system, the primary "code for conduct" was "diffuse, enduring solidarity"—that is, "love":

> *Solidarity* because the relationship is supportive, helpful, and cooperative; it rests on trust and the other can be trusted. *Diffuse* because it is not narrowly confined to a specific goal or a specific kind of behavior. . . . Two members of the family cannot be indifferent to one another, and since their cooperation does not have a specific goal or a specific limited time in mind, it is *enduring.* (Schneider 1980: 52)

Schneider's analysis identifies an essential difference between *family* and *friends* in American culture: whereas friendship is understood by definition to be optional and susceptible to rupture, and thus is not necessarily enduring, his material suggested that for Americans, family cannot be chosen. Family ties endure whether one wants them to or not, no matter how a given relative behaves. The structural similarity between this model and the cultural logic that allows for the idea of "lost Jews"—that even if they or their ancestors convert to another religion, their membership in the Jewish "extended family" cannot be severed—is unmistakable. As Shavei Israel's website explains, "We believe the Jewish People is a family with links that never vanish completely; our endeavor is to strengthen the links wherever they may have been weakened by history, distance or social parameters."[3] While Schneider (1980: 120–21) cautions that his analysis is based on white, middle-class Americans and should not be applied in other cultural contexts without careful consideration, here its resonance is clear. In practice, the fundamental "family" obligation of Jews and roots-seeking crypto-Jewish descendants to one another and to Portuguese urban Marranos seemed to be no more and no less than diffuse, enduring solidarity.

Thus the vast majority of tourists and outreach workers came with a preexisting conceptual framework for the interactions they would have with the urban Marranos. As "family"—*primos,* brethren, kin—the people visited would automatically be recipients of their interest and affection. The encounter was, in effect, a fleeting materialization of a presupposed feeling of relatedness. For roots-seekers, part of the process of gaining self-knowledge as descendants of crypto-Jews was to meet and connect with other descendants like themselves, even if only for a few days on a tour bus or an hour at a reception. For both Jews and crypto-Jewish descendants, meeting local people was a mode of concretizing an abstract feeling, one that had little to do with the living, breathing individuals they met along the way. It was a generalized, *categorical* affection.

Cousins and Siblings

However Jewish tourists and outreach workers may have perceived them, the members of Menorá and HaShalom did not feel that they were part of the Jewish world. The effect of their blatant rejection by the normative Jewish communities, arbiters of Jewishness in their immediate setting, could not be overcome entirely by the warmth shown them in heady flashes by foreigners who arrived and disappeared within the span of an hour. Nonetheless they continued to welcome the visits, because they heard in the tourists' expressions of relatedness and familial affection a willingness to help them resolve their local situation. Recall that they distinguished between "tourists" and "friends," where "friends" were those who stayed in touch or even returned. They hoped that their visitors would become "friends," as the warmth and interest so many showed during their encounters suggested they would, both because they longed for a sense of Jewish belonging and because they needed social ties to the Jewish world. Their desire for belonging was, of course, emotional; but their desire for social ties was instrumental, stemming from a basic belief across the Portuguese social spectrum that one must rely upon such ties in order to get much of anything done, particularly in situations that require access to closed networks. I return to this point below, but first let us examine the meanings of *primo* and other kin terms for the Portuguese.

Early in my fieldwork, I was surprised at how often I heard Portuguese friends mention their cousins. Most seemed to have a large number whom they saw regularly at family gatherings, and they socialized with those in their age cohort. They counted among their *primos* individuals related to them by descent and by marriage, or, in the nomenclature of kinship studies, consanguineal and affinal kin. Hence, in Portugal, both one's mother's sister's daughter and, if known personally, the wife of a fellow descendant of one's great-great-great-grandfather (in American parlance, a fourth cousin's wife) would be called *prima* (Callier-Boisvert 1968). In addition to socializing, cousins appeared to rely upon each other for all sorts of things. Take the case of Manuel Teixeira, from HaShalom. Having been made *padrinho* (godfather) to the son of one *prima* and the daughter of another, he was routinely called to participate in birthday parties, school events, and the like. Although he identified strongly as Jewish, like most members of the Marrano associations Manuel still participated in Catholic cultural practices like the ritual role of *compadrio* (godparenthood) or celebrating Easter and Christmas with kin. He was raised in Viseu, a city of one hundred thousand in central Portugal, close to the town where his mother's extended family lived—including her parents, her parents' siblings and their offspring, four of her six brothers and sisters and their spouses, their spouses' extended families, and all of their children. Growing up, Manuel played with *primos* and *primas* with whom he shared grandparents or great-grandparents, especially during summer vacation, and they remained in contact as adults. One afternoon I learned in casual conversation that his computer had stopped working. To my amazement, he said he planned to drive it to Coimbra, a city two hours away, to have one such cousin fix it. The cousin was a computer programmer, he said, currently unemployed, and it wouldn't be right to take it to a stranger instead. While his commitment to his cousin's well-being may have been greater than most, throughout my research I heard stories in which cousins figured in everything from choosing a vacation spot or hosting a party to finding employment or locating a cosignatory for a major loan.

Unlike the United States, Canada, England, South Africa, and Israel, the source of many of the Marrano associations' foreign visitors, Portugal has not historically absorbed a large number of immigrants. Because families have roots reaching back hundreds of years in the same soil, extended kin networks remain a central aspect of social organization (Brettell 1986; Willems 1962). Even when families migrate from rural areas to Porto or Lisbon or as far away as Paris or Frankfurt, they typically maintain kin networks through lengthy summer visits, siblings and cousins returning in droves to the towns and ancestral villages where their parents or grandparents live. HaShalom and Menorá members had many *primos* at multiple degrees of genealogical and emotional distance; for them, the roots tourists' delight at finding "cousins" in Portugal was an entirely foreign sentiment. What they heard in the latter's use of *primo* was a declaration of a diffuse (metaphorical) familial tie, an expression of common identification and interest, which in the Portuguese context carried with it the logical entailment that one could call upon them if there were some way they could be of help in the future. That, at a minimum, is the obligation Portuguese kin hold to one another.[4]

I do not mean to suggest that Portuguese Marranos reflected consciously upon the entailments of these and other kin terms I discuss below. My point is rather that their reactions and affect both during and after the encounter suggested that they were reasoning on that basis. As I noted in chapter 2 with regard to the logic of genealogical causality, cultural models are so powerful in part because they operate below the level of conscious thought. While they do not *determine* how we think and behave, they do provide familiar paths along which thoughts can run and inferences can be made. The word *primo*, used metaphorically in conjunction with expressions of warmth and affection, invokes the conceptual framework of a family tie, and it is entirely intelligible to a Portuguese speaker in those generic terms. However, because the word does not name a particular degree of closeness or distance—in fact, it can be used for any relative for whom there is not a more specific Portuguese kin term—that conceptual framework does not entail great emotional intensity or any particular set of obligations and responsibilities beyond general warmth, solidarity, and readiness to give assistance if needed, like all Portuguese familial relationships in the abstract.

Brother and *sister*, terms Jewish tourists and outreach workers occasionally used in English during their encounters, are significantly different. As in English, in Portuguese these words are used to index relationships beyond literal siblings. But where the foreign visitors intended the terms to be a *categorical* expression of solidarity and desire for connection, drawing on the conceptual framework of "the Jewish family," for the Portuguese the metaphor of siblings has a far more intense and personal emotional valence. To say that someone is one's *irmão* (brother) or *irmã* (sister) means that one feels a profound connection to that specific individual, one that is deeper than friendship and literally like that of immediate family. Significantly, in Portuguese one does not say, "You are like a sister to me." The phrasing is "You are my sister" (*És minha irmã*). A friend becomes one's sister or brother, for example, when the friend and oneself have gone through a transformative life experience together and have "felt each other's emotions," as it is said in Portuguese, achieving an unusually deep level of understanding.

A case in point arose during a Nostálgia Conference-Tour. Seemingly out of the blue, participants decided to bestow a Jewish ritual name upon Joaquim Martins, the HaShalom member of *chueta* origin. The impromptu ceremony took place in a newly restored medieval synagogue that Joaquim, an architectural historian by training, had discovered several years earlier being used as a garage. Our local guide for the past two days, he had led us through *judiarias* in several towns, including this one on the Spanish border, and told us his life story over lunch. Once we were inside the small, bare room, Anshel called for attention, put his arm around Joaquim, and announced that it was time he had a Hebrew name. He nodded to Yaniv, an Israeli retiree, who sang a prayer in Hebrew bestowing Joaquim's ritual name, Natanel. Then the two broke into a round of "Simon Tov u'Mazal Tov" (Good Signs and Good Fortune), a joyous song of congratulations sung at weddings and bar mitzvahs. Others joined in, some clapping in time. Joaquim was speechless, standing in the ancient synagogue he had discovered, as Jews from around the world sang in his honor—five hundred years after his ancestors had been forced to relinquish their identity. Participants hugged him as he brushed away tears, some wiping away tears of their own.

Thereafter, Joaquim addressed Anshel, Graciana, me, and one or two others with whom he maintained contact as "*meu irmão* Anshel," "*minha irmã* Naomi" (my brother Anshel, my sister Naomi). When I returned to Portugal for long-term fieldwork he regularly reminded me that I was his *irmã*, inviting me for dinner at his home with his mother and siblings and repeatedly offering his help, should I need it. I had noted that after the naming ceremony he corrected Graciana whenever she called him *primo,* saying he was her brother. Two years later, I asked him to explain.

> NL: I noticed when Graciana called you *primo,* you corrected her. You said "No, no, I am your brother, you are my sister."
>
> JOAQUIM: Obviously, yes. It's because after I received my name I suddenly felt very connected [*de repente fiquei muito ligado*]. Very, very connected. I became very connected to you, I became very connected to Anshel, I became very connected to Graciana, in such a way that the three of you are my siblings, you're definitely not cousins. [laughs] The rest of the people on the trip [gestures dismissively], they can be cousins.

For Joaquim, the words *brother* and *sister* brought with them a conceptual framework of deep emotional connection, mutual trust, and—as his subsequent behavior toward Anshel and me suggested—responsibility for assistance, hospitality, and care.

At the time, mid-2004, Joaquim was one of a very small number of members of HaShalom and Menorá who had spent more than an hour or two with tourists and outreach workers at any given time. Most did not have the opportunity to forge the kind of bond he formed with Anshel, who returned several times and on one trip even stayed in Joaquim's home. Consequently, they did not mistake foreigners' use of *brothers* and *sisters* as referring to the kind of deep friendship entailed by those terms in Portuguese. Their use did, however, evoke the feelings of warmth and loyalty inherent to it. Several participants told me that they were quite touched by being called "brother"; said one member of Menorá, "It tells me that they would like to have a closer relationship [*relação de mais proximidade*]. There's an intimacy there that touches me."

Whether they heard themselves called *primo*, "a member of the family," or "brother" or "sister," many of the urban Marranos rightly interpreted their visitors to mean that they felt affection toward them. Where things became confused, however, was in their assessment of the specificity of that affection. None mistook it for personal affection, the kind that would develop between two individuals over time; but a significant percentage initially thought—or hoped—that their visitors felt something particular for them, the urban Marranos, that specific group of people in that time and place, and that consequently they might act to help them. Let us return now to the matter of family, social ties, and the problem of getting things done, for it is here that the framing of relationships in terms of kinship and affection becomes particularly significant.

Family, Social Networks, and the Logic of Cunha

In Portugal, one is struck by the disparity between the formal structure and the manner in which decisions are actually made.

JOYCE RIEGELHAUPT
"Saloio Women"

Quem quer bons padrinhos, arranja-os.
He who wants good "godfathers" finds them for himself.

PORTUGUESE PROVERB

Walking through downtown Lisbon one day, I noticed a sign in the window of a bank touting the company's commitment to customer service. Above the head of a smiling thirty-something woman were the words, "If I have concerns, I go in and ask. It's my right." (*Se tenho dúvidas, entro e pergunto. Estou no meu direito.*) In Portugal, this is not self-evident. Throughout my fieldwork I was struck by a pervasive sense that official bureaucratic channels—in whatever sphere of life those channels might be—did not work as they should. Absolute strangers could not be trusted to attend thoroughly to one's situation, no matter what their job duties required. In matters of finance, employment, access to education and services, or membership in social organizations, people typically assumed that there was something inherently wrong with the system, starting from the premise that one must have an "in," a personal tie of some kind, to achieve one's goals. Although this is partly a class-based phenomenon—working-class and lower-middle-class individuals are far more likely to describe themselves as being kept outside of closed networks and denied access to social benefits because of a lack of personal contacts—the underlying pattern of reliance upon social ties is consistent throughout Portuguese society.

Seeing the sign in the bank window, I was reminded of an awkward moment at a Menorá meeting some months earlier. I had commented that I needed to open a bank account, and Ricardo immediately suggested I go to a branch managed by his cousin. When he told me where it was, several miles outside the city center, I was perplexed. Why would I go there, when the same bank had a branch just a block from my apartment? "In case you have any concerns or problems later," he replied, as if it were obvious. Ricardo seemed offended at my lack of interest. I was baffled as to why I would need a personal connection for what seemed to me a straightforward transaction. Similarly, when I mentioned that I had to renew my research visa, a routine matter of compiling and submitting paperwork, another Menorá member offered that he had a cousin in the Office of Immigration Services who could handle it for me; here, too, there was a momentary social hiccup when I declined to pursue the connection. Much later I realized that both men were offering me access to their personal networks of family and friends, the networks they turned to when they needed help to get things done.

Although Portugal was a very different place at the time of their fieldwork, Joyce Riegelhaupt (1967, 1979) and José Cutileiro (1971) documented similar attitudes and practices in their ethnographies of peasants in the 1960s and 1970s, as did both Estellie Smith (1976, 1980) in her work on Portuguese migrants to North America and, more recently, Manuel Carlos Silva (1998) in his study of peasants in the northern Minho province. All four noted a persistent cultural tendency toward finding contacts through personal networks in order to accomplish everything from minor administrative tasks, such as filing for a permit at a local government office, to major matters like securing employment. While the precise details of their ethnographic materials vary—the contacts may be primarily kin, friends (*amigos*), acquaintances (*conhecimentos*), or all three, as I found in my own research— the pattern remains the same (cf. Gerry and António 2002). People already known to oneself or to family or friends are perceived as being more likely to help, and more trustworthy, than those with whom one has no social tie.[5] Even a tenuous tie is better than none. As a result, when faced with a task that appears to rely upon chance or that would require the goodwill of absolute strangers (*desconhecidos;* literally, "unknown ones"), a common response is to search one's mental roster for someone who could be of help or to spread the word to family and friends, who in turn tell others, who tell others, until a connection is found. According to this logic, the wider one's extended network of social ties, the better.

Consider the case of a man looking for work. He does not search classified ads or go to an employment agency; instead, his wife pursues a solution through personal ties:

> Mrs. Pereira tells various women whom she knows that her husband does not like his job (or has been laid off); the friends and kin pass this message on to their friends and kin; word ultimately comes back to Mrs. Pereira of a job here or there; she then tells her husband that she hears there are openings at X-factory; "Maybe you should give Joe Gomes a call—tell him that you heard *through* Pete Alves that there might be an opening at his place." Thus, when Mr. Pereira calls Joe Gomes he does not mention the entire information network, merely Pete Alves. (Smith 1976: 23)

Although this is a working-class example, reliance on personal ties operates at all levels of Portuguese society, whether or not it is actually necessary. Even if one does not use such ties oneself, the general assumption is that everyone else does, and so the entire system is taken a priori to be inherently dysfunctional. An interviewee quoted in a study of personal networks and employment patterns in northern Portugal explained it this way:

> People have got it into their heads that they won't get anywhere in life without "knowing someone." So they make a point of talking to Mr. X, or Dr. Y, or Mrs. Z about some employment opportunity or other . . . for their son or daughter. And these people reply, "Don't worry, I'll talk to so-and-so,

everything will turn out OK." And even if the intermediary doesn't do anything or hasn't really got any influence, maybe the young person concerned
gets the job. So the whole thing becomes an accepted and normal procedure.
(Gerry et al. 2004: 216)

In both of these examples, a family member is the first node in the network,
and he or she undertakes the role of "agent" (Smith 1976) without being
asked. This is an essential obligation of "family" in Portugal, one repeated to
me by numerous friends in the field and demonstrated in multiple instances:
a parent, child, sibling, close cousin, or godparent should act on one's behalf
upon hearing there is a need, without an explicit request being made.

The case of Dona Ermelinda, a friend's mother, is instructive. Dona
Ermelinda had severe abdominal pain and was diagnosed with gallstones. A
working-class woman without substantial savings, she needed surgery urgently
but could not afford a private clinic. The nearest state hospital placed her on a
nine-month waiting list. Concerned, her niece's husband called a friend who
knew someone who had a relative who worked in the state hospital administration, and that person was able to have her moved up the list by several
months. No money changed hands to make this happen, no explicit exchange
of favors. Although Dona Ermelinda and the person who ultimately helped
her did not know each other, it was relations connecting each node in the
network between them—starting with her motherly relationship to her niece's
husband and ending with his friend's friend's relative—that mattered.

The Portuguese term for what Dona Ermelinda's niece's husband did for
her is *meter uma cunha,* "to place a wedge," referring to the act of using a
contact in one's network to circumvent official channels or bypass an administrative hurdle. Though rarely discussed openly, the institution of *cunha* is a
pervasive aspect of Portuguese society. Colloquially called *o factor-C* (the
C-factor), it encompasses a spectrum of practices ranging from relatively
benign acts of assistance in bureaucratic problem-solving or access to otherwise closed social networks, to full-blown favoritism, nepotism, and financial
corruption (Gerry et al. 2004: 214; cf. Silva 1993). The term has become an
epithet in Portugal, particularly among the middle classes; few will admit
that they have benefited from it themselves, but most will readily suggest that
others do. Nonetheless, the basic structure of *cunha*—wherein one relies
upon one's extended social network for ad hoc solutions to bureaucratic problems or to gain professional advancement—remains in place.[6]

Let us return to Ricardo and his cousin, the bank branch manager. As it
turned out, Ricardo's offer proved useful after all. When I went to the nearest

branch to open the account, without which I could not draw on my research grant, I learned I needed a *número de identidade fiscal* (NIF), roughly equivalent to the American social security number. Processing the NIF application would take three weeks. Counting time for the bank account application to be processed thereafter, it would be at least five weeks before I would have access to the grant. Hearing of my troubles, Ricardo mentioned once again that his cousin managed a branch. This time, I accepted. A few days later he escorted me to his cousin's bank for an appointment. Duarte, an imposing man in his mid-forties wearing a well-cut suit, ushered me into his inner office. He was brisk and professional as he went over the forms, explaining each and helping me fill them in. He waved away my concerns about the missing NIF and instructed me to email it to him as soon as it arrived. He would personally approve my new account now, on the spot, and fill in the missing information when it came. I could access my grant within a week. As I left his office, Duarte leaned out and greeted Ricardo, who was waiting in the lobby. "Come for dinner soon," he said to Ricardo. "Diogo wants to show you his new video games." As we walked back to the metro, Ricardo explained that he was *padrinho* to Duarte's twelve-year-old son.

Here, again, no explicit exchange of favors was made. A single favor, one that clearly involved overlooking certain legalities, was requested and granted on the basis of a strong family tie between the two men. In the background was a far greater favor, Ricardo's commitment as *padrinho* to care for Duarte's son as his own, should tragedy strike, and, as the proverb at the beginning of this section suggests, to draw on his personal networks to help Diogo find employment or resolve any intractable issues that might arise during his lifetime. Whether either man consciously took that aspect of their relationship into account when deciding respectively to request and grant this particular favor, we cannot know for certain. But Duarte's decision to help was certainly not about me. We had no prior relationship; I had nothing to offer him, nor did he know enough about me to have any sense of whether I did. I was a bystander to the transaction. It was Ricardo, his cousin and his son's godfather, who asked the favor of him, and it was Ricardo who did a favor— placed a *cunha*—for me. Unless Duarte and I developed a friendship of our own, it was unlikely he would grant me another favor without Ricardo's intercession. In the past, my elderly neighbor explained, *cunhas* like this one could be secured openly with "money or wine, even sausages"; but today most Portuguese would prefer to distance themselves from the "premodern" institution of *cunha*, increasingly understood negatively as *corrupção* (corruption, i.e., clientelism or nepotism), and present themselves positively as granting *favores* (favors) as one does for close friends and family, out of love.[7]

Often, of course, official channels do work as they should. Bureaucracies function according to stated rules and procedures; people apply for jobs through a depersonalized process and await a result; research visas like mine are approved quickly and efficiently without anyone placing a *cunha*. In practice, the Portuguese rely upon anonymous institutional structures on a daily basis. At a conceptual level, however, the role of personal connections looms large. Upon seeing what appears to be unwarranted success or unfair advancement, people routinely invoke *cunha* as the culprit. *Cunha,* I was told, was responsible for everything from awkward translations of tourist materials ("a tourism official hired a friend's kid, obviously, that's why it's so bad") to celebrities' children appearing in lucrative cameo roles on television ("obviously they had an 'in' at casting; they can't even act!"). One friend surmised that my application to a Portuguese granting institution had been unsuccessful because I didn't mention a connection to any of the "big names" associated with it. These are situations in which fairness is increasingly equated with dispassionate anonymity: ideally an applicant would be judged on aptitude, not the breadth of his or her personal network. But what of membership in social organizations, where decisions to include or exclude can be entirely personal, even capricious? Here preexisting ties are crucial, and sometimes explicitly required. Ironically, even the Marrano associations required that prospective members have their application endorsed by a current member.

The major problem facing members of HaShalom and Menorá, as we have seen, was that they lacked any social tie to the normative Jewish communities. These were closed networks, as far as they were concerned; on attempting to enter they were repeatedly rejected. Many were familiar with stories of the handful of self-identified descendants of Portuguese Jews who had managed to become integrated into those communities. All of them, they assured me, had preexisting professional, personal, or familial ties to someone in that world and shared that person's class position. As such, they could use their connections for initial acceptance and, if necessary, to ensure full incorporation into the community. There was the case of a high-profile lawyer, a prominent Marrano activist in the 1980s and 1990s, who married into one of Shaaré Tikvá's leading families; there were the two young men who became leaders in CIL's youth group even while studying to "return"; there was the Marrano psychologist who joined the board of the Porto synagogue without being Jewish according to halakhah. Lacking the social ties and class standing of these men, how were those left outside the gates to gain access? From whom could they request the favor of help?

Were it any other sphere of life, they would have mentioned to family and friends that they were having difficulty, consciously or unconsciously drawing upon the deeply ingrained logic of social networks to find a way around what was for them an inherently unfair system. In essence, the logic of *cunha*—that wedge supplying "leverage [for] manipulating the system" (Riegelhaupt 1979: 83)—is this:

1) official institutional channels frequently do not work as they should;

2) when they do not work, one can attempt to circumvent them;

3) one can (even should) rely upon family and friends for help in such matters;

4) social ties are key, because what really matters is who you know and who your family and friends (and their family and friends) know;

5) the more social ties one has and the larger one's extended social network, the better;

6) there is nothing wrong with giving a family member or close friend (or their family members or friends) a contact that will help them overcome a problem in an inherently dysfunctional or patently unfair system (cf. Cutileiro 1971: 205).

Now, my use of the term *cunha* is shorthand for the entire conceptual framework that encompasses and contains it, according to which institutions are never entirely impersonal, nor do they function well. Hence personal relationships—family and friends—are the most effective and trustworthy means of getting things done. It is this general conceptual framework, what I am calling the *logic of cunha,* that gives rise to the twin social practices of *cunha* (in the narrow sense of nepotism or clientelism) and *favores* (favors done for loved ones), and more broadly to reliance on social networks to accomplish one's goals. Beyond outright corruption, these assumptions and practices are so taken for granted as to go unremarked in daily life.

In pursuing connections with foreign visitors, urban Marranos engaged in a largely unconscious, international application of the logic of *cunha*. The reasons for this were both structural and interpersonal. There was no way for them to enter the Portuguese Jewish community through the official institutional channels of membership or conversion. In this sense, the system was not functioning as they felt it should. But neither could they gain access through their existing personal networks. Enter the foreign visitors, who showed them affection, who called them kin, and who bore the promise of new social ties stretching far beyond the local situation. Small wonder the Marranos hoped the tourists and outreach workers would become "friends" who would stay in touch and help them out of the impasse in which they were trapped. Whether by offering a social tie to someone in the normative Jewish community who had power to admit them, by connecting them with an organization that would facilitate their "return," by sending them educational materials, by coming back to teach classes on Jewish life and thought, by guiding them in creating their own Jewish communities, or simply by putting them in touch with other people who could do the same, there were many ways their foreign visitors could have assisted them, and indeed eventually some did. I never heard anyone ask for these things explicitly, however. What they did instead was precisely what they would have done when asking a favor of a family member or close friend: they mentioned the problem— they told their stories—to what appeared to be a very sympathetic audience, and then hoped that assistance would be forthcoming. This is the logic of *cunha* at work.

Although their engagement with foreign Jews was partly instrumental, the urban Marranos' reliance on the cultural logic of *cunha* was neither mercenary nor cynical, any more than Dona Ermelinda's actions were when she told loved ones that she faced an unconscionably long wait for much-needed surgery. They had an embryonic expectation, based on their visitors' expressions of interest and warmth, that *pessoas de fora* might act on the information they had shared, that they might pull whatever strings they could to help them. Said Dulce,

> We were always hoping that someone would look at us and see—"Oh, wow, it's about time, yes sir, I will help your group." We always thought Nostálgia [members] were going to help us, that they were going to bring us in. Because the Nostálgia forum was created by and for people who are searching like we are, so they should help everyone who is in that same situation.

In this sense the urban Marranos' orientation was quite different from that of their visitors. What brought them to meetings with foreign Jews and crypto-Jewish descendants was a specific need, a desire for belonging and acceptance and above all integration into the Jewish world, not a celebration of a sense of kinship already achieved.

"IT'S BY TALKING THAT PEOPLE COME TO AN UNDERSTANDING"

Amidst the language of kin, it is important to remember that encounters between urban Marranos and their visitors were essentially interactions between tourists and toured. Whether heritage tourists or outreach workers, whether in a group or independently, all first-time visitors were travelers discovering new worlds during a temporary break from everyday life (cf. Smith 1989: 1). The local people, on the other hand, remained in place; their fleeting interactions with traveling Jews were a window onto a different way of being, one that opened briefly and then just as quickly closed. The two met in what Bruner (2005: 17) calls "the touristic borderzone," a space of interaction where the local people "engage the tourists in structured ways in predetermined localities for defined periods of time." Where their encounters diverged from more common forms of scheduled tourist-toured interaction was in the nature of the exchange. This was not a costumed performance of ethnic dance, rehearsed and presented for tourists; nor was it an ethnic crafts market, traditional wares spread out on blankets for them to buy. There was no formal presentation, no prepared remarks, no master of ceremonies to shape and guide the visitors' experience. In format, it was much closer to a social mixer or a reception, or sometimes a question-and-answer session. The primary mode of interaction was talking. Not dancing, not displaying, not buying and selling—just talking.

Visitors to the Marrano associations generally arrived with an overarching assumption of mutual intelligibility and an enormous amount of goodwill. They were eager to talk with the locals, to hear their stories. There was just one problem: only three members of HaShalom and two members of Menorá spoke English with anything approaching true fluency. A few others had good comprehension but limited speaking ability. The majority could manage basic conversation with a limited vocabulary and minimal subtlety. A remaining few understood very little and could convey even less. And yet I was repeatedly struck by tourists and outreach workers speaking to their hosts very quickly, in English, without first ascertaining their level of comprehension. Even visitors who were non-native English speakers did this. It was especially pronounced among those volunteer outreach workers who used family metaphors most effusively, suggesting that they had a high level of built-up imagining and anticipation that shaped their experience and made the specific life stories of the individuals standing before them less important. Often there was no translator available during their interactions, resulting in partial communication at best. Even when I or one of the local fluent English speakers was called upon to translate, a great deal of nuance was lost.

A common Portuguese saying has it that "it's by talking that people come to an understanding" (*a falar é que a gente se entende*). Over the months in Portugal I found that proverb increasingly ironic, for the more visitors spoke with local people, the less they appeared to understand. There was continual slippage on multiple levels—emotional, linguistic, conceptual. This, even as both parties appeared to think that they were communicating well. The miscommunication was detectable only to the few who spoke both English and Portuguese fluently. The problem first dawned on me in the midst of translating during a tour-group reception. It was Anshel's first visit, and he was full of love and effusive appreciation for his categorical "lost brothers and sisters," the Marranos. Speaking very quickly to a member of HaShalom, barely slowing for me to translate, he listed his ideas for generating international attention for the Marrano cause. Orlando's response was receptive and warm, but not overly so. Portuguese has multiple forms of address that convey at least four different levels of social distance and politeness, depending on context, and their forms vary by speaker, relative age, and social class. When answering Anshel, Orlando used the polite *você* (you), signaling slight social distance; an adult uses *tu,* the least formal "you," only with close friends, within families, and among peers who meet socially. Anshel's affect, on the other hand, was that of a loving grandfather or uncle. He stood quite close to Orlando, repeatedly touched his arm, and made asides to me and others nearby about how close he felt to the whole group and how he felt he had found long-lost cousins.

I was at a loss as to how to translate "you" and its corresponding verb forms. Had he been speaking Portuguese, Anshel would clearly have used *tu;* everything about his affect suggested that he brought much informal affection to the interaction. But I had not yet started using *tu* with Orlando myself, as he was a decade older and we had met only recently, and so even in my role as translator I felt awkward addressing him informally. I was also certain that in a similar situation between Portuguese-speaking strangers the *você* form would be used, even if only initially, no matter how close their felt familial connection. I had experienced as much when meeting my own Portuguese cousins for the first time earlier that year. In the end, I opted for the Portuguese-appropriate form, translating Anshel's "you" as *você*. In English, on the other hand, Orlando's *você* became the ambiguous

English "you." In the process, I later realized, I allowed each to preserve his own reading of the situation. The slippage in emotional content went unremarked. Anshel was convinced he had bonded with a local person; Orlando had had a straightforward conversation with a unusually warm, even loving stranger. He did not share the emotional intensity that Anshel professed to feel.

As it turned out, I was not the only one to note this translation conundrum and handle it as I did. As a fluent English speaker at HaShalom pointed out to me, though, it didn't much matter how one translated that sort of thing: visitors came in with an expectation of what they would find—warmth, connection, a feeling of relatedness—and they were virtually never disappointed. As she described it,

> They come, and it's like they drift in on clouds and then we're there, ... we bring food, and sometimes they come bearing gifts, and we feed them, and we're *exactly the way they thought we would be.* So many people come, and yet everyone leaves fully satisfied. But if they really *saw us,* they wouldn't—they couldn't possibly be as satisfied. But they are, because they come expecting something and whether it's there or not, they get it.

It was precisely the lack of communicative transparency that allowed visitors' perceptions of emotional and conceptual intelligibility to continue. The warm welcome, the food placed out for them, the relaxed body language and unstructured time to converse freely (if across language barriers), and the intensity of such a brief visit combined to create a feeling of meeting long-lost friends and family, a feeling the urban Marranos also sought and welcomed.

What was lost in the process was a clear sense on either side of who the individuals in the room really were, what they actually felt, and what assumptions they made about the encounter. Expecting a homogeneous group, visitors would hear one person's story and assume it applied equally to everyone; and the most likely to share theirs at length were those who, like Tomás, had an especially dramatic Marrano story to tell. Few imagined that their hosts might include people who identified neither as Marranos nor as B'nai Anusim. Yet among those they so effusively greeted as "kin" were two or three Portuguese participants with no known Jewish ancestry, who wanted to convert and had been unable to do so through the normative Jewish communities. Visitors saw a room filled with "Marranos," people just a few generations removed from crypto-Jews like those in Belmonte, the long-lost "family" they had come to meet. For their part, the urban Marranos consistently confused the nationality, background, and intentions of their visitors. In part because most visitors spoke English to them, in part because most had their first tour-group encounter with Graciana's Conference-Tours, they repeatedly misremembered groups and individuals as having been American or crypto-Jewish descendant when in fact they were Ashkenazi or Sephardic Jews from South Africa, Israel, England, even Mexico. I heard outreach volunteers described as ultra-Orthodox whom I knew to be secular, personal ties assumed between individuals I knew had neither met nor had contacts in common, motives attributed to people whom I knew from prior conversations to be thinking in another direction entirely. And, as we have seen, they assumed from their visitors' affect and expressions of support that these *pessoas de fora* were committed to helping them find a solution to their local difficulties. Much was misconstrued on both sides.

Why, then, did these encounters almost invariably go so smoothly and produce so much good feeling in the moment? There is a phenomenon at work here that I call *productive miscommunication,* a delicately calibrated balance between communicative clarity and opacity where just enough is transmitted to establish a sense of common ground and mutual understanding, but not so much as to reveal that the two sides' imaginings of each other are flawed.[8] Although urban Marranos and their visitors made sense of their encounters according to different structures of reasoning, there was sufficient congruence between them—the language of kinship and expressions of emotional engagement—that they seemed superficially to be operating within the same conceptual framework. And, because both sides had a substantial if unconscious investment in a harmonious, positive exchange, neither probed too deeply into the other's personal history, motivation, or intentions. During these very brief encounters, visitors talked with several local people, and vice versa. It is to be expected that most came away from the interaction without having their expectations shaken. In the moment of encounter, at least, everyone got more or less what they had hoped: the urban Marranos achieved a feeling of Jewish belonging, however fleetingly, and heard expressions of sympathy and support from foreign Jews; and the tourists and outreach workers were able to meet and hear the stories of "Marranos" (or "B'nai Anusim"), the treasured remnants of pre-Inquisition Portuguese Jewry.

There is a broader principle here, one that applies to any interaction in the touristic borderzone where presumed mutual intelligibility is part of the attraction: parties to the encounter must not communicate sufficiently to

disrupt the appearance of mutual understanding about the nature and meaning of the exchange. Too little information, and common ground cannot be
established; the parties remain alien to each other. Too much information,
and points of communicative slippage become obvious, the assumption of
commonality proven incorrect. Whether in instances of "roots" journeys,
solidarity tours, volunteer vacations, or even sex/romance tourism couplings,
the emotional effectiveness of the encounter typically relies upon limited
communicative clarity and even outright misunderstanding. A great deal of
mutual imagining both preceded and followed meetings between urban
Marranos and their visitors. Each side had a vested interest in keeping their
image of the other intact. There was an exquisite tension, a communicative
tightrope, that both parties to the encounter walked.

Shortly before I returned to the United States, a visitor to HaShalom
provided the exception that proved the rule. Vacationing in Lisbon, the
Brazilian rabbi had heard about the city's "Marrano synagogue" and was
curious, as a similar phenomenon had been under way in Brazil for some time
(Ramagem 1994). We gathered at Anshei Emet on a freezing night just after
Christmas, everyone expecting the usual pleasantries and informal chitchat.
But while the rabbi was friendly, it was the friendliness of a stranger. He
offered little about himself beyond his birth in Eastern Europe and migration to Brazil as a child during the Holocaust, nor did he inquire about their
backgrounds. Instead, he asked each one, including me, to describe what we
saw as our personal strength vis-à-vis Judaism and the Jewish people. Unsure
what was really being asked, each answered hesitantly. Manuel named his
love of scholarship; Pedro, his "tribalism"; Catarina, her facility with
languages. It was an awkward exchange, the group becoming increasingly
uncertain why the rabbi had come. Suspecting that he was doing reconnais-
sance for CIL, as he mentioned having visited Shaaré Tikvá that morning, or
that he had been sent by any of the numerous rabbis who had passed through
and promised to explore possibilities for a *beit din*, Dulce waited impatiently
for him to explain. When he did not, she burst out angrily, "All these people
come, and they want to know about us. You want to know about us. How
will you *help* us? That's what we want to know. What can you do to help?" So
rare was it for the group to receive Portuguese-speaking visitors that I was
momentarily stunned, not only at Dulce's outburst but at realizing that the
rabbi understood her perfectly. There was an awkward pause. Although
something of a firebrand in her native Portuguese, Dulce rarely spoke at any
length with visitors because of her limited English. "Help you? I don't know

how I could," said the rabbi, taken aback. After a few moments of strained conversation, he left. Over dinner afterward, Nuno voiced what we all had thought: "Maybe it's better when we can't actually understand each other."

IMAGINATION, EXPERIENCE, AND THE SPACE BETWEEN

In this chapter I have traced the format and character of interactions between urban Marranos and their foreign Jewish visitors. Their encounters point up a difficult question about belonging in our globally interconnected world: What happens when people who have long imagined each other from afar in terms of commonality, connectedness, or kinship come face-to-face in the form of a tourist encounter? To what extent does the lived experience of contact confirm or disrupt participants' imaginings about the people they meet? What factors come into play? These questions extend well beyond the case of Marranos and Jews; they are crucial for understanding the interpersonal and emotional dynamics of tourist-toured interactions when one or more of the parties is seeking a space of human connection, solidarity, or belonging. Transnational adoptees returning to their birth country on "motherland tours," for example, may discover to their dismay that they hold radically different perceptions of the obligations of kinship—to birth parents, biological relatives, or the nation at large—than those held by locals, potentially leading to disappointment on all sides (Howell 2007; Kim 2010). Diasporic tourists, too, may find their anticipated experience of "homecoming" undermined when local people treat them as foreign vacationers like any others—an economic resource, to be engaged only in commercial transactions—rather than as compatriots or kin (Bruner 1996). And yet many such tourists do have the experience they had hoped. From feminist solidarity tours to individual travelers seeking romance abroad, numerous cases in the anthropological literature reveal a delicate tension between imagination and experience. Given the ever-present possibility of contradictory framings of the encounter, under what conditions can a sense of interpersonal communion and belonging be achieved?

The ethnographic material presented in this chapter suggests that in situations with sufficient mutual intelligibility to give rise to productive miscommunication—that delicate balance between communicative clarity and opacity that maintains the impression of shared understanding—brief encounters do little to challenge pretour narratives on either side. Tourists and other short-term visitors who have a great deal of emotional investment in a particular framing will encounter exactly what they hope to find: here, crypto-Jewish descendants came looking for *primos,* and found them; outreach workers came to "bond" with lost Jews, and did; heritage tourists came to be moved by the rebirth of Jewish life from the Inquisition's ashes, and indeed they were. In each case, imagination was a continuously present force, coloring every interaction. The urban Marranos also brought powerful imaginings to the encounters, and they too found what they were looking for: warmth, momentary belonging, an apparent promise of assistance. Had they shared the same cultural schemas or spoken the same language, as members of HaShalom did with the Brazilian rabbi, it would have been clear that neither party was exactly as the other had thought.

Paradoxically, then, it would seem that despite their expressed desire for "real" interaction with Portuguese Marranos, for foreign visitors less communicative clarity was better than more. Indeed, as anthropologist Julia Harrison (2003: 46) suggests, from the traveler's perspective it may be of little consequence if "what [is] communicated between a tourist and a local person through a few words, gesture, body language, laughter... [has] nothing to do with what was intended to be communicated. Such details hardly matter if all the tourist is interested in is the perception that some form of positive connection was made." Although partial miscommunication was initially positive for the urban Marranos, too, theirs was a very different position. Staying in place, they stood before a revolving door of foreign arrivals; while the encounters continued to be brief and effervescent, emotionally uplifting while under way, cumulatively they conveyed a different message. Over time members of Menorá and HaShalom came to understand that most visitors had no real intention of helping them, despite enthusiastic promises in the moment. At times they confessed that a particular visit had left them feeling like exotic creatures, inspiring fascination and awe. The space between imagination and experience began to grow, as did an awareness of the gap between their impression of the encounter and that of their visitors. No matter how powerful their desire for belonging, global imaginings of Jewish peoplehood could not counteract the stark facticity of face-to-face encounter.

The ethnographic material presented in this chapter represents a particular period, roughly from 2002 to mid-2005. Thereafter, a small number of outreach workers, rabbis, and former tourists returned again and again, a development that irrevocably upset the balance of productive miscommunication.

The opacity that had long characterized the Marranos' interactions with their visitors cleared; they began to see one another more and more as individuals, with particular, complex, messy life stories that diverged from the potent imaginings and neat historical metanarratives they had originally held. Rather than falsifying their presumed common ground and goodwill, however, in this case the increased communication led to something else altogether. Emerging friendships and, ultimately, something approaching kinship—relations of mutual obligation and care (Borneman 2001)—between the Marranos and their repeat visitors opened a new arena of relatedness: that of love. But that is the subject of the next chapter.

FIVE

From Ancestors to Affection

MAKING CONNECTIONS, MAKING KIN

> Humans . . . are not blind egos following deterministic sequences
> of events, of cultural paradigms and rules. They plot sequences of
> experiences in narratives organized around for whom and what
> they care.
>
> JOHN BORNEMAN
> "Caring and Being Cared For"

IN DECEMBER, PORTUGAL'S CITIES AND TOWNS come alive with holiday lights. Woven into metal-framed arches that span the cobbled streets of each historic city center, adorning every narrow lane of Lisbon's eighteenth-century Baixa district, the lights trace the shape of bells, shooting stars, and candles. In the final weeks of my fieldwork, the great square in front of Porto's city hall boasted an enormous, multistory conical scaffold covered in tens of thousands of tiny lights: the city's "Christmas tree." The lights blinked on and off in a looping series of patterns—bells, stars, candles, trees, snowmen—accompanied by the Christmas carol croonings of Frank Sinatra and Bing Crosby. With nightfall came a carnival atmosphere, as hundreds milled around taking pictures, laughing, eating snacks purchased at stalls that ringed the square. But in António Abreu's middle-class residential neighborhood, just a few blocks from the great synagogue built for Barros Basto's Marrano revival, there were few lights decorating the street. Christmas was the furthest thing from António's mind.

It was Friday evening, and António needed to leave shortly for services. Darkness was fast falling and opening prayers would begin momentarily. He would walk—driving on Shabbat is forbidden—and he did not want to be late. Since we met, early in 2004, António had become increasingly committed to making his return to Judaism through the Orthodox path offered by Shavei Israel, guided by the soft-spoken, gentle rabbi the organization had placed in Porto shortly after I began my fieldwork there. At the time António, whose story appears in chapter 2, had been a gregarious, excitable young man who was always interested in meeting tourists. Like most founding members of Menorá, he had been committed to righting the historical wrongs done to his ancestors, ideally through a formal rite of "return," and he had long seen visitors as a way to connect with the Jewish world and perhaps chart a path toward his and the others' reincorporation. But two years on, António's attitude had changed. He was tired, physically tired. Tired of the endless visitors, all asking the same questions; tired of being looked at; tired of the promises to remain in touch that came to naught. With the rabbi from Shavei Israel, he had found what appeared to be a direct path to "return": a multiyear process of study and strict adherence to the prohibitions and directives of Jewish law that would culminate in Orthodox conversion under the supervision of a *beit din* in Israel.

It had been months since we last spoke at length, and we had much catching up to do. When I arrived earlier that afternoon, António made tea and we sat together in his tiny living room. He recounted the biggest change that had taken place since my move to Lisbon: over the past several months there had been a protracted struggle at the synagogue, and in the end the Israeli brothers who had run the community for two decades effectively ceded the building to the urban Marranos and their rabbi. It was now a regional center for resuming Barros Basto's "work of redemption."[1] But other things had changed, as well. When António spoke of how he felt about tourists now, his voice was sad, even disillusioned. He mentioned an Israeli tour group that had joined them for Shabbat services a few weeks earlier. The rabbi explained in Hebrew to the visitors that most of the people in the synagogue were B'nai Anusim making their "return." Upon hearing that, António said, the tourists' affect changed:

> We started noticing that the group was looking at us as if we were a rare species, a lost species, like, "Oh! Oh! They are so beautiful!" They weren't practicing Jews, not at all. They drove up in the tour bus on Shabbat, then drove away. They got so emotional! It was like being a monkey in the zoo. A monkey in the zoo.

He sighed. He wished the rabbi wouldn't tell everyone who came to the synagogue what their background was, he said. "We don't need to tell them everything. Look, I have a policy of truth. If they ask us, we say who we are. But I'd rather not volunteer it."

But why? I asked. Hadn't the interest of foreign visitors been helpful for his own journey, in the long run? Hadn't Shavei Israel come to Portugal through the intervention of Graciana Mayer, the globe-trotting activist for the B'nai Anusim, who had twice brought a busload of tourists, educators, and other descendants of Portuguese Jews to meet with members of Menorá? True, he acknowledged, but most of the time, even when foreign Jewish visitors took the time to talk to them, they looked at them like exotic creatures. "Ohhhhh, the little monkeys [*macaquinhos*] are so beautiful!" he said, adopting an enraptured voice. "When they do that, I feel bad. It's uncomfortable. We all feel like children, with them looking at us indulgently." What was wrong with being looked at that way? I asked. António sighed again. "They don't look at us like *brothers*, you know, 'brothers in the faith'; they look at us like a thing. A beautiful thing, but a thing."

The distinction António made between being looked at as a "beautiful thing" and being treated as a "brother in the faith" is crucial for the argument I develop in this chapter. There were, in fact, two primary trends in interaction style among the foreign visitors, corresponding neatly to the two ways of seeing that António specified. These two trends were not necessarily characteristic of tourists, on the one hand, and volunteer outreach workers and rabbis, on the other; some tourists clearly interacted with the Marranos as individuals and equals, while some visiting rabbis seemed much more interested in them in the categorical sense as "B'nai Anusim." The reverse, of course, was also true. The critical difference was the relative weight a visitor gave to their collective status as a reflection of the metanarrative of Jewish destruction and survival. That difference, in turn, led to different suggested means by which the urban Marranos could become (re)incorporated into the Jewish people and to varying degrees of likelihood that they would feel an enduring sense of belonging as a result.

In this chapter, I explore the repercussions of these two ways of seeing through the story of a subset of the original members of HaShalom and Menorá, who set about forming their own Jewish community. Over the course of ten months, coinciding with the latter half of my fieldwork, they developed a close relationship with a network of rabbis, Jewish educators, outreach workers, and former tourists that spanned three continents and gave them a sense of having finally joined "the Jewish family." As we will see, that close relationship resulted in their achieving halakhic status as Jews, but by unexpected means and with unanticipated results for the way they understood themselves relative to the Jewish people. In the end, the shift from a national frame of reference to a global one, from an identity based on ancestry to one steeped in relations of the present, proved transformative.

I described earlier an interaction between three members of HaShalom and a tour leader whom they met one evening after services at Shaaré Tikvá. Upon being told by a sympathetic congregant that the three men were B'nai Anusim, descendants of the Inquisition's survivors, the tour leader was enchanted. "This is history, right in front of us!" he exclaimed. Although he meant well and was genuinely interested in hearing their stories, it was precisely the repeated implication that the urban Marranos were an embodiment of "history" for their foreign visitors that led them to feel they were being viewed "like a thing." For many tourists, as we have seen, to come into contact with a descendant of the storied Inquisition-era Marranos was to have an encounter with the extraordinary. Even as they presumed that there would be sufficient common ground to communicate freely, it was difficult for them to see past their own enchantment. They were, above all, moved.

In this sense they were no different from most tourists, as John Urry's (2002) concept of the *tourist gaze* suggests. Urry coined the term to capture how leisure travelers apprehend objects and people differently when away from home than they would in non-touristic contexts. He drew inspiration from Michel Foucault's (1973) concept of the *medical gaze,* a historically situated mode of viewing the human body that arose in conjunction with the medical clinic. Like Foucault's, Urry's concept "is not necessarily ocular and is not concerned only with spectacle as some claim, but relies on mental perceptions" (Maoz 2006: 222). We focus our attention on different things when traveling, in markedly different ways, than at home or at work. The tourist gaze picks out that which has been anticipated, dreamed about, pictured on postcards and in guidebooks, featured in novels and in films, invoked in rumor, fiction, and myth—in short, the assemblage of images that make up tourism imaginaries (Salazar and Graburn 2014). These things are rarely extraordinary for local people. The tourist gaze transforms ordinary people going about their lives into delightful objects to behold; it renders an assortment of buildings a long-imagined cityscape; it makes a picturesque landscape of what is for the locals simply a village and surrounding fields.

In early twenty-first-century Portugal, the tourist gaze rendered the urban Marranos "family"—but of a very particular kind. They became an embodiment of a collective past, one theoretically shared by tourist and toured. Filtered through imagination and narrative, they were a point of connection, a remnant, even a relic of a tragic and pivotal event in the history of the Jewish people. The metanarrative of Jewish destruction, survival, and rebirth, the pretour narrative of getting to meet "Marranos" (crypto-Jews) in Portugal, and eventually face-to-face contact with the urban Marranos themselves converged to produce an utterly overdetermined encounter. For international tourists who traced their own ancestry to Portuguese crypto-Jews, there was a similar convergence of narratives around ancestral loss, genealogy, and discovery of long-lost kin. In both cases, the specificity of the individual people at the destination mattered little. What was important was that they were Marranos, B'nai Anusim, "descendants of the forced ones." It was in light of that confluence of narratives and imaginaries—of destruction, of loss, of survival, of discovery, of contact—that most visitors perceived and experienced the local people. Theirs was a *narrative gaze,* one that privileged history over the present.[2]

Like António, local people in tourist destinations often become aware of the touristic nature of the gaze being directed at them, even when the traveler is not (Bunten 2008; Evans-Pritchard 1989). As Urry (2002: 145) explains, "Such gazes implicate both the *gazer* and the *gazee* in an ongoing and systematic set of social and physical relations." Merely by looking with such obvious interest and appreciation at António and others in the synagogue that day, the Israeli tourists participated in a common pattern of interaction between Portugal's urban Marranos and their foreign visitors. This would have been so even had they interacted with them directly, as did the tour groups whose visits I described in the previous chapter. Rather than offering the local people a bridge to the Jewish world at large, encounters like these tended instead to maintain the distance between the two. In large part because of the publicity disseminated about them online, but also because of their discursive positioning by travel writers, tour guides, and outreach organizations like Shavei Israel, António, Dulce, Catarina, and the rest had become something to be visited, gazed upon, photographed, consumed: they had become a tourist site.

In the previous chapter I introduced the concept of productive miscommunication, a phenomenon in which a shared perception of mutual intelligibility between tourist and toured obscures communicative slippage on a deeper level, yet it is precisely that slippage that enables the encounter to proceed smoothly. As long as members of HaShalom and Menorá felt that their visitors' interest and affection was in fact directed *at them,* a living community of individuals, the encounters left a positive glow from having been momentarily accepted and suggested the possibility of being helped out of their in-between state as Marranos. But productive miscommunication is by nature an unstable phenomenon. It rests upon a limited amount of information being exchanged and, ideally, none at all that could disrupt the expectations of either party. While the foreign visitors came and went with their imaginings intact, rarely to return, the urban Marranos remained in place, accumulating experience from each encounter. Over time they realized that despite their visitors' continual invocation of kinship and emotional connection, the vast majority did not feel any particular obligation to help them, nor did they remain in contact after the visit. The nature of the miscommunication became apparent. Like António, participants in both associations began to speak of their experience as feeling like exotic animals or creatures in a circus. Among themselves they developed a shorthand expression for the dynamic when they felt the tourist gaze most keenly: *o jardim zoológico dos marranos*—the Marrano zoo. That dynamic was equally likely to transpire with visiting rabbis and volunteer outreach workers as with Jewish heritage tourists; as Dulce explained, it was a matter of the difference between *olhar* (to look) and *ver* (to see). Many visitors, she felt, looked at them without seeing them at all.

Although it may sound pejorative in English, their description of interactions as zoo-like was not necessarily critical or cynical. More often than not, it was said in a self-mocking, ironic tone, indicating frustration at their own inability to break through the visitors' imaginings sufficiently to be *seen,* truly seen, rather than remaining objects of the tourist gaze. "They think it's romantic, 'the resistance of the Anusim,'" Tomás told me. "But for us it's just a really frustrating situation." Why, then, did they continue to welcome tourists and other visitors? Tiago used the zoo analogy to explain:

TIAGO: Look, people aren't coming here with bad intentions. They just come to look. But just looking is already something good, right? Because if not, if the children didn't come to the zoo, if they didn't pay for the tickets, there would be no money in the zoo and the critters [*bichos*] would starve [*morriam à fome*]. So the critters have to be happy to receive the children's visits, right?

NL: You're saying without the visits, this group would starve?

TIAGO: Of course.

NL: What's the food, then?

TIAGO: The food is the pleasure of knowing there are people who value us. It's good, especially when visitors treat us as equals. And I do think the majority of people who come treat us like equals. Even if they come and don't do anything for us. If they do, so much the better, because we need it, right?

For Tiago, the metaphor of the zoo did not necessarily mean that they were treated as inferiors, nor was it inherently negative; it meant simply that they had become a tourist destination. People were coming to look at them, but they meant no harm. On the contrary, Tiago felt—as did most participants, António's objections notwithstanding—that the feeling these visits imparted of being valued and, for a moment, of belonging made it worth their while, even if they were sometimes objectified and occasionally greatly misunderstood.

Where the narrative gaze became problematic was in discussions with rabbis and outreach workers over possible schemes to resolve their liminal status, trapped between non-Jews and Jews. Recall that their problem was twofold. First, they needed some form of ritual of (re)incorporation, typically called conversion but which they insisted should be a "return," for which all major branches of Judaism require a three-member rabbinic court, or *beit din*. At no time were there more than two rabbis or other qualified individuals resident in Portugal.[3] Second, they needed a Jewish community that would accept them as members, but as we saw in chapter 3 the doors of Portugal's "mainstream" communities were shut tightly against them. From the perspective of conversion, becoming a Jew is not simply a matter of adopting a new religion; it is simultaneously one of becoming incorporated into a *people*. One must join a community to learn from its members how to live as—how to *be*—a Jew. According to the metanarrative of destruction and survival, however, the urban Marranos were already Jews, in spirit if not according to Jewish law. Hence most proposals devised to help them completely side-stepped their present-day need for a community to join. Instead, the solutions were conceived with an eye to the past, responding to the Marranos' ancestral articulation of their Jewish identity and emphasizing a symbolic righting of wrongs done to their distant forebears.

A single example will suffice to show the powerful influence of the narrative gaze. In late 2005, researchers announced that they had located the site of an Inquisition-era Marrano synagogue in Porto's historic center, in a private home now owned by the Catholic Church. The find generated considerable international publicity, for although there is substantial historical documentation of hidden synagogues in Portugal, to date little archaeological evidence has been found. Early in 2006, a rabbi who had devoted much of his career to working with "lost Jews" around the world developed a plan. As a sign of acceptance for all who had not yet reclaimed their ancestral identity and as a dramatic declaration that a rekindling of the Jewish spirit was taking place in Portugal after five centuries, the rabbi proposed to gather a small group from Lisbon and Porto for a ceremony of return. It would be held in none other than the newly discovered Marrano synagogue—rabbinic court and all. Moreover, he proposed to hold the event just before Passover, the holiday commemorating the Israelites' freedom from slavery in Egypt, adding another layer of poignancy to this celebration of the Portuguese Marranos' emergence after centuries of hiding. This, he felt, would be an appropriately momentous way to conduct their reincorporation into the Jewish people.

Proposals like this one certainly promised satisfying narrative closure, marking the Marranos' "return" to their ancestral faith and transforming their halakhic status from Gentile to Jew. But while such an event would have incorporated them into the Jewish world ritually and symbolically, it would have done nothing to bring them into that world in the concrete sense of human relationships. Instead, such solutions held the Marranos fast in a kind of historical amber, still isolated in their national context with few tools for living a Jewish life among other Jews, in the present. There was little acknowledgment of the concrete problems they faced—the complex dynamics of being Jewish in contemporary Portugal, particularly exclusion from the local normative communities—despite their attempts to explain the situation to their visitors. To be fair, the narrative gaze was partly of their own making. For in stressing a historically rooted, genealogical framing of their identity as essential Jews, by using the terms *Marranos, crypto-Jews,* and *B'nai Anusim* interchangeably, they had inadvertently transformed themselves into a collective symbol of Jewish survival—*netsach yisrael,* the eternal spirit of the Jewish people—in bodily form. Small wonder that they attracted so much emotion-laden attention from abroad, attention that obscured their personal histories behind the singular image of "the Marrano"—with all the weight of centuries of Jewish imaginings that image bore.

The urban Marranos walked a difficult path in their encounters with foreign visitors. Nearly all felt strongly that their ancestors had been persecuted for their Jewish faith and they did not want to relinquish that aspect of their background. It provided an explanatory context they felt must be preserved.

And yet to emphasize that history rendered them "the living past," as Dulce put it after an especially disappointing encounter with a visiting rabbi, which in turn made it difficult for them to gain concrete assistance toward the future. Shavei Israel, for example, petitioned the Israeli Chief Rabbinate in 2004 to have them officially recognized as descendants of Jews, a move that would have qualified them for an accelerated Orthodox "Return to Judaism" program rather than ordinary conversion. That program had originally been developed in the 1990s to resolve the case of the Feres Mura, a subgroup of Ethiopian Jews whose ancestors had converted to Christianity (Seeman 2003, 2009); it required only months, whereas the standard Orthodox conversion process took years to complete. In response to Shavei Israel's petition, the chief Sephardic rabbi traveled from Jerusalem to Lisbon to meet directly with urban Marranos. The meeting was disappointing; once again members of Menorá and HaShalom told their Marrano stories, this time gathered in the apartment of Lisbon's rabbi, a Shavei Israel emissary. Although the local rabbi was warm and encouraging, the chief rabbi said only that he would form a commission in Israel to consider the matter. Rabbinic wrangling over the Marranos' status and proper procedures to be followed went on for years, with no apparent progress.[4] Members of HaShalom and Menorá wondered aloud if it would have been simpler not to have mentioned ancestry in the first place.

Therein lay the paradox, for had they omitted the ancestral component and presented themselves simply as would-be converts, very likely no one would have visited.[5] Yet despite their compelling narratives of hidden ancestry, urban Marranos did not quite register on the roster of "exotic" Jewish communities routinely supported by Jewish charitable and outreach organizations based in the United States and Europe. One group, for example, gave years of support to ancestrally Jewish communities throughout Africa and Asia, but did not offer educational and logistical help to Menorá or HaShalom after its board members participated in a Nostálgia Conference-Tour. One explanation that circulated among urban Marranos at the time was that they were not sufficiently "different" to warrant interest. Commented a member of Menorá,

> You know, probably one of the reasons we're not getting very much help from the Jewish world is that we're not exotic, not like Burmese Jews, Kaifeng [Chinese] Jews, Ethiopian Jews. We're almost all white Europeans, and we don't plan to emigrate to Israel. We don't offer proof of the Lost Tribes. So we're not interesting.

Had they lived in a country like the United States, where there are hundreds of Jewish communities, it would have been a relatively simple matter to go to a synagogue of their choosing, explain their situation to the rabbi, and pursue an individual program of conversion or "return" that would acknowledge the experiences of their ancestors. Their initial journey toward a Jewish identity had been solitary; there was no inherent reason why their case should be resolved collectively. Several Nostálgia members, descendants of crypto-Jews in the Portuguese diaspora, had already made their "return" in American Reform synagogues, and they posted about the process online. Members of the Marrano associations read their accounts with interest. But in Portugal, with just two synagogues, neither of them welcoming, no such direct approach was possible. A few considered correspondence courses with sympathetic rabbis abroad, but they could offer only guidance from afar and, eventually, a "certificate of return," leaving the individual a Jewish community of one.

The urban Marranos were effectively consigned to waiting for the right visitors to appear, people who would see them simultaneously as B'nai Anusim—descendants of the forced converts—and as historically situated individuals living very much in the Portuguese present. As we will see, the few visitors who were able to hold those two aspects of their condition in tension realized that their primary need, more than an appropriate ritual of reincorporation, was a concrete program of face-to-face instruction, guidance, and community building before they could live as full-fledged Jews. Ultimately, what proved most important was for them to forge lasting bonds with visitors who would incorporate them into the global "Jewish family" through personal relations of love and care. For a visitor to offer this, however, required that rare gaze of assumed equality, individuality, and contemporaneity—rather than "the living past"—that António glossed as "looking at us like brothers."

EXPERIENTIAL AFFINITIES AND EMOTIONAL BONDS

> Analogies are relations of resemblance; that does not mean their fancifulness is idle. On the contrary, much of culture is a fabrication of resemblances, a making sense through indicative continuities.
>
> MARILYN STRATHERN
> Kinship, Law and the Unexpected

Not all tourists are content to remain on the surface of things. There is a long history of writing in the anthropology of tourism on authenticity, how it is determined, what it is, and whether tourists seek it or prefer superficial entertainment (Leite and Graburn 2009: 43–44), but that need not occupy us here. We have already seen that most visitors were not concerned with judging the "authenticity"—by whatever the criteria—of the urban Marranos' ancestral Jewishness, despite their fears to the contrary. Let us consider instead the character of interpersonal engagement during the visit. While the compressed time frame of most package tours precludes in-depth discussion or the creation of lasting bonds, a great many travelers do seek sociability, and even a sense of intimacy, with local people (Harrison 2003). For them, the feeling of becoming "separated out from the generic category of 'stranger' and seen as a real person" and seeing a local person as a "real person," as well, is a way "to affirm or to strengthen a sense of common humanity" and thus have an experience of lasting meaning (Harrison 2003: 65, 90; see also Simoni 2014). It is this particular point, the traveler's desire to strengthen or affirm a sense of commonality, that is most important for understanding the dynamic that evolved between urban Marranos and a small group of their visitors. Unlike those who came primarily to be moved and to experience difference, those tourists and outreach workers who drew analogies between their own life experiences and those of their hosts, who saw a glimmer of resemblance in their dreams and struggles, and who felt an emotional or spiritual resonance in their presence were much more likely to empathize with and care about them as distinct individuals. Indeed, as Signe Howell and Diana Maare (2006) argue with regard to transnational adoption, seeking "resemblances" is a fundamental element in the work of transforming strangers into kin.

Resonance, Commitment, and Love

Bernard Lévy was deeply affected by the story of the Portuguese Marranos, past and present. For him, the survival of the Jewish people was personal. The French rabbi had survived the Holocaust as a small child in hiding, sheltered by a Catholic family. Having had to relinquish and then regain his own Jewishness, he was sensitive to the plight of marginal Jews worldwide. During his long career he had served as an outreach mentor to people claiming Jewish descent in Africa, Latin America, the Caribbean, and the American Southwest, online and face-to-face. When he first traveled to Portugal, it was as scholar-in-residence on one of Graciana Mayer's Conference-Tours.

Thereafter, he returned several times to offer weekend seminars on Jewish religious and intellectual history, free of charge, at Menorá and HaShalom. Our paths crossed repeatedly in Portugal and the United States over the years of my research, and on one of his trips to Lisbon I asked him to explain why he had spent so much of his career teaching would-be "returnees" to Judaism. He responded by comparing his experience during the Holocaust with that of the historical Marranos:

> I was in hiding myself. I understand people being in hiding for five hundred years. It's very important to me. When I was thirteen, after the war, I remember reading a story in a magazine [adopts wonderstruck tone] *about those Marranos.* It was about a Marrano family that was about to celebrate Passover. They were going to have their seder in the basement, but upstairs, on the main floor, they had prepared another kind of banquet to give the impression that they were going to—There was pork on the table, and everything. So downstairs they were, they were about to begin, and there was a knock on the door. Quickly they go up, they pretend to be eating, they open the door. It's a priest, an agent of the Inquisition. And he says, "Don't be afraid. I'm one of you. I came because I knew you would be celebrating Passover. I want to celebrate with you. Will you allow me?" [slaps knee, laughs loudly] *That* is in my mind every day of my life!

The former hidden child had never forgotten that image of the Marranos: outwardly seeming to be one thing while maintaining a very different identity within, terrified that they would be discovered. He was enchanted by the idea that there could be millions of people who "have Jewish blood in their veins," as he put it, and he wanted to help anyone seeking to connect with their religious roots. He emphasized that he didn't want their pursuit to be merely ethnic or cultural; to be Jewish, he felt, spirituality and scholarship were essential. A liberal rabbi himself, he was not concerned with what branch of Judaism they chose as long as they found some spiritual home.

Rabbi Lévy was one of the few visitors who from the outset engaged with urban Marranos as individuals. Their experience of reclaiming a lost identity and lost world resonated for him; at the same time, his approach as an educator had always been to work with each student independently. It may also be that having himself lived a life many would celebrate as an example of *netsach yisrael,* the eternal survival of the Jewish people, he was more likely to approach Marranos as individuals than as symbols of something else. After his first visit to Menorá and HaShalom he maintained personal correspondence with any member who wished, readily and fluently communicating in

French, Spanish, or English. On return visits he spent many hours with the two associations, at their headquarters and informally over restaurant meals. He was a lively and humorous conversationalist, enthusiastic and engaged. Many of the local people considered him a mentor and friend.

When members of HaShalom and Menorá decided in 2005 to create an autonomous congregation of B'nai Anusim, as they increasingly called themselves, it was to Rabbi Lévy that they turned for guidance. They had no idea that he was already working on their behalf, drawing on his many social ties in the Jewish world to find a way of helping them "return." As we have seen, the urban Marranos had long hoped that someone from abroad would have the connections to surpass the institutional blocks in their national context and, to use the Portuguese phrase, "place a *cunha*" for them. Earlier that year, Rabbi Lévy had begun making calls to Canada, the United States, England, France, Israel, reaching out to everyone he knew at high levels of leadership in the liberal branches of Judaism, particularly Reform and Masorti/ Conservative. "It's not what you know, but who you know!" he exclaimed, recounting the thirty-odd calls he had made to friends and acquaintances before finally arriving at a potential intermediary with the Israel-based head of the international Masorti movement. Just as the logic of *cunha* would predict, shortly thereafter the Masorti leadership sent two prominent rabbis, one from Israel and one from England, to meet with the urban Marranos and assess their situation. I return to these developments below.

The year 2005 proved tumultuous for the Marrano associations, particularly in Porto. That April, Shavei Israel held a much-publicized three-day seminar at the Porto synagogue, bringing Orthodox outreach workers from as far as South Africa and Canada face-to-face with dozens of B'nai Anusim from throughout Portugal and Spain. Nearly all of Menorá's members attended, and thereafter several decided to study solely with Shavei Israel's Porto rabbi, who by that time had already gathered half a dozen people to pursue Orthodox "return" under his tutelage. The remaining members preferred to affiliate with a more liberal branch of Judaism, if at all; those who had time and freedom to travel to Lisbon on a regular basis began to collaborate with members of HaShalom to create a national, liberal congregation, while a few others opted to go abroad for a simple, one-day rite of return at a willing Reform synagogue in New York and did not seek affiliation thereafter with a Jewish community in Portugal. Menorá faltered and then dissolved, riven by leadership struggles and discord over which branch of Judaism to pursue. A handful of Menorá's original participants created a new Marrano association, but within a few months it too had split in two, and eventually its successor associations ceased meeting as well.

By May 2005, efforts to start an egalitarian congregation, to be named Kehilá (Heb.; community), were well under way. With a group of some twenty founding members from Menorá and HaShalom—among them Dulce, Catarina, Tiago, Miguel, Pedro, Ricardo, Joaquim, Nuno, and Luisa—and the support of Rabbi Lévy, they chose to locate it in Lisbon. They had the crumbling Anshei Emet synagogue as a meeting space, and they surmised that there were significantly more potential members in greater Lisbon than in the smaller cities of the north, given the metropolitan area's population of 2.5 million. Two other foreign visitors, Anshel Rappaport and Frank Albertson, would prove instrumental in the developments to come. They too connected with the urban Marranos on a personal level, finding affinity based on their own life experiences.

Like Rabbi Lévy, eighty-year-old Anshel had been enchanted by Marranos since his boyhood in 1930s Montreal, and he too had long been an outreach worker among groups whose Jewish status was under debate—among them the Black Jews and Black Hebrew Israelites in the United States (Fernheimer 2014), various groups in Uganda and Ghana, Soviet émigrés in New York and Israel, and most recently Marranos in Iberia and crypto-Jewish descendants in the American Southwest. With each group, he articulated his stance as one of love and acceptance, categorically, collectively, and individually; "human relationships," he told me, were much more important than "working on an ideological level." Anshel was a resolutely secular Jew, but he firmly believed that anyone who claimed to be Jewish must have a Jewish soul and so was worthy of being embraced—often literally—as a member of "the Jewish family." His commitment to sustaining the vitality of the Jewish people was deeply personal. He had lost his maternal grandparents and most of his aunts, uncles, and cousins to the gas chambers at Treblinka, and both his paternal grandfather and his older sister were murdered in a pogrom in Poland before his parents fled to Canada. "But," he told me, "those things made me stronger to say, 'Damn you all!' to the Inquisition, and to all the anti-Semites: 'We're still around!' All my life, wherever I felt Jewish individuals or communities should be strengthened, should be encouraged, should be welcomed, I stepped in." Despite his advanced age Anshel was extraordinarily energetic, his effusively positive attitude infectious.

After visiting HaShalom and Menorá on the 2004 Nostálgia Conference-Tour, Anshel was captivated. He had traveled to Portugal twenty years earlier in search of Marranos and met crypto-Jews in Belmonte, but the Nostálgia tour brought him to something quite different: a group of Portuguese young adults in search of Jewish education and belonging who had no one to help them. A trained Jewish educator, he returned to Lisbon three times in the subsequent eighteen months, each time offering classes and sharing every meal at a casual restaurant with urban Marranos, often six or more at a time. The ability to see each person as an individual came easily for Anshel; his goal, he often repeated, was "to connect, to bond." To my delight, he did so with me as well. By his second visit, in August 2004, I had become his personal driver and translator, ferrying him from airport to hotel and from meeting to meeting. From then on, when I collected him at the airport he would breathlessly fill me in on correspondence he had had with HaShalom and Menorá members since his last visit. He was always impatient to show me the small wrapped gifts he had brought for everyone, each neatly labeled with the recipient's name: a Star of David pendant or key ring, a box of Hanukkah candles, a Jewish calendar.

Each time Anshel traveled to Portugal he brought along an old friend, Frank Albertson. Frank was not an outreach activist; quite the opposite. He knew very little about Judaism. He became involved entirely at Anshel's urging and then continued because he developed a profound affection for, and sense of experiential identification with, the urban Marranos as individuals. An elderly New Yorker, already in his late eighties, Frank had been raised upstate in an entirely secular household; although he always knew he was Jewish by birth, that was all, and as an adult he rarely mentioned that background. It was not until quite late in life that he began exploring his roots. Like the urban Marranos, he found himself searching to claim something that felt both alien and intrinsically his own. When Anshel invited Frank to accompany him on the Conference-Tour, he decided "on a lark" to go along. Frank was a wealthy man with a long history of supporting American social and political causes—indeed, it may have been his potential as a donor that prompted Anshel to invite him—but he never expected to become involved in Portugal's Marrano movement. In fact, he had never heard of Marranos, and he knew next to nothing about the Inquisition and its aftermath. But once he spent time talking with members of HaShalom, Menorá, and later Congregation Kehilá, he told me, something inside him changed. He found that his and the leaders' personalities meshed beautifully; they approached Judaism with the same tentativeness, intelligence, gentle irreverence, and emotional sincerity that he did, and he delighted in their conversations.

Ultimately, a year after my fieldwork concluded, he underwrote the expense of moving Anshei Emet and its new congregation, Kehilá, out of the condemned apartment and into a building that was structurally sound. Later he added the community to his will.

Explaining his motivation for becoming involved, he told me,

> I loved the people. And I felt they liked me. I enjoyed them and I felt I was accepted from the first moment. I wasn't much of a Jew, I wasn't anything like a Jew, but I knew I was Jewish *from that first trip*. It was the people, how strongly they felt. I feel like we speak the same language emotionally. This is a perfect space for me, 'cause I feel something here. It's given me a mission to come back and reorganize myself around it. *This* is where I feel very Jewish. [long pause] And very touched.

Frank's identification with the group was manifold. He was touched by their distance from their Jewish heritage, a distance that he too felt, and by their desire to connect with it; by their rejection by the "mainstream" synagogues, a feeling he too had experienced in other settings; and, above all, by their obvious enjoyment of his presence among them. He noted small kindnesses they showed him—Pedro or Catarina offering him an arm to lean on when his cane wasn't enough, Dulce bringing a plate of cookies to the car where he sat when his arthritis was too painful to make it up Anshei Emet's rickety stairs for a meeting, Nuno and Luisa sending him emails to ask after his health. They greeted both him and Anshel with hugs and *beijinhos* and stayed in contact long after the two men returned home. The affectionate relationship between Frank, Anshel, and the people of Kehilá proved crucially important for their evolving identity as Jews, in ways both interpersonal and practical.

Until the period of rapid change that began in mid-2005, visitors like Rabbi Lévy, Anshel, and Frank were a rarity. What set these men apart from the great majority of foreign visitors was, first, their obvious interest in the associations' members as individuals and, second, that they remained in contact by email and returned repeatedly. However, although each traveled to Portugal several times during my stay and continued to do so thereafter, I do not mean to give the impression that they were a continuous presence in the minds of the urban Marranos. There were many long months between their visits, typically with no indication of when or whether they would return. Even with the feeling of connection engendered by their intermittent appearances, little changed for the urban Marranos until Rabbi Lévy drew on his network of social ties to connect them with the leadership of a major branch of Judaism.

Individual Relations

The members of the nascent Congregation Kehilá presented a challenge to any organization wanting to help them become a viable Jewish community, religiously and culturally: none of them knew how to live as Jews. The eclectic assemblage of knowledge and practices they had accumulated over the years as "Marranos" hardly constituted being Jewish from the perspective of normative Judaism, never mind the problem of their status according to Jewish law. Moreover, far from being a matter of simply adopting a set of beliefs or committing to a set of practices, becoming a member of the Jewish people is, as one rabbi who had participated in a *beit din* many times explained to me, "first and foremost, socialization into a social group. Most people convert by coming to a Jewish community, they live in that Jewish community, and over a period of time, they adopt the ways of thinking, the ways of behaving of that group. That's really what conversion is. That's how it works. At the end of the day a successful conversion is about people just living a Jewish life." With no one to show them, how would they learn?

That was the primary concern facing the two leading rabbis from the Masorti movement who came to meet with members of Kehilá at Anshei Emet in June 2005. Rabbi Martin Axler, an American, was a director of the organization's worldwide leadership, based in Jerusalem; Rabbi Asher Siegel was head of the London-based *beit din* that would likely be tasked with handling the urban Marranos' ritual incorporation into the Jewish people. There was already a system in place to help Europeans new to Masorti Judaism with establishing a congregation, as it was a relatively new movement outside North America.[6] In that system, a young-adult volunteer from Israel or the United States would live locally and meet regularly with the new congregation, providing instruction in the practices and stances that distinguish Masorti/Conservative Judaism from Reform and Orthodox. But elsewhere, the new congregations had been constituted largely of people who were Jewish by birth, and by families as well as individuals. Kehilá would be made up entirely of newcomers to Judaism, nearly all of them single, and most of them the only person in their natal family to become involved. Much of Jewish religious and cultural life centers around the family and the home, not the synagogue. Would it be possible, Rabbi Asher wondered aloud during their first meeting, to achieve something so complex? Neither he nor the Marranos were interested in having the outcome be little more than a certificate of "return." They wanted to create a functioning Masorti community made up of Jews, like any other. Hence the question was how to achieve that transformation: absent a Jewish community, how would the urban Marranos become Jews?

It is important to note here that leaders of the Masorti movement did not visit Portugal out of a desire to find and reconnect Marranos with their ancestral faith, nor did they intend to convert the people of Congregation Kehilá en masse, as a collective endeavor. They came at the personal request of fellow rabbis who had identified a need for assistance. Their task was to help a group of individuals learn to live as Jews, to become Jewish according to halakhah, and to create a living community that would someday also include "born" Jews among its members. While the group's collective designation as "Marranos" or "B'nai Anusim" was the reason the Masorti rabbis had been contacted and the reason they came, whether the participants were truly of Jewish descent was effectively immaterial. For these new visitors, the essential factor was each person's sincerity and commitment to being Jewish—not only in honor of their ancestry, but in all ways, as it would be for any newcomer to the religion—in accordance with the practices and beliefs of Masorti Judaism. Based on their assessment from that first meeting, where they explained options and heard from the twenty-odd urban Marranos in attendance about the local situation, their motivation, and their concerns, the rabbis decided to proceed.

When Rabbi Asher returned two months later, in August, approximately fifteen people assembled once again around the large table in Anshei Emet's meeting room. Each man wore a *kipá,* as they always did when meeting with a rabbi. Rabbi Asher was in his forties, one of the youngest rabbis to visit the group, and he arrived with a backpack slung over one shoulder, dressed casually in a T-shirt, jeans, and a small, colorful knitted yarmulke. Although he was reserved and slow to speak, the lanky, bearded rabbi's affect was warm and friendly. As he explained how he and his colleagues had determined the process should be handled, he stressed that he would speak with each person individually to discuss his or her background and reasons for pursuing this path. Each would fill in an enrollment questionnaire for the Masorti conversion program and commit to taking classes and reading books from a recommended list, as well as attending Shabbat services regularly. The men would have to be circumcised. The per-person cost for the program was £100. Immediately there was a flurry of concern and frustration. Why should they convert when they were already Jews? Their ancestors had suffered for their Jewishness, and now they were to be treated like run-of-the-mill converts? How were they to attend the required classes? None could afford to relocate to London. The enrollment fee was prohibitively expensive. And where would they attend Shabbat services, when they could never predict whether they would be allowed to enter Shaaré Tikvá? It seemed this, too, would be yet another misguided proposal.

Rabbi Asher hastened to reassure them. He and his colleagues had thoroughly explored options for handling this unprecedented situation. They had decided to send teachers to Lisbon who would visit periodically, several weeks at a time, and the classes would be held right there at Anshei Emet. Participants were to begin observing Shabbat to the best of their ability, again at Anshei Emet, reciting those parts of the service that did not require a *minyan;* the teachers would show them how. The enrollment fee would cover a tiny fraction of the teachers' travel, lodging, and work. As for conversion, it was an absolutely necessary step if they sought to become Jews according to halakhah, and their new congregation could not affiliate with the Masorti movement unless they did so. If they wanted to consider it a "return," rather than conversion, that was entirely acceptable. The details of the wording on their certificates could be worked out later. Most were comforted by his reply; they later confided, importantly, that they felt he had truly heard their concerns and understood their feelings—a rarity after rabbinic visits. They were enthusiastic about the proposed program, but for the enrollment fee. At then-current exchange rates it was €150 (US$180), around one-sixth the average monthly wage in Portugal, and for most of the participants far more than that. Several were students with no income at all; the rest were primarily hourly employees or independent contractors. Few felt they could afford it.

Two weeks later, Anshel and Frank returned to Lisbon. As always, the local people—now united as Kehilá—gathered to prepare for the visit, tidying the space beforehand and setting out snacks. After the usual flurry of greetings, with Anshel presenting gifts and describing the many people to whom he had told their story, Tiago and Nuno recounted the latest developments. Anshel and Frank were visibly thrilled for the group. When Dulce took the two men aside, gesturing for me to translate, and quietly explained that the situation was not wholly joyful because several members would have difficulty with the enrollment fee, Frank's response was swift: he would pay for everyone. For a group of people who had felt profoundly rejected at every turn, some of them for years, it was an extraordinary moment. They would be able to make their return and be recognized as Jews at last. Some looked at Frank in disbelief, eyes brimming; a few whispered among themselves to make sure they had understood; the more demonstrative members jumped up to hug him and Anshel.

At the end of the meeting, as we prepared to leave for dinner, I noticed that someone had written "WE ♥ FRANK & ANSHEL!" on the whiteboard that hung on the back wall. Later that night Catarina expressed the group's gratitude on her English-language blog. Under two photos, one of the whiteboard and the other a snapshot of everyone posing happily with Anshel and Frank, she wrote,

> We are making history. We have just received yet another amazing donation which will allow us to once again burst through closed doors. We thank our American cousins for that. We call each other that, *cousins,* and we ARE family. Our people think nothing of oceans and deserts, distance doesn't faze us, we've done it before, we could do it again. We are theirs, they are ours, we ARE one in that which matters. Love is thicker than water.

This is a very different invocation of the relationship of "cousins" and "family" than the abstract, categorical version we saw in chapter 4. Here, it is a local person using the language of kin, rather than a visitor, and it is in reference to a specific instance of affection—even "love"—between the urban Marranos and two men who supported them, delighted in them as individuals and as a group, and nurtured their collective growth. In their own way, the local people supported, delighted in, and nurtured Frank and Anshel in turn, sharing their time, energy, and emotions with the elderly men, socializing with them, and continuously offering small acts of kindness. In the eyes of both the local people and these visitors, those were the actions and emotions of "family." The words they used—*family, cousins, love*—were not poetic metaphors; they indexed deeper currents of emotion and reasoning that were common to all involved and that would have profound implications for the particular configurations of Jewish identification and belonging experienced by the local people.

"You Were Like Our Own Children"

Rabbi Ezra and Chaya Kaplan arrived in Lisbon with no idea what to expect. The seasoned educators had traveled to Moscow and Leningrad to work with Soviet Jewish refuseniks in the 1970s and then to Warsaw to teach Polish Jews after the fall of communism, but they had never been involved in outreach efforts to "lost" communities like this one. An internationally respected rabbi and professor, widely considered the chief liturgist of the American Conservative movement, Rabbi Ezra had devoted his career to teaching and to making the Jewish prayers accessible and meaningful in the modern world. He had never been a pulpit rabbi, however, nor had he been responsible for overseeing the education of what would effectively be converts. Nor had Chaya, a medical professional, been involved in such work. But when one of the directors of the worldwide Masorti movement invited them to visit a group of Marranos in Lisbon, they did not hesitate. Both had first heard of Marranos as young children and were fascinated and moved by the idea of generation after generation feeling a mysterious call to continue practicing rituals for which they had no explanation. With this in mind, the two New Yorkers were eager to meet the founding members of Kehilá.

They were given little information, only that they would be teaching approximately twenty Marranos who had been turned away by the local Orthodox synagogues. During their first twelve-day visit the Kaplans' role would be to offer nightly classes, at the same time assessing whether it would in fact be possible to create a viable congregation, whether the people were merely seeking an easier route to conversion than Orthodox Judaism or actually understood what Masorti/Conservative Judaism entailed, and whether they were sincere in their desire to become Jews in ways other than ancestry. To prepare, the couple sought to become both historically and emotionally situated for the work. They wanted to understand the multigenerational legacy of suffering on which they understood the group's identity was built. As Chaya later explained, "We became immersed in the history of the Jews of Portugal and the history of the Inquisition, so that when we came, we were also immersed in the *feelings* we needed to understand when we met this group." Although they were Ashkenazi, they found recordings of Sephardic prayer melodies and listened to them during their daily commute, singing along until they learned them well enough to teach them to the urban Marranos. Given that the historical Portuguese Jews were by definition Sephardic, they assumed that would be what the local people would want to learn. Beyond that, it was difficult to prepare; they had no idea what level of Jewish knowledge they would find and no sense of whether Rabbi Asher's plan for the community could succeed.

From the moment they arrived on a sunny September morning, Chaya asked questions. She was fearlessly curious and unabashedly informal. Over lunch with Nuno and Luisa, who had met them at the airport, she peppered them with questions about the group while Ezra listened. Nuno had requested that I come along as a translator and fellow American, thinking that my presence might make things go more smoothly. On discovering the nature of my research, Chaya did not hesitate to question me as well. She was on a fact-finding mission, doing "fieldwork," she later told me. Hers were not the ordinary questions asked by foreign visitors: How many are there? How long have they been gathering? Is "Marrano" the right word to use? How old are they? Are there families? And on and on. Nuno answered to the best of his ability, but as a relative newcomer he often referred her questions to me; Luisa, who spoke little English, sat by quietly. By the time everyone gathered that night at Anshei Emet for their first class, the Kaplans were fully oriented, except for the one thing virtually every other visitor asked about first: their Marrano stories. Although Chaya raised the question as soon as the group was assembled, it did not stay the focus for long. Crypto-Jewish customs and family histories were not her and Rabbi Ezra's primary concern. They felt, she said, that they were there to help create a future, not to revisit the past.

In addition to teaching and assessment, their role during that first visit was to demonstrate, as much as possible, how to *live* as Jews. Chaya met the challenge with gusto. An energetic, emotionally demonstrative woman, she had brought photographs of her family, her children's weddings, and their Jewish holiday celebrations over the years to share. She continuously referred to how things were done in their own congregation in New York and in their home. When Rabbi Ezra announced that we would meet at Anshei Emet for a Shabbat learning service the following Friday evening, Chaya added that we would have a community potluck dinner afterward. The weekly Shabbat dinner is a fundamental family practice in Jewish homes around the world, and it was one that she was eager to impart. When the evening came, everyone brought a dish to share. After the prayer service Chaya walked the group through each step in real time—from the ritual hand-washing, *netilat yadayim,* to the tradition of not speaking before the blessing for bread and wine, to the prayers and songs sung before and after the meal. "This is how *we* do it at home," she would say before explaining what to do next, and she shared funny anecdotes about how her own children reacted or made mistakes in Jewish rituals growing up.

It was the first Shabbat dinner the group had held at Anshei Emet, in fact the first many had ever attended, and the air was charged with excitement and possibility. Chaya's enthusiasm and obvious interest in each person in the room, combined with Rabbi Ezra's quiet warmth, were infectious. At this point Kehilá was a new organization, its membership drawn from the two associations, and some members were not yet well known to the others. But after twelve consecutive nights of four-hour classes on Jewish thought and religious practice with the rabbi, Chaya translating difficult concepts into Spanish and periodically grounding the lesson in examples from the Kaplans' own life, something changed in the atmosphere. Already tentatively united around creating a congregation, the urban Marranos came together as an intensive learning community, one that ate together, studied together, and listened as others asked questions, expressed doubts, and talked about their own spiritual journeys with the rabbi and his wife. The Kaplans encouraged this mutual engagement, for in the absence of Jewish families of their own, Kehilá's members would need one another to create a Jewish life. Indeed, after that first visit Nuno and Luisa began hosting weekly Shabbat dinners at their modest apartment on the outskirts of Lisbon, attended by a rotating selection of people from the new community and conducted exactly as Chaya had taught them. In Portugal, as I noted in an earlier chapter, socializing is often done outside the home, typically in restaurants; dinner parties happen much less frequently than in America or England, as home-cooked meals are generally for very close friends or family. Consequently, the Shabbat dinners Luisa so painstakingly prepared, always with conversation and laughter late into the evening, not only heightened participants' feeling of Jewish involvement but generated a new sense of intimacy among them.

On returning to New York, the Kaplans submitted their enthusiastic recommendation that the program go forward. Several members had shown the necessary knowledge and commitment to be ready to go before the Masorti *beit din* within the year, perhaps even the next few months. They had discerned, they felt, a realistic likelihood that the community would develop into a viable congregation. Thereafter they sent Kehilá's members a weekly group email with reflections on the community's progress, their feelings about working with them, and guidance for the coming week. In each one Rabbi Ezra acted as their long-distance rabbi, sending a mini-sermon on the weekly Torah portion and points for discussion after the service. This they were to conduct in abbreviated form, including only those portions of the Shabbat service permitted without a *minyan*. Chaya also corresponded with some of them individually, responding promptly to anyone who wrote, including me, always encouraging, chiding, clucking over something or other. To both American and Portuguese eyes, she was nothing if not motherly.[7]

The couple returned to Lisbon three months later, on a chilly Friday morning in December. During their September visit, I had mentioned to Chaya that no one in the group had tasted a bagel; some had no idea what one was. She burst out laughing. "How can you be *Jewish* without bagels?" she joked. "I'll bring some!" So was planted the seed of an idea: Chaya would bring Jewish food to Lisbon, made in her own kitchen in New York. A week before the next visit, she prepared a classic Ashkenazi holiday casserole, sweet noodle kugel (Yid., *kugl*), and froze it solid. Into her suitcase it went, kept cold in the baggage hold during the flight. She also slipped in a bag of bagels and a tub of cream cheese from her favorite bagel shop. The group was scheduled to meet for Shabbat services and another potluck dinner that night, so with Nuno's help, that afternoon Chaya took the food to Anshei Emet, placed the kugel in the oven to defrost, and waited there for evening to fall. That night's dinner was a warm, relaxed, often playful reunion. Chaya and I demonstrated the American preparation of bagels and cream cheese topped with sliced tomato and onion that I had brought, and passed a tray around for all to taste. Once again everyone had made food to share—salads, vegetable side dishes, desserts. Dulce's offering was a caramel custard (*pudim flan*) made expressly for Rabbi Ezra, since he had exclaimed over her flan at the first Shabbat dinner in September, and she presented it to him with a great show of honor and affection.

Both commensality, the act of eating together, and the sharing of food are powerful means by which human beings create, express, and solidify feelings of mutual trust, intimacy, and kinship (Carsten 2000, 2004; Sahlins 2013; Weismental 1995). While the group's many restaurant meals with Anshel and Frank and with Rabbi Lévy had been memorable experiences of social connection and bonding, this new situation struck a deeper chord. Chaya's decision to bring home-cooked food across three thousand miles of ocean was an explicit act of motherly nurturance, one that did not go unremarked. So too was Dulce's preparation of a dish specifically for the rabbi, remembering that he had liked it so. These acts of care were magnified by the brief window of time they were together, and made all the more more special because the roles were reversed: in the past HaShalom and Menorá members had offered snacks to their foreign visitors, strangers who arrived, ate while standing and chatting for an hour, and vanished back down the building's rickety stairs. Now it was Chaya who awaited them in the synagogue's tiny kitchen, food warming in the oven as they arrived. Although the local people also brought food, it was to be shared along with Chaya's offerings, literally breaking bread together around the same table. The next day, having realized that Anshei Emet's drafty, unheated rooms would be much too cold and damp for their "old bones" on December evenings, the Kaplans offered to hold the rest of the classes in their hotel suite. From then on, the entire group squeezed into the couple's little sitting room for lessons on Jewish thought and ritual practice, four or five to a sofa, while Chaya passed cookies and other treats she had bought for the occasion. By hosting the urban Marranos in their own space, even if a hotel room, and by offering them food, knowledge, and affection, the couple engaged in a direct form of nurturance no other visitors had.

Several factors made it easy for the Kaplans to slip into a parental role. They were grandparents, with adult children around the same age as most members of Kehilá. They had come to Portugal as teachers for this specific group of individuals, rather than as tourists or outreach workers generically in search of Marranos. Perhaps it was a combination of these factors, as well as Chaya's outgoing, expressive nature, that predisposed them to interact with their Portuguese students in a familial manner. Whatever the reason, by the middle of the second visit they were articulating their feelings explicitly in terms of the parent-child relationship. Upon teaching the men the difficult practice of putting on *tefillin,* with leather straps that must be wound just so around the arm and head, Rabbi Ezra was delighted at how quickly they learned. When we gathered in the hotel suite the following evening he said, "Last night, watching you put on the *tefillin* was very important for us, very exciting. It ranks up there with the first time we heard our children recite the four questions at the Passover seder" (a role assigned to the youngest able person at the table). The comparison was so important to them that Chaya insisted I translate his words immediately into Portuguese, to be absolutely certain everyone had understood. And after returning to New York, Chaya sent an email copied to all, repeating that she and Ezra were as proud of their "family in Lisbon" as if they had been the parents and stressing that they had received as much love in return as if the group had been their own respectful, loving children:

> We arrived home safely after spending ten extraordinary days with you, our family in Lisbon.... We have come to take pride in your achievements and increasing knowledge, as parents take pride in their children when they begin to walk, then run, then jump. You are almost ready to jump! And you took care of us with love and respect as children relate to the parents whom they love.

Although she was unaware of it, from a Portuguese perspective Chaya acted like a parent in yet another way: not only had she offered nurturance, not only was she taking pride in their progress, but she had "placed a *cunha*" on behalf of members of the group who particularly needed it. Two of the men had not yet been circumcised, a major stumbling block if they were to go before the *beit din* within the next few months, which the Kaplans felt they were ready to do. When they explained to Chaya that the procedure was not covered by the national health service unless there was an urgent medical problem and that they lacked financial resources to pay a private surgeon, she turned to her network of social ties in New York. Through a series of connections, she discovered a friend of a friend who knew a leading urologist in Lisbon. Drawing on that contact, she scheduled an appointment to meet with the doctor on her next visit to Portugal. When the day came they chatted for ten or fifteen minutes about topics of mutual professional interest before she raised the subject, asking his advice. Although she had no idea that she was working within the framework of *cunha,* the two young men involved noted that she had performed brilliantly: she talked with the doctor first about other professional matters, inviting him to New York, where, she promised, she would introduce him to one of America's leading urologists—who happened to be a friend—and only then did she make her request. The young men had their circumcisions performed at his hospital shortly thereafter. I never did learn how the surgeries were billed; it was not discussed. Like a loving parent, Chaya had taken care of everything.

A few weeks later, a member of Kehilá also made explicit the parent-child framing of their relationship. In a letter of gratitude to the director of the worldwide Masorti movement, Nuno wrote in English, "No one here can express exactly the huge and complex feelings we've built between ourselves and these two unique human beings. But I'm sure we can call it LOVE, since we see them not as teachers but as parents—the best teachers anyone can ever have." Here, for the first time, we have an instance in which the local people and their foreign visitors used exactly the same kin relation to describe their feelings for one another. Rabbi Ezra, Chaya, and members of Kehilá used the parent-child framing on multiple occasions beyond those I have quoted here, primarily conversationally but also in writing, and the local people did so in Portuguese as well as in English. As we saw in the case of Anshel and Frank, here too the urban Marranos drew on the language of kinship to articulate their feelings about *specific* relationships, bonds with individual people that they described in terms of "love."

What, precisely, did they mean by speaking about each other as kin? Rabbi Ezra and his wife had adult children of their own, with whom they had rich and active relationships that reached into most aspects of their everyday life back in New York. For their part, the members of Kehilá all had at least one living parent, none of them estranged; four even shared a home with their mother, a common Portuguese practice. The relationship they developed with these special visitors, and vice versa, was quite different from the existing ties that they called by the same name. But neither was the terminology mere metaphor. It was, instead, a highlighting of significant resemblances. In referring to one another as parents and children, these American educators and their Portuguese students expressed feelings that evolved within a very particular social space: the Jewish world. They would not have used those kin terms in reference to one another in any other context, despite their obvious mutual affection. In relation to Judaism, however, the urban Marranos were orphans, lacking Jewish families of their own; they were in need of parental stand-ins who could offer them hands-on guidance, assistance, encouragement, and support, as actual parents would do.

Having thought they were coming primarily to teach a group of Marranos and to guide them in the logistics of creating a Jewish community, the Kaplans found themselves needed for a more fundamental activity: that of *kinning,* of bringing unconnected persons "into a significant and permanent relationship with a group of people that is expressed in a kin idiom" (Howell 2006: 63). As the parents to Kehilá's Jewish "family," they lovingly helped shape each member-orphan into a full-fledged Jewish adult. In the process they and the local people genuinely came to care for one another, and it was in this light that the couple embraced the weighty responsibility of guiding them individually and collectively as they made their way from the Portuguese Jewish past into the global Jewish "family" of the present. The urban Marranos' transition from one frame of reference to the other—from past to present and from the nation to the world at large—would come about through nothing else but human caring.

JEWISH FAMILIES, OLD AND NEW

"One Jew is no Jew," as the saying goes.... The first and most difficult "community" gap for converts to bridge is the most obvious: they did not come from a Jewish family. Since so much of Jewish religious life centers around home rituals and celebrations, converts have [to find] unique ways to supply the missing experiences.... Some converts, especially those who are single, have adopted themselves into a Jewish family.

CATHERINE MYROWITZ
Finding a Home for the Soul

In all branches of Judaism, conversion generally involves two levels of "adoption." First, many converts develop an informal relationship with a Jewish family—typically their future in-laws—from whom they can learn to live as Jews in the day-to-day sense of practices in the home, at holidays, and among kin.[8] The second is the codified, ritual form of spiritual adoption in which the convert receives a new ancestral lineage, binding him or her to the Jewish people in its entirety as a common descent group. Although these modes of incorporation operate on different registers, they reinforce each other. From a religious perspective, Jewishness operates through the idiom of family, writ large and writ small (Boyarin 2013). There is *am yisrael*, "the People Israel" or "the Jewish people," who share common mythical descent from the biblical patriarchs and matriarchs; and there is also the central institution of "the Jewish home," in which Judaism is practiced and perpetuated religiously, culturally, and genealogically. It is the Jewish nuclear family that reproduces the Jewish people, generation after generation (Sharlin 1999: 52).

Because the convert's parents are by definition not Jewish, but he or she is henceforth to be considered a full member of the Jewish people, a new lineage must be granted. When a child is born into an observant Jewish family, he or she receives a Hebrew or Yiddish ritual name that includes a patronymic: "son/daughter of" followed by the father's ritual name, and sometimes the mother's as well, as in *Hannah bat Natan* (Anna, daughter of Nathan) or *Yonatan ben Adam ve-Ruth* (Jonathan, son of Adam and Ruth).[9] This ritual name is used in life-cycle rituals and in the synagogue, should the individual be called to read from the Torah or to play some other ritual role. For the convert, however, the ritual name works differently. Following a successful interview with the *beit din*, this "orphan" is deemed a son or daughter of Abraham *avinu* (Heb.; our father) and Sarah *imeinu* (Heb.; our mother), biblical progenitors of the Jewish people: *ben* or *bat Avraham avinu ve-Sarah imeinu*.

The convert is thus adopted into the Jewish family, ritually renamed as if he or she shared the collective ancestral origin (Washofsky 2000: 216). Following conversion, the newcomer is to be treated in nearly all respects identically to those born into Judaism. In a remarkable conflation of the relationships North Americans would call "by blood" and "in law" ("substance" and "code," in the vocabulary of kinship studies), in taking the vow of affiliation the convert *becomes* a descendant of the Jewish forefathers, in body as well as spirit. This is again reflected in the articulation of lineage, as the patronymic *ben/bat Avraham avinu* is used only for the convert. His or her children and subsequent generations bear lineages formed with the birth parents' ritual names, according to standard Jewish practice, provided that the Jewish maternal line is not broken. Once deemed a member of the Jewish people by the *beit din*, that is, the female convert gives birth to "born" Jews, like any Jewish woman; and the male convert fathers them, like any Jewish man. Moreover, once taken, the vow of affiliation is irreversible. Having decided to become one with the Jewish people, bodily and spiritually, from the perspective of halakhah the convert never ceases to be a Jew, even if he or she later chooses a different religion.

I have addressed the matter of conversion and lineage in detail because it proved a major point of contention between urban Marranos and those who came to help them. In chapter 2 I discussed their vehement opposition to the idea of "conversion," given that their ancestors were Jews, and their preference for conceptualizing their acquisition of a Jewish identity as a process of ancestral and spiritual "return" on a genealogical basis. The more they learned about what conversion entailed, the more opposed to it they became, for they realized that the ritual adoption of a new lineage would mean relinquishing their own ancestral line—the very thing to which they traced their Jewishness in the first place. In stressing ancestry as a determinant of their sense of self, they were hardly unique. As Eleana Kim notes in her study of transnational Korean adoptees in Europe and the United States, the contemporary Western "injunction to search for and know one's genealogical and cultural roots" points up "the degree to which kinship knowledge has become central to personhood" (Kim 2010: 88; see also Cannell 2011). If the conversion process meant urban Marranos would have to take on a new lineage, it would require effectively the same erasure of kinship knowledge undertaken in many literal adoptions, where the child's biogenetic background is "torn away," blotted out, and replaced by the "as-if genealogical" model typical of adoptive kinship throughout the Western world (Yngvesson 2010: 12–13; Modell 1994).

The matter came to a head on a September evening at Anshei Emet. It was only a few days after the Kaplans had arrived for their first visit, and the group was seated around the table for a class on *kashrut* with Rabbi Ezra. The atmosphere was still a bit tense; everything had gone smoothly to that point, but no one wanted to say the wrong thing. Unaware that she might touch a nerve, Chaya made an offhand comment about the group being in preparation for conversion. Immediately, several people protested that conversion would be redundant because they were *already* Jewish, and their ancestors were Jews before them. But Chaya was adamant. "Just as we have to be strict about the tradition of our texts, we have to be strict about the tradition of halakhah," she said. "We must be able to follow the maternal bloodline. If you cannot prove the bloodline, you must do what halakhah says to become a Jew. And that is conversion. When you convert, you enter a *new* bloodline, within the Jewish people. It has to be that way. It's black and white."

"We know about taking a new bloodline," replied Dulce in Portuguese, rising to her feet, her face coloring, "but it's not right. We say one thing for born Jews, and another for converts—they are *ben Avraham avinu*—but what about B'nai Anusim? Our ancestors *were* Jews. Why do we have to deny them and have a new bloodline? I'm shocked by this." Her voice grew louder. "The B'nai Anusim are not included in any way. We are not recognized. We are survivors of the Inquisition! It was another Holocaust!" David Orta, one of the earliest members of HaShalom and a Brazilian immigrant, protested that he knew if he were called *ben Avraham avinu* he would forever be a second-class Jew at the Portuguese synagogues. And anyway, he insisted firmly, "my forefathers have been Jewish since the beginning! How can I deny them? I am *David ben Yosef*! I will never be *David ben Avraham avinu*!" Tiago, who spoke fluent English, added vehemently: "No one can ever make me say that I am a *goy*. I cannot prove that I am B'nai Anusim, but I am *not* a *goy*! I will not be *Yaakov ben Avraham avinu*!"

Taken aback, Chaya said quietly, "This is the first time we've heard of this. This is the first time I feel we can begin to understand the pain and sadness of the B'nai Anusim." She paused. "We're grateful to you for being so honest. I don't think anyone knows how you feel." Rabbi Ezra followed suit: "You have a problem I suspect does not exist anywhere else in the world. We'll bring it to the Masorti/Conservative law committee, to see if they can find an opinion. They'll study the question." Because Judaism does not have a worldwide religious leader or single authority, decisions like this one are made by rabbis within a given branch of the religion, through close study of relevant aspects of Jewish law and review of prior rabbinic judgments—"opinions," or *responsa*—much as would a secular court of law.

When the Kaplans returned to Lisbon three months later, in December, Rabbi Ezra announced that he and Rabbi Asher, head of the European Masorti *beit din,* had consulted with three respected rabbis, two Orthodox, one Masorti/Conservative. Following the lead of one of the Orthodox rabbis—who, Chaya assured the group, was a great legal scholar—they had deemed it a matter of *kibbud av va'em,* the commandment to "Honor thy father and mother." In their judgment, the urban Marranos would be following this commandment if they preserved their parents' names in their ritual lineage, and hence there would be nothing wrong with doing so. From the moment of the "return" ceremony, their birth parents' names could be rendered in Hebrew and used for all ritual purposes, including the *beit din* certificate affirming their Jewishness. Hence when the time came, David, for example, would be named *David ben Yosef*—David, son of José—"of the remnants of the families of the B'nai Anusim of Portugal."

This decision proved a watershed moment for members of Kehilá. After being promised so much by so many visitors and having so often been misunderstood, they were slow to trust. That Rabbi Ezra listened carefully to their feelings, reflected upon them, presented their concerns to leading rabbinic authorities, and ultimately decided in favor of their wishes marked a turning point. Knowing that their commitment to their ancestry would be respected, they consented wholeheartedly to go through an otherwise standard conversion ceremony, conducted in accordance with halakhah, as a means of reclaiming the identity they felt had been "stolen" so many generations before. The *beit din* for the first group was set for March 2006, three months later. There would be seven: Dulce, Pedro, David, and Tiago would be the first of the B'nai Anusim. Nuno and Luisa, the only two who did not consider themselves already Jewish, would accompany the group and undergo conversion at the same time, followed by a Jewish wedding ceremony to resolemnize their four-year civil marriage according to halakhah. Cécile, too, would go, for the slightly different ritual confirming her Jewish status. The next group was expected to be ready by the end of the year.

In allowing the Marranos to retain their parental lineage for ritual purposes, the Masorti/Conservative law committee's decision neatly satisfied multiple definitions of Jewishness at once. It preserved their own version, rooted in the logic of genealogical causality, while overlaying it with the requirement of conversion in the absence of unbroken matrilineal descent, as enshrined in Jewish law. That such an agreement could be reached, however, was made possible only through their participation in a growing number of nurturing relationships with Jews from abroad. It was upon realizing that they had already been accepted on their own terms that they were willing to meet their supporters' conditions. At the same time, those relationships helped them become Jews according to a third common definition, that of living a Jewish life. In the end, their ancestral, essential Jewishness would not be denied; augmented by their newfound fluency in Jewish religious and cultural practices, it would be affirmed and made incontrovertible under the aegis of halakhah.

While those going before the *beit din* would not be called upon to relinquish their lineage and could thus maintain their ties to the ancestral past, as time went on they became increasingly oriented toward the present. In large part this was due to the emotional bonds they had forged with the small group of visitors I have introduced here, bonds that in turn brought them into broader spheres of belonging. Through regular contact extending over months and then over years, through the exchange of material gifts, and, in the case of Frank's donations, monetary ones, through acts of kindness and expressions of love, and through multiple forms of nurturance, large and small, the urban Marranos and their inner circle of foreign supporters began to develop something approaching what Rupert Stasch (2009), in his analysis of Korowai kinship, calls *mutuality of being* or *intersubjective belonging*—terms taken up by anthropologist Marshall Sahlins (2013) to characterize the very core, in the most distilled sense, of kinship cross-culturally. This network of individuals constituted the urban Marranos' Jewish kin in the present, based not on descent but on love. In practice, relatedness is never entirely given; kin connections may arise and disappear, and there are multiple modalities beyond descent and alliance through which people *become* kin (Cannell 2013; Carsten 2004; Weston 1991).[10] While the analysis of relatedness I offer here applies only within the Jewish domain of urban Marranos' lives and the Portuguese domain of their supporters' time, with other forms of kinship becoming more salient at other times for all involved, it was precisely this familial dynamic that fostered the incorporation of the members of Congregation Kehilá into the Jewish "family" in the concrete sense of lived experience.

The group's foreign supporters were well aware of the importance of fostering bonds between the Marranos and Jewish families abroad, whether or not they articulated their goal in terms of kinship. Anshel, for example, convinced friends in New York and Toronto to vacation in Portugal and urged them to spend time with Kehilá, hoping that ongoing ties would result. And Rabbi Asher, who occasionally organized Jewish heritage tours of his own, arranged one for Portugal, bringing a dozen London retirees to Lisbon. In addition to seeing the medieval *judiarias* and synagogues in surrounding towns, the group spent an entire Shabbat—from sundown on Friday to sundown on Saturday—with the urban Marranos, complete with meals, prayer services, and extensive one-on-one conversation in the group's own space,

Anshei Emet. In both cases the goal was the same: to provide an opportunity for additional bonds to form, so that the Marranos could be brought into active identification with the *present-day* Jewish world, in an ever-widening sphere of belonging.

Chaya, too, sought ways of increasing the number of Jews with whom her charges had meaningful contact. Knowing that there was no local source of Judaica in Portugal, and wanting to ensure that they had the material items needed to set up a Jewish home, she enlisted the help of her own congregation to supply them with prayer shawls, *tefillin,* seder plates, matzo covers, kiddush cups for the blessing over wine, and the like. The large-scale procurement and distribution of such items is standard practice for outreach programs involving "lost" Jewish communities; organizations will purchase dozens of identical mezuzahs at a time, for example, to distribute to isolated populations. The Kaplans, on the other hand, kept their focus on helping the Marranos feel they were joining the Jewish people on a very personal level. Chaya wanted the items to come as *gifts,* given by specific individuals with whom the recipients could correspond thereafter. To that end she encouraged anyone donating a ritual object to attach a letter introducing themselves and sharing the story of how they came to have it. She also asked that donors include their email address, so that the urban Marranos would know, she explained, "that there are people in America who know about them and who care, and to create a bond between them."

On a damp December afternoon during their second visit, Chaya gathered everyone together in Anshei Emet's worn meeting room. Reaching under the table, she produced a pair of oversized shopping bags filled with gifts, each neatly wrapped. She explained that they came from members of her own congregation, sent in response to an announcement she and Rabbi Ezra had made during Shabbat services. Some had been purchased new, but the majority came from the donors' own families. "Now, they all know about you," she said. "We've told them about you. And everything has a story. I'll read them out loud. Everybody who wanted to send something, we said, 'You must write the story, tell who you are, because we want our family in Lisbon to know who our friends are.'" She read each donor's letter slowly but with dramatic emphasis, pausing often for me to translate. She wanted to be certain that each gift giver's words came alive.

First came a prayer shawl and *tefillin* that had been used every day for nearly thirty years by a member of the Kaplans' congregation. "This is embroidery from Israel," Chaya began, lifting up the embroidered velvet zippered pouch that held them. "The *tallit*, it's beautiful, amazing embroidery. It's from a very dear friend of ours, Fred Fischer, F-I-S-C-H-E-R.[11] Now, listen to this story." And then she read:

> The enclosed tallit and tefillin were mine. I am a seventy-one-year-old man liv-ing in New York, and I used both tallit and tefillin on a daily basis for many years. I cannot be sure exactly how many, but probably for 25 or 30 years I used this tallit every day, until nine years ago, when I set out to buy a tallit and tefil-lin for my new son-in-law. The occasion of a young couple starting a new life together seemed like the right time for me to start a new chapter for myself. The tallit and tefillin represented an important part of my personal spiritual and religious life, and I hope that they will provide the same meaning to whoever becomes their new user. May they become a symbol both of my good wishes and the continuing strength of our Jewish tradition.

She presented the gift and card to Nuno, who stood mute, overwhelmed. He later confessed that he had been bowled over by the idea that someone could be so kind and generous to a complete stranger. Even had they been available in Portugal, these ritual objects would have been well beyond the means of most Kehilá members. Finely made *tefillin*, for example, cost approximately US$250 at the time; a prayer shawl, particularly of the quality and decorative beauty of this one, could easily have reached US$400.

But there was more. The next item was a true heirloom, a prayer shawl that had belonged to the donor's father.

> The enclosed tallit was bought by my father, David Gottesman, in the 1970s, for his personal use around the same time that me and my sister were celebrating our bar and bat mitzvah. I saw my father use it on a number of occasions when he was praying in our synagogue in Brooklyn, New York. My father died in 2002, and I am glad that his tallit will be able to enable someone else to enjoy it for the purpose it was meant for.

"Now that is from Michael Gottesman," continued Chaya, "a young man like you, Tiago; he's in his thirties. This is for you—with his email address." Tiago, too, was speechless as he accepted the gift and card from Chaya's out-stretched hand. After a pause, another of the men said, "They're giving us all these gifts. What can we send in return?" Chaya's reply was immediate: Write to them. Send a photo of yourself. Tell them your story. The gifts, she implied, were an opening for becoming connected to one another.

More and more gifts came out the bag. There were cloths to cover matzo on Passover, seder plates, a kiddush cup for the new congregation, more *tefillin* for the men. Each came with a story, some funny, some heartwarming, some heartbreaking. The group was most affected by the story accompanying a priceless, solid silver challah knife, intended for use on Shabbat, that had been passed down within a single family for generations. The woman who sent it had married into the family and, Chaya explained, her husband, Samuel Waxman, had died when he was just forty, leaving her alone with two small boys. Now she and her sons were giving the heirloom to the newly founded Kehilá.

> *This challah knife is given to you from the Waxman family in New York. Rabbi Ben Zion Waxman, who was a rabbi in Queens, New York, for 50 years, and Rabbi Professor Samuel Waxman, a professor of Talmud at the Jewish Theological Seminary, are memorialized as we give this gift in their memory. We think of you as you will be using this knife. May you share many Sabbath meals with friends and family. We look forward to hearing from you and perhaps visiting.*

When she finished reading, the room was absolutely silent. The memory of a deceased young man and his father had made its way to Lisbon, to a battered synagogue in a condemned building, where it could be perpetuated by the group that received it amidst an outpouring of generosity and support from abroad. When all the gifts had been distributed, Chaya told more stories about each family that had sent an item, again encouraging the recipients to write. Later that evening Manuel commented that he had been especially touched by the family stories that came with the objects, "because before we didn't have any Jewish family memories of our own. Now we do."

Objects like these are potent points of connection, traveling from one pair of hands to another, accompanied by stories that give them added dimension and heft, or "density" (Weiner 1994). As gifts from named individuals, rather than anonymous charitable donations, the items Chaya carried across the Atlantic brought their recipients into a web of social relations. The gifts did not initiate a system of exchange (Mauss 1967); there was no expectation of reciprocity here, beyond perhaps written correspondence and someday a personal visit. Instead, they were material emissaries that connected the local people to specific Jewish families abroad, making them bearers of those families' good wishes, their thoughts, and their memories, as well as stewards of the treasured objects themselves. Like Frank's donations and Anshel's trinkets, the gifts from abroad were signs of awareness, attention, and caring. The offerings created new social ties for the members of Kehilá, whether in imagination or in practice, and the more engaged with those new ties they became, the less they spoke of their ancestry. The nature of their identification as Jews began to change.

Appropriately, it was during the weekend of the first group's appearance before the Masorti *beit din* that their "adoption" into their foreign supporters' families reached its most explicit form. Let us begin at the end, with Nuno and Luisa's Jewish wedding. It was held in the multipurpose room of a London synagogue, adjacent to the room in which the *beit din* had met that morning. Rabbi Ezra and Rabbi Asher performed the ceremony together. Luisa wore a cream-colored silk gown and veil painstakingly sewn for the occasion by her older sister. In place of Luisa's parents, it was Chaya who accompanied her down the aisle and stood at her side under the *huppah* (Heb.; wedding canopy). During the ceremony, Rabbi Ezra spoke of his and Chaya's feelings. "It's a privilege," he said, "it's a joy, for us to be able to celebrate this day with you! It's wonderful, wonderful, especially since Chaya and I both feel that you are a part of our family. We feel the same for the other members of Kehilá as well. And as a symbol of the fact that we do feel you're a part of our family, the ring used in the ceremony today *is* part of our family. It belonged to Chaya's grandmother and it's been used in weddings in our family through the generations."[12]

In offering Chaya's grandmother's ring, a family heirloom, to be used in Luisa and Nuno's Jewish wedding ceremony, Rabbi Ezra and Chaya provided an explicit, material indication of their acceptance and affection for the couple and, by extension, for the rest of the group that went before the *beit din* that day. So too did Cecilia Samuels, a member of the London synagogue's congregation, who had participated in Rabbi Asher's tour to Lisbon a few weeks earlier. While spending Shabbat with Kehilá's members, she and her husband had decided that they would host a wedding reception for the couple—a casual affair of white wine and hors d'oeuvres, complete with dancing the hora and toasts to the bride and groom. They welcomed Luisa and Nuno into their suburban London home for the weekend, having them stay in their adult son's former bedroom. Other families also offered home hospitality, all of them, like the Samuels, taking in the urban Marranos, including them at the table for every meal, and showing them how an observant (but not Orthodox) Jewish family lives, from the kosher food in their refrigerator to the ins and outs of celebrating Shabbat in the home. Each host family's Shabbat dinner was a warm, welcoming event; the one I joined at the Samuels' home that weekend, along with several other members of Kehilá, also included our hosts' adult children and extended late into the evening with conversation and song.

This full-scale welcome into "the Jewish family," here writ small, occurred in tandem with the group's ritual incorporation into "the Jewish family," writ large. Where the former was vibrant, full of conversation, physical and verbal effusiveness, and continuous interpersonal engagement, the latter was a solemn, individual process—until the final moments, that is. On March 30, 2006, seven members of Kehilá gathered in the basement café of the nineteenth-century building housing the Masorti *beit din.* One by one, Chaya led them up the stairs to a large room on the second floor, where each had a thirty-minute interview with the rabbinic court. Rabbi Asher and Rabbi Ezra remained in place throughout, with others making up the third seat on the *beit din* over the course of the morning. The court asked each one to tell their story and then posed a series of questions intended to gauge their knowledge, commitment, and sincerity—none of which, in truth, was in doubt. Afterward, each made their way to the *mikvah,* the ritual bath housed in the same complex, for the solitary immersion that marked the passage point from Marrano to Jew.[13] The final stage of the ritual of "return" was the recitation of the *Shema,* the Jewish affirmation of faith. Standing in the same room where they had met with the *beit din* just a few hours earlier, now bright with afternoon sunlight streaming through stained-glass windows, one by one the former Marranos read the prayer aloud and heard themselves called by their Hebrew name and lineage for the first time, as Rabbi Asher handed them the certificate affirming their full membership among the Jewish people. They were, at last, *judeus de carteirinha*—Jews with papers.

The recitation and certificate ceremony was open to observers. Already in the building to set up for Nuno and Luisa's wedding, several members of the London congregation came to show their support and acceptance. Initially, the presence of outsiders made participants uncomfortable; they momentarily worried that they were, once again, to be creatures in "the Marrano zoo." But then, as Dulce explained later that evening,

> the moment I realized that the people watching weren't there as spectators, but that they were moved [*estavam emocionadas*], their presence became important to me. Because I saw that they were *really moved*—not by the ritual itself, but *by our emotion.* For the first time I feel like I belong, like I'm actually part of the Jewish world.

The realization that others viewed them with empathy was a second watershed moment, for it opened the possibility of genuine connection, even intimacy: here was that rare gaze, at last, of assumed equality, individuality, and temporal coexistence, of "looking at us like brothers." The balance of the urban Marranos' identification as Jews was progressively shifting from past to present, from their rigorously Portuguese, ancestral way of understanding Jewishness to a global vision of communal, mutually supportive Jewish life.

GUT SHABBOS IN LISBON

I do not mean to suggest that members of Kehilá ceased to identify as ancestrally Jewish, for they did not. But having moved from a national frame of reference to a global one, many began to focus more on experiential affinity, empathy, and acceptance as crucial elements of Jewish identification. Menorá's Ricardo Carvalho once commented that he felt the greatest connection with assimilated American Ashkenazi Jews, and they often seemed especially comfortable with Marranos, because they shared a similarly distanced relationship to their Jewish heritage. Here we might think of Frank and his adoration of the people he met in Portugal for precisely that reason. So, too, did "hidden children" like Rabbi Lévy feel a special connection with these descendants of hidden Jews, who also had to struggle to reclaim a Jewish identity. Feelings of friendship and mutual understanding arose quickly in encounters between the local people and visitors who felt this way, just as they did with Masorti Jewish tourists who spent Shabbat at Kehilá, specifically because they were all members of the same branch of Judaism. Simply put, for urban Marranos these interpersonal bonds offered far more lasting experiences of belonging than did biological descent.

From a historical perspective, of course, their Jewish ancestors would have been Sephardic, and that is why it was the chief Sephardic rabbi who came from Israel to evaluate their situation; and yet it was precisely their claim of Sephardic descent that led to years of unresolved rabbinic debate over their status. Many Jewish tourists and other foreign visitors were baffled by their exclusion from Portugal's "mainstream" synagogues, both of which followed Sephardic liturgical practice and were formally identified as Sephardic institutions. The urban Marranos' Jewish ancestry was by definition Iberian, so why, their visitors wondered, were they not accepted as fellow Sephardic Jews? What were they doing at Anshei Emet, which was still recognized as an Ashkenazi synagogue? If their Jewishness was grounded purely in terms of descent, it made no sense at all.

Recall that Rabbi Ezra and Chaya spent many hours in their car singing along to Sephardic prayer melodies, expecting that their students would want to learn them. To their amazement, when they arrived in Lisbon they found that the urban Marranos wanted their new congregation to follow Ashkenazi rite, instead. They were insistent that the Kaplans should teach them not only Ashkenazi prayer melodies, but customs. When asked why, Dulce said simply, "I've never felt the slightest human warmth from the Sephardim." Her attitude was not surprising, given the deep antipathy many of the group's members had developed toward the Sephardic synagogues after their repeated rejection, not to mention their feeling of having been put off indefinitely by Israel's chief Sephardic rabbi. Where they *did* experience great warmth, on the other hand, was from Ashkenazi Jews, from the elderly Polish men who first opened the door to Anshei Emet and welcomed them in, to the foreign visitors who promised to keep in touch and actually did so. Indeed, the vast majority of those who offered affection and support to the people of Kehilá were Ashkenazi, whether Canadian, American, Israeli, French, or British— including Frank, Anshel, Rabbi Lévy, Rabbi Asher, Rabbi Ezra, Chaya, the leadership of the Masorti movement, the New York congregation who sent gifts, the London congregation who welcomed them into their homes and witnessed their "return," and on and on.

Having looked beyond their national borders for Jewish role models and connections of any kind, many of the urban Marranos found their closest "kin" among the Ashkenazim. Tiago, Nuno, and a few others decided that they wanted to *be* Ashkenazi, and pursued new cultural practices to that end. Luisa learned to make gefilte fish, challah, and cholent, staples of Ashkenazi cooking; Tiago, who had long studied Yiddish, the language of the Eastern European Jews, taught the others a few words; and some members started greeting each other playfully at Friday night services with "*Gut shabbos*"—the *Ashkenazi* way of wishing someone a good Shabbat. This, even as they continued to understand the core of their Jewishness as stemming from their Portuguese ancestry. Rather than a simple matter of either/or—Sephardic or Ashkenazi, descent or affiliation, biology or love—these individuals found it possible to define themselves simultaneously along multiple pathways of identification and belonging. That such a hybrid was possible is due in no small part to the peculiarly global moment in which we find ourselves, marked by an apparently unceasing supply of alternative ways of being and heightened attention to the project of self-making, not only in North America and Western Europe, but well beyond (Mathews 2000; Pieterse 2007). As the material presented in this chapter suggests, the possibility of face-to-face inter-action over vast distances is rapidly transforming and expanding the figured worlds within which we might situate ourselves, offering new modes and materials for imagining the self and enabling a transition—for some—"from a world of roots to a world of choice" (Mathews 2000: 179).

LOCAL IDENTITY, GLOBAL IDENTIFICATION

Upon hearing that Portuguese Marranos had gone before an Ashkenazi *beit din* in London and were forming an Ashkenazi congregation of their own, rather than joining one of Portugal's Sephardic synagogues, some former tourists and outreach workers were baffled, even outraged. Postings lambast-ing whoever had been behind such an inappropriate decision appeared on Nostálgia and other social media. Individuals from a wide array of Jewish and Jewish-descendant backgrounds, including some Ashkenazim, argued that the proper way for descendants of the Inquisition's victims to reclaim their Jewish identity would be to adopt the religion of their ancestors, which would be "traditional" (Orthodox) Sephardic Judaism. While overlooking that these were knowledgeable adults, entirely capable of deciding which branch of Judaism they wanted to affiliate with, those who complained missed a crucial point. These former "Marranos" continued to identify with the experiences of their ancestors, maintaining a resolutely local identity as descendants of Portuguese Jews, but they had no desire to be zoo animals, as it were, caged by the past. When it came time to affiliate with the Jewish world of the present, they made their choice on the basis of love and nurtur-ance, not in terms of blood and birth. The previous four years had seen Jews from around the globe passing through the doors of their associations, and they had noted that those who returned again and again to help and guide them in making their "return" were not Sephardic, but Ashkenazi.

Both before and after their "return," the urban Marranos saw no contra-diction in holding two axes of identification in tension with each other. Vertically, on the basis of descent, their sense of self was firmly rooted in the logic of genealogical causality: they were attracted to Judaism and things Jewish because their ancestors had once been Jews. Horizontally, however, they understood themselves in terms of a logic of affinity, in the vernacular sense of a mutual attraction on the basis of shared interests, analogous experiences, or sympathies. The people of Kehilá chose to affiliate with Ashkenazi Judaism, that is, because those were the people with whom they had forged personal bonds of mutual affection and care, the people who saw something important in their experience, the people who became their "Jewish family," writ small. For all their initial protestations that they should be accepted as Jews on the basis of descent and history, it was ultimately the latter form of identification, the logic of affinity operating in the global present, that hastened their incorporation into the Jewish world and helped them to become halakhic Jews.

Portugal's urban Marranos and their Ashkenazi supporters abroad revealed something profound when they referred to each other in the vocabulary of kinship and concretized their feelings in micropractices of mutual care. In taking each other on and identifying with one another as *kin,* at least within circumscribed domains of their lives, they reworked the widely presumed basis of Jewish relatedness and belonging: from descent and shared history to love and choice. But this was not "choice" in the sense of conversion, of electing to *become* a Jew. For, as we have seen, the urban Marranos felt emphatically that they were already Jewish, and even those foreign Jews who subscribed to halakhic definitions of Jewishness tended to view Marranos as "lost brethren" who needed to be returned to the whole. Although they carried the *pintele yid,* the Jewish spark said to burn inside anyone who has strayed from the Jewish people, theirs was a "self-conscious" kinship (Howell 2001), a "choice" that privileged a horizontal axis of belonging based on affinity over a vertical axis of belonging based on genealogical descent. Regardless of their abstract imaginings of Jewish belonging at the outset, it was face-to-face relations, the concrete ways in which individuals treated one another, that in turn offered them an entirely new sense of identification, and reconfigured vision of belonging, on a global scale. In the end, as Catarina put it in her inimitable way, here love—not blood—proved the thicker stuff.

Conclusion

STRANGERS, KIN, AND
THE GLOBAL SEARCH FOR BELONGING

> Questions of belonging and kinship are universal as well as cul-
> turally specific, and rarely as simple as bureaucratic taxonomies
> would have us believe.
>
> DON SEEMAN
> *One People, One Blood*

ONE MORNING AS I NEARED the end of this writing, a dear friend and
fellow anthropologist sent me the link to an article she had just read in
Tablet, an American online magazine. *"Bem Vindos, Judeus!"* (Welcome,
Jews!), exclaimed the unlikely banner headline. The subtitle read, "After 500
years, Portugal wants its Jews back, and some are coming."[1] The subject was
Portugal's Sephardic "Right of Return" (*direito de retorno*), passed by
Parliament in 2013 and now fully in effect, restoring Portuguese nationality
to descendants of Jews who fled the Inquisition centuries ago. Given the difficulty of verifying that descent, the law assigns the task of vetting applicants
to two institutions: the Comunidade Israelita de Lisboa and the Comunidade
Israelita do Porto. These are, of course, the very communities that so openly
and effectively maintained their boundaries against urban Marranos' bids to
local Jewish belonging. What will the new law mean for the Marranos, not
to mention their counterparts overseas, the crypto-Jewish descendants of the
Portuguese diaspora, who are equally unable to furnish proof beyond their
own convictions?

The text of the law is surprisingly broad, stipulating only that applicants
must "demonstrate a familial tradition of belonging to a Portuguese-origin
Sephardic community, based on family names, family language, direct
descent, or collateral familial connection to an ancestor originating in a

Portuguese-origin Sephardic community."[2] In addition to birth and death certificates and synagogue records, permissible documentation includes a letter from a leader of a Portuguese-identified Sephardic community attesting to the applicant's legitimacy, or even testimonial evidence from witnesses to the family's oral tradition of Sephardic descent and connection to Portugal. In fact the law explicitly lists "family memory" as potential evidence, and nowhere does it indicate that applicants must themselves have been raised Jewish. Thus it would seem that the ancestral logic and forms of "proof" underpinning many urban Marranos' claims to Jewish belonging have been officially validated.

So it would seem. But because certification of candidates' legitimacy falls to the normative Jewish communities, each has been allowed to develop its own criteria, and here we can see that little has changed. In Porto, in fact, where the community is ironically made up largely of expatriates, the grounds for acceptance—and hence certification for Portuguese citizenship—are stricter than ever. I quote here from the Porto Jewish community website, which provides a lengthy English-language overview of the application process and criteria for certification:

Factors that will be taken into account in interpreting the spirit and letter of the law

1. The law requires a traditional connection to a Sephardic Community of Portuguese origin, which means that there must still exist today an emotional connection to that distant time, preserved over the centuries in family traditions, memories, heirlooms, or language.

2. The law intends to cover not all descendants of Portuguese Sephardic Jews, but only those who retain the status of Jews in the light of halakhah and, in special cases, non-Jews whose parents or grandparents were Sephardic Jews, and descendants of Portuguese Jews whose families had for a long time been distanced from the official chain of Judaism, but that later came to renew their ties with Judaism through an Orthodox *beit din* and halakhah, which is the same.

3. The basic questions in the certification process are the following: whether the applicants are Jews in the light of halakhah; whether the candidates are Sephardim or descendants of Sephardim; whether the candidates are of Portuguese origin. The first two questions must be affirmatively answered by the [candidate's] local Orthodox Rabbinates and, ultimately, by the Orthodox Rabbinate of Porto, recognized by the Chief Rabbinate of Israel. Finally, the Portuguese origin of the candidate must be determined.[3]

Consider the vast difference between the law's modest minimum requirement of a familial tradition of affiliation and the Porto community's stringent insistence upon Orthodox-certified Jewish status, via maternal descent (whatever the applicant's degree of observance) or Orthodox conversion after multigenerational estrangement.[4] In practice, this is a question not of restoring Portuguese nationality to documented descendants of Portugal's exiled Jews, but instead of offering citizenship to Jews of Portuguese descent who meet the local Jewish communities' criteria for belonging. We have returned, once again, to social categories, to the profound entanglement of kinship (here, descent), exclusion, and belonging even in the supposedly rationalized domain of citizenship law, and to the contested power to define Jewish belonging and enshrine that definition in bureaucratic decisions that matter. Is it enough to be a descendant? Or must one also be an observant Jew? Why should those descendants recognized as Jewish by Orthodox Jews have greater claim to Portuguese national belonging and ancestral restitution than those who are not?

Two additional developments shed light on the logic at work here. First, as the *Tablet* article explains, while Lisbon's Jews appear not to be terribly invested in the new law, treating their gatekeeping role "as largely functional, a part of government bureaucracy that just happens to have a cultural and religious flavor," for Porto's still-tiny, barely viable congregation the law represents "an opportunity for revival." Seeing in it a source of desirable future members, the leadership has used it as a pretext for raising international awareness of the congregation and the city as a whole. Indeed, the article quotes a member of the synagogue's Law of Return Committee, himself a British expatriate, as expressing hope that Portuguese citizenship will appeal to Jewish nationals of countries with increasing anti-Semitic rhetoric, such as Turkey, as well as from elsewhere in Europe. Not surprisingly, the online overview of the certification process concludes with a portrait of Porto as an ideal place for Jews to live—and, in the same breath, starkly delineates the community's limits to belonging:

> Although the true city of return of the Jews is Jerusalem, Porto is perhaps the best "safe haven" for Jews in Europe. There is no anti-Semitism in the city of Porto, the second largest city in the country. The Mayor of Porto is the grandson of German Jews and has a high regard for the Jewish people. A large part of the population is descended from Jews persecuted by the Church and the monarchy between 1496 and 1821. (Obviously the fact that Portuguese citizens are descendants of Jews—and descendants of many other people—

does not confer on them the status of "B'nai Anusim." Please visit the page "Review Commission for purported Portuguese B'nai Anusim.")

Why the pointed reference to "B'nai Anusim"—that is, the urban Marranos—in this seemingly unrelated context, complete with a link to an official statement on the matter? The answer seems to lie in the second development: a concerted effort to change the synagogue's public image. One result of Shavei Israel's well-publicized efforts to revive Barros Basto's *obra do resgate,* the "work of redemption" of northern Portugal's "lost" Jews, was that the Porto synagogue became inextricably linked in the Jewish imagination with the centuries-long saga of the Marranos. For over a decade, journalists and travel writers have published accounts in international media erroneously describing the congregation's primary membership as Marranos who have "returned" to Judaism. After regaining control of the synagogue in the late 2000s, the local leadership publicly and vociferously denied any support of Shavei Israel's presence, dismissing it as a "proselytizing organization" and forming a commission to develop a policy on newcomers presenting themselves as Marranos or B'nai Anusim. The resulting statement, released on October 14, 2014, makes the Jewish community's position abundantly clear:

> It is the opinion of the Religious Committee of the Jewish Community of Porto, as well as of reputable scholars, that there are no longer any B'nai Anusim (crypto-Jews) in Portugal, just as there are no longer any Samurai warriors in Japan, and it is misleading to imply that there are. The matter is now one for the history books, local culture, and tourism. The discourse of proselytizing organizations, which uses abstract terms like "Jewish roots" and "return to the religion of their ancestors," is misleading and deceptive, because all Portuguese have "Jewish roots."[5]

Hence, according to the report, looking for Marranos in Portugal today is a fool's errand—not because there are no descendants left within the country's borders, but, ironically, because "it is virtually impossible to have a single Portuguese that is not a descendant of converted Jews."[6] Among Portugal's mainstream Jewish communities, as among the Portuguese public, both Portuguese citizenship and the status of Marranos (or B'nai Anusim) are couched in terms of kinship. Here, however, that kinship is understood not as a matter of lineage, but of continuous identification and affiliation. Descendants of the Jews who fled may yet be Jewish enough to become Portuguese, that is, but descendants of the Jews who stayed are now too Portuguese to be Jewish.

The question of who is or is not a Jew is less significant for people engaged in thinking about Marranos from beyond Portugal's borders. While any local Jewish population must presumably decide who will or will not be welcomed into the community, a question with concrete and immediate consequences, the stakes are much lower for those observing from a distance. Other than the network of international travelers discussed in the previous chapter, most tourists and outreach workers I encountered were operating under an abstract assumption of categorical belonging for any and all "Marranos" they might meet, reaching out to them collectively as "lost kin." Leaders of Portugal's normative Jewish communities, on the other hand, were regularly faced with the presence of known individuals who clearly fell outside the bounds of their membership. Given the considerable interpersonal tension involved in assessing the newcomers' claims, small wonder they opted instead for a blanket statement of categorical exclusion—whatever we might think of their reasoning.

While the cliché that things look different from afar certainly applies, this is not a simple matter of the beholder's physical location. In his classic essay "The Stranger" (1950), Georg Simmel argues that all human relations involve both proximity and distance, literal and metaphorical: we are "near" and "remote" in different ways, to differing degrees, in every social setting. To understand his theory and why it is relevant to the urban Marranos, let us take a step back to consider the concept of *social space*. For Simmel, modern life, particularly urban life, was characterized by changed relations of proximity and distance: those who were physically close were not necessarily part of one's social world, and vice versa. This observation has come to seem all the more prescient over the past half century, as global interconnectivity enables human relations to stretch across vastly expanded geographical distances (Appadurai 1996; Rouse 1991). In a world on the move, spheres of interaction and identification are uncoupled from fixed locations, a state captured by the proliferation of social-scientific terms like "social spheres," "cultural flows," "social landscapes," and, as here, "social spaces"—all intended to capture both the ephemeral realms within which interactions increasingly take place and the complex interplay of social and geographical location in diverse forms of sociality (Reed-Danahay 2015). This is not to say that social life is now necessarily deterritorialized. We can speak equally of the "social space" of the Porto synagogue, a physical location, and the "social space" of the

Nostálgia social media platform, a virtual one. Either way, Simmel's writings on the sociology of space allow us to recognize that we can be socially close to others who are not in immediate physical proximity, and that "the immediate copresence of subjects is no longer considered to be the necessary basis of community relations" (Allen 2002: 58). The reverse is also true: being socially close to someone *may* require physical proximity in some instances, and the copresence of subjects *is* sometimes a necessary basis of community relations. Here, context is everything.

This was Simmel's great insight: all human interactions are constituted by differing degrees of social and physical proximity, and a given party's relative social and physical distance from others will vary from one social space to another. The figure of the Stranger, at one extreme, indexes a particular form of interaction, defined by physical proximity to a group of people while remaining socially distant from it. Writes Simmel, "[The Stranger] is fixed within a particular spatial group, or within a group whose boundaries are similar to spatial boundaries. But his position in this group is determined, essentially, by the fact that he *has not belonged to it from the beginning,* that he imports qualities into it, which do not and cannot stem from the group itself" (1950: 402; emphasis added). We can readily see that within the social space constituted by Portugal's normative Jewish communities—what I refer to elsewhere in this book as "the figured world of Portuguese Jews"—the urban Marranos were strangers par excellence, physically near and yet profoundly socially distant: they had never belonged and never would. As an illustration we need only recall the painful Sukkot dinner described in the introduction, an incident mirrored in other community events in Lisbon and Porto throughout the early 2000s.

The cognitive dissonance of being simultaneously present and seeing themselves as rightfully belonging, on the one hand, and being continuously and explicitly marked as outsiders, on the other, presented one of the greatest stumbling blocks for the urban Marrano movement. In addition to the practical problem of physical access, there was the conceptual problem of never articulated but clearly divergent understandings of Jewishness, a confusion only exacerbated by the unexpectedly warm reception they received from foreign visitors and online correspondents. The stubbornly concrete experience of face-to-face rejection, week after week, by individuals whose names they knew and remembered had far greater impact than did fleeting encounters with affectionate strangers. Hence the puzzle with which we began: if the Jewish people are a globally dispersed family, united by common ancestry or by "adoption" via conversion, how could this small group of self-designated Jews-by-descent—so flatly dismissed in their out-of-the-way corner of the world—possibly find belonging among them? Or, to put the question more broadly, how can strangers in a local setting ever become kin to the imagined community represented by the very people who hold them at a distance?

The previous chapter offered one answer to this question, through the story of how one group of urban Marranos unexpectedly moved from the proximate social space of Portugal's synagogues, in which it seemed they could never belong, to an ephemeral, deterritorialized social space that encompassed both them and an international network of supporters in relations of nurturance and care. Given that these relations stretched over many hundreds and even thousands of miles, their example would seem to lend credence to the argument that in a globalizing age, physical proximity is no longer essential for engendering feelings of *social* closeness. However, the developments traced in this book reveal the reverse to be true: direct, one-on-one interaction remains an essential component both in enacting exclusion and in fostering identification, kinship, and belonging with collectivities that transcend the local—perhaps not only for Portugal's Marranos, but for all of us living in a profoundly interconnected and yet still undeniably material world.

ANCESTRAL JEWS / UNWELCOME STRANGERS / FELLOW OUTSIDERS / LOST KIN

One goal of this book has been to shed light on the dynamics of *identification:* how people come to identify with a particular social category, how they act within specific figured worlds to embody that category through practice, and how interactions with others shape their sense of belonging to or exclusion from the collectivity it represents. This has entailed an examination of the social life of the categories "Jews," "non-Jews," and "Marranos" as they arose in distinct social spaces—Portuguese history, the Portuguese family, the mainstream synagogues, Marrano associations, interactions between urban Marranos and foreign Jewish visitors, and the "family" that emerged among Kehilá's members and their Ashkenazi supporters—with attention in each case to available resources for self-making, experiences of proximity and distance, and consequent feelings of affinity or alienation. Within the immediate family (the context in which many first came to think of themselves as Jews-by-descent), for example, prevailing logics of cross-generational "continued identities" and genealogical causality made the attribution of ancestral Jewishness entirely reasonable. Recall that in Portugal, "from the very moment the baby is out of the womb ... there is a constant preoccupation to root the baby's identity in the familial past," in particular by noting resemblances between the individual and his or her forebears (Pina-Cabral 1997: 87). Here we might think of how Dulce first discovered her Jewish ancestry: "You really are Jewish," her uncle told her. "You're Jewish just like your grandmother." With Jewishness anchored in family history—whether presumed, implied, or relayed directly—the urban Marranos' relationship to it was colored by identification with ancestors and relatives, as well as by positive interactions with Jews they met in their own cities or abroad. It resonated with who they felt they were, and there seemed no reason they could not claim it as their own.

When they ventured into the synagogues in Lisbon and Porto, Dulce and the others encountered a remarkably different set of assumptions about Jewishness and its origins. There, physical proximity brought swift and unequivocal rejection. Precisely because they were face-to-face with those who had the authority to welcome or deny them, interactions with the normative Jewish community affected them profoundly, above all because it positioned them so differently than they had expected based on their understanding of Portuguese Jewish history and their imaginings of the Jewish world at large. Finding each other and forming *associações* provided an alternative social space, one in which they came to think of themselves collectively as *Marranos*—"Catholics without faith, Jews without knowledge" (Carvalho 1999: 31–32)—the available (historical) social category that most closely resembled who they felt they were. As Marranos, they worked collaboratively to develop and adopt practices and dispositions that would make them legitimately the Jews they felt they already were. All the while, they understood themselves to be Jews by descent and inclination, ancestry and attraction, criteria accepted within their associations as sufficient to make one Jewish.

Beyond Portugal's borders, as we have seen, the category "Marrano" carries very different meaning. Throughout the Jewish world, it refers narrowly to secret Jews, those who persist in practicing Judaism (or some form thereof) at great risk while outwardly professing a different faith. In this sense, few if any Jews today will ever meet a Marrano, for by now they exist primarily in historical texts and in the imagination as objects of continuing fascination.

Collectively and categorically, "Marranos" are the lost brethren of any Jew, anywhere. Thus they are socially near in the Jewish imagination—indeed, "kin"—and yet remarkably distant in concrete cultural and physical terms, located by definition well outside the social spaces of ordinary life. It is hence through tourism, so often a pathway to the extraordinary, the enchanted, and the transcendent (Selwyn 2007; Whittaker 2012; Picard and Di Giovine 2014), that foreign Jews find an opportunity to meet the storied Marranos, "the living past"; and they bring with them the expectation of a moving encounter, replete with stories of poorly understood rituals and mysterious phrases, hidden practices and familial legacies of secrecy and fear. They arrive primed to embrace those they meet as offshoots of "orphaned branches of the Jewish people" (Sola Pool 1934: 247), and embrace them they do.

International tourism encounters generate a social space of a unique kind, transitory and yet emotionally charged out of all proportion to its duration. Typically, its potency is in direct proportion to the intensity with which it is anticipated by either or both parties. By virtue of its brevity and the complexity of cross-linguistic interaction, it allows only the most minimal communication—what one scholar of sex/romance tourism describes as "radical simplification" (Askew 1999: 117)—even as it offers intense moments of felt connection across difference. This is perhaps why so many tourists were happy to listen without skepticism to the Marrano life stories shared during their brief visits, even generously identifying further clues of Jewish origins in the details they heard (cf. Moore 1976: 199). It was precisely through such radically simplified interactions that tourists could connect with a living remnant of Jewish near-destruction and survival, just as trekkers in the Himalayas find mysticism and enchantment in encounters with Sherpas (Adams 1996) or spiritual seekers find the same in the unfamiliar, even unintelligible rituals of Hindu temples in India. Writing of encounters between "primitivist" tourists and Korowai people in West Papua, Indonesia, Stasch (2013: 13) notes that inherent to this dynamic is a semi-conscious "process of misapprehension, the noticing and suppressing of alternative understandings ... or the slipping in and out of a plurality of different understandings across the flow of an overall range of interactions. People often know more than they know, in other words." Or, as one Canadian tourist whispered during a synagogue service in Lisbon when his companion attempted to translate, "Shhh! I feel more spiritual when I don't understand."

It is not difficult to imagine the impact of such warmhearted credulity for a group whose claims to belonging had repeatedly been denied by the only other Jews with whom they had regular personal interaction. No amount of supportive correspondence online could counterbalance "the real world," as one man described it, of their face-to-face rejection at the mainstream synagogues in Porto and Lisbon; but face-to-face acceptance from tourists offered an antidote, at least in the short term. This was true even as urban Marranos became increasingly aware that their foreign visitors, whether tourists or outreach activists, did not fully understand who they were and why they welcomed their company. Because brief visits to foreign destinations are inevitably governed by maps, guidebooks, and itineraries that saturate the landscape with particular themes, visitors encounter a curiously two-dimensional destination. Local differences, internal discord, and cultural complexity are, again, radically simplified: things do, after all, look different to those who are socially removed as much as to those who are physically distant. Thus a great many visitors conflated "Portuguese Jew" with "Marrano," continuously confused one site on the itinerary with another, and had difficulty fathoming why those peopling "Jewish Portugal" couldn't all just get along in one large, inclusive community. One outreach activist tried repeatedly to build bridges between leaders of the Marrano associations and the nominally Orthodox synagogues, thinking the sticking point was a difference in degrees of religious observance. "She thinks we're all one big Jewish family here," sighed Ricardo, "like our problem getting into the synagogues is some kind of family squabble. But it's not. It's two completely different families."

Nonetheless, it is perhaps better to be collectively misunderstood and categorically welcomed than to be turned away, again and again, as individuals. In search of enchantment, most foreign visitors took the urban Marranos at face value, greeting them with warmth, affection, and occasionally even awe. Here again we find the work of productive miscommunication, that fragile balance between communicative clarity and opacity that enables cross-cultural interactions to run smoothly: within the transient social space of the touristic encounter, it was great anticipation, limited communication, and desire for meaningful contact that allowed the *feeling* of kinship, whatever the reality of what would (or would not) follow. As Catarina put it when asked whether she felt an affinity with the endless visitors who came and went, "I do, I actually do. I think we're all moved by the same things. We're all pushed forward—and touched, really—by looking for kin. We're all trying to build some kind of extended family of people we can relate to." Still, she admitted, it was a generic affinity she felt, and the interactions afforded at best a transient affirmation of her Jewishness. Again, as a social space the tourist encounter is by definition fleeting. One cannot find genuine belonging in an interaction that lasts just an hour or two. However great the feeling of a common quest for kin, what urban Marranos and tourists shared was not kinship in a lived sense, enacted in practice; it was kinship of the imagination, a discursive but not experiential phenomenon, and there is a vast difference between the two.

By what alchemy, then, were some participants in the Marrano associations transformed into members of the Jewish family? As we saw in the previous chapter, a crucial factor was the development of ongoing, face-to-face relations with people who came to know and care for them as individuals, and for whom the latter came to feel lasting affection and appreciation. For all the urban Marranos' assertions of a Jewishness transmitted by descent and claimed through voluntary affiliation, it was only through relations of mutual human caring that they were ultimately able to forge a "Jewish family" with their closest supporters and thus find a place among the Jewish people. The necessity of direct personal interaction for fostering a sense of belonging should not surprise us. Indeed, writes sociologist Vanessa May, "belonging is an intersubjective experience that necessarily involves other people. We make claims for belonging which others either reject or accept, and therefore mere familiarity with a place, a group of people, or a culture is not enough for us to gain a sense of belonging" (May 2011: 370; cf. Candea 2010). Nor is merely having one's presence tolerated. Affect, too, is key.

CONNECTION, KINNING, AND FORGED BELONGING

Joaquim Martins, the HaShalom member of *chueta* origin, attended Lisbon's Shaaré Tikvá synagogue as a teenager in the 1960s. Although the rabbi at the time welcomed him, after a hiatus for college and then a period working in another city Joaquim returned to find new leadership and a far less open environment. His personal connection with the synagogue lost, he sought links with Judaism elsewhere, volunteering on archaeological projects related to Portuguese Jewish history and eventually finding kindred spirits online through Graciana Mayer's Nostálgia network. Recall that Joaquim served as one of the local guides on the second Nostálgia Conference-Tour, sharing his story and taking participants to the newly restored medieval synagogue he, a trained architect, had discovered some years before. It was there that Anshel Rappaport led an impromptu ceremony giving Joaquim a Hebrew name.

The moment was profoundly moving, in no small part because the tour group had just spent the day visiting medieval quarters where long-absent Jewish communities once flourished and pausing in leafy squares to remember those who perished there in the grotesque pageantry of an auto-da-fé. Already steeped in intense emotions, participants could not help but be touched by the symbolism of one descendant's recognition and effective incorporation as a member of the Jewish people—not by local Jews, observed from a tourist's distance, but by the tour group itself.

Amidst the hugs and group photos that followed, several participants were visibly affected. Said one man over dinner that evening, to nods of agreement from others, "You know what moved me most? It was being there with Joaquim, seeing *his* feelings, his reactions, his—well, it moved me to tears." As we saw in chapter 4, the experience was indeed a powerful one for Joaquim, who later recounted a flood of emotions—an almost physical sensation of his Jewish identity deepening, an awareness of the great weight and responsibility of his ancestral past, and a sudden, profound sense of connection with the people around him. Those of us who subsequently returned and spent more time with him became his siblings, he said, with whom he felt particular closeness (*proximidade*) and intimacy (*intimidade*) from that point on. Although he did not specify why the more general feeling of connection arose, I suspect it had much to do with realizing that those present were moved, too, and that the reason they were moved was precisely because he was. What is empathy, after all, if not an act of concentrated emotional engagement? And is that emotional engagement, however briefly expressed, not a potential step toward a lasting bond?

In many cultural contexts, shared emotion is a potent medium through which people come to feel connected and, over time, to see one another as kin. For urban Marranos, encountering Jews who would listen, absorb, reflect upon, and even mirror their emotions in face-to-face encounters was a great gift. In a statement of thanks read aloud in the London synagogue the morning following the *beit din,* Dulce wrote, "Rabbi Ezra and Chaya were our parents, who taught us to live as Jews, felt our suffering, lived through it all with us, learned our feelings, and gave us the strength to persevere." Her experience of connection—indeed, of kinship—lay in the perception that the group's emotions were felt and understood by the Kaplans, their "parents," who accompanied them on their journey and took on their pain as their own. Returning to Sahlins's universal definition of kinship as "mutuality of being," consider his provocative claim that "where being is mutual, experience itself is transpersonal" (2013: 44). The reverse, we might say, is also true: just as urban Marranos reasoned that their Jewish ancestry caused them to experience their forebears' feelings as their own, reflecting a mutuality of being with prior generations, so too did they recognize in the empathy of others a sign of mutuality of being on the basis of love.

Kinship is a temporal phenomenon, a process, as much as it is a system for organizing persons and relationships. This is because it is *performative:* the actions kin are expected to undertake in relation to one another produce the very ties they express (Lambek 2013). This is why rhetorical invocations of kinship do not have the same effect as those concretized in practice, over time. To think of and describe someone as kin is not the same as treating them as if they are. Hence categorical descriptions of Marranos as "lost kin" could not, in the long run, render them members of "the Jewish family" on an individual level. Familial relationships arise through acts of *kinning,* social practices by which existing kin transform a newcomer—newborn, adoptive child, spouse, in-law—into a relative (Howell 2006). Nurturing, feeding, cohabitating, exhibiting interest and empathy, giving gifts, sharing stories, providing material support, and incorporating the newcomer into existing kin-based networks are common cultural practices through which kinship may be enacted and thus congealed into an enduring relationship. Certainly such acts transpired between Kehilá members and their Ashkenazi supporters, individually and collectively, just as they did for the handful of members of the Marrano associations who moved abroad and married into local Jewish families.[7] And, in both cases, participants articulated a sense of belonging to a collectivity well beyond the immediate relationships those acts fostered, so long as their interactions continued.

But how are such interpersonal relations transposed to the level of the imagined community? At work here is a process similar to "forged transnationality" (Schein 1998), the creation of transnational ties among members of diasporic populations, or between ethnic descendants and the ancestral homeland, when such links have been lost. Government- or community-sponsored "roots tours" for young adults, for example, operate on the principle that direct contact with the land and its people will generate identification and even future financial or political engagement (Louie 2004; Aviv and Shneer 2005). In the case of urban Marranos, the goal seems to have been the less instrumental process I call *forged belonging,* achieved through embodied, concrete relations with individuals over time that modeled for collective attachment with the Jewish people at large. In his analysis of personal and collective ties among Freemasons, anthropologist Danny Kaplan (2014) shows that a similar rescaling occurs in ritual and social contexts as participants extend logics of interpersonal friendship and intimacy to communal solidarity, and vice versa. The two levels of affiliation are not separate, he argues, but exist on an experiential continuum. Just as Freemasonry is founded on the concept of generalized, non-instrumental friendship, its members forming "a community of strangers trusted as friends" (Kaplan 2014: 87), Jewish peoplehood is founded on the idea of generalized relatedness, its members forming, extending Kaplan's insight, a community of strangers envisioned as kin. And, as with Masonic friendship, the saga of Portugal's urban Marranos suggests that to feel a part of "the Jewish family" one must first have concrete experience of what such relatedness entails, one-on-one: global kinship makes sense only if grounded on a human scale (Herzfeld 2007: 319).

BELONGING, MYSTICAL AND MUNDANE

Throughout this book I have grappled with questions of identification and belonging, both existential and interpersonal. What is it to know oneself? To work to become the person one feels one already is? To encounter those to whom one feels one *should* belong? To long for kin? To feel connected? To find belonging? These are perennial questions of the modern condition, of course, questions that have been explored in a great many genres beyond ethnography. Nonetheless, this true story of a particular group of people in a small European country offers poignant material for exploring how people come to identify with far-flung others; how they seek and find glimmerings of mystical connection in a world said to be disenchanted; how the horizons of kinship expand in a globally interconnected era; and how relatedness emerges and gathers strength as a lived condition over time. Tracing transformations in Marrano imaginings of self in relation to others has also helped us grasp the profound role of affect in shaping identity and sociality across domains and scales—from personal encounters to the imagined community and back again.

However unique the conditions of their search for belonging, Portugal's urban Marranos illustrate broader currents of meaning-seeking and self-making in the contemporary world. Amidst the seemingly limitless range of identities and values around which one might shape one's life—immersed as we are in what Gordon Mathews (2000) calls the "global cultural supermarket"—each of the individuals whose trajectory we have followed in this book drew upon diverse models, both local and foreign, for making sense of yearnings and attachments that seemed to emerge from within. In anchoring their sense of intrinsic Jewishness in the idiom of descent and imbuing that lineage with ineffable causality, they echoed mystical ideas about kinship and the self found in diverse populations today (Basu 2007; Sturm 2010; vom Bruck 2005). In this reputedly secular age, advances in genetics and reproductive technologies may seem to have shifted public understanding of descent and inheritance entirely into the modern, disenchanted realm of science. Nonetheless, as Fenella Cannell (2013: 234) cogently observes, listening to what our respondents have to say about cross-generational transmission suggests instead "a space of mystery," one that "permits the expression of feelings about kinship as what is mysterious, yet intimate, in the human condition; the sense of connectedness to and yet separateness from others, both past and present, living and dead; the sense of something patterned, not arbitrary, yet too complex to be amenable to any complete or reductive explanation."

Cannell's analysis of Mormon kinship provides a glimpse into an enchanted domain that is closer to the Marrano case than it might initially seem. According to Mormon doctrine, one "belongs" to one's mortal family before birth, in the pre-mortal heaven; to "choose" one's kin, as in adoption or marriage, is not an individual decision but a recognition of something already determined, for kin connections preexist this lifetime (Cannell 2013: 227). Broadening her scope to received assumptions about "Western" kinship in general, Cannell notes that such mystical models "may also reveal something truthful about the modern world that is otherwise difficult to see, [for] modern disenchantment may be partially transcended through a language and practice of kinship understood as ineffable, a third term, one that . . . remains embedded . . . in our metaphors of human transmission" (Cannell 2013: 238). Reading Cannell's work, I am reminded of how Chaya Kaplan described her feelings about urban Marranos, whose Jewishness, too, evidently preexisted their birth, transmitted across generations:

So what made them do this? What was this calling? It was something that was transmitted in some mysterious way. It is *netsach yisrael,* the eternity of the People Israel. It can never be obliterated, despite all odds, it's there. There's a flame. And sometimes it dwindles, and sometimes it flickers, but it seems always to remain and to grow stronger with time. Here we have descendants, and people who truly believe they are descendants, of ancestors from the time of the Inquisition, who have Jewish heritage but nothing that would make them halakhically Jewish. And something motivates them, and something is pushing them, and that flame is being fanned! And the flickering flame is getting stronger, and stronger, and burning within them. And that is *netsach yisrael*. There's a mystery we don't understand. There *is* something that we don't understand.

Whether articulated in terms of an ancestrally transmitted Jewish spark (the *pintele yid*) or a divinely bestowed Jewish soul (*neshamah*), the Jewishness that Chaya and other foreign visitors recognized in the urban Marranos was grounded in descent, transmitted, just as in the Portuguese model of transgenerational "continued identities," via "some sort of common substance . . . [that was] not limited to a corporal, 'physical' dimension" (Pina-Cabral 1997: 89–90; cf. Boyarin 2013:124). That recognition was itself a kinning device, identifying the urban Marranos as legitimately "lost" members of the Jewish family and hence worthy of the effort of reincorporation.

Who we feel an affinity with is not predetermined, however "natural" it may seem. Narrative, emotion, desire, expectation, interaction, perceived resemblance, common experience, and reciprocity may all have a role to play, and can themselves engender feelings of affinity that seem embodied, even existential. In their efforts to connect with the Jewish world, Portugal's urban Marranos were not alone in the search for belonging. Imagined communities, after all, are not themselves kin networks in practice, though they may rely upon idioms of blood and common ancestry. Belonging—whether familial, ethnic, religious, or otherwise—is an ongoing, reciprocal relation, one that must be continuously renewed in direct encounter (May 2011). The foreign Jews who traveled to meet Marranos, too, were in search of human connection, however fleeting, that would affirm their sense of self and community. Said one secular American outreach worker after a warm exchange with members of Menorá, "I love visiting these groups. I feel so much more Jewish here, so much more connected, so much prouder of the Jewish people." This is the "work" urban Marranos and their visitors did for one another, even if unaware: they reciprocally fanned the Jewish flame within.

Yet, as we have seen throughout this book, the encounter itself was far simpler and more mystically infused for tourists and outreach workers than for their hosts. Being (and becoming) a Marrano was not an easy experience. It entailed continual self-consciousness, a palpable awareness that one's sense of self could be challenged at any turn. This was equally true whether interacting with people at the mainstream synagogues, immediate family and friends, tourists, or outreach workers. While Menorá and HaShalom offered a space in which participants could safely explore Jewish religion, history, and culture, it was also a place of continuing self-consciousness, where they looked for and learned to identify clues in their family histories and even their own hearts that offered corroboration of Jewish roots. Even their collective self-designation as "Marranos" was a conscious act, levied in response to their interstitial position in the figured world of Portuguese Jews. Nevertheless, most believed that they would eventually leave that in-between, self-aware status and be recognized as "just Jewish"—not "the living past" tourists sought, but Jews like any other.

Belonging is an intersubjective accomplishment, a relaxed sense of mutual identification that, some say, is characterized above all by a lack of self-consciousness: one belongs when one has achieved an "everyday mode of being" that does not require conscious reflection (May 2011: 370). This is quite different from a claim to Jewish belonging on the basis of mystical affiliation; it is, rather, a matter of mundane coexistence. Not all of the people who appear in this book have found such Jewish belonging, despite having made their "return," and others have not yet found a path to a *beit din* or even remained active in an association. But for a few members of the fledgling Kehilá, a first taste of that belonging came on a Saturday evening in September 2005, in the form of six French young adults on a cycling trip through Portugal. Most of them were affiliated with the Masorti movement, but they were not on a Jewish-themed tour, nor were they interested in attending local religious services. The just-inaugurated Kehilá had been listed online as Portugal's Masorti congregation, and since they would be passing through Lisbon on a Saturday, one of the cyclists inquired on a whim whether there might be a social gathering for Havdalah, the informal ritual marking the end of Shabbat. The answer, of course, was yes.

When the evening came, Catarina, Tiago, Pedro, Nuno, Luisa, and the rest were all present at Anshei Emet, the table laden with snacks as usual. Conversation was lively, mostly in French and English, with an easy camaraderie that continued well past the brief Havadalah ceremony. It spilled over into a nearby restaurant for a three-hour dinner, followed by a late-night stroll through Lisbon's historic Baixa district. The atmosphere was different from any other encounter with *pessoas de fora,* though at first I could not put my finger on the cause. And then it dawned on me: our visitors had no idea that their hosts, founders of Kehilá, were "Marranos." It was only later in the evening, when one asked about the Inquisition and Portugal's secret Jews, that the group's story emerged. But these visitors were not inclined to probe further; they were more interested in talking about Portugal today, about their hosts' lives and travels, about what else they should see on their journey. With breathtaking simplicity and ease, the founders of Kehilá had unexpectedly found a space of belonging—not as Marranos, not even foremost as Jews, just twelve young adults, they and their French guests, swapping stories and laughing as they walked the cobbled streets of a warm Lisbon evening.

NOTES

INTRODUCTION

1. Definition compiled from several standard dictionaries and rephrased.

2. See "A Note on Translation and Terminology." Although in Hebrew *anusim* is a plural noun (singular, *anous*), the term *B'nai Anusim* has been taken up in colloquial English as both a singular noun and an adjective, a usage I follow in this book. In Portuguese, too, *anusim* has been imported as the singular form (Pt., *anussim*), with the plural derived according to Portuguese pluralization rules as *anussins*.

3. In some exceptional cases, such as in seventeenth-century Amsterdam, they formed their own congregations (chap. 1), guided by rabbis who traveled from as far as Greece and Turkey to help them return to normative Judaism (Melammed 2004).

4. HaShalom and Menorá are pseudonyms, as are all names of individuals in this book. At least ten similar associations have formed and disbanded over the past three decades, most of them based in Lisbon or Porto.

5. *Israelita* (Pt.; Israelite) is an archaic Portuguese term meaning "Jewish," whereas the word for a citizen of the modern nation of Israel is *israelense*.

6. In 2002 compulsory education ran only through Grade 9 (age fifteen). Just 10 percent of the adult population had completed twelve years of schooling and had some form of higher education; 40 percent left secondary school by the ninth year, and 9 percent of those age ten or older were entirely illiterate (Reis 2007: 228–29). Until the mid-1970s more than half of the population left school at or before Grade 4 (Lubkemann 2003: 84). Attendance through Grade 12 became compulsory in 2012.

7. I am indebted to Paula Mota Santos (personal communication) for this observation.

8. See, e.g., Cannell 2013; Carsten 2000; Thomas et al. forthcoming; Weismantel 1995.

9. Consider, for example, the *Avot* (Heb.; forefathers), the opening section of the prayer (the *Amidah*) congregants read silently during daily services: "Praised

are you, Lord our God and God of our Ancestors, God of Abraham, of Isaac and of Jacob, great, mighty, awesome, exalted God who bestows lovingkindness, Creator of all. You remember the pious deeds of our ancestors and will send a redeemer to their children's children."

10. For recent anthropological analyses, see studies of "Feres Mura" in Ethiopia (Seeman 2003, 2009), Lemba in southern Africa (Tamarkin 2014), and Bene Menashe and Bene Ephraim in India (Egorova and Perwez 2013).

11. The resulting accounts of "exotic" Jewish communities in unexpected places continue to be a popular genre. See, e.g., Dan Ross, *Acts of Faith: A Journey to the Fringes of Jewish Identity* (New York: Schocken, 1982); Ken Blady, *Jewish Communities in Exotic Places* (New York: Jason Aronson, 2000); James Ross, *Fragile Branches: Travels through the Jewish Diaspora* (New York: Riverhead Books, 2000); and Ben Frank, *The Scattered Tribe: Traveling the Diaspora from Cuba to India to Tahiti & Beyond* (Guilford, CT: Globe Pequot, 2011).

12. Poem by Abraham Reisin, included here by kind permission of the Reisin family. I am grateful to linguist José Claudio Costa for his translation from the original Yiddish, to which I have made a few stylistic and rhyming modifications. I am solely responsible for any errors introduced.

13. David Gitlitz and Linda Davidson, *A Drizzle of Honey: The Lives and Recipes of Spain's Secret Jews* (New York: St. Martin's Griffin, 1999).

14. Original emphasis. All emphasis in quoted material is in the original, unless noted otherwise.

15. Nostálgia is a pseudonym.

16. I am often asked about urban Marranos' relationship to Israel, and particularly whether they hoped to move there. Although both associations' meeting spaces were decorated with posters of Israeli landscapes, donated by the embassy's cultural attaché, Israel was effectively a non-issue—politically, practically, or spiritually. It came up only when association members who had traveled, worked, or studied there mentioned their experiences during broader conversations about Jewish identity or practice internationally, or when the subject was broached by foreign visitors. As their Jewishness was initially constituted in relation to the particularities of the Portuguese past and present, Israel was not a central reference point. In this they were not necessarily unique. As Caryn Aviv and David Shneer (2005: 28) note in their analysis of the decreasing importance of Israel as a "homeland" for a younger generation worldwide, the presumption that the Israel/diaspora framing is always, everywhere central to Jewish identity "has prevented [scholars] from exploring the diversity of Jewish experiences and the ways that Jews craft their identities in the places that they live."

17. Here my experience was similar to Jewish ethnographers of Orthodox communities, who report encountering the expectation that they too will become Orthodox (e.g., Benor 2012: 37). In general, anthropologists of Jewish origin whose work involves Jewish communities often find themselves positioned in the field foremost as "fellow Jews," rather than as researchers (Lehrer 2013; Klein 2012; Markowitz 2006).

1. The caretaker told me the story in Portuguese. During my fieldwork I heard it from numerous others, in several languages. Versions have appeared in many historical and folkloristic publications (e.g., Bethencourt 1903: 252n1; Roth 1941: 398n8; 1964: 249–50; Sachar 1994: 180; Siporin 1993: 143). The detail of yellow hats as required Jewish dress is historically accurate, but centuries earlier, during the reign of Afonso IV (1325–57). See Martins 2006: 1:120.

2. For an overview of population estimates and supporting data, see Soyer 2007a: 103–6; Martins 2006: 2:122.

3. Zimler's novel, set during these events, initially appeared in translation in Portugal—where it became a best-seller within a month—before finding a publisher in the United States. It subsequently topped best-seller lists in thirteen countries and was translated into over twenty languages. Its impact has been remarkable, sparking international fascination in Portuguese Jewish history and Portugal's hidden Jews.

4. The term *Sephardic* is often erroneously applied to all Jews from Muslim countries or to those of "non-European" origin. It derives from the ancient Hebrew *Sefarad,* meaning "Iberia"; *Sephardic diaspora* refers to the historical dispersion of Spanish and Portuguese Jews and their descendants throughout the Mediterranean, North Africa, and the Middle East (Benbassa and Rodrigue 2000). Although augmented by Iberian migrants throughout the Moorish and early Christian eras, the original North African and Middle Eastern Jewish communities long predated the Sephardic diaspora and maintained distinct cultural and religious traditions.

5. Representative lists are reproduced in Canelo 2004: 27 and Saraiva 2001: 178–80. Saraiva notes that these practices were not unique to hidden Jews during that era. Many remain widespread in Portugal today, e.g., slaughtering animals via a single slash to the throat and draining blood completely before butchering.

6. For eyewitness accounts and a moment-by-moment description of an auto-da-fé, see Saraiva 2001: 100–115.

7. These claims are seemingly corroborated by a 2008 study published in the *American Journal of Human Genetics.* Focusing on genetic signatures on the Y-chromosome common to Sephardic Jews, researchers found that as many as 20 percent of Spanish and Portuguese men who did not identify as Jews nonetheless bore distinctive markers of Jewish ancestry. From an anthropological perspective tests of this kind are inherently problematic, as they locate "real" Jewishness in genes, using biological criteria to assign what is a fundamentally socially constituted identity (Azoulay 2003; Schramm, Skinner, and Rottenburg 2012).

8. For examples, see Canelo 2004: 41–44; Caro Baroja 1961: 225–37.

9. Schwarz 1925, 1926. Additional publications of crypto-Jewish prayers and practices include Alves 1925; Canelo 1990; Garcia 1993; Gitlitz 1996; Mea 2005; Novinsky and Paulo 1967; Sola Pool 1934.

10. Schwarz's usage was not a reflection of local terminology: "to the common masses in Portugal the word *Marano* [*sic*] is totally unknown" (Schwarz 1926: 145).

It has since entered the Portuguese lexicon, though it is more common among scholars to hear *cripto-judeus* or, in everyday speech, simply *judeus.*

11. Wolf's report describes a pervasive intellectual philosemitism among aristocratic descendants of New Christians that contrasted sharply with the rural Marranos' ritual-based Jewishness. He quotes one such man, a high-ranking provincial official who read avidly about Judaism and the Jewish people, as saying, "I am not and probably never will become a believer, an observer of the Hebrew religion, but every day I feel more profoundly a compassionate and intimate sympathy, an intense solidarity with the Jewish race—the eternal victim." "It is probable," comments Wolf, "that this feeling is very widely spread in Portugal" (1926: 14).

12. After an international campaign to restore his name, in 2012 the Portuguese Parliament declared Barros Basto's dismissal from the army to have been politically and religiously motivated, unanimously passing a bill reinstating his full rank and honors (Assembleia da República Processo Nº 119/2012).

13. See Portuguese Marranos Committee 1938.

14. *Time* magazine published one of the first post-revolution accounts, devoting several pages to the community. See "Catholics Who Celebrate Passover," *Time,* April 11, 1977.

15. "New Emissary to Crypto-Jews of Portugal Named." Posted at http://www .shavei.org/, retrieved August 11, 2010. The rabbi has since returned to Belmonte full-time.

16. The most prominent was a three-part National Public Radio series, "The Hidden Jews of New Mexico." First broadcast nationally in 1987, it generated more mail than any previous NPR program (Kessel 2000: 33). Throughout the 1980s and 1990s the *Los Angeles Times,* the Santa Fe *New Mexican,* and other regional newspapers reported about crypto-Jews in the Southwest, as did the *New York Times.*

17. Full text of speech retrieved at www.saudades.org/soares.html on June 14, 2003.

18. More recently, this discourse has also been invoked in relation to Portugal's pre-1497 Muslims, the "Moors" (Vakil 2003).

19. Assembleia da República Processo Nº 27–PL/96.

20. See Policarpo, "Purification of Memory," Address at XIII International Meeting of Peoples and Religions, Lisbon, September 24–26, 2000, retrieved at www.santegidio.org/uer/lisbona2000/policarpoebrei_en.htm; and "Catholics Apologize to Portugal's Jews." *Christianity Today,* October 2000, retrieved at www .christianitytoday.com/ct/2000/octoberweb-only/56.0.html.

21. The stamps and book, *A herança judaica em Portugal,* were part of a long-standing philatelic series. A previous set recognized Portugal's "Arab" heritage (*A herança árabe em Portugal,* 2001).

22. *Recenseamento Geral da População, Resultados Definitivos, Censos 2011,* 6.49, "Resposta à Pergunta sobre Religião." Instituto Nacional de Estatística, www.ine.pt.

23. Census statistics at www.ine.pt. See Martins 2006: 3:107–10 for a graph of 2001 data.

24. *Público* (Lisbon), July 3, 2008.

1. Observant Jews affix a *mezuzah,* the small decorative case containing a parchment scroll inscribed with passages from Deuteronomy, on the doorposts of their houses.

2. The article was Nuno Guerreiro's "O regresso dos judeus," *Visão,* June 1994.

3. In all, I documented the life histories of more than forty participants. Formal interviews were semistructured and wide-ranging, conducted in Portuguese except with two individuals who spoke English with near-native fluency.

4. *Davening* (Yid.-Eng.; praying) is a term used by American Jews for the distinctive forward-backward rocking of Orthodox Jews in prayer.

5. Tiago's summary of Hasidic thought was correct. As Henry Goldschmidt (2009) explains, Hasidic Jews maintain that all Jews carry an inherited "godly soul," one that predates the material form of the Jewish people but was transmitted to them via the biblical patriarchs and matriarchs, to whom it was bestowed directly by the divine. Not all who inherit this soul are "born" Jews: "According to Hasidic understandings of the transmigration of souls, Jewish souls are nearly always reborn in Jewish bodies, but sometimes—by the inscrutable workings of divine providence—one may find its way into the body of a Gentile, who is thus drawn to Judaism. Conversion is thereby imagined as a realignment of one's 'religious' commitments with one's 'racially' fixed inner self" (Goldschmidt 2009: 563). The Jewish soul, that is, is racial, inherited, and determinative of one's ultimate religious affiliation. More broadly, according to Talmudic interpretation of Deuteronomy 29:14, "all Jewish souls, past, present, and future, were present at the revelation on Mount Sinai. The Talmud . . . interprets this verse to include converts, whose spirits were in attendance as well, implying that converts have Jewish souls that got misdirected into non-Jewish bodies, and returned to their destiny upon conversion" (Kessel 2000: 119–20; see also Klein 1996: 203).

6. Even in the 2000s, Protestantism was only sometimes included in "Religion" sections. Evangelical Christianity has since made significant inroads but remains far from mainstream. According to Teixeira (2012), evangelical Protestants make up just 2.3 percent of the population.

7. On Portuguese religious adherence and diversity, see Dix 2009, 2010; Teixeira 2012; Vilaça 2006.

8. A northerner can become a southerner by settling permanently in the south. In idiomatic Portuguese, that change is described with a metaphor of ethnoracial transformation: one is said to "become a Moor" (*tornar-se mouro*). There is no such term for making the reverse move.

9. This idiom mirrors terms used for thoroughbred horses (*cavalo de raça*) and pedigreed dogs (*cão de raça*).

10. Writing of urban, upper-middle-class and aristocratic Portuguese families, Pina-Cabral (1997: 78) notes that family members inevitably share "identities derived from the joint association to earlier moments of the cycle of social reproduction (that is, to primary social units now extinct or in the process of extinction)."

From birth, one's identity is intimately connected with that of previous generations, and that connection is revealed in ways that can be seen and commented upon by others. Moreover, as in the case discussed here, an individual may show signs of "continuing" the identity of more than one ancestor, not only physically but behaviorally.

11. For related discussions of multiple and ambiguous modes of cross-generational transmission, see Charmé 2012; Goldschmidt 2009; Lambek 2013; Pina-Cabral 1997.

CHAPTER THREE. OUTSIDER, IN-BETWEEN

1. Jewish services do not require a rabbi. Any ten people (men, if the proceedings are Orthodox) can perform the full Shabbat prayer service, provided that they are Jewish according to the definition used by that branch of Judaism. A subset of the prayers can be performed even by a single individual, in any location.

2. The Jewish Community of Faro was composed of Anglophone expatriates who had retired to Portugal's southern Algarve coast. Although its presence registered among the normative communities to the north, it was not a major player.

3. These distinctions operated very differently in Belmonte than elsewhere in the country. There, the Orthodox community coexisted with a large, still-active crypto-Jewish community; in many cases members of a single family were divided between the two. On Jewish/crypto-Jewish divergence in Belmonte, see Canelo 1990, 2004: 197–206; Garcia 1993, 1999.

4. Such a low level of observance is not at all exclusive to Portugal, and reflects the complex nature of Jewishness as simultaneously a religion and an ethnocultural identity worldwide.

5. I stress "widely assumed" here, because in Portugal there are "born" Jews across the class spectrum, certainly from an economic if not social perspective, just as there are among Jews anywhere in the world. The perception that all Jews are upper-middle to upper class in Portugal is, as elsewhere, based on who is visible and socially identified as Jewish, not the socioeconomic conditions of the entire Jewish population (cf. Klein 2012: 99–131).

6. The book was Lydia Kukoff's *Choosing Judaism* (New York: UAHC Press, 1981).

7. Sometimes another symbolic universe, that of Jews from abroad, came into play. French Jews, male and female, frequently wear similar pendants; American women also often do (Heilman 1988: 269). At scheduled visits with foreign tourists, both male and female leaders of Belmonte's Orthodox Jewish community wore visible Stars of David. In addition, self-identified ancestral Jews who interacted regularly with foreign tourists—for example, attendants at the Jewish museums in Tomar and Belmonte, as well as other professionals in the tourism industry—wore them openly.

8. *Kashrut* prohibits eating meat of animals that do not have cloven hooves and do not chew their cud, any fish or seafood lacking fins or scales, and carnivorous birds. Rabbinic authorities have historically interpreted "You shall not cook a kid in its mother's milk" (Exodus 23:19) to mean that meat and milk cannot be eaten together. Although observant Jews vary in the degree to which they implement these rules, avoiding shellfish and pork and never combining meat and milk in one meal are widely considered the baseline of "keeping kosher."

9. The same type of logic underpins the identity claims of descendants of Spanish and Mexican crypto-Jews in the American Southwest (Neulander 1996). For indicative narratives, see, e.g., Jacobs 2002; Kessel 2000; Kunin 2009.

10. Kunin (2009: 197–99) makes the related observation that in the absence of surviving religious traditions among "crypto-Jews" in the American Southwest, "the most significant element of crypto-Jewish practice is the narrative presentation of self."

11. See, e.g., Brandes 2002; Cain 1991; Holland et al. 1998; Stromberg 1993.

12. See, e.g., Barker 2002; Benor 2012; Zimman 2009.

13. On the *pintele yid* and the Jewish soul (*neshamah*), see Goldschmidt 2009; Hoffman 2005.

14. While this is an extreme position, one not shared by the Reform or Conservative movements, it is not unheard of in some types of Orthodox Judaism (Klein 1996).

15. The criteria for inclusion abruptly relaxed when two of the new community's founding members dropped out. Portuguese law requires twelve signatories for incorporation as a legal entity; as there were now only eleven members whom the leaders trusted with that responsibility, I was made the twelfth signatory and hence a founding member after all.

CHAPTER FOUR. "MY LOST BROTHERS AND SISTERS!"

1. Tour vignettes in this chapter are written from the position in which I experienced them. The 2004 Conference-Tour, on which I was a participant observer, was my first visit to Anshei Emet. The 2005 tour described below took place during my long-term fieldwork as a member of Menorá and HaShalom.

2. While visitors came from numerous countries, I do not address the constructions of kinship operative in their specific national contexts. Instead, I generalize on the basis of common patterns observed over several years of fieldwork among North American, British, Israeli, South African, French, Italian, and Brazilian travelers.

3. See www.shavei.org. Some ultra-Orthodox groups, such as Chabad, delimit *am yisrael* more narrowly. For rabbinic rulings on the status of descendants of converts to other religions, many of which closely mirror the conceptual framework discussed here, see Corinaldi 1998; Klein 1996.

4. My field observations diverge here from Cutileiro's (1971) among peasants in the Alentejo. There, he wrote, "ideally a man should always help a brother in distress,

but for a cousin no such ideal obligation exists, and each case is judged on its merits" (1971: 128). I found to the contrary that although each case was judged on its merits, there *was* an ideal obligation. Those who mentioned having declined to help a cousin in need expressed guilt, indicating that a code of conduct had been broken.

5. This was particularly true during the Salazar dictatorship, the era of Riegel-haupt's and Cutileiro's fieldwork, when bureaucracy was extraordinarily complex and any stranger could be an informer. Riegelhaupt 1979 provides an insightful analysis of this phenomenon.

6. The Portuguese institution of *cunha* rarely appears in the anthropological literature. Although some scholars (e.g., Smith 1976) explicitly distinguish *cunha* from patronage or clientelism based on their different power dynamics, others see all three as falling along the spectrum of a single system (e.g., Riegelhaupt 1967, 1979). Silva, in particular, situates *cunha* in the context of clientelism in Portugal and worldwide (for extensive citations, see Silva 1993: 491n4). The closest analogues, where "favors" are performed on an ad hoc, personal basis to circumvent established rules and procedures, have been described in Brazil (Barbosa 1995) and Chile (Lom-nitz 1971). More broadly, patronage and clientelism have long been a defining theme of southern European ethnography, generally in conjunction with analyses of class structures.

7. I am indebted to Miguel Vale de Almeida (personal communication) for this observation.

8. Related phenomena have been identified elsewhere, most relevantly by Stasch (2014, 2015), who writes of working misunderstandings in "primitivist tourism," and Simoni (2016), on the generative potential of ambiguity in touristic encounters in Cuba. For other useful theorizations, see Cole 2014; Livingston 2007; Pina-Cabral 2002, 2010; Tsing 2005.

CHAPTER FIVE. FROM ANCESTORS TO AFFECTION

1. This situation was short-lived. By 2010 the rabbi had long since been transferred back to Belmonte, and in October 2014 the Jewish Community of Porto publicly and vociferously disputed any suggestion that they had ever been associated with Shavei Israel.

2. This analysis is intended to capture the quality of how many visitors inter-acted with local people, not to portray them as automatons entirely determined by preexisting narratives. While remarkably few could be characterized as developing a "questioning gaze" (Bruner 2005), there were of course alternative perspectives and engagements from both sides of the encounter.

3. Strictly speaking, the *beit din* must include at least one rabbi who is knowl-edgeable in the matter of conversion; the remaining two members may be educated and religiously observant members of the community under whose auspices the conversion is performed (Diamant 1997: 114).

4. As of this writing I have been unable to locate any indication that the matter was resolved, beyond the formal statement by the Jewish Community of Porto discussed in the next chapter.

5. In this sense their dilemma was quite like that faced by the "Feres Mura" on their arrival in Israel, as Seeman (2009: 193) explains: "The more 'Feres Mura' claimed an essential and unchanging Jewishness, the more their commitment to real religious change was undermined by the taint of historical apostasy, but the claim to be essentially converts [to Judaism] would have undermined their claim to be in Israel as descendants of Jews."

6. The Conservative movement coalesced in North America in the nineteenth century, occupying the space between Reform Judaism on one side and Orthodoxy on the other, often with an explicitly egalitarian approach to tradition. Its overseas counterpart, the Masorti movement, emerged in the United Kingdom a century later, in the 1960s; in Israel the first congregations were established in the 1970s. There are now Masorti synagogues throughout Europe and South America.

7. Several individuals routinely forwarded me their correspondence with Chaya, both to confirm they had understood her and to further my research.

8. While those converting out of religious conviction are helped by finding a family to include them in home rituals and provide mentorship as they become enculturated into Jewish life, there is no stipulation that converts-to-be should be matched with families. Individual congregations do sometimes coordinate pairings, but according to *beit din* rabbis with whom I spoke the vast majority of converts in Europe and North America do so in order to marry their Jewish partner and so have a ready-made Jewish family in their spouse and in-laws.

9. The child's Hebrew name is ceremonially given during the *brit milah* (Heb.; circumcision ceremony), for boys, or in a baby-naming blessing for girls. Because the language of the ritual name is essentially a marker of ethnic/religious inclusion, if the child's given name is already Hebrew or Yiddish a separate ritual name would be unnecessary.

10. As Howell (2006: 64) argues, *kinning*—the transformation of strangers, including newborns, into relatives—is a universal activity: "While those involved in biological birth may think of [creation of the kin relation] as an automatic process, ... it is always a deliberate one, and it is one that is engaged in intersubjectively between existing kin and new kin (whether they are biological babies, affines subsequent to a marriage, adoptees, or other adoptive families)." All kin, that is, *become* kin through human social interaction.

11. This is a pseudonym, as are all names in the donor letters quoted here.

12. In traditional Jewish wedding ceremonies, a plain gold band is briefly placed on the bride's right forefinger. After the wedding it is replaced with a ring of the couple's choosing.

13. I, too, participated in each stage of the process, translating during one individual's appearance before the *beit din* and later returning alone to discuss my

relationship to Judaism and its relevance to my research with the rabbis. I was also permitted to immerse in the *mikvah,* which can be used by Jews for purposes other than conversion. My goal was to experience the entire process bodily and emotionally, as well as conceptually.

CONCLUSION

1. Rod James, "Bem Vindos, Judeus!" *Tablet,* April 15, 2016. www.tabletmag.com.

2. Ministério da Justiça Decreto Lei Nº 30-A/2015; my translation. Freer translation posted at http://jewishcommunityofoporto.blogspot.co.uk, December 15, 2014, with Porto application procedure updated March 2016; original Portuguese text and Lisbon application procedure posted at www.cilisboa.org, February 27, 2015. Spain passed a similar law in June 2015.

3. http://jewishcommunityofoporto.blogspot.co.uk/2014/12/portuguese-nationality-for-sephardic.html.

4. The Porto document also names children and grandchildren of Sephardic Jews as eligible for consideration even if they are not Jewish according to *halakhah,* as in the case of individuals with a Jewish father or grandfather but a non-Jewish mother. This mirrors Israel's Law of Return, which recognizes Jewishness through a single grandparent.

5. http://jewishcommunityofoporto.blogspot.co.uk/2014/10/t-mikvah-of-oporto-synagogue.html. Posted October 14, 2014.

6. Ibid.

7. Over the past decade members of Menorá and HaShalom have relocated to America, England, Holland, Czech Republic, Switzerland, and Israel. Not all have married.

REFERENCES

Abu-Lughod, Lila. 1991. "Writing against Culture." In Richard Fox, ed., *Recapturing Anthropology,* 137–62. Santa Fe, NM: SAR Press.

Adams, Vincanne. 1996. *Tigers of the Snow and Other Virtual Sherpas: An Ethnography of Himalayan Encounters.* Princeton, NJ: Princeton University Press.

Allen, John. 2002. "On Georg Simmel: Proximity, Distance, and Movement." In Mike Crang and Nigel Thrift, eds., *Thinking Space,* 54–70. London: Routledge.

Alves, Francisco. 1925. *Os judeus no distrito de Bragança.* Braganza: n.p.

Anderson, Benedict. 1991. *Imagined Communities: Reflections on the Origin and Spread of Nationalism.* London: Verso.

Appadurai, Arjun. 1996. *Modernity at Large: Cultural Dimensions of Globalization.* Minneapolis: University of Minnesota Press.

Askew, Marc. 1999. "Strangers and Lovers: Thai Women Sex Workers and Western Men in the 'Pleasure Space' of Bangkok." In Jill Forshee et al., eds., *Converging Interests: Traders, Travelers, and Tourists in Southeast Asia,* 109–48. Berkeley: International and Area Studies.

Austin-Broos, Diane. 1994. "Race/Class: Jamaica's Discourse of Heritable Identity." *New West Indian Guide* 68: 213–33.

Aviv, Caryn, and David Shneer. 2005. *New Jews: The End of the Jewish Diaspora.* New York: New York University Press.

Azoulay, Katya. 2003. "Not an Innocent Pursuit: The Politics of a 'Jewish' Genetic Signature." *Developing World Bioethics* 3(2): 119–26.

Barbosa, Lívia. 1995. "The Brazilian Jeitinho." In David Hess and Roberto DaMatta, eds., *The Brazilian Puzzle,* 35–48. New York: Columbia University Press.

Barker, Kristin. 2002. "Self-Help Literature and the Making of an Illness Identity." *Social Problems* 49(3): 279–300.

Barth, Frederik, ed. 1969. *Ethnic Groups and Boundaries.* London: George Allen & Unwin.

Bastos, José. 2000. *Portugal Europeu.* Oeiras: Celta Editora.

Bastos, José, and Susana Bastos. 1999. *Portugal Multicultural.* Lisbon: Fim do Século Edições.

Basu, Paul. 2007. *Highland Homecomings: Genealogy and Heritage Tourism in the Scottish Diaspora*. New York: Routledge.

Battaglia, Debbora, ed. 1995. *Rhetorics of Self-Making*. Berkeley: University of California Press.

Bauman, Zygmunt. 2001. "Identity in the Globalising World." *Social Anthropology* 9(2): 121–29.

Behar, Ruth. 1996. "The Story of Ruth, the Anthropologist." In Jeffrey Rubin-Dorsky and Shelley Fishkin, eds., *People of the Book*, 261–79. Madison: University of Wisconsin Press.

Bellah, Robert, Richard Madsen, William Sullivan, Ann Swidler, and Steven Tipton. 1985. *Habits of the Heart*. Berkeley: University of California Press.

Ben-Dor Benite, Zvi. 2009. *The Ten Lost Tribes*. Oxford: Oxford University Press.

Benbassa, Esther, and Aron Rodrigue. 2000. *Sephardi Jewry*. Berkeley: University of California Press.

Benor, Sarah Bunin. 2012. *Becoming Frum: How Newcomers Learn the Language and Culture of Orthodox Judaism*. New Brunswick, NJ: Rutgers University Press.

Bethencourt, Cardozo. 1903. "The Jews in Portugal from 1773 to 1902." *Jewish Quarterly Review* 15(2): 251–74.

Birmingham, David. 1993. *A Concise History of Portugal*. Cambridge: Cambridge University Press.

Bloch, Maurice. 1996. "Internal and External Memory: Different Ways of Being in History." In Paul Antze and Michael Lambek, eds., *Tense Past: Cultural Essays in Trauma and Memory*, 215–33. New York: Routledge.

Bodenhorn, Barbara, and Gabriele vom Bruck, eds. 2006. *The Anthropology of Names and Naming*. Cambridge: Cambridge University Press.

Borges, Dulce, ed. 1999. *Guarda: História e cultura judaica*. Guarda: Museu da Guarda.

Borneman, John. 2001. "Caring and Being Cared For: Displacing Marriage, Kinship, Gender and Sexuality." In James Faubion, ed., *The Ethics of Kinship*, 29–46. Lanham, MD: Rowman & Littlefield.

Bouquet, Mary. 1993. *Reclaiming English Kinship: Portuguese Refractions of British Kinship Theory*. Manchester: Manchester University Press.

Bourdieu, Pierre. 1993. *The Field of Cultural Production*. New York: Columbia University Press.

Boyarin, Jonathan. 2013. *Jewish Families*. New Brunswick, NJ: Rutgers University Press.

Boyarin, Jonathan, and Daniel Boyarin. 1995. "Self-Exposure as Theory: The Double Mark of the Male Jew." In Debbora Battaglia, ed., *Rhetorics of Self-Making*, 16–42. Berkeley: University of California Press.

Brandes, Stanley. 2002. *Staying Sober in Mexico City*. Austin: University of Texas Press.

———. 2003. "Kol Nidre in Spain." *Kroeber Anthropological Society Papers* 89–90: 168–75.

Brennan, Denise. 2004. *What's Love Got to Do with It? Transnational Desires and Sex Tourism in the Dominican Republic*. Durham, NC: Duke University Press.

Brettell, Caroline. 1986. *Men Who Migrate, Women Who Wait: Population and History in a Portuguese Parish*. Princeton, NJ: Princeton University Press.

Brink-Danan, Marcy. 2008. "Anthropological Perspectives on Judaism: A Comparative Review." *Religion Compass* 2(4): 674–88.

Bruner, Edward. 1996. "Tourism in Ghana: The Representation of Slavery and the Return of the Black Diaspora." *American Anthropologist* 98: 290–304.

———. 2005. *Culture on Tour*. Chicago: University of Chicago Press.

Bunten, Alexis. 2008. "Sharing Culture or Selling Out? Developing the Commodified Persona in the Heritage Industry." *American Ethnologist* 35(3): 380–95.

Cabral, Maria Luísa, ed. 1999. *Testemunhos do judaísmo em Portugal*. Lisbon: Ministério da Cultura.

Cain, Carol. 1991. "Personal Stories: Identity Acquisition and Self-Understanding in Alcoholics Anonymous." *Ethos* 19(2): 210–53.

Callier-Boisvert, Collette. 1968. "Remarques sur le système de parenté et sur la famille au Portugal." *Homme* 8: 87–103.

Campbell, John, and Alan Rew, eds. 1999. *Identity and Affect: Experiences of Identity in a Globalising World*. London: Pluto Press.

Candea, Matei. 2010. "Anonymous Introductions: Identity and Belonging in Corsica." *Journal of the Royal Anthropological Institute* 16(1): 119–37.

Canelo, David Augusto. 1990. *The Last Crypto-Jews of Portugal*. Portland, OR: IJS.

———. 2004. *O resgate dos marranos portugueses*. 2nd ed. Belmonte: Câmara Municipal.

Cannell, Fenella. 2011. "English Ancestors: The Moral Possibilities of Popular Genealogy." *Journal of the Royal Anthropological Institute* 17(3): 462–80.

———. 2013. "The Re-Enchantment of Kinship." In Susan McKinnon and Fenella Cannell, eds., *Vital Relations,* 217–40. Santa Fe, NM: SAR Press.

Carlisle, Steven, and Gregory Simon. 2012. "Believing Selves: Negotiating Social and Pyschological Experiences of Belief." *Ethos* 40(3): 221–36.

Caro Baroja, Julio. 1961. *Los judíos en la España moderna y contemporanea*. Madrid: Ediciones Arion.

Carroll, Michael. 2002. "The Debate over a Crypto-Jewish Presence in New Mexico: The Role of Ethnographic Allegory and Orientalism." *Sociology of Religion* 63: 1–19.

Carsten, Janet. 2004. *After Kinship*. Cambridge: Cambridge University Press.

———, ed. 2000. *Cultures of Relatedness*. Cambridge: Cambridge University Press.

Carvalho, António. 1999. *Os judeus do desterro de Portugal*. Lisbon: Quetzal Editores.

Causey, Andrew. 2003. *Hard Bargaining in Sumatra: Western Travelers and Toba Bataks in the Marketplace of Souvenirs*. Honolulu: University of Hawai'i Press.

Charmé, Stuart. 2012. " Newly Found Jews and the Politics of Recognition." *Journal of the American Academy of Religion* 80(2): 387–410.

Clifford, James. 1988. *The Predicament of Culture*. Cambridge, MA: Harvard University Press.

Cohen, Anthony. 1994. *Self-Consciousness: An Alternative Anthropology of Identity*. London: Routledge.

Cohen, Erik. 1971. "Arab Boys and Tourist Girls in a Mixed Jewish-Arab Community." *International Journal of Comparative Sociology* 12: 217–33.

Cohen, Shaye. 1999. *The Beginnings of Jewishness: Boundaries, Varieties, Uncertainties.* Berkeley: University of California Press.

Cole, Jennifer. 2014. "Working Mis/understandings: The Tangled Relationship between Kinship, Franco-Malagasy Binational Marriages, and the French State." *Cultural Anthropology* 29(3): 527–51.

Comaroff, Jean, and John Comaroff. 2003. "Ethnography on an Awkward Scale." *Ethnography* 4(2): 147–79.

Conran, Mary. 2006. "Beyond Authenticity: Exploring Intimacy in the Touristic Encounter in Thailand." *Tourism Geographies* 8(3): 274–85.

Cooper, Alanna. 2006. "Conceptualizing Diaspora: Tales of Jewish Travelers in Search of the Lost Tribes." *AJS Review* 30(1): 95–117.

Corinaldi, Michael. 1998. *Jewish Identity.* Jerusalem: Hebrew University/Magnes Press.

Costa, Carlos. 2004. Preface to *A herança judaica em Portugal,* by Maria José Ferro Tavares. Lisbon: CTT Correios.

Costa, Pedro. 2002. "The Cultural Activities Cluster in Portugal." *Sociologia, Problemas e Práticas* 38: 99–114.

Costa Pinto, António, ed. 2003. *Contemporary Portugal: Politics, Society, and Culture.* Boulder, CO: Social Science Monographs.

Cutileiro, José. 1971. *A Portuguese Rural Society.* London: Oxford University Press.

Davidman, Lynn. 1991. *Tradition in a Rootless World: Women Turn to Orthodox Judaism.* Berkeley: University of California Press.

Diamant, Anita. 1997. *Choosing a Jewish Life.* New York: Schocken.

Dias, Jorge. 1990 [1950]. *Estudos de antropologia.* Lisbon: Imprensa Nacional.

Dix, Steffen. 2009. "Religious Plurality within a Catholic Tradition: A Study of the Portuguese Capital, Lisbon, and a Brief Comparison with Mainland Portugal." *Religion* 39: 182–93.

———. 2010. "As esferas seculares e religiosas na sociedade portuguesa." *Análise Social* 45: 5–27.

Dominguez, Virginia. 1989. *People as Subject, People as Object: Selfhood and Peoplehood in Contemporary Israel.* Madison: University of Wisconsin Press.

dos Santos, Maria Helena, ed. 1994. *Os judeus portugueses entre os descobrimentos e a diáspora.* Lisbon: Fundação Calouste Gulbenkian.

Egorova, Yulia, and Shahid Perwez. 2013. *The Jews of Andhra Pradesh: Contesting Caste and Religion in South India.* Oxford: Oxford University Press.

Elazar, Daniel. n.d. "Statement on Jewish Continuity." Daniel Elazar Papers Index, Jerusalem Center for Public Affairs. www.jcpa.org/. Retrieved March 18, 2011.

Errante, Antoinette. 2003. "White Skin, Many Masks: Colonial Schooling, Race, and National Consciousness among White Settler Children in Mozambique." *International Journal of African Historical Studies* 36(1): 7–33.

Espírito Santo, Moisés. 1993. "O que é um judeu." Introduction to facsimile edition, *Os Cristãos-Novos em Portugal no século XX*, by Samuel Schwarz. Lisbon: Universidade Nova de Lisboa.

Evans-Pritchard, Deirdre. 1989. "How 'They' See 'Us': Native American Images of Tourists." *Annals of Tourism Research* 16: 89–105.

Ewing, Katherine. 1990. "The Illusion of Wholeness: Culture, Self, and the Experience of Inconsistency." *Ethos* 18(3): 251–78.

Fernheimer, Janice. 2014. *Stepping into Zion: Hatzaad Harishon, Black Jews, and the Remaking of Jewish Identity*. Tuscaloosa: University of Alabama Press.

Ferro Tavares, Maria José. 1982. *Os judeus em Portugal no século XV*. Lisbon: Universidade Nova de Lisboa.

———. 1995. *Os judeus na época dos descobrimentos*. Lisbon: Edição ELO.

Foucault, Michel. 1973. *The Birth of the Clinic*. New York: Pantheon Books.

Frank, Gelya. 1995. "Anthropology and Individual Lives: The Story of the Life History and the History of the Life Story." *American Anthropologist* 97(1): 145–48.

Franklin, Sarah, and Susan McKinnon, eds. 2001. *Relative Values: Reconfiguring Kinship Studies*. Durham, NC: Duke University Press.

Garcia, Maria Antonieta. 1993. *Os judeus de Belmonte*. Lisbon: Universidade Nova de Lisboa.

———. 1999. *Judaísmo no feminino: Tradição popular e ortodoxia em Belmonte*. Lisbon: Universidade Nova de Lisboa.

———. 2001. *Fios para um roteiro judaico da Covilhã*. Covilhã: Universidade da Beira Interior.

Gay, Ruth. 1971. "Counting Jews." *Commentary* 52(5): 71–80.

Gerry, Chris, and Patrícia António. 2002. "Social Networks and Employment Opportunities among Rural Youth in the Douro Valley, Portugal." In *Desenvolvimento e ruralidades no espaço europeu*, 125–42. Coimbra: APDR.

Gerry, Chris, José Portela, Patrícia António, Carlos Marques, and Vasco Rebelo. 2004. "Social Networks, Labour Market, and Policy Impact in Santa Marta de Penaguião." In Birgit Jentsch and Mark Shucksmith, eds., *Young People in Rural Areas of Europe*, 186–235. Aldershot: Ashgate.

Gitlitz, David. 1996. *Secrecy and Deceit: The Religion of the Crypto-Jews*. Philadelphia: Jewish Publication Society.

Glenn, Susan. 2002. "In the Blood? Consent, Descent, and the Ironies of Jewish Identity." *Jewish Social Studies* 8(2–3): 139–52.

Goldschmidt, Henry. 2009. "Religion, Reductionism, and the Godly Soul: Lubavitch Jewishness and the Limits of Classificatory Thought." *Journal of the American Academy of Religion* 77(3): 547–72.

Gonçalves, Albertino. 1996. *Imagens e clivagens: Os emigrantes face aos residentes*. Porto: Edições Afrontamento.

Graburn, Nelson. 1982. "Tourism, Leisure, and Museums." Paper presented at the annual meeting of the Canadian Museums Association, Halifax, Nova Scotia.

———. 1989. "Tourism: The Sacred Journey." In Valene Smith, ed., *Hosts and Guests*, 2nd ed., 21–36. Philadelphia: University of Pennsylvania Press.

———. 2001. "Secular Ritual: A General Theory of Tourism." In Valene Smith and Maryann Brent, eds., *Hosts and Guests Revisited: Tourism Issues of the 21st Century,* 42–52. Elmsford, NY: Cognizant Communications.

———. 2002. "The Ethnographic Tourist." In G. M. S. Dann, ed., *The Tourist as a Metaphor of the Social World,* 19–39. New York: CABI.

Gray, Lila. 2007. "Memories of Empire, Mythologies of the Soul: Fado Performance and the Shaping of Saudade." *Ethnomusicology* 51(1): 106–30.

Grünewald, Rodrigo. 2001. *Os índios do Descobrimento.* Rio de Janeiro: Contra Capa.

Hage, Ghassan. 2005. "A Not-So-Multi-Sited Ethnography of a Not-So-Imagined Community." *Anthropological Theory* 5(4): 463–75.

Halstead, Narmala. 2001. "Ethnographic Encounters: Positionings Within and Outside the Insider Frame." *Social Anthropology* 9(3): 307–321.

Hannerz, Ulf. 2003. "Being there ... and there ... and there! Reflections on Multi-Site Ethnography." *Ethnography* 4(2): 201–16.

Harrison, Julia. 2003. *Being a Tourist: Finding Meaning in Pleasure Travel.* Vancouver: University of British Columbia Press.

Heilman, Samuel. 1988. "Jews and Judaica: Who Owns and Buys What?" In Walter Zenner, ed., *Persistence and Flexibility: Anthropological Perspectives on the American Jewish Experience,* 260–79. Albany: SUNY Press.

Herskovits, Melville. 1927. "When Is a Jew a Jew?" *Modern Quarterly* 4(2): 109–17.

Herzfeld, Michael. 2005. *Cultural Intimacy: Social Poetics in the Nation State.* 2nd ed. New York: Routledge.

———. 2007. "Global Kinship." *Anthropological Quarterly* 80(2): 313–23.

Hespanha, António Manuel, ed. 1997. *Diáspora e expansão: Os judeus e os descobrimentos portugueses.* Special issue. *Oceanos* 29.

Hoffman, Betty. 2001. *Jewish Hearts: A Study of Dynamic Ethnicity in the United States and the Soviet Union.* Albany: SUNY Press.

Hoffman, Matthew. 2005. "From *Pintele Yid* to *Racenjude:* Chaim Zhitlovsky and Racial Conceptions of Jewishness." *Jewish History* 19: 65–78.

Holland, Dorothy, and Naomi Quinn, eds. 1987. *Cultural Models in Language and Thought.* Cambridge: Cambridge University Press.

Holland, Dorothy, William Lachicotte Jr., Debra Skinner, and Carole Cain. 1998. *Identity and Agency in Cultural Worlds.* Cambridge, MA: Harvard University Press.

Holy, Ladislav. 1996. *Anthropological Perspectives on Kinship.* London: Pluto Press.

Hom Cary, Stephanie. 2004. "The Tourist Moment." *Annals of Tourism Research* 31(1): 61–77.

Hordes, Stanley. 2005. *To the End of the Earth: A History of the Crypto-Jews of New Mexico.* New York: Columbia University Press.

Howell, Signe. 2001. "Self-Conscious Kinship: Some Contested Values in Norwegian Transnational Adoption." In Sarah Franklin and Susan McKinnon, eds., *Relative Values,* 203–23. Durham, NC: Duke University Press.

———. 2006. *The Kinning of Foreigners: Transnational Adoption in a Global Perspective.* Oxford: Berghahn.

———. 2007. "Imagined Kin, Place, and Community: Some Paradoxes in the Transnational Movement of Children in Adoption." In Marianne Lien and Marit Melhuus, eds., *Holding Worlds Together,* 17–36. Oxford: Berghahn.

Howell, Signe, and Diana Marre. 2006. "To Kin a Transnationally Adopted Child in Norway and Spain." *Ethnos* 71: 293–316.

Jacobs, Janet. 2002. *Hidden Heritage: The Legacy of the Crypto-Jews.* Berkeley: University of California Press.

Kaplan, Danny. 2014. "The Architecture of Collective Intimacy: Masonic Friendships as a Model for Collective Attachments." *American Anthropologist* 116(1): 81–93.

Kessel, Barbara. 2000. *Suddenly Jewish.* Hanover, NH: Brandeis University Press.

Kim, Eleana. 2010. *Adopted Territory: Transnational Korean Adoptees and the Politics of Belonging.* Durham, NC: Duke University Press.

Klein, Emma. 1996. *Lost Jews.* New York: St. Martin's Press.

Klein, Misha. 2012. *Kosher Feijoada and Other Paradoxes of Jewish Life in São Paulo.* Gainesville: University Press of Florida.

———. 2014. "Anthropology." In Nadia Valman and Laurence Roth, eds., *Routledge Handbook to Contemporary Jewish Cultures,* 17–34. London: Routledge.

Kondo, Dorinne. 1986. "Dissolution and Reconstitution of Self: Implications for Anthropological Epistemology." *Cultural Anthropology* 1(1): 74–88.

———. 1990. *Crafting Selves: Power, Gender, and Discourses of Identity in a Japanese Workplace.* Chicago: University of Chicago Press.

Kovecses, Zoltan. 2006. *Mind, Language, and Culture.* Oxford: Oxford University Press.

Koven, Michèle. 2007. *Selves in Two Languages: Bilingual Verbal Enactments of Identity in French and Portuguese.* Amsterdam: John Benjamins.

Kugelmass, Jack. 1994. "Why We Go to Poland: Holocaust Tourism as Secular Ritual." In James Young, ed., *The Art of Memory,* 175–83. Munich: Prestel.

Kunin, Seth. 2009. *Juggling Identities: Identity and Authenticity among the Crypto-Jews.* New York: Columbia University Press.

Lakoff, George, and Mark Johnson. 1980. *Metaphors We Live By.* Chicago: University of Chicago Press.

Lambek, Michael. 2013. "Kinship, Modernity, and the Immodern." In Susan McKinnon and Fenella Cannell, eds., *Vital Relations,* 241–60. Santa Fe, NM: SAR Press.

Lave, Jean. 1991. "Situating Learning in Communities of Practice." In Lauren Resnick, John Levine, and Stephanie Teasley, eds., *Perspectives on Socially Shared Cognition,* 63–82. Washington, DC: American Psychological Association.

Lave, Jean, and Etienne Wenger. 1991. *Situated Learning: Legitimate Peripheral Participation.* Cambridge: Cambridge University Press.

Leal, Joao. 2000a. *Etnografias portuguesas (1870–1970): Cultura popular e identidade nacional.* Lisbon: Dom Quixote.

———. 2000b. "The Making of *Saudade:* National Identity and Ethnic Psychology in Portugal." In Ton Dekker et al., eds., *Roots and Rituals,* 267–87. Amsterdam: Het Spinhuis.

Lehrer, Erica. 2013. *Jewish Poland Revisited: Heritage Tourism in Unquiet Places.* Bloomington: Indiana University Press.

Leite, Naomi. 2005. "Travels to an Ancestral Past: On Diasporic Tourism, Embodied Memory, and Identity." *Antropológicas* 9: 273–302.

———. 2007. "Materializing Absence: Tourists, Surrogates, and the Making of Jewish Portugal." In Mike Robinson, ed., *Things That Move: Material Worlds of Tourism and Travel,* 1–21. Leeds: Centre for Tourism and Cultural Change.

———. 2014. "Locating Imaginaries in the Anthropology of Tourism." In Noel Salazar and Nelson Graburn, eds., *Tourism Imaginaries,* 365–91. Oxford: Berghahn.

Leite, Naomi, and Nelson Graburn. 2009. "Anthropological Interventions in Tourism Studies." In Mike Robinson and Tazim Jamal, eds., *Sage Handbook of Tourism Studies,* 35–64. London: Sage.

Linde, Charlotte. 1993. *Life Stories: The Creation of Coherence.* New York: Oxford University Press.

Lindquist, Galina, and Simon Coleman, eds. 2008. *Against Belief?* Special issue. *Social Analysis* 52(1): 1–18.

Lipiner, Elias. 1985. "O cristão-novo: Mito ou realidade?" In Yosef Kaplan, ed., *Jews and Conversos,* 124–38. Jerusalem: Magnes Press.

———. 1999. *Terror e linguagem: Um dicionário da Santa Inquisição.* Lisbon: Contexto.

Little, Walter. 2004. *Mayas in the Marketplace: Tourism, Globalization, and Cultural Identity.* Austin: University of Texas Press.

Livingston, Julie. 2007. "Productive Misunderstandings and the Dynamism of Plural Medicine in Mid-Century Bechuanaland." *Journal of Southern African Studies* 33(4): 801–10.

Loeb, Laurence. 1989. "Creating Antiques for Fun and Profit: Encounters between Iranian Jewish Merchants and Touring Coreligionists." In Valene Smith, ed., *Hosts and Guests,* 2nd ed., 237–45. Philadelphia: University of Pennsylvania Press.

Loewe, Ronald, and Helene Hoffman. 2002. "Building the New Zion: Unfinished Conversations between the Jews of Venta Prieta, Mexico, and Their Neighbors to the North." *American Anthropologist* 104(4): 1135–47.

Lomnitz, Larissa. 1971. "Reciprocity of Favors in the Urban Middle Class in Chile." In George Dalton, ed., *Studies in Economic Anthropology,* 93–106. Washington, DC: American Anthropological Association.

Louie, Andrea. 2004. *Chineseness across Borders: Renegotiating Chinese Identities in China and the United States.* Durham, NC: Duke University Press.

Lowenthal, David. 1998. *The Heritage Crusade and the Spoils of History.* Cambridge: Cambridge University Press.

Lubkemann, Stephen. 2003. "Race, Class, and Kin in the Negotiation of 'Internal Strangerhood' among Portuguese Retornados, 1975–2000." In Andrea Smith, ed., *Europe's Invisible Migrants,* 75–93. Amsterdam: Amsterdam University Press.

Machado, Diamantino. 1991. *The Structure of Portuguese Society.* New York: Praeger.

Mair, Jonathan. 2013. "Cultures of Belief." *Anthropological Theory* 12(4): 448–66.

Maoz, Darya. 2006. "The Mutual Gaze." *Annals of Tourism Research* 33(1): 221–39.

Marcus, George. 1998. *Ethnography through Thick and Thin*. Princeton, NJ: Princeton University Press.

Markowitz, Fran. 2006. "Blood, Soul, Race, and Suffering: Full-Bodied Ethnography and Expressions of Jewish Belonging." *Anthropology and Humanism* 31: 41–56.

Martin, Denis-Constant. 1995. "The Choices of Identity." *Social Identities* 1(1): 5–20.

Martins, Jorge. 2006. *Portugal e os judeus*. 3 vols. Lisbon: Nova Vega.

Mathews, Gordon. 2000. *Global Culture / Individual Identity: Searching for Home in the Cultural Supermarket*. London: Routledge.

Mauss, Marcel. 1967 [1925]. *The Gift*. New York: Norton.

May, Vanessa. 2011. "Self, Belonging and Social Change." *Sociology* 45(3): 363–78.

———. 2013. *Connecting Self to Society: Belonging in a Changing World*. New York: Palgrave Macmillan.

McCabe, Scott. 2009. "Who Is a Tourist? Conceptual and Theoretical Developments." In John Tribe, ed., *Philosophical Issues in Tourism,* 25–42. Bristol: Channel View.

McIntosh, Janet. 2015. "Autochthony and 'Family': The Politics of Kinship in White Kenyan Bids to Belong." *Anthropological Quarterly* 88(2): 251–80.

McKinnon, Susan, and Fenella Cannell, eds. 2013. *Vital Relations: Modernity and the Persistent Life of Kinship*. Santa Fe, NM: SAR Press.

Mea, Elvira. 1998. "Ha-Lapíd: Orgão da Comunidade Israelita do Porto, espelho da obra do resgate." In Maria Helena dos Santos and Maria Graça Bachmann, eds., *O património judaico português,* 239–49. Lisbon: APEJ.

———. 2005. "O renascimento do judaísmo em Portugal: O movimento marrano no século XX." In Armando Silva and Rui Centeno, eds., *Museu Judaico de Belmonte,* 79–117. Belmonte: Câmara Municipal.

Mea, Elvira, and Inácio Steinhardt. 1997. *Ben Rosh: Biografia do Capitão Barros Basto, o apóstolo dos marranos*. Porto: Edições Afrontamento.

Mead, George Herbert. 1934. *Mind, Self, and Society*. Chicago: University of Chicago Press.

Mead, Margaret. 1928. *Coming of Age in Samoa*. New York: William Morrow.

Melammed, Renee. 2004. *A Question of Identity: Iberian Conversos in Historical Perspective*. Oxford: Oxford University Press.

Milgram, Avraham. 2011. *Portugal, Salazar, and the Jews*. Jerusalem: Yad Vashem.

Miller, Daniel. 2008. *The Comfort of Things*. London: Polity Press.

Modell, Judith. 1994. *Kinship with Strangers: Adoption and Interpretations of Kinship in American Culture*. Berkeley: University of California Press.

Monteiro, Isabel. 1997. *Os judeus na região de Viseu*. Viseu: Região de Turismo Dão-Lafões.

Moore, Kenneth. 1976. *Those of the Street: The Catholic-Jews of Mallorca*. Notre Dame, IN: University of Notre Dame Press.

Mucznik, Esther. 1999. "Presença e memória: Comunidade israelita em Portugal." *História* 15:32–41.

Myrowitz, Catherine. 1995. *Finding a Home for the Soul*. Northvale, NJ: Jason Aronson.

Nash, Catherine. 2005. "Geographies of Relatedness." *Transactions of the Institute of British Geographers*, n.s., 30: 449–62.

Neulander, Judith. 1996. "The New Mexican Crypto-Jewish Canon: Choosing to be 'Chosen' in Millennial Tradition." *Jewish Folklore and Ethnology Review* 18(1–2): 19–58.

Novinsky, Anita, and Amílcar Paulo. 1967. "The Last Marranos." *Commentary* 43(5): 76–81.

Nuñez, Theron. 1977. "Touristic Studies in Anthropological Perspective." In Valene Smith, ed., *Hosts and Guests*, 207–16. Philadelphia: University of Pennsylvania Press.

Orlove, Benjamin. 1997. "Surfacings: Thoughts on Memory and the Ethnographer's Self." In Jonathan Boyarin and Daniel Boyarin, eds., *Jews and Other Differences*, 1–29. Minneapolis: University of Minnesota Press.

Palmié, Stephan. 2007. "Genomics, Divination, 'Racecraft'" and "Rejoinder: Genomic Moonlighting, Jewish Cyborgs, and Peircian Abduction." *American Ethnologist* 34(2): 205–22; 245–51.

Parfitt, Tudor, and Emanuela Semi. 2002. *Judaising Movements*. New York: Routledge.

Peacock, James, and Dorothy Holland. 1993. "The Narrated Self: Life Stories in Process." *Ethos* 21(4): 367–83.

Picard, David. 2012. "Tourism, Awe and Inner Journeys." In David Picard and Mike Robinson, eds., *Emotion in Motion: Tourism, Affect and Transformation*, 1–19. Farnham: Ashgate.

Picard, David, and Michael Di Giovine, eds. 2013. *Tourism and the Power of Otherness: Seductions of Difference*. Bristol: Channel View.

Pieterse, Jan Nederveen. 2007. *Ethnicities and Global Multiculture*. Lanham, MD: Rowman & Littlefield.

Pimentel, Irene, and Sandra Monteiro. 1999. "Estudos judáicos: Memórias e fontes (Entrevista: Maria Ferro Tavares)." *História* 21: 10–16.

Pina-Cabral, João de. 1986. *Sons of Adam, Daughters of Eve: The Peasant Worldview of the Alto Minho*. London: Oxford University Press.

———. 1991. *Os contextos de antropologia*. Lisboa: Difel.

———. 1997. "Houses and Legends: Family as Community of Practice in Urban Portugal." In Marianne Gullestad and Martine Segalen, eds., *Family and Kinship in Europe*, 77–102. London: Pinter.

———. 2002. *Between China and Europe: Person, Culture, and Emotion in Macao*. London: Continuum.

———. 2010. "The Dynamism of Plurals: An Essay on Equivocal Compatibility." *Social Anthropology* 18(2): 176–90.

Pina-Cabral, João de, and Susana Veigas, eds. 2007. *Nomes: Género, etnicidade e família*. Coimbra: Edições Almedina.

Pinho, Patricia. 2008. "African-American Roots Tourism in Brazil." *Latin American Perspectives* 10(3): 70–86.

Pinto, Ralf. n.d. "Jewish Events in Portugal in the 1990s." Typescript. Portimão, Portugal.

Portuguese Marranos Committee. 1938. *Marranos in Portugal: Survey by the Portuguese Marranos Committee, London, 1926–1938.* London: Bevis Marks.

Ramagem, Sonia. 1994. *A fênix de Abraão: Um estudo sobre cristãos-novos retornados ao judaísmo de seus ancestrais.* Brasília: Cultura Gráfica e Editora.

Reed-Danahay, Deborah. 2015. "Social Space: Distance, Proximity and Thresholds of Affinity." In Vered Amit, ed., *Thinking through Sociality,* 69–96. Oxford: Berghahn.

Reis, António, ed. 2007. *Retrato de Portugal.* Lisbon: Instituto Camões.

Richard, Analiese, and Daromir Rudnyckyj. 2009. "Economies of Affect." *Journal of the Royal Anthropological Institute* 15(1): 57–77.

Riegelhaupt, Joyce. 1967. "Saloio Women: An Analysis of Informal and Formal Political and Economic Roles of Portuguese Peasant Women." *Anthropological Quarterly* 40(3): 109–26.

———. 1979. "Peasants and Politics in Salazar's Portugal." In Lawrence Graham and Harry Makler, eds., *Contemporary Portugal,* 167–90. Austin: University of Texas Press.

Rocha-Trindade, Maria Beatriz. 1987. "As micropátrias do interior português." *Análise Social* 23(98): 721–32.

Roof, Wade. 1999. *Spiritual Marketplace: Baby Boomers and the Remaking of American Religion.* Princeton, NJ: Princeton University Press.

Rosaldo, Renato. 1989. "Imperialist Nostalgia." *Representations* 26: 107–22.

Roth, Cecil. 1941. *A History of the Marranos.* Rev. ed. Philadelphia: Jewish Publication Society.

———. 1964. *The Spanish Inquisition.* New York: Norton.

Roth, Sol. 2007. *The Jewish Idea of Ethics and Morality.* New York: Yeshiva University Press.

Rouse, Richard. 1991. "Mexican Migration and the Social Space of Postmodernism." *Diaspora* 1(1): 8–23.

Rowland, Robert. 2001. "New Christian, Marrano, Jew." In Paolo Bernardini and Norman Fiering, eds., *The Jews and the Expansion of Europe to the West, 1450–1800,* 125–48. London: Berghahn.

Saa, Mario. 1925. *A invasão dos judeus.* Lisbon: Imprensa da Silva.

Sachar, Howard. 1994. *Farewell España: The World of the Sephardim Remembered.* New York: Knopf.

Sahlins, Marshall. 2013. *What Kinship Is—and Is Not.* Chicago: University of Chicago Press.

Salazar, Noel, and Nelson Graburn, eds. 2014. *Tourism Imaginaries: Anthropological Approaches.* Oxford: Berghahn.

Salomon, Herman. 1998. "Crypto-Judaism or Inquisitorial Deception?" *Jewish Quarterly Review* 89(1–2): 131–54.

Saraiva, António José. 2001. *The Marrano Factory: The Portuguese Inquisition and Its New Christians, 1536–1765.* Boston: Brill.

Sardinha, João. 2014. *Immigrant Associations, Integration, and Identity: Angolan, Brazilian, and East European Communities in Portugal.* Amsterdam: Amsterdam University Press.

Schein, Louisa. 1998. "Forged Transnationality and Oppositional Cosmopolitanism." In Michael Smith and Luis Guarnizo, eds., *Transnationalism from Below,* 291–313. New Brunswick, NJ: Transaction Publishers.

Schneider, David. 1977. "Kinship, Nationality, and Religion in American Culture." In Janet Dolgin et al., eds., *Symbolic Anthropology,* 63–71. New York: Columbia University Press.

———. 1980. *American Kinship.* 2nd ed. Chicago: University of Chicago Press.

———. 1984. *A Critique of the Study of Kinship.* Ann Arbor: University of Michigan Press.

Schramm, Katharina, David Skinner, and Richard Rottenburg, eds. 2012. *Identity Politics and the New Genetics.* Oxford: Berghahn.

Schwarz, Samuel. 1925. *Os cristãos-novos em Portugal no século XX.* Lisbon: Empresa Portuguesa de Livros.

———. 1926. "The Crypto-Jews of Portugal." *Menorah Journal* 12: 138–49, 283–97.

Seeman, Don. 2003. "Agency, Bureaucracy, and Religious Conversion: Ethiopian 'Felashmura' Immigrants to Israel." In Andrew Buckser and Stephen Glazier, eds., *The Anthropology of Religious Conversion,* 29–42. Lanham, MD: Rowman & Littlefield.

———. 2009. *One People, One Blood: Ethiopian-Israelis and the Return to Judaism.* New Brunswick, NJ: Rutgers University Press.

Segal, Daniel. 1999. "Can You Tell a Jew When You See One?" *Judaism* 48(2): 234–41.

Selwyn, Tom, ed. 1996. *The Tourist Image.* Chichester: John Wiley & Sons.

———. 2007. "The Political Economy of Enchantment." *Suomen Antropologi* 2: 48–70.

Sharlin, Shlomo. 1999. "The Family in Jewish Tradition." In Barbara Settles et al., eds., *Concepts and Definitions of the Family for the Twenty-First Century,* 43–54. New York: Haworth Press.

Silva, Manuel Carlos. 1993. "Camponeses, mediadores, e estado." *Análise Social* 28(122): 489–521.

———. 1998. *Resistir e adaptar-se: Constrangimentos e estratégias camponesas no noroeste de Portugal.* Porto: Afrontamento.

Simmel, Georg. 1950. "The Stranger." In Kurt Wolff, trans., *The Sociology of Georg Simmel,* 402–8. New York: Free Press.

Simoni, Valerio. 2014. "From Tourist to Person: The Value of Intimacy in Touristic Cuba." *Journal of Tourism and Cultural Change* 12(3): 1–13.

———. 2016. *Tourism and Informal Encounters in Cuba.* Oxford: Berghahn.

Siporin, Steve. 1993. "The Sephardim: Field Report from Portugal." *Jewish Folklore and Ethnology Review* 15(2): 142–44.

Smith, Estellie. 1976. "Networks and Migration Resettlement: Cherchez la Femme." *Anthropological Quarterly* 49(1): 20–27.

———. 1980. "The Portuguese Female Immigrant: The 'Marginal Man.'" *International Migration Review* 14(1): 77–92.

Smith, Valene, ed. 1989. *Hosts and Guests: The Anthropology of Tourism.* 2nd ed. Philadelphia: University of Pennsylvania Press.

Sobral, José Manuel. 2004. "O norte, o sul, a raça, a nação: Representações da identidade nacional portuguesa (séculos XIX–XX)." *Análise Social* 39: 255–84.

Sola Pool, David. 1934. "The Marranos." *Jewish Quarterly Review* 24(3): 247–50.

Soyer, François. 2007a. *The Persecution of the Jews and Muslims of Portugal.* Leiden: Brill.

———. 2007b. "The Massacre of the New Christians of Lisbon in 1506." *Cadernos de Estudos Sefarditas* 7: 221–44.

Stasch, Rupert. 2009. *Society of Others: Kinship and Mourning in a West Papuan Place.* Berkeley: University of California Press.

———. 2011. "Textual Iconicity and the Primitivist Cosmos." *Journal of Linguistic Anthropology* 21(1): 1–21.

———. 2014. "Powers of Incomprehension: Linguistic Otherness, Translators, and Political Structure in New Guinea Tourism Encounters." *Hau* 4(2): 73–94.

———. 2015. "Double Signs and Intrasocietal Heterogeneity in Primitivist Tourism Encounters." In Rupert Stasch, ed., *Primitivist Tourism.* Special issue. *Ethnos* 80(4).

Steinhardt, Inácio. 2003. "Contando a nossa história." *Tikvá* 39(4): 6–8.

Strathern, Marilyn. 2005. *Kinship, Law and the Unexpected.* Cambridge: Cambridge University Press.

Stromberg, Peter. 1993. *Language and Self-Transformation: A Study of the Christian Conversion Narrative.* Cambridge: Cambridge University Press.

Sturm, Circe. 2010. *Becoming Indian: The Struggle over Cherokee Identity in the Twenty-First Century.* Santa Fe, NM: SAR Press.

Tamarkin, Noah. 2014. "Genetic Diaspora: Producing Knowledge of Genes and Jews in Rural South Africa." *Cultural Anthropology* 29(3): 552–74.

Teixeira, Alfredo. 2012. "Identidades religiosas em Portugal." Paper presented at the Portuguese Episcopal Conference, Fátima, Portugal.

Thomas, Todne, Asiya Malik, and Rose Wellman, eds. 2017. *New Directions in Spiritual Kinship.* London: Palgrave.

Tomlinson, John. 1999. *Globalization and Culture.* Chicago: University of Chicago Press.

Tsing, Anna. 2000. "The Global Situation." *Cultural Anthropology* 15(3): 327–60.

———. 2005. *Friction: An Ethnography of Global Connection.* Princeton, NJ: Princeton University Press.

Tsuda, Takeyuki. 2003. *Strangers in the Ethnic Homeland.* New York: Columbia University Press.

Turner, Victor. 1974. *Dramas, Fields, Metaphors.* Chicago: University of Chicago Press.

Urry, John. 2002. *The Tourist Gaze.* 2nd ed. London: Sage.

Vakil, Abdoolkarim. 2003. "From the Reconquista to Portugal Islâmico: Islamic Heritage in the Shifting Discourses of Portuguese Historiography and National Identity." *Arqueologia Medieval* 8: 5–15.

Vilaça, Helena. 2006. *Da Torre de Babel às terras prometidas: Pluralismo religioso em Portugal.* Porto: Edições Afrontamento.

Visweswaran, Kamala. 1994. *Fictions of Feminist Ethnography.* Minneapolis: University of Minnesota Press.

vom Bruck, Gabriele. 2005. *Islam, Memory and Morality in Yemen: Ruling Families in Transition.* New York: Palgrave.

Wang, Ning. 1999. "Rethinking Authenticity in Tourism Experience." *Annals of Tourism Research* 20(2): 349–70.

Washofsky, Mark. 2000. *Jewish Living.* New York: UAHC Press.

Waters, Mary. 1990. *Ethnic Options: Choosing Identities in America.* Berkeley: University of California Press.

Weiner, Annette. 1994. "Cultural Difference and the Density of Objects." *American Ethnologist* 21(1): 391–403.

Weismantel, Mary. 1995. "Making Kin: Kinship Theory and Zambagua Adoptions." *American Ethnologist* 22(4): 685–709.

Weston, Kath. 1991. *Families We Choose: Lesbians, Gays, Kinship.* New York: Columbia University Press.

Whittaker, Elvi. 2012. "Seeking the Existential Moment." In David Picard and Mike Robinson, eds., *Emotion in Motion,* 73–84. Farnham: Ashgate.

Willems, Emilio. 1962. "On Portuguese Family Structure." *International Journal of Comparative Sociology* 3: 65–79.

Williams, Brackette. 1993. "The Impact of the Precepts of Nationalism on the Concept of Culture." *Cultural Critique* 24: 143–92.

Wolf, Lucien. 1926. *Report on the "Marranos" or Crypto-Jews of Portugal.* London: Anglo-Jewish Association.

Yerushalmi, Yosef. 1982. *Assimilation and Racial Anti-Semitism: The Iberian and the German Models.* New York: Leo Baeck Institute.

———. 1992. "Les derniers marranes." In Frederic Brenner, ed., *Marranes,* 17–44. Paris: Éditions de la Différence.

Yngvesson, Barbara. 2010. *Belonging in an Adopted World.* Chicago: University of Chicago Press.

Zerubavel, Eviatar. 1996. "Social Memories." *Qualitative Sociology* 19: 283–99.

———. 2012. *Ancestors and Relatives: Genealogy, Identity, and Community.* Oxford: Oxford University Press.

Zimman, Lal. 2009. "The Other Kind of Coming Out: Transgender People and the Coming Out Narrative Genre." *Gender and Language* 3(1): 53–80.

Zoloth, Laurie. 2003. "Yearning for the Long Lost Home: The Lemba and the Jewish Narrative of Genetic Return." *Developing World Bioethics* 3(2): 127–32.

INDEX

HaShalom, Kehilá, Menorá, Anshei Emet, and Nostálgia are pseudonyms for organizations. Individuals whose stories appear in this book are indexed by first name or title and have also been given pseudonyms.

183, 196, 233–234, 284n7; urban Marranos and, 42, 93, 124, 181. *See also* Beira provinces; crypto-Jews, Portuguese; Trás-os-Montes province

belonging: affect and, 8, 27–28, 36–38, 256–257, 276–277; and Ashkenazi Jews, urban Marrano affinity for, 257–260; connectivity and lack of sense of, 26–28; empathy/shared emotion and, 256–257, 271–273; and exclusion, 3, 5–6, 13–14, 36–38; experiential vs. rhetorical, 27–28, 38, 273, 277–278; face-to-face rejection, impact of, 27–28, 36–38, 132–133, 268, 270; face-to-face relations as essential to, 260, 267, 271; forged, 273–274; imagined communities and, 17–20, 38, 273–274; intersubjective belonging/ mutuality of being, 251, 271, 272–273, 277; and self-consciousness, lack of, 277–278; tourist encounters and experience of, 5, 200, 211, 215, 217–219, 270–271. *See also* identity; interpersonal connection; kinning/making kin; nurturance and care between foreign supporters and urban Marranos; relatedness; urban Marranos, associations of

Bevis Marks synagogue (London), 50, 61

biogenetic substance: in reckoning kinship/ relatedness and personhood, 14–16, 25, 103–104, 109, 114, 257–258, 259–260, 276; in urban Marrano self-narratives, 86, 87, 91, 93, 95, 102–105, 115–116. *See also* blood; cross-generational transmission; Jewishness; relatedness

biological determinism, 103–104, 109, 112

biology. *See* biogenetic substance; biological determinism; blood; Jewishness; kinship; relatedness

blood: hypodescent ("blood logic"), 51, 103; Jewish, 16, 103–104, 116–117; Jewish, among Portuguese people at large, 13, 39–40, 51–53, 71–72; Portuguese, 9, 15–16, 109; purity of (*limpeza de sangue*), 46, 51; as symbol of relatedness, 15–16, 109. *See also* biogenetic substance; kinship

B'nai Anusim: definition of, xv, 171, 279n2; foreign visitors and use of term, 30, 76,

168, 180–183, 222; Porto Jewish community's official statement on, 264; as social category, 168; urban Marranos and use of term, 3, 138–139, 141, 143, 168–169, 171–172, 181–182, 227, 237

B'nai Brith, 62

books: and becoming/being a Marrano, 142, 145–146; as source of Jewish knowledge, 88, 89, 135, 142, 143, 145–146, 169, 188

borderzone, touristic, 212, 215–216, 269

Brazil, historical Marranos and, 47, 50

Bruner, Edward, 32, 179, 182, 212, 217, 286n2

Buddhism, 85, 86, 100, 101

Cannell, Fenella, 15, 248, 251, 275

care. *See* kinning/making kin; kinship; nurturance and care between foreign supporters and urban Marranos

Catarina (HaShalom member): and foreign visitors, 164, 185, 189–192, 216, 270, 277; on identity, 107, 109, 111, 112; life story, 77–78, 92–95, 145–146; on Marranos and Jewishness, 92, 102–103, 104, 113, 115–116, 142, 145, 153, 170; relations with Kehilá's supporters, 235, 239, 260

Catholicism: anticlericalism and, 54–55, 84; cultural, 101, 154, 201; during First Republic, 54–55; during Salazar dictatorship, 63, 92; forced conversion to, 2–3, 8–9, 42–47, 71–72, 128, 159; godparenthood (*compadrio*) roles of, 201, 204, 207, 208; Inquisition and, 47–49, 50; syncretic, 48, 51, 63, 72, 281n5; in twentieth- and twenty-first c. Portugal, 53, 72, 101; urban Marranos and, 80, 84, 88, 89, 92, 93, 95, 165, 166, 169, 172, 201. *See also* Catholic-Jewish identity; religion

Catholic-Jewish identity, 60–61, 71–75, 84, 146–147, 162–163, 282n11

Cécile (HaShalom member), 169–171, 250

Chabad, 192–193, 285n3

Chaya (Jewish educator). *See* Kaplan, Chaya and Rabbi Ezra

Cherokees, "white," 103, 114, 173

choice: vs. essence, 79, 98–99, 104, 106; rhetoric of, 98, 101, 102. *See also* conversion vs. "return," urban Marranos and; Jewishness; Jewishness of urban Marranos

chuetas (Majorca), 83–84, 146–147

CIL. *See* Comunidade Israelita de Lisboa

circumcision: Inquisition-era abandonment of, 47; in Judaism, 90, 144, 287n9; twentieth c. resumption of, 61, 63; urban Marranos and, 144, 162, 237, 245

citizenship, Portuguese: granted freedom of religion, 53; Sephardic Right of Return law, 261–264, 288n4; social difference and, 10, 13, 53, 68–69

class. *See* social class

colonial settlers, 16, 50; *retornados* and descendants, 10, 12–13, 89–91

commensality: and kinning/making kin, 243–244; and nurturance and care, 234, 241–244, 255–256

communication. *See* misunderstanding; translation

Comunidade Israelita de Lisboa (CIL), 68, 127, 129, 130, 131, 261. *See also* Lisbon Jewish community (normative)

Comunidade Israelita do Porto, 10, 261. *See also* Porto Jewish community (normative)

connectivity: definition of, 27; vs. proximity, 26–28, 265–266; technological, 32–34. *See also* globalization

Conservative Judaism. *See* Masorti/Conservative Judaism

continued identities, 110–111, 268, 276, 283–284n10

conversion: to Catholicism, forced, 2–3, 8–9, 42–47, 71–72, 128, 159; narratives of, 98, 102, 160–161. *See also* conversion to Judaism

conversion to Judaism: as adoption, 38, 197–198, 246–249, 255–256, 287n8; barriers to, 19, 61; branches of Judaism and differing approaches to, 19; circumcision, requirement of, 61, 237; community participation as necessary for, 19, 226, 236; as incorporation into Jewish people, 226; and Jewish relatedness, 197–198, 199, 247–248; and Jewish ritual name,

197–198, 247; Jewish soul and, 97, 166, 283n5; Jewish study as prerequisite for, 132; to Orthodoxy, in Belmonte, 65–67, 135, 284n3; to Orthodoxy, of "born" Jews (*ba'alei teshuva*), 98, 102, 173; process of, 132, 145–146, 226, 247, 256, 286n3, 287n8, 287n13; rabbinic court (*beit din*) necessary for, 132, 221, 226, 256, 286n3; as recognition of "lost" Jewish ancestry, 170, 228, 250, 285n14; and Sephardic "Right of Return" law of Portugal, 261–264, 288n4; and subsequent generations, Jewishness of, 247–249; vow of, as irreversible, 248. *See also* conversion to Judaism, urban Marranos and; Jewish law

conversion to Judaism, urban Marranos and: access to Jewish community as problem in, 131–134, 174–175, 210–211, 226, 229, 236–238; adoption as framework for, 246, 248–249, 255–256; choice and, 98, 101–103, 169, 214, 260; circumcision and, 237, 245; converts as social category, 127, 133, 137–139, 287n5; higher standard of observance required of converts, 153–154, 156; lack of *beit din* in Portugal, 132; as (re)incorporation into Jewish people, 188, 197–198, 226–227, 229, 236, 247–248, 276. *See also* conversion to Judaism, urban Marranos and— approaches to; conversion vs. "return," urban Marranos and

conversion to Judaism, urban Marranos and—approaches to: correspondence courses, 229; marriage into Jewish families, migration abroad and, 273, 288n7; multiyear study/strict adherence, under Shavei Israel, Orthodox, 221, 232; one-day rite of return, Reform (New York), 232; proposed ceremony of Marrano return, 226–227; "Return to Judaism" program, Orthodox (Israel), 228, 287n4; visiting teachers, under Masorti (London), 237–238. *See also* Masorti/Conservative Judaism, and urban Marranos; Shavei Israel

conversion vs. "return," urban Marranos and: and ancestral loss of Jewish identity, 85, 94–95, 97, 112–113, 221; and

cunha, logic of: definition and entailments of, 210; as explanation for inaccessibility of normative Jewish community, 209–211; as underpinning hope for help from foreign visitors, 200, 210–211. *See also* social class

Cutileiro, José, 205–206, 285–286nn4–5

Davidman, Lynn, 98, 101–102

demographics: of Portuguese Jews, 73–74; of Portuguese Marranos, 56–57, 60–61, 63–64; of religious affiliation in Portugal, 100–101, 283n6

descent group(s), 14–16, 17–18, 113. *See also* descent group, Jews as

descent group, Jews as: biblical lineage of, 17–18, 197–198, 247, 279–280n9; conversion and, 197–198, 247–248; and global Jewish relatedness, 16, 22, 183, 197–198; and ritual names, 197–198, 247–248. *See also* ancestral Jews, urban Marranos as; Jewish family, global; Jewishness; kinship; "lost" or "marginal" Jews; peoplehood, Jewish

Dias, Jorge, 72

diaspora: forged transnationality and, 273; and Israel as homeland, 280n16; Jewish people as, by definition, 21, 38; Sephardic, 9, 47, 50, 279n3, 281n4. *See also* crypto-Jewish descendants; peoplehood, Jewish

dietary laws, Jewish (*kashrut*), 285n8; and becoming/being Marranos, 152–156; Inquisition-era abandonment of, 47; traces of, in the "Marrano story," 162, 165; variation/nonobservance across branches of Judaism, 153–154

divinatory logic (abduction), 159, 285n9

donations: anonymous, differentiated from gifts, 187, 254; for *obra do resgate,* 3, 60–63; on tours, 177–178, 190, 198; for urban Marrano movement, 235, 238–239, 251, 254–255. *See also* gifts from foreign supporters

Dulce (HaShalom member): and foreign visitors, 161–163, 177, 185, 189–192, 211, 216, 225, 228; life story, 89–91, 113, 134–136, 151, 250, 258, 268; on Marranos,

124, 138, 148, 249; relations with Kehilá's supporters, 235, 238, 243, 256, 272

Edict of Expulsion: apologies for, 69–70; Portuguese, 44–45, 66, 69–70; Spanish, 43–44

educators. *See* outreach workers/volunteer educators, Jewish

Elsa (HaShalom member and tour guide), 180–181, 183–184

emotion: shared, 256–257, 272–273; tourist display of, 3–5, 8, 22, 184–188, 190–192, 213–214, 272. *See also* affect

empathy, 257, 272, 273

enchantment: of Jewish world, with Marranos, 57–58, 63–65, 68; kinship as domain of, 275–276; tourism as domain of, 269; of tourists, with Marranos, 4–5, 163–164, 186, 221, 223–224, 269, 270. *See also* mystical beliefs

England, historical Marranos and, 50, 61

Erasmus, 52

Espírito Santo, Moisés, 72

essence: vs. choice, 79, 98–99, 104, 106; Jewishness in, 82, 83, 85, 101–106, 112–114, 116–118, 227; rhetoric of, 102–103

Ethiopian Jews, 176, 228, 280n10, 287n5

evangelical Christianity, 95, 101, 161, 283n6

exoticism: "marginal" Jews and, 189, 228; "Marrano zoo" (feeling of), 218, 221–222, 225–226, 256; touristic desire for, 22, 179, 181, 186, 269, 280n11; traveler narratives of "first contact" and, 57–58

expatriate Jews in Portugal, 36, 132, 284n2; Porto synagogue and, 3, 63, 140–141, 262

family: vs. friends, 199; Jewish, nuclear, 236, 245–246, 247, 255–256, 260, 273, 287n8; metaphors of, 194, 197–198, 202–204, 239; natal, response to urban Marranos' pursuit of Judaism, 82, 84, 90–91, 94, 115; urban Marranos as sole member of, to pursue Judaism, 5, 78, 101–102, 104–105, 125, 236. *See also* Jewish family, global; kinship; peoplehood, Jewish

Faro (Portugal), 127, 284n2

Ferdinand (king of Spain), 44

fieldwork (ethnographic): locations, 6–7, 29–32; methods, 28–36, 81, 283n3; multisited ethnography, 29, 32–36; "native" and "halfie" anthropologists, 34–36; online, 30, 33; participant observation, 29; researcher's positionality, 29, 32–36, 140, 153, 170–171, 205, 207–208, 213–214, 234, 240–241, 280n17, 285n1, 285nn1,15, 287n13; and time, ix, 30. *See also* anthropological study

figured worlds, theory of, 125–126, 258–259, 267

folklore: Jewish, Marranos in, 23–25, 68; Portuguese, Jews in, 39, 52, 86, 158, 281n1; proverbs, Portuguese, 89, 131, 204, 213

food. *See* commensality; dietary laws

foreign supporters of urban Marranos: and Ashkenazi vs. Sephardic affinity of urban Marranos, 257–260; *cunha* unknowingly enacted by, 232, 235–236, 244–245; and mutual expression of kinship, 239, 245–246, 251, 260, 271, 272–274; and mutuality of being/ intersubjective belonging, 27, 251, 271, 272–273; and shift of urban Marrano Jewish identification from ancestry/past to affinity/present, 28, 246, 257, 260. *See also* Masorti/Conservative Judaism, and urban Marranos; nurturance and care between foreign supporters and urban Marranos

foreign visitors (*pessoas de fora*): blurring together over time of, for urban Marranos, 191, 215; definition of, 20; distinctions among, as (not) made by urban Marranos, 20, 188–189, 193, 203; imaginaries of Marranos brought by, 9, 23–26, 68, 223–224; and Inquisition, significance to urban Marranos vs., 49, 226–227, 249; Kehilá and, 241–242, 257, 277–278; misunderstanding of local situation, 214–215, 224–227, 257–258, 259, 270, 286n2; and self-image of urban Marranos, development of, 125; snacks offered to, 189, 238, 243, 277; as source of Jewish knowledge, 6, 26–28, 104, 177,

188–189; study in preparation for trip, 49, 182. *See also* foreign supporters of urban Marranos; foreign visitor–urban Marrano interactions; outreach workers/volunteer educators, Jewish; tourist(s)

foreign visitor–urban Marrano interactions: acceptance of urban Marranos as ("lost") Jews, 3, 5, 166, 177, 193, 211, 230, 260, 265, 266, 269–271; affective display in, 3–5, 8, 22, 184–188, 190–192, 213–214, 272; assistance from abroad as hope of urban Marranos, 188–189, 193–194, 200, 204, 210–211, 216–217, 218; and belonging, urban Marrano hope for, 5, 17, 193–194, 200, 211, 215, 217–219, 270–271; and the collective past, urban Marranos seen as embodiment of, 223–229, 259, 269, 286n2; donations given by tour participants, 177–178, 190, 198; kinship expressed by visitors, 4–5, 183, 187–188, 194–200, 201–202, 213–215, 270–271, 273, 285n2; and kinship, meaning of to urban Marranos, 200–204, 210–211, 213–214, 285–286n4; logic of *cunha* and, 200, 210–211; multiple exposures to foreign visitors, effect of, 179, 191, 215, 218, 225; and mutual intelligibility, presumption of, 177–178, 179, 212–215; ongoing contact, urban Marrano hope for, 193–194, 200, 211; promises by visitors of support vs. silence after returning home, 186–187, 192, 218, 225; rejection as non-Jews, as risk for urban Marranos, 189, 192–193; single exposure to urban Marranos, effect of, 179, 225; vignettes of visits, 1–5, 184–187, 189–193, 285n1. *See also* foreign supporters of urban Marranos; gaze; "Marrano story"; misunderstanding; tourist site, urban Marrano associations as

forged belonging, 273–274

framing. *See* cultural logics; cultural models

France, historical Marranos and, 50

Frank (donor): donations, 238–239, 251, 254–255; life story, 234; relations with urban Marranos, 234–235, 239, 257, 258 friends: family vs., 199; tourists vs., 193–194, 200, 211. *See also* foreign supporters of urban Marranos

gaze: coeval, of "looking at us like brothers," 229, 257; medical, 223; narrative, 224, 226–227, 286n2; questioning, 286n2; tourist, 223–226
genealogical causality, logic of, 106–114, 115, 250, 259, 268; definition of, 111–112. *See also* ancestral Jews, urban Marranos as; cross-generational transmission; cultural logics
genes. *See* biogenetic substance
gifts from foreign supporters: differentiated from anonymous donations, 187, 252, 254; of heirlooms, and family memories, 253–255; and kinning, role in, 239, 251–255; of mementos, 234, 238, 251; monetary, 238–239, 251. *See also* donations
Glenn, Susan, 16, 104, 116–117
global cultural supermarket, 274–275
globalization, 6–8, 26–28; and global cultural supermarket, 274–275; imaginaries and affinities and, 25–26; and scale of fieldwork, 32–36; self-making and, 99, 258–259; shift of urban Marrano frame of reference from national to global, 222, 246, 257. *See also* connectivity; Nostálgia forum; proximity; social media; social spaces
global Jewish family. *See* Jewish family, global
global vs. local, as matter of scale, 28, 32–33, 273–274
godparenthood (*compadrio*), 201, 204, 207, 208
Graciana (outreach activist): life story, 181; Nostálgia and, 31, 76–77, 181, 196; outreach activism of, 67–68, 181, 222; relations with urban Marranos, 203, 221–222; as tour leader, 182–183, 183, 184. *See also* Nostálgia Conference-Tours; Nostálgia forum

Harrison, Julia, 22, 187, 218, 230
HaShalom Jewish Association: founding of, 10–11, 136–137; as learning environment, 144–145, 156; in life stories of urban

Marranos, 86, 89, 96; and material culture, 148, 149; membership, 11–14, 133–134, 137–139, 167–171, 190; and Menorá, relationship with, 120, 232, 233; methodology of study and, 29, 30; mission statement of, 136–137; and Nostálgia network, 30, 31; as pseudonym, 279n4; relations with Lisbon Jewish community, 124, 153. *See also* Anshei Emet synagogue; foreign supporters of urban Marranos; foreign visitors; foreign visitor–urban Marrano interactions; Kehilá; tourist site, urban Marrano associations as; urban Marranos, associations of
Hasidic Judaism, 97, 98, 116, 283n5. *See also* Chabad
hazzan (cantor), 127–128
Hebrew: abbreviation used to identify, xv; attraction to/aptitude for, in urban Marrano life stories, 86, 89, 93, 95, 112; chosen name in, 90, 151–152; as identity marker, 90, 146, 150, 151–152, 168, 287n9; lost to Portuguese Jews, 44, 56; ritual name in, 203, 247, 250, 256, 271–272, 287n9
heritable identities, 106–111, 115. *See also* genealogical causality, logic of
heritage tourism, Jewish: Belmonte as fixture of, 64, 66–67, 177; development of, 70, 177, 180; differences between local populations elided by, 180–182; "Jewish Portugal" as destination, 2, 31–32, 33, 44, 64; meeting Marranos, anticipation of, 178–179; meetings with local Jewish communities, expectation in, 177–178; package tours, 2–5, 31–32, 163–164, 177–179, 180–181 (*see also* Nostálgia Conference-Tours); pretour narrative and, 218; toponyms as clues in finding sites, 44, 76. *See also* foreign visitor–urban Marrano interactions; Nostálgia Conference-Tours; tourism; tourist(s); tourist site, urban Marrano associations as
hidden Jews. *See* crypto-Jews; Marranos; secret practice of Judaism
historical Marranos, Portuguese. *See* crypto-Jews, Portuguese; New Christians

Holland (Netherlands), historical Marrano migration to, 50, 61, 279n3

Holland, Dorothy, 7, 79, 81, 107, 119, 125–126, 160

Holocaust: analogy with Inquisition, 24, 231, 249; foreign visitors' experience of, 230, 231, 233; refugees from, in Portugal, 54

Howell, Signe, 14, 217, 230, 246, 260, 273, 287n10

hypodescent, 51, 103

identification: definition of, 8, 79; hybrid, 258–260. *See also* belonging; identity; self-making; social categories

identity: adult acquisition of, 78–79, 144, 173; and affect, 8, 274; anthropological study of, 7, 18–19, 79; as choice vs. fixed essence, 79, 98–99, 104, 106; claims to, 16, 17–18, 104, 159; collective vs. individual, 141, 144; as constituted through interaction, 7, 8, 79; continued, 110–111, 268, 276, 283–284n10; figured worlds and, 125–126, 258–259, 267; globalization and, 99; heritable, 106–111, 115; individualization and, 99–100; intersubjectivity and, 251, 271; Jewish (*see* Jewishness); and kinship, knowledge of, 217, 248–250; and life stories, 81, 159, 160–161, 165; material culture and, 146–147, 151; as multiple, 79, 141, 173–174; names and naming and, 151–152, 158, 159, 249–250; national, as relatedness, 109; Portuguese (*see* Portuguese identities; Portugueseness); as process of becoming, 78–79, 99–100, 105–106, 144; as the self's core truth, perception of, 80; social categories and, 41, 141; typifications and, 18–19. *See also* ancestral Jews, urban Marranos as; Catholic-Jewish identity; cross-generational transmission; identification; life stories; narrative(s); self; self-making; urban Marranos, becoming a Marrano

imaginaries: definition of, 23; of historical Jewish presence, Portuguese, 52; of Jews, urban Marranos and, 23, 26; of Marranos, Jewish visitors and, 9, 23–26, 68; pretour narratives as intersecting with, 182–183, 217–219, 223–224, 269

imagined communities, belonging and, 17–20, 38, 273–274. *See also* Jewish family, global; peoplehood, Jewish

India, historical Marrano migration to, 47

Ingathering of the Exiles, 25, 68

Inquisition, Portuguese, 2–3, 47–52; asset seizure and, 48, 50; end of, 52, 53; forced conversion of Jews to Catholicism, 2–3, 8–9, 42–47, 71–72, 128, 159; Jewish identity perpetuated by, 51; Judaizers (secret practitioners of Jewish rituals) as target of, 48, 49–50, 51, 281n5; and "Marrano" as term, xv; prehistory of, 8–9, 42–47; process of, 47–49

Inquisition, Portuguese—as history: analogy of Holocaust and, 24, 249; ancestral surnames in records of, 48–49, 86, 158; apologies for, 69–70; and Belmonte synagogue, inauguration of, 66; commemoration of, 70–71, 72; foreign visitor knowledge of, 49, 182, 230–231, 233, 234, 240; as global Jewish heritage, 24, 49, 223–224; significance of, to foreign visitors vs. urban Marranos, 49, 226–227, 249; tourism and, 4, 5, 76, 181, 218, 223–224; urban Marrano knowledge of, 91, 124, 134, 157–158

Inquisition, Spanish, 42, 43, 44; analogy of Holocaust and, 24; and "Marrano" as term, xv

intermarriage: in contemporary Jewish community, 130; mandated for New Christians, 46, 51; Portuguese history of, 51, 128–129, 159

internet: fieldwork on, 30, 33; as social space, 26–28, 33–34; as source of Jewish knowledge, 6, 26, 86, 96, 143, 158, 169. *See also* connectivity; Nostálgia forum; social media

interpersonal connection: with Ashkenazi vs. Sephardic Jews, 257–260; forged belonging and, 273–274; tourism and desire for, 4–5, 21–23, 185–186, 193–194; tourism and sense of commonality in, 230, 231–232, 233–234, 235–236, 276. *See also* belonging; foreign supporters of urban Marranos

Isabella (queen of Spain), 44

Islam, 59, 100, 113–114. *See also* Moors (medieval Muslims)

Israel: chief Sephardic rabbi of, 89, 161, 193, 228, 257, 258, 262; government representatives, in Portugal, 66, 70; images of, in Marrano spaces, 119, 146; Jewish Agency, 65; and Jewish identity/homeland, 280n16; Law of Return, 288n4; living in, 93–95, 102; migration to, 102, 146, 228, 280n16, 287n5, 288n7; significance of, for urban Marranos, 280n16; travel to, for conversion, 132, 221; travel to, for vacation, 93. *See also* Israeli embassy

Israeli embassy (Lisbon): in author's fieldwork, 32; Belmonte crypto-Jews and, 65; Jewish community and, 128, 132, 153; Menorá and collaboration with, 120

Italy, historic Marrano migration to, 50

Jewish community, Portuguese (normative): CIL as public face of, 68; defined as primary "Portuguese Jews," 53, 54; establishment by immigrants, 3, 53–54, 63, 135–136, 140–141, 262; as figured world, 125–128; historical reluctance re: conversion, proselytism accusations and, 59, 60–61; historical role in Marrano outreach, 60, 62, 63, 65; institutions of, 68, 127, 129; Jews/non-Jews distinction, 127, 128–129; leaders and roles of, 127–128; low level of religious observance, perception of, 129–130, 153–154, 284n4; religiously observant/nonobservant distinction, 127, 129–130; and self-image of urban Marranos, development of, 125, 134; and social category "Marranos," 127, 183; and social category "outsiders," 133–134, 136; and social category "potential converts," 127, 131, 133; socioeconomic position of, 127, 130–131, 209–210, 284n5; and surnames, significance of, 128–129, 131, 133, 261; and tourists/visitors, interactions with, 4, 122–123, 128, 130, 132, 183. *See also* Jewish community, Portuguese (normative)—rejection of urban Marranos by

Jewish community, Portuguese (normative)—forms of inclusion/exclusion: allowing/denying access to services and events, 36–37, 84, 123, 129, 131–133; counting for *minyan*, or not, 122–123, 124, 128, 171, 284n1; forbidding urban Marrano use of prayer shawl, 128, 149, 171; invitation to read aloud from Torah, or not, 128; Sephardic "Right of Return" law, text of vs. implementation of, 261–264, 288n4; social and spatial isolation of urban Marranos, 36–38, 123–125, 132–133. *See also* Jewish community, Portuguese (normative)—rejection of urban Marranos by

Jewish community, Portuguese (normative)—rejection of urban Marranos by: and Ashkenazi vs. Sephardic affinity, 136, 257–258; and community acceptance as necessary for conversion, 131–134, 226–227, 229; *cunha* as explanation for, 209–211; face-to-face rejection, impact of, 27–28, 36–38, 132–133, 268, 270; and intervention from abroad as hope of urban Marranos, 188, 193–194; and lack of other resources for urban Marranos to live as Jews, 26, 144; and "Marrano" as self-designation, adoption of, 171, 172, 173–175, 277; norms and expectations as unfamiliar to urban Marranos, 36–38, 123; outsider status of urban Marranos, 133–134, 138, 139, 141, 169, 265–267; and physical proximity vs. social distance, 27–28, 265–267; sense of kinship not reciprocated, 13–14; social class/social networks and, 130–131, 209–210, 284n5; synagogue services and, 121–124, 132–133; vs. welcome given to tourists, 4, 122–123, 128, 130, 132; vs. welcome of other "returnees" with Jewish antecedents, 131, 133, 174–175, 209–210. *See also* foreign supporters of urban Marranos; Jewish community, Portuguese (normative)—forms of inclusion/exclusion

Jewish diversity, 17–20, 21, 230, 233

Jewish family, global: and biblical lineage, basis in, 17–18, 197–198, 247, 279–

Jewishness of urban Marranos *(continued)*
    106, 117; shift in articulation of, from
    ancestry/past to affinity/present, 28,
    246, 257, 260. *See also* ancestral Jews,
    urban Marranos as; conversion vs.
    "return," urban Marranos and; cross-
    generational transmission; descent
    group, Jews as; genealogical causality,
    logic of; heritable identities
Jewish soul *(neshamah)*: and ancestry,
    91–97, 105; inherited/divinely delivered,
    97, 283n5; recognition of prayers by, 166;
    as source of Jewishness, 18, 166, 233,
    275–276, 283n5. See also *pintele yid*
    (Jewish spark)
Jews. *See* Ashkenazi Jews; crypto-Jews;
    descent group, Jews as; foreign visitors;
    Jewish community, Portuguese (norma-
    tive); Jewishness; Jews, Portuguese;
    "lost" or "marginal" Jews; secular Jews;
    Sephardic Jews
Jews, Portuguese: definitions of, 53–54, 75,
    263, 270; 18th–20th c. history, 52–54;
    medieval and early modern history, 8–9,
    42–47; population estimates, 73; pre-
    Inquisition, in national memory, 9,
    69–72; and Sephardic "Right of Return"
    law of Portugal, 261–264; as social cat-
    egory, 40–41, 46, 47–48, 51, 51–52, 53–54,
    68–69, 73–75, 267; social distinctions
    between Christians and, 42–43, 46, 51,
    69. *See also* crypto-Jews, Portuguese;
    Inquisition; Jewish community, Portu-
    guese (normative); Marranos, Portu-
    guese; New Christians; Sephardic Jews
Jews, Spanish: medieval and early modern
    history, 42, 43–44, 47. *See also*
    Sephardic Jews
João II (king of Portugal), 44
João III (king of Portugal), 47
Joaquim (HaShalom member): and foreign
    visitors, 203–204, 271–272; life story,
    83–85, 146–147, 151; on Marranos and
    Jewishness, 112–113
José I (king of Portugal), 39, 281n1
Judaica. *See* books; gifts from foreign
    supporters; material culture
Judaism. *See* conversion; dietary laws;

Jewish law; Jewishness; Jews; Judaica;
    Judaism, types of; religious observance,
    Jewish; secret practice of Judaism
Judaism, types of. *See* Ashkenazi Jews;
    Chabad; Hasidic Judaism; Masorti/
    Conservative Judaism; Orthodox
    Judaism; Reform Judaism; secular Jews;
    Sephardic Jews
judiarias (medieval Jewish quarters), 42,
    44, 46; Marrano-led walking tours of, 1,
    2, 62, 180–181, 203; as setting, 62, 69; as
    tourist sites, 70, 76, 251. *See also* medi-
    eval Jewish sites

Kadoorie, Sir Ely, 62
Kadoorie synagogue. *See* Porto synagogue
Kaplan, Chaya, and Rabbi Ezra (educators),
    239–257, 275–276; and encouragement of
    bonds with Jewish families abroad,
    252–256; and food and food sharing,
    241–242, 242–244; and Nuno and
    Luisa's Jewish wedding, 255; parental role
    of, 244–246, 272; prior outreach activi-
    ties, 239–240; relations with urban
    Marranos, 154–155, 240–246, 258, 275–
    276, 287n7; and rituals of "return"/
    conversion, 249–250, 256; study in prepa-
    ration for role, 240; teaching in prepara-
    tion for "return"/conversion, 241–246
Kehilá: and community-building as neces-
    sary to live as Jews, 229, 236–237; dona-
    tions/underwriting for, 235; foreign
    supporters unknowingly enacting logic
    of *cunha* to help, 232, 235–236, 244–245;
    founding of, 232–237; Masorti/Con-
    servative tourists visiting, 251–252, 255,
    257, 277–278; membership, 233, 236; and
    move to global vs. national frame of
    reference, 222, 257; narrowing of criteria
    for membership, 170–171, 285n15; new
    building, 235. *See also* foreign supporters
    of urban Marranos; Masorti/Conserva-
    tive Judaism, and urban Marranos
kinning/making kin: adoption and, 14,
    230, 273, 287n10; as aspect of all kin
    relations, 14, 251, 273, 287n10; definition
    of, 246, 273, 287n10; nurturance and
    care in, 8, 14, 239, 246, 259–260, 271,

273; recognition/seeking resemblances as, 14, 230, 246, 268, 272, 275–276; (re-) naming in, 151, 203–204, 247–248; role of empathy and shared emotion in, 256–257, 271–273; role of food in, 243–244; role of gift-giving in, 239, 252–255, 273; social incorporation into kin networks as, 251–252, 254–255, 273; as temporal phenomenon, 8, 28, 251, 271, 272–273. *See also* kinship

kinship: across scales and domains of sociality, 8, 15–16, 38, 247–248, 256–257, 261–264; biogenetic substance as means of reckoning personhood and, 14–16, 25, 103–104, 109, 114, 257–258, 259–260, 276; as conscious choice, 14, 260; cultural logics of, 5, 7–8, 13, 14–16, 17, 79, 194, 259–260, 261–264, 274 (*see also* genealogical causality, logic of); descent group(s), 14–16, 17–18, 113 (*see also* descent group, Jews as); as determinant of personhood (*see* cultural models); genealogical distance, 103; Jewish, collective (*see* Jewish family, global); knowledge of, and identity, 217, 248–250; limits to, as culturally determined, 15, 17–18, 261–264; making (*see* kinning/making kin); metaphors of (*see* kin terms); mutual expression of, between foreign supporters and urban Marranos, 239, 245–246, 251, 260, 271, 272–274; mystical beliefs regarding, 16, 80, 115–116, 117, 274–276; narratives of lineage, 16, 17–18; obligations and roles of, 14, 194, 196–202, 207–208, 217, 219, 273, 285–286n4; as performative, 273; and personhood, 13; Portuguese, 13, 200–204, 207–208, 285–286n4; predestined, 275; rhetorical vs. experiential, 38, 200, 239, 270–271, 273; self-conscious, 260; tourist/outreach-worker expressions of, 4–5, 183, 187–188, 194–200, 201–202, 213–215, 270–271, 273, 285n2; tourist/outreach-worker expressions of, and meaning to urban Marranos, 200–204, 210–211, 213–214, 285–286n4; and transpersonal experience (the "kinship I"), 112–116, 272–273.

See also adoption; belonging; cross-generational transmission; *cunha* (social leverage); *cunha*, logic of; family; Jewish family, global; kin terms; relatedness; self

kinship, anthropological study of: across cultural domains and scales, 15–16; as enchanted domain, 275; kinship narratives, in claims to collective belonging, 16; mutuality of being, 113–114, 251, 272–273; relatedness as alternative term, 14–15. *See also* cross-generational transmission

kinship "I," 113

kin terms: as (more than) metaphor, 194, 195, 197–198, 202, 239, 245–246; categorical vs. personal use of, 202, 204, 211, 239, 273, 274; in Portugal, 200–204, 285–286n4; used by foreign visitors, 194–200, 201–202, 203–204, 212, 285n2; used by foreign visitors, and meaning to urban Marranos, 200–204, 210–211, 213–214, 285–286n4; used on Nostálgia forum, 195–196; used reciprocally between the Kaplans and members of Kehilá, 245–246

kipá (yarmulke), 149, 237

klal yisrael (the whole of the Jewish people). *See* Jewish family, global; peoplehood, Jewish

Kondo, Dorinne, 173–174

kosher food. *See* dietary laws

Kulanu, 21, 30, 34, 67

language: abbreviations used in text, xv. *See also* Hebrew; misunderstanding; translation; Yiddish

Last Kabbalist of Lisbon, The (novel, Zimler), 46, 281n3

Last Marranos, The (film, Brenner), ix–x, 65–68, 77

Lave, Jean, 126, 143–145

learning: anthropological study of, 143–144; as component of becoming/being a Marrano, 142–143, 144–145, 154, 156, 157–159

leisure travel. *See* tourism; tourist(s)

Lévy, Rabbi Bernard. *See* Rabbi Lévy

life histories: distinguished from life stories, 81; sources for compiling, 81; of urban Marranos' paths to Jewish identity, 81–97, 283n3

life stories (life history narratives): convergence in, 161, 165; as culturally patterned, 160; discursive structure of, 80, 102–104; distinguished from life histories, 81; as evolving over time, 81, 165, 166; implicit causal connections in, 80–81, 97, 102, 160; and self-making, 159–161; shared on Nostálgia forum, 157. *See also* "Marrano story"; narrative(s)

Lisbon (Portugal): Massacre of 1506, 46–48, 281n3; mass baptism of Jews (1497), 45. *See also* Anshei Emet synagogue (Lisbon); HaShalom; Kehilá; Lisbon Jewish community (normative); Shaaré Tikvá synagogue (Lisbon)

Lisbon Jewish community (normative): Comunidade Israelita de Lisboa (CIL), 68, 127, 129, 130, 131, 261; exclusive grounds and events, 129–130; immigrant and expatriate Jews and, 53–54, 135–136; prospective converts with social ties to, welcomed in, 131, 209; religious observance of members, 130, 153–154; and Sephardic "Right of Return" law, 263. *See also* Shaaré Tikvá synagogue (Lisbon)

local vs. global, as matter of scale, 28, 32–33, 273–274

logics, cultural. *See* cultural logics

"lost" or "marginal" Jews: exoticism of, 176, 228, 233, 280n10; Jewishness of, 17–18, 19–20, 285n13; Jewish outreach workers as focused on finding, 20–21, 25, 62, 67–68, 198, 199, 230, 233; Marranos as, 2, 25, 178, 213, 231, 260, 265; offspring of Holocaust-era converts to Catholicism as, 116–117, 169–170, 285n14; in Portuguese history, 2, 8–9, 40–41, 51–52, 63–64, 70, 72, 279n3; Portuguese identity and, 9, 40–41, 70–72, 75; rabbinic rulings on, xv, 228, 249–250, 257, 285n3; tourism among, and presumption of Jewish peoplehood, 17, 21–22, 176, 178, 198–199, 260, 265, 269. *See also* crypto-

Jews; descent group, Jews as; Ingathering of the Exiles; Jewish family, global; outreach organizations, Jewish

love. *See* kinning/making kin; nurturance and care between foreign supporters and urban Marranos

Luisa (HaShalom member): and foreign visitors, 189–192; life story, 168–169, 242, 250; relations with Kehilá's supporters, 235, 240–241, 255–256, 258, 277

Malinowski, Bronislaw, 35

Manuel (HaShalom member), 190–192, 201, 216, 254

Manuel (king of Portugal), 44–45, 46–47, 69

Marrano(s), as term: as controversial/pejorative, xv; etymology of, xv–xvi; HaShalom definition of, 137–139; interchangeably used with "crypto-Jews" and "Anusim," 29–30, 76, 180–182, 227; as Jewish-world referent, 172; New Christians and, 57, 281–282n10; as self-designation by urban Marranos, xv–xvi, 138–142, 168–172, 268, 277; as social category, 41–42, 57, 125, 141, 170–172, 268; as symbol, 24–26, 141. *See also* B'nai Anusim; crypto-Jews; Marranos, Portuguese

Marranos, Portuguese: historical (*see* crypto-Jews, Portuguese; Inquisition; New Christians); population estimates, 56–57, 60–61, 63–4; representations of, 23–26; rural (*see* Beira provinces; Belmonte; Trás-os-Montes province); urban (*see* urban Marranos)

"Marrano story": components of, 165–166; contexts of narration, 161–162, 163–164, 179, 185, 186, 191, 192, 211, 228; declining importance of, 221–222, 241, 255; definition of, 160; divinatory logic and, 159, 285n9; elicitation of, 161–163; forming narrative, process of, 157–163; as generalized by foreign visitors to entire group, 186, 212, 214–215; as outreach tool, 166–167; role in identity, 125, 160–161, 163–165; self-discovery and, 157–159; as shaped by interaction with visitors,

161–164, 166–167, 269; shared narrative pattern of, 160–161, 164–166; as "staking a claim," 164, 174–175, 228; and surnames, 158, 159, 160. *See also* life stories

Masorti/Conservative Judaism: conversion and, 19; dietary laws and, 154; history of movement, 19, 236, 287n6; system for creating new congregations, 236. *See also* Kaplan, Chaya, and Rabbi Ezra (educators); Masorti/Conservative Judaism, and urban Marranos

Masorti/Conservative Judaism, and urban Marranos: and Ashkenazi vs. Sephardic affinity of Kehilá, 257–260; community building as priority of, 236–237; conversion vs. "return" as issue, 237–238, 248–251; and development of bonds with Jewish families abroad, 251–257; Jewish education provided, 239–246; and Kehilá, role in founding of, 236–238, 257; "return"/conversion process, 237–238, 256, 287–288n13; tourists affiliated with, visiting Kehilá, 251–252, 255, 277–278. *See also* Kaplan, Chaya and Rabbi Ezra (educators); Kehilá

Massacre of 1506, Lisbon, 46–48, 281n3

material culture: becoming/being a Marrano and, 142, 145–151, 284n7; commemorating crypto-Jewish experience, 24–25; home display of Judaica, 146–147, 150; identity and, 146–147, 151; and kinning, role in, 251–255; as life story element, 165; ritual objects, learning to use, 156, 244; secular American Jews and, 150. *See also* gifts from foreign supporters

Mathews, Gordon, 274–275

Mayer, Graciana. *See* Graciana (outreach activist)

Mead, Margaret, 33

medieval and early modern history of Portuguese Jews, 8–9, 24, 42–47. *See also* Inquisition

medieval Jewish sites: absence of, 44, 76; as setting, 69, 226–227, 271–272; as tourist sites, 39–40, 44, 180–181, 251. See also *judiarias*

memory, sociobiographical, 17

Menorá Jewish Cultural Association: dissolution of, 232–233; founding of, 10–11, 83, 119–120; and HaShalom, relationship with, 120, 232, 233; Israeli embassy and, 120; as learning environment, 120, 144–145, 156; in life stories of urban Marranos, 83, 88; membership, 11–14, 120–121, 133–134, 167–168; methodology of study and, 29; mission of, 119; and Nostálgia network, 31; as pseudonym, 279n4; relations with Porto Jewish community, 36–38, 83, 121–125. *See also* foreign supporters of urban Marranos; foreign visitors; foreign visitor–urban Marrano interactions; HaShalom; Kehilá; tourist site, urban Marrano associations as; urban Marranos, associations of

mezuzah, 76, 146, 150, 252, 283n1

migration: to Israel, 102, 146, 228, 280n16, 287n5, 288n7; Jews, to Portugal, 18th–20th c., 3, 53–54, 73, 75, 141, 262; in Marrano life histories, 13, 82, 89–91, 95–96, 288n7; Portuguese Jews and New Christians, from Portugal, 15th–18th c., 47, 50; Portuguese laborers, returning to Portugal, 20th c., 13; postcolonial *retornados*, to Portugal, 20th c., 10, 12–13, 89–91; Spanish Jews, to Portugal, 15th c., 43–44; urban Marranos, abroad, 273, 288n7

Miguel (Menorá member), 3–4, 5, 151, 193

Miller, Daniel, 147

minyan, 122–123, 124, 128, 171, 284n1

misunderstanding: communicative slippage and, 179–180, 196–197, 212–215, 224–225, 269–270; of foreign visitors' nationality and intentions, by urban Marranos, 215, 216–217; of local situation, by foreign visitors, 214–215, 224–227, 257–258, 259, 270, 286n2; as productive miscommunication, 215–219, 224–225, 269, 270, 286n8; radical simplification and, 269–270. *See also* translation

Moors (medieval Muslims), 9, 72, 109, 111, 282n18, 282n21, 283n8 multiculturalism, 69–72

multisited ethnography, 29, 32–33; local (mis)readings of researcher's positionality in, 33–36

mutuality of being, 113–114, 251, 272–273. *See also* cross-generational transmission; kinship; relatedness

mystical beliefs: ancestry and the self, 16, 80, 112–116, 166, 275; kinship, 16, 80, 115–116, 117, 274–276; predestination, 98, 106. *See also* cross-generational transmission; essence; Jewish soul; *pintele yid* (Jewish spark)

names and naming: becoming/being a Marrano and, 151–152; conversion and, 197–198, 247–250, 256; forced baptism and, 45–46; Hebrew/ritual, 90, 151–152, 197–198, 203, 247–250, 256, 271–272, 287n9; identity and, 151–152, 158, 159, 249–250; Marrano choice of, 152, 249–250; Portuguese conventions of, 111; pseudonyms, 279n4, 287n11; of tourists, forgetting, 4, 191. *See also* surnames, ancestral

narrative(s): and affinity, role in generating, 220, 276; of conversion, 98, 102, 160–161; of "first contact," by tourists and travel writers, 57–58; of Jewish destruction and survival, 24, 49, 186, 222, 224, 226, 269; kinship, 16, 17–18; in tourism, role of, 182–183, 186–188, 214–215, 217–219, 222–224, 269

narrative gaze, 224, 226–227, 286n2

Nederlandsch Marranen Comité, 61

netsach yisrael (eternal spirit of the Jewish people), 227, 231, 275–276

New Age spirituality, 100–101

New Christians (*cristãos-novos*): abolition of distinctions between Old Christians and, 52; as ancestry, and claim of Jewishness, 59; considered Jews by contemporaries, 46–48, 49, 51; cultural assimilation and, 45–46, 47, 51–52; definition of, 45, 57, 61–62; emigration of, and return to Judaism, 47, 50; forced conversion and, 2–3, 8–9, 42–47, 71–72, 128, 159; Lisbon Massacre (1506) of, 46–48,

281n3; secret Jewish practices maintained by, 46, 47, 48, 49–50, 51, 231, 281n5; surnames of, 39–40, 56, 158, 166. *See also* crypto-Jews; Inquisition; Portuguese

normative Jewish community. *See* Jewish community, Portuguese (normative)

Nostálgia Conference-Tours, 180–182, 233–234; impromptu Hebrew naming ceremony during, 203–204, 271–272; and kinship, expressions of, 187–188, 196–197, 200, 203–204; normative Jewish Community in Portugal and, 183; pretour narratives and, 182–183; researcher's positionality and, 31–32, 35, 76–78

Nostálgia forum: American conversions by members of, 229; and Ashkenazi affiliation of urban Marranos, as controversial, 259; and assistance from abroad as hope of urban Marranos, 211; and becoming a Marrano, 143; founding of, 181; as international nexus, 30–31, 50; kinship terms used on, 195–196; life stories shared via, 157; researcher and, 30–31, 76–77; significance of, for individuals, 75, 78, 271; as social space, 265–266

nostalgia, imperialist, 71

Nuno (HaShalom member): and foreign visitors, 189–192, 217; on Jewishness, 130–131, 155, 156; life story, 168–169, 242, 250; relations with Kehilá's supporters, 235, 238, 240–241, 243, 245, 253, 255–256, 258, 277

nurturance and care between foreign supporters and urban Marranos: Anshel and Frank and, 203–204, 233–236, 238–239, 271–272; commensality and, 234, 241–244, 255–256; empathy/shared emotion and, 256–257, 271–273; face-to-face relations as essential to, 260, 267, 271; gifts from Jewish families abroad and, 252, 254–255; hybrid identification and, 257–260; mutual expressions of kinship and, 239, 245–246, 251, 260, 271, 272–274; Rabbi Ezra and Chaya Kaplan and, 242–246, 255, 272; Rabbi

Lévy and, 231–232. *See also* kinning/
making kin

obra do resgate. See Barros Basto, Artur
"one-drop" racial classification (hypodescent), 51, 103
Orthodox Judaism: anthropological study
of, 280n17; and Belmonte crypto-Jews,
65–67, 133, 135, 183, 284n3, 284n7;
conversion requirements of, 19, 221, 228;
conversion to, of "born" Jews, 98, 102,
173; conversion to, "Return to Judaism"
program, 228, 285n3; Jewishness criteria
of, 19, 285n3, 285n14. *See also* Jewish
law; Judaism, types of; Porto synagogue;
Shaaré Tikvá synagogue (Lisbon);
Shavei Israel
outreach organizations, Jewish, 21, 30, 34,
67. *See also* Ingathering of the Exiles;
Jewish family, global; peoplehood,
Jewish; Shavei Israel
outreach workers/volunteer educators,
Jewish: and Belmonte/northern provinces, 21, 42, 57, 66–68, 122, 176; classes
taught by, 21, 29, 89, 132, 143, 231; definition of, 20–21; international social
networks of, 30–31, 33–34, 181, 221–222,
232; social media and, 30, 31. *See also*
foreign supporters of urban Marranos;
foreign visitors; foreign visitor–urban
Marrano interactions; tourist(s)

Paula (Menorá member), 33–34, 87–89, 151
Pedro (HaShalom member): and foreign
visitors, 162–163, 190, 216; life story,
85–87, 250; on Marranos and Jewishness, 103, 139, 155; relations with Kehilá's
supporters, 235, 277
peoplehood, Jewish: as community of
strangers envisioned as kin, 274; conversion and, 247–248, 285n3; definition of,
198; imaginaries of, 23–26, 218; and
Jewish diversity, 18; mystical beliefs and,
275–276; secular Jews and identification
with, 198; and tourism, 21–22, 176, 178,
197–200; and urban Marrano identification with Jews, 7–8, 86, 88. *See also*
imagined communities; Ingathering of

the Exiles; Jewish family, global; kinship; outreach organizations, Jewish;
relatedness
personhood, 13. *See also* cross-generational
transmission; identity; self
pessoas de fora. See foreign visitors (*pessoas
de fora*)
philosemitism, 71–72, 282n11
Pina-Cabral, João de, 13, 15, 110, 111, 129,
268, 276, 283–284n10
pintele yid (Jewish spark), 166, 260, 275–
276, 276, 285n13
Policarpo, D. José (Patriarch of Lisbon), 70
Pombal, Marquis of, 39, 52, 53
Porto (Portugal): Municipal Council of
Communities, 10–11. *See also* Menorá;
Porto Jewish community (normative);
Porto synagogue
Porto Jewish community (normative):
disavowal of Shavei Israel, 264, 286n1;
immigrant and expatriate Jews and, 3,
63, 140–141, 262; invitation-only events
of, 129; as member of Porto Municipal
Council of Communities, 10; and
Sephardic "Right of Return" law, text of
vs. implementation of, 261–264, 288n4.
See also Jewish community, Portuguese
(normative); Porto synagogue
Porto synagogue: and Barros Basto's "work
of redemption" (*obra do resgate*), 82, 221,
286n1; founding of by Barros Basto,
2–3, 62–63; leadership of, 3, 221, 264; in
life stories of urban Marranos, 82–83,
88; and Orthodox Judaism, affiliation
with, 122, 132, 270; and rabbi, historical
lack of, 2, 128; Shavei Israel and, 67,
220–221, 232, 264, 286n1; as tour stop,
2–5, 121, 177, 221–222; urban Marranos
and, 1–5, 36–38, 82–83, 88, 120–124, 141,
209, 221
Portugal: blood of, 9, 15–16, 109; bureaucracy, navigation of (see *cunha*); class
system in, 2, 12–13, 100, 110; education
in, 11, 279n6; ethnic and cultural diversity in, 100; First Republic of, 54–55, 63;
and "foreign" religions, recognition of,
10–11, 68–69, 73, 75, 100–101, 283n6;
freedom of religion in, 53, 54–55, 64–65;

Portugal *(continued)*
greeting of *(beijinhos)*, 184; Jewishness/
Jewish blood among people at large, 13,
39–40, 51–53, 71–72, 281n7; kin terms
and obligations in, 200–204, 207–208,
285–286n4; and messianic mentality,
72; norms of social gatherings in, 12,
147, 242; and religion, popular attitudes
toward, 94, 100–101, 154–156, 283n7;
Revolution of 1974, 64–65, 69, 70;
Salazar dictatorship, 63, 64, 92, 100,
286n5. *See also* anti-Semitism; citizenship, Portuguese; demographics; Inquisition; Jews, Portuguese; Marranos,
Portuguese; Portuguese identities;
Portugueseness; race; social differentiation; surnames, ancestral; urban
Marranos
Portugal-Israel Friendship Association, 127,
134
Portuguese Association for Jewish Studies,
127
Portuguese identities: continued, 110–111,
268, 276, 283–284n10; and genealogical
causality, 111–112, 268; heritable, 106–
111, 115; naming conventions and, 111;
regional *(terra)*, 107–108, 109–110, 111.
See also Portugueseness; social categories; social class; social differentiation
Portuguese National Tourist Office, 70,
177, 180
Portugueseness: as absolute, 110; as carrying
a hidden Jewish heritage, 9, 13–14,
71–72, 75; as ethnogenealogical, 15–16,
109, 283nn8–9; as grounded in mixed
ethnicity, 71–72. *See also* Portuguese
identities
prayer shawl *(tallit)*: and becoming/being a
Marrano, 149–150, 165, 171; as gifts from
families abroad, 252–253; use reserved
for "Jews," 128, 149, 171
productive miscommunication, 215–219,
224–225, 269, 270, 286n8; definition of,
215–216
Protestantism, 100, 101, 283n6. *See also*
evangelical Christianity
proximity: and connectivity, 26–28, 259,
265–266, 265–267; and exclusion,

27–28, 38, 266, 268; and inclusion, 17,
28, 260, 270–272; and intimacy, 27–28.
See also belonging; foreign visitor-
urban Marrano interactions; Jewish
community, Portuguese (normative)—
rejection of urban Marranos by; nurturance and care between foreign supporters and urban Marranos; social space(s)
pseudonyms, 279n4, 287n11

Rabbi Asher Siegel, and urban Marranos,
236–237, 249, 251–252, 255, 256, 258
Rabbi Ezra (Jewish educator). *See* Kaplan,
Chaya and Rabbi Ezra
Rabbi Lévy (outreach worker): life story,
230–232; on Marranos, 231; prior outreach activities, 230; relations with
urban Marranos, 231–232, 233, 235–236,
257–258
Rabbi Martin Axler, and Kehilá, 236
rabbinic court *(beit din)*, as requirement of
conversion, 132, 221, 226, 256, 286n3
race: hypodescent ("blood logic"), 51, 103;
Jewishness and discourses of, 57, 104,
117, 283n5; north/south distinction in
Portugal and, 108–109, 283n8; racial
homeopathy, 103. *See also* biological
determinism
Reform Judaism, 19, 229, 232
relatedness: across scales and domains of
sociality, 8, 15–16, 38, 247–248, 256–257,
260, 261–264, 273–274; of all Jews, as
descent group, 16, 22, 183, 197–198;
definition of, 14–15; limits to, as culturally determined, 15, 17–20, 261–264,
266–267. *See also* belonging; Jewish
family, global; Jewishness; kinning/
making kin; kinship; peoplehood,
Jewish; Portugueseness
religion: attitudes toward, in contemporary
Portugal, 94, 100–101, 154–156, 283n7; by
birth vs. by choice, 97–99, 101–106;
Buddhism, 85, 86, 100, 101; evangelical
Christianity, 95, 101, 161, 283n6; "foreign," recognition of, 10–11, 68–69, 73,
75, 100–101, 283n6; freedom of, 53, 54–55,
64–65; individualization of, 98–101;
Islam, 59, 100, 113–114; Protestantism,

100, 101, 283n6; spiritual marketplace, 99–101, 106. *See also* Catholicism; Catholic-Jewish identity; conversion; Judaism; Moors (medieval Muslims)

religious observance, Jewish: belief vs. practice, 19, 35, 154, 236; differing forms of, across branches of Judaism, 130, 136, 153, 220–221; differing levels of, among urban Marranos, 143, 144, 153–156, 220–221; experimentation with, by urban Marranos, 85–86, 95–96, 154; Havdalah, 156, 189–192, 277–278; higher adherence to, required of converts, 153–154, 156; lower adherence by normative Jewish community, perception of, 129–130, 153–154, 284n4; *minyan*, 122–123, 124, 128, 171, 284n1; prayers/praying, 17, 93, 143, 166, 191, 203, 256, 258, 279–280n9, 283n4, 284n1; public expression of, as issue for urban Marranos, 148–149, 154–156, 284n7; Shabbat dinner, 130, 155–156, 241–242, 243, 254; Shabbat prohibitions, 88, 144, 220; Shabbat services, 121–124, 237–238, 242, 251–252, 257, 284n1; Sukkot, 36–38, 130, 266; weddings, 35, 255, 287n12. *See also* conversion to Judaism; dietary laws; Jewish law; material culture; secret practice of Judaism

retornados, 10, 12–13, 89–91

"return" to Judaism. *See* conversion vs. "return," urban Marranos and

Revolution of 1974 (Portugal), 64–65, 69, 70

Ricardo (Menorá member): and foreign visitors, 1–5, 23, 177, 188, 189, 193, 257, 270; life story, 1–2, 119–120; on Marranos and Jewishness, 3, 128–129, 131, 148, 153; and social networks, 205, 207–208

"roots" tourism: forged transnationality and, 273; government sponsorship of, 273; imagination vs. experience and, 217; and productive miscommunication, 216; seeking contact with local coethnics, as commonality, 22, 217; transnational adoptees and, 217. *See also* "roots" tourism of crypto-Jewish descendants; tourism; tourist(s)

"roots" tourism of crypto-Jewish descendants: crypto-Jewish descendants defined

in relation to, xv, 50; and pretour narrative, 182–183, 185, 199–200, 217–218; and productive miscommunication, 216, 218; seeking contact with urban Marranos, 179, 200; and surnames, comparison of, 185, 196; and viewing of urban Marranos as "cousins," 186, 188, 196–197, 200, 201–202. *See also* crypto-Jewish descendants; Nostálgia Conference-Tours; Nostálgia forum; tourism; tourist(s)

rural Marranos. *See* Beira provinces; Belmonte (Portugal); Trás-os-Montes province

Sadah (Yemen), 113–114

Sahlins, Marshall, 113, 243, 251, 272–273

Salazar, António Oliveira, dictatorship of, 63, 64, 92, 100, 286n5

Sampaio, Jorge (prime minister of Portugal), 70

Schneider, David, 14, 16, 103, 194, 198, 199

Schwarz, Samuel, 55–58, 59–61, 63–64, 67, 70, 176

secret practice of Judaism (crypto-Judaism): Barros Bastos and, 59; Belmonte crypto-Jews and, 65, 66, 67, 281n9, 284n3; foreign visitor expectation of, among urban Marranos, 36, 68, 162–163, 269; Inquisition and New Christians, 46, 47, 48, 49–50, 51, 231, 281n5; lack of, as distinction between historical populations termed "Marranos," 60–62, 282n11; lack of, in urban Marrano families, 5, 78, 87, 139; and the "Marrano story," 163–165; in media, 65, 68, 93, 282n16; and secrecy as lifestyle, 77; syncretism of, 41, 48, 51, 62–63, 67, 72; and term "Marrano," xv, 41, 137, 139, 171; women as leaders in, 55–56

secular Jews: among foreign supporters, 233–234; conceptions of Jewishness, 19–20, 104, 117; and display of Judaica, 150; and Jewish peoplehood, identification with, 198; as not concerned with Jewish law, 153, 193; as outreach workers, 21, 193, 233, 276; selective holiday observance of, 17, 35, 98

self: alternative, in tourist interactions, 5–6, 7, 22–23; as arbiter of spiritual fulfillment, 98–101; as emergent, 172; as fixed/essential, 79, 102–103; as intersubjectively produced, 125, 167, 258–259; as plural, 79, 141, 173–174; Portuguese cultural model of, 80, 110–111; as predetermined vs. self-determined, 98–100, 101–106, 259–260; as requiring discovery, 78, 92, 105, 117, 166; and social categories, 13, 125–126, 134, 138–141, 168–172, 174–175, 268; and tourism, 5–6, 7, 22–23, 125, 159, 161–162, 166, 200, 276; "true" self, 22–23, 105–106, 146. *See also* cross-generational transmission; essence; figured worlds; identification; identity; self-making

self-consciousness: belonging as lack of, 277–278; continual, among urban Marranos, 276–277

self-making, 26, 99–100, 159–161, 258–259. *See also* becoming; identification; identity; life stories; "Marrano story"; self; urban Marranos, becoming a Marrano

Sephardic Jews: definition of, 281n4; diaspora, 9, 47, 50, 279n3, 281n4; distinctive practices of (vs. Ashkanazi), 54, 240, 258; immigration to Portugal, 53, 54; relationship to Marranos, 47, 50, 140–141, 257–258; surnames of, 84, 97, 129, 158, 261. *See also* Jewish community, Portuguese (normative)

Sephardic "Right of Return" law (Portugal), 261–264, 288n4

Shaaré Tikvá synagogue (Lisbon): and Anshei Emet synagogue, relationship to, 135–136, 157–158; architecture and grounds of, 53; Barros Basto and, 59, 62; CIL as administrator of, 68, 127, 129, 130, 131, 261; in life stories of urban Marranos, 84, 86, 91, 96, 271; and Marrano boarding school project, 60; and Orthodox Sephardic Judaism, affiliation with, 54, 132, 270; questioning/exclusion of newcomers/urban Marranos, 132–133, 238, 271; and rabbi, periods of lack of, 128; Sephardic/

Ashkenazi congregants of, 54, 135–136; and Sephardic "Right of Return" law, 263; in state commemoration of Inquisition, 70; as tour stop, 177, 183, 223. *See also* Jewish community, Portuguese (normative); Jews, Portuguese

Shavei Israel, 21, 30, 199; and Belmonte outreach efforts, 67, 122; disseminating publicity about Marrano outreach, impact of, 68, 181, 198, 199, 224, 264; guiding Orthodox "return" in Porto, 166, 220–221, 232; Judaism classes offered by rabbi-emissaries, 67, 122, 143, 169; and Porto Jewish community, relations with, 37, 122, 221, 264, 286n1; and Porto synagogue as base for Iberian outreach, 67–68, 221, 232, 264, 286n1; urban Marranos and rural crypto-Jews represented as of a piece by, 181, 264

Shearith Israel synagogue (New York), 50

Simmel, Georg, 265–266

slippage, communicative. *See* misunderstanding

Soares, Mário (president of Portugal), 69–70

social categories, 40–42; converts to Judaism, 127, 133, 137–139, 287n5; figured worlds and, 125–126; as malleable, 41; Marranos, 41–42, 57, 125, 141, 170–172, 268; mass forced conversion and reclassification of, 45–46; outsiders, 133–134, 136; Portuguese Jews, 40–41, 51, 73–75; as self-ascribed, 103; typifications, 18–19. *See also* Jewishness

social class: of foreign visitors, 20, 179; and Jews, stereotypes of, 43, 284n5; and normative Jewish community of Portugal, 127, 130–131, 209–210, 284n5; in Portugal, 2, 12–13, 100, 110–111, 112, 174; and social mobility, 2, 10–11, 110; urban Marranos and, 2, 12–13, 130–131, 169, 195, 209–210, 284n5. See also *cunha* (social leverage); *cunha*, logic of; social categories; social differentiation

social differentiation, 12–13; accent and, 12, 13, 75, 110; north-south origins, 108–109, 283n8; of Portuguese Jews (historic), 42–43, 46, 51; religiously observant vs. secular, 127, 154–156. *See also* social class

social media, 26–27, 30, 31. *See also* Nostálgia forum

social networks, closed, 12, 130–131, 169, 174. See also *cunha* (social leverage)

social space(s), 7–8, 26–28, 265–267, 269–271

Society for Crypto-Judaic Studies, 157, 167

sociobiographical memory, 17

soul, Jewish. *See* Jewish soul

Spain. *See* Inquisition, Spanish; Jews, Spanish; Sephardic Jews

spiritual marketplace, 99–101, 106

Star of David, 38, 40, 74, 84–85, 147–149, 150, 152, 234, 284n7

Stasch, Rupert, 251, 269, 286n8

"Stranger, The" (essay, Simmel), 265–266

surnames, ancestral: Ashkenazi, 129; comparison of, in tourism encounters, 4–5, 185, 191, 196–197; in Inquisition records, 48–49, 86, 158; "Marrano," in early 20th c. Belmonte, 56; and the "Marrano story," 158, 159, 160; "New Christian," 39–40, 158, 166; in Portugal, significance of, 10, 111, 158; in Portuguese Jewish community, significance of, 128–129, 131, 133, 261; recognized as "Jewish" in Portugal, 129, 158, 174; Sephardic, 84, 97, 129, 158, 261. *See also* names and naming

synagogues. *See* Anshei Emet synagogue (Lisbon); Belmonte: synagogue; Porto synagogue; Shaaré Tikvá synagogue (Lisbon); Tomar synagogue

tefillin, 244, 252, 253–254

Ten Lost Tribes, 17–18, 21, 228

Tiago (HaShalom member): and foreign visitors, 162, 163–164, 185, 225–226; life story, 95–97, 133, 250; on Marranos and Jewishness, 116, 249, 283n5; relations with Kehilá's supporters, 253, 258, 277

Tomar synagogue, 39–40, 284n7

Tomás (HaShalom member): and foreign visitors, 163–164, 185, 186, 190–191, 225; life story, 138, 185, 191, 193, 214; on Marranos and Jewishness, 138–139, 172

toponyms, as sign of former Jewish presence, 44, 76

tour guide(s): Barros Basto as, 62; normative Portuguese Jewish community members as, 4, 183; urban Marranos as, 1–2, 180–181, 183–184, 203, 284n7

tourism: as alternative social space, 5, 7, 22–23, 269, 270–271; authenticity in, question of, 230; definition of, 20; and desire for interpersonal connection, 4–5, 21–23, 185–186, 193–194, 217, 230, 276 (*see also* foreign visitor–urban Marrano interactions); as domain of enchantment, 269; the gaze and (*see* gaze, the); Jewish peoplehood and, 21–22, 177–178, 197–200; radical simplification in, 269, 270; reasons for local involvement, question of, 22–23, 177–178; and the self, 5–6, 7, 22–23, 125, 159, 161–162, 166, 200, 276; as temporal and experiential break, 187, 269. *See also* foreign visitor–urban Marrano interactions; heritage tourism, Jewish; "roots" tourism; tourism, anthropological study of; tourism materials; tourist(s); tourist site, urban Marrano associations as; tourist-toured interaction

tourism, anthropological study of: as alternative realm of experience, 187, 269; and authenticity, 230; methods, 28–29, 31–32. *See also* productive miscommunication; tourist-toured interaction

tourism materials: government-sponsored, for Jewish heritage tourism, 70, 177; representation of "lost" Jews/Marranos in, 41, 43, 55, 69, 182; role in shaping tourist experience, 233, 270

tourist(s): crypto-Jewish descendants as, 31, 50, 76–77, 182–186, 196, 200, 218; definition of, 20; display of emotion by, 3–5, 8, 22, 76, 178, 184–188, 190–192, 203, 213–214, 221, 272; expectations of, role of imaginaries/narratives in, 23, 182–183, 217–219, 223–224, 269; experience of, 182–183, 187, 212, 214–215, 217–218, 224, 269; as fixed component of local dynamic, 20; independent,

tourist(s) *(continued)*
 31–32, 122, 177, 179, 180; interactions with
 normative Jewish community, 4, 122–123,
 128, 130, 132, 183; interest in meeting local
 Jews, 21–22, 177–178, 197–200; metanarratives as framework for journey, 182–183,
 186, 188, 222, 224; national origin of,
 generally, 20; and study in preparation for
 trip, 49, 182. *See also* foreign visitors;
 foreign visitor–urban Marrano interactions; tourism; tourist site, urban Marrano associations as; tourist-toured
 interaction; tours, package
tourist gaze. *See* gaze
touristic borderzone, 212, 215–216, 269
tourist site, urban Marrano associations as:
 in context of independent travel, 31–32,
 179, 182, 216–217; in context of package-
 tour itineraries, 29–30, 31–32, 76–77,
 177, 178–179, 181, 182–183; development
 of, 6, 177, 178–181; impact of being, for
 urban Marranos, 164, 192–193, 200,
 218–219, 221–222, 224; "Marrano zoo"
 (feeling of), 218, 221–222, 225–226, 256;
 package-tour visits, vignettes of, 183–187,
 189–193, 285n1; and risk of rejection as
 "non-Jews," 189, 192–193; "the living
 past," urban Marranos as, 223–229, 259,
 269, 286n2; tourist expectations of,
 177–178, 182–183, 194, 200, 214–215, 269.
 See also *cunha*, logic of; foreign visitor–
 urban Marrano interactions; "Marrano
 story"; Nostálgia Conference-Tours
tourist-toured interaction: cultural difference emphasized in, 179; meetings of
 urban Marranos and foreign visitors as,
 212–213; mutual intelligibility presumed
 in, 212, 215–216; pretour narratives and,
 182–183, 214–215, 217–218, 224, 269;
 rote performances and, 177. *See also*
 foreign visitor–urban Marrano interactions; gaze; misunderstanding; tourism,
 anthropological study of
tours, package. *See* heritage tourism, Jewish; Nostálgia Conference-Tours; tourism, anthropological study of
translation: abbreviations of languages in
 text, xv; chain of, 190–192; lack of, 22,

212–213; and productive miscommunication, 215–217, 269; researcher role in
 and positionality of, 29, 30, 213–214,
 240–241, 287–288n13; and slippage of
 meaning, 196–197, 212–215. *See also*
 misunderstanding
transnationality, forged, 273
Trás-os-Montes province: ancestral Jewish
 identity in, 73–74; hidden Jews in, 53,
 56–64, 176; Jewish outreach workers
 and, 21; as place of family origin, 108,
 158–159, 165. *See also* Belmonte
 (Portugal)
truth. *See* belief
Tsur Israel synagogue (Brazil), 50
typifications, 18–19

urban Marranos: Barros Basto as model
 and precedent for, 59, 120–121, 135,
 137–139, 157, 158, 174, 221; Belmonte
 crypto-Jews and, 42, 93, 124; characteristics of, 5, 6, 9–14; definition of term, 9;
 desire to leave status of "Marrano"
 behind, 172, 175, 277–278; independent
 Jewish congregation begun by (*see*
 Kehilá); marginality/existential difference as common feeling for, 12–14;
 "Marrano" as term of self-designation
 by, xv–xvi, 138–142, 168–172, 268, 277;
 rabbinic debate and rulings on, 228,
 249–250, 257; as sole members of family
 pursuing Judaism, 5, 78, 101–102, 125,
 236. *See also* ancestral Jews, urban
 Marranos as; conversion vs. "return,"
 urban Marranos and; foreign supporters
 of urban Marranos; foreign visitors;
 foreign visitor–urban Marrano interactions; Jewish community, Portuguese
 (normative)—rejection of Marranos by;
 Jewishness of urban Marranos; Kehilá;
 urban Marranos, associations of; urban
 Marranos, becoming a Marrano
urban Marranos, associations of, 9–14; as
 alternative community of practice,
 143–145, 156, 173; coherent social
 space formed by, 11; interstitial
 character of, 10–11; members of, 11–14,
 167–172; Menorá's dissolution and

attempts to start new, 232–233; and self-consciousness, 277; and social class, 130–131; social media and, 31; voluntary associations as common feature in Portugal, 10. *See also* HaShalom; Kehilá; "Marrano story"; Menorá; tourist site, urban Marrano associations as

urban Marranos, becoming a Marrano, 172–175; alternative community of practice, Marrano associations as, 143–145, 156, 173; components of, 145; dietary laws, 152–156, 285n8; and discomfort with fanaticism, 154–156; Hebrew names, contextually distinct use of, 151–152; historical Marranos, study of, 157; hybrid practices becoming norms, 173; learning as component of, 142–145, 154, 156, 157–159; mass-media imagery of Jews and, 142; material culture and, 145–151, 284n7; and

narrative of life story (*see* "Marrano story"); observance of Jewish law, higher standard required of, 153–154, 156; rejection by normative Portuguese Jewish community as driver of need to become, 171, 172, 173–175; search for clues to Jewish roots, as practice of, 157–159; self-consciousness and, 276–277

Urry, John, 223–224

Wolf, Lucien, 60–61, 176, 178, 282n11

"work of redemption". *See* Barros Basto, Artur

Yiddish: abbreviation used to identify, xv; ritual name in, 247, 287n9; urban Marrano use of, 93, 97, 162, 249, 258; "Zog, Maran" (song), 23–25, 280n12

Zimler, Richard, 46, 281n3

"Zog, Maran" (song), 23–25, 280n12